DEFINING DVĀRAVATĪ

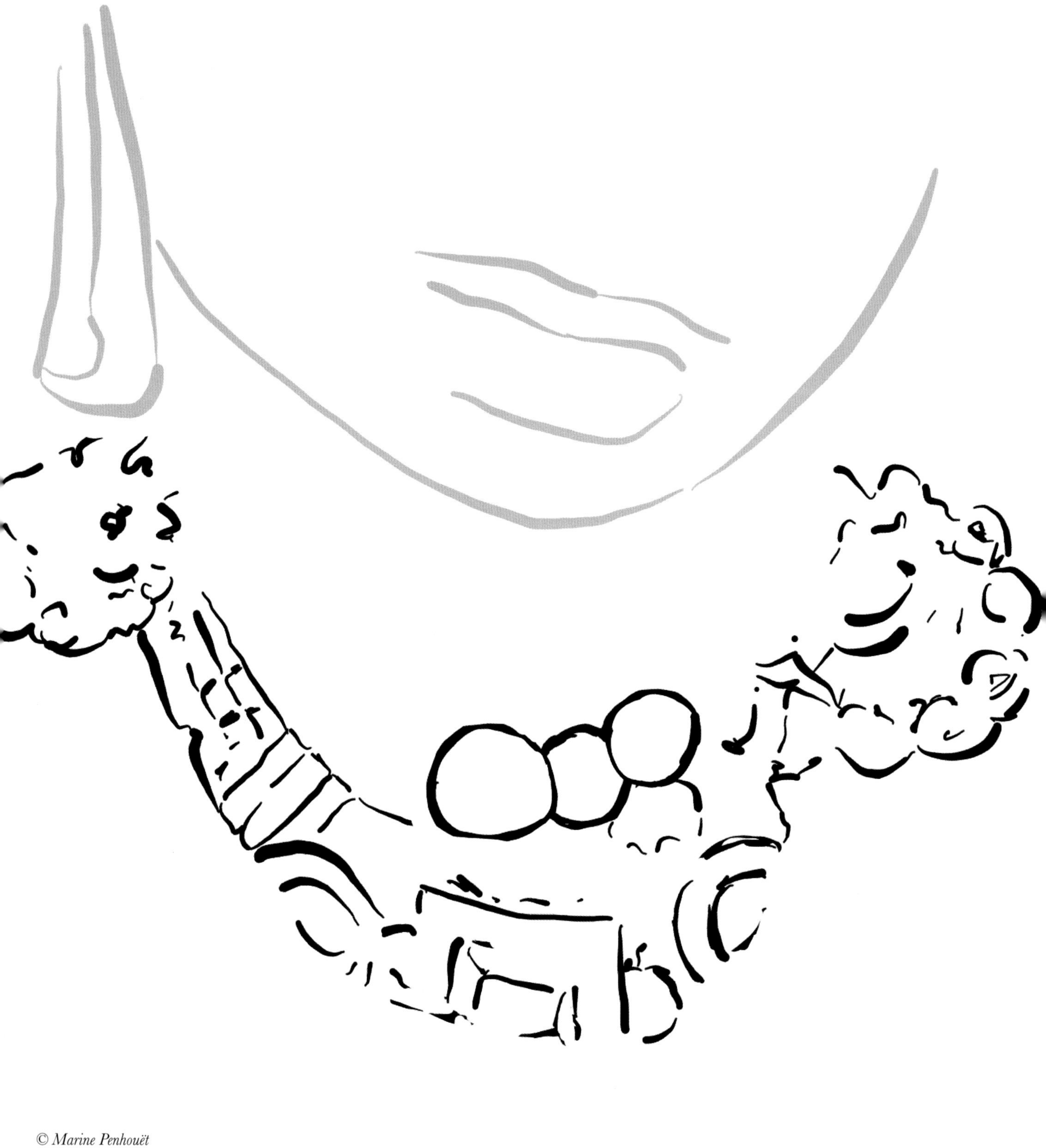

DEFINING DVĀRAVATĪ

Silkworm Books

Essays from the U Thong International Workshop 2017

Published by DASTA, Designated Areas for Sustainable Tourism Administration
(Public Organization) and BIA, Buddhadasa Indapanno Archives
ISBN 978-616-215-157-6

Worldwide distribution: Silkworm Books
430/58 M. 7, Soi Ratchaphruk, T. Mae Hia, Chiang Mai 50100, Thailand
info@silkwormbooks.com http://www.silkwormbooks.com
Edited by Anna Bennett and Hunter Watson
Layout by Anna Bennett, Pairot Singbun and Marine Penhouët

Cover image: Terracotta relief, U Thong National Museum, 30/2543, 1/24, 2002/2518. Courtesy Musée Guimet, Paris. Design by Anna Bennett
Typset in Baskerville 11 pt. by Anna Bennett and Pairot Singbun

Printed and bound in Thailand by Pimdee Company Limited, Bangkok

This book is dedicated to Ian Glover.

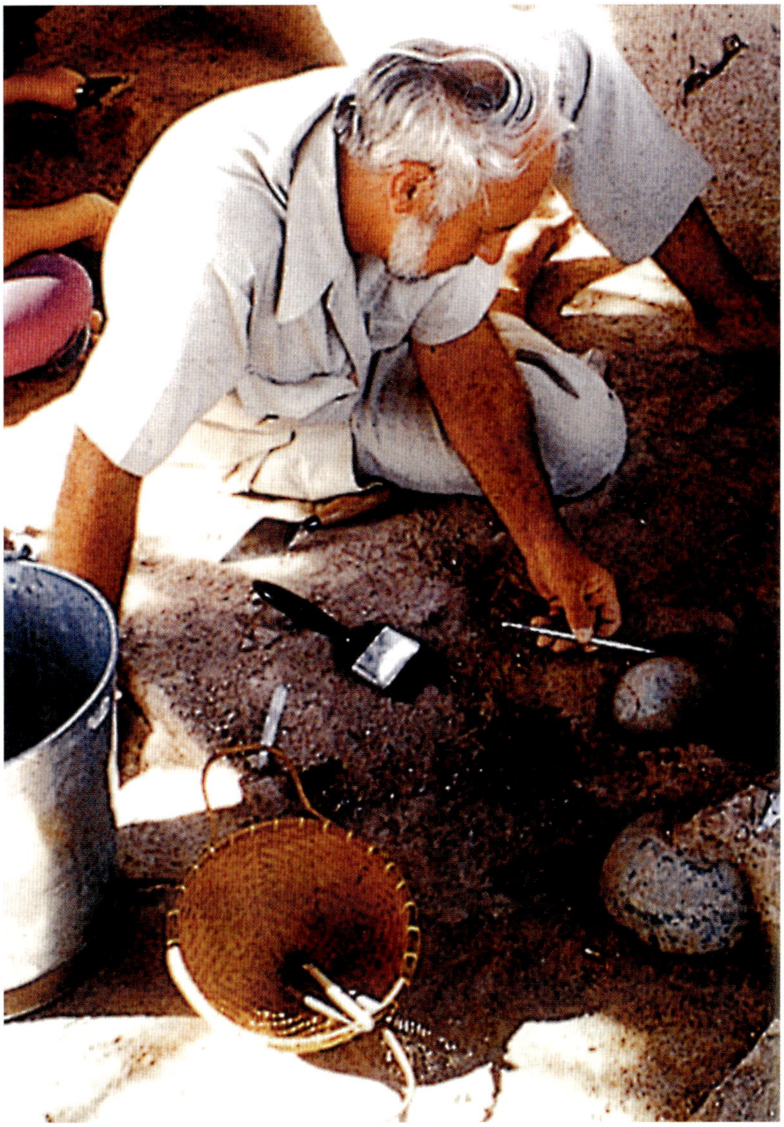

Ian Glover excavating at Ban Don Ta Phet, west-central Thailand in 1984.

IAN CARVEL GLOVER (1934–2018)

Ian Glover will always be remembered as a great pioneer of Southeast Asian archaeology, with a breadth of fieldwork which took him from the Ulu Leang caves in South Sulawesi in the 1970s, to Ban Don Ta Phet in west-central Thailand in the 1980s, to Tra Kieu in Vietnam in the 1990s, and many other sites in-between. Those of us lucky enough to have known Ian have all in some way been influenced by his life.

Born in Lancashire, England, Ian never quite lost some of its linguistic traits, saying 'uzz' instead of 'us'. In the years leading up to the Second World War, his family lived in Grange-over-Sands in a wonderful house overlooking Morecambe Bay with the Lake District National Park beyond. Those hills in the north of England remained important to him throughout his long life and he often returned to them, celebrating his eightieth birthday on a walking holiday. That love of the outdoors, of the hills and exploring the unknown, shaped him and, to a huge extent, his family as well.

Ian went to school in the Lake District, and then to Stowe in Buckinghamshire. This shaped and honed his mind as an independent, scholarly and intelligent young man. He was amongst the last of his generation to do National Service, which he hated. He then swapped the Yorkshire gloom for the Cyprus sunshine on a sort of surveillance duty, which he would only describe mysteriously as 'secret'. He was in fact attached to MI7 and his family are convinced that his job involved intercepting 'enemy' Russian telegraphic messages, but he once told his eldest son that the British actually spent much of their time intercepting American messages, too. More importantly, it was in Cyprus that Ian's interest in archaeology began, a passion which would last his whole life.

In 1959, Ian's wanderlust overtook him, and he left London to head East, when that was still a rare thing to do. The hippies would only follow a decade later. He hitch-hiked across Europe, through Pakistan to Asia, and then on to Australia, with many mishaps and adventures along the way, including a night in an Iranian jail. Once in Australia, he tried his hand at film editing for a TV channel, for which he had a natural ability, but something in his mind told him it was time to attend university. Ian would say he chose archaeology and anthropology because the lectures were in the afternoon, so he could continue to work in the television industry. In reality, he did it because he loved the subject matter. He also said that it was one of the few professions that caused no harm to anyone.

After graduating from Sydney University with top honours, Ian went on to study for his PhD at the Australian National University in Canberra and work in (what was then) Portuguese Timor on early prehistoric sites. In 1963, he met his future wife, Emily, whom he married in 1968—a marriage that was to last for fifty years. They set up their home in London, where Ian had been offered a permanent teaching position in archaeology at the Institute of Archaeology, a college of London University, which later became part of University College London (UCL). They had two sons, of whom he was extremely proud and whose academic successes delighted him immensely. His eldest, Julian Glover OBE, is an English author, journalist and speech-writer. The younger, Adrian, is a research leader in the Life Sciences Department of the Natural History Museum, London, with a particular focus on deep-sea biodiversity. As a family, they shared many interests, led in many ways by Ian and his imagination.

As one of the founding members in the field of Southeast Asian prehistory, his legacy is not only in his fieldwork, having conducted excavations in Timor, Thailand, and Vietnam, but also in his publications and books about early Southeast Asia. In 1986, he and Per Sorensen founded the European Association of Southeast Asian Archaeologists (EurASEAA), which held its inaugural meeting in London. One of his greatest contributions to Southeast Asian archaeology is in terms of the large number of his students who have gone on to work in this field. The enormous feeling of sadness and the great number of expressions of gratitude and appreciation for his steadfast support, vis-à-vis his colleagues and students from all over the world, is testimony to the great number of people he inspired.

Although Ian was structured in his work, and his research was carefully conducted, he did not cling to preconceived ideas. He allowed the archaeology and the material to speak for itself. In that respect, his research attitude was exemplary. He was a great site director, and he would provide the framework and the basis on which to let his students and colleagues operate freely, allowing them to put their talents to good use. Occasionally, a student might fail to appreciate the extraordinary opportunity that Ian's support offered and might fail to rise to the level required. While Ian was always ready to guide and encourage his students, he would never do their work for them. He might obtain research funding for students' work but would never dictate how that money should be spent. Rather, he would demand that his students think for themselves and produce their own original research. At times, he might even disagree with their methodology or hypotheses, but for him that was secondary. He was like a generous gardener who allowed plants and trees to flourish independently.

Knowing when to show humility, Ian was not afraid to change his mind or admit when he may have been incorrect. In the 1980s, Ian had suggested that the high tin bronzes he excavated at the protohistoric site of Ban Don Ta Phet in west-central Thailand, dating to the 4th century BCE, were products of workshops in what is now Thailand. He later came to believe that these were, in fact, more likely to be products of Indian manufacture, albeit with the raw tin coming from Southeast Asia. However, he also would never fail to stand his ground when his strongly held opinions about fairness were challenged. A particular example caused him to take early retirement two years prior to his sixty-fifth birthday because of his views concerning the equality of treatment of staff members and his refusal to be bullied by the university authorities.

After he retired from teaching prehistory at UCL, Ian continued contributing to the field by inspiring new students and imparting advice and valuable knowledge with boundless generosity. Easily bored, he was constantly busy with new ideas and projects, and, as a consequence, he did not publish as much as he should have. Those of us lucky enough to have worked with him could take advantage of his great intellect. Being in his company meant that the resources of his mind and his formidable powers of reflection were on tap and at our disposal. How fortunate we were!

Ian was a true polymath, widely read and with an impressive memory. His interests in literature, history, architecture, cooking and early music made him an intellectual guide to his family and friends. After his retirement from teaching, he spent more time at his country house in Shropshire, where he was as happy strimming the weeds and making bread and cider in season as he was in London, attending the theatre and classical music concerts and having dinner with friends, or in a Soi off Sukhumvit, in Bangkok. His zest for life showed through in every aspect.

In his eighties, Ian was still travelling the world, not only for his Southeast Asian research, attending conferences, giving talks and keeping in touch with his old colleagues and former students, but because he decided that there were too many places in the world with which he was still unfamiliar. To his dying day, he pursued new adventures, gaining new knowledge with the same unfailing curiosity. This unadulterated enthusiasm meant that his circle of friends ranged down through the generations to those just setting out on their paths in the world. His ease and talent for befriending people of all ages and walks of life rested on his singular capacity to learn from others. His appreciation of people translated into a symbiotic relationship of mutual exchange.

At the time of his death on the 23rd April in Catania, Sicily, on the eve of his eighty-fourth birthday, he was still on an adventure. Ian died on stage with sword in hand.

Anna Bennett

CONTENTS

INTRODUCTION 11
Bunchar Pongpanich
Buddhadasa Indapanno Archives (BIA), Bangkok

THE PRE-DVĀRAVATĪ GAP 14
Ian Glover
Institute of Archaeology, University College London

DVĀRAVATĪ FROM THE BOTTOM UP 24
Wesley Clarke
The Castle Museum, Marietta, Ohio

NEW KNOWLEDGE ON DVĀRAVATĪ 34
Phuthorn Bhumadhon
Rearn Phra Lop and Lop Buri Conservation Committee

MAKING SENSE OF DVĀRAVATĪ 48
John Guy
The Metropolitan Museum of Art, New York

DVĀRAVATĪ IN INSCRIPTIONS AND MANUSCRIPTS 64
Peter Skilling (Bhadra Rujirathat)
École française d'Extrême-Orient and Fragile Palm Leaf Society, Bangkok

OLD MON INSCRIPTIONS AND THE EXTENT OF DVĀRAVATĪ 82
Hunter Watson
National University of Singapore

A CLAY TABLET FROM U THONG INSCRIBED IN OLD MON 94
Hunter Watson and Peter Skilling (Bhadra Rujirathat)
National University of Singapore and École française d'Extrême-Orient and Fragile Palm Leaf Society, Bangkok

PRECIOUS METALS IN DVĀRAVATĪ CULTURE **98**
Anna Bennett
Conservation and Technical Services, Brussels

THE REQUEST FROM DVĀRAVATĪ FOR FINE HORSES **126**
Lin Ying and Huang Jiaxin
Sun Yat-Sen University, Guangzhou

THE FALL OF DVĀRAVATĪ **136**
U-tain Wongsathit, Kangvol Katshima, and Chatupohn Khotkanok
Silpakorn University, Bangkok

EXHIBITION OF PRE-DVĀRAVATĪ ARTEFACTS AND POST WORKSHOP VISITS **144**

BIBLIOGRAPHIES **152**

APPENDIX 1: ENGLISH–THAI LIST OF PLACE NAMES **179**

APPENDIX 2: ARCHAEOLOGICAL SITES AND AREAS IN THAILAND MENTIONED IN THE TEXTS **180**

Transliterations and names

This book includes vocabulary and place names from various languages. Notably, numerous Pāli and Sanskrit words are used, and these have been transliterated following the IAST/ISO 15919 convention. All Thai words and place names have been transliterated following the current standard of the Royal Institute of Thailand. Appendix 1 is a list of English–Thai place names; Appendix 2 is a list of archaeological sites and areas in Thailand mentioned in the texts. This book uses British English, although American spelling conventions have been followed by some authors.

Abbreviations

BCE	Before Common Era
BDTP	Ban Don Ta Phet
BE	Buddhist Era
BIA	Buddhadasa Indapanno Archives
c.	circa
Cat.No.	Catalogue Number
CE	Common Era
cm	centimetre
d.	diameter
DASTA	Designated Area for Sustainable Tourism Administration
ed.	editor
e.g.	exempli gratia, for example
et al.	et alia, and others
etc.	etcetera
FAD	Fine Arts Department of Thailand
Fig.	Figure
g	gram
ht.	height
i.e.	id est, in other words
ibid.	bidem, in the same source
idem.	the previously cited person
km	kilometre
m	metre
mm	millimetre
n.d.	not dated
No.	number
P.	Province
r.	reign
trans.	translator
Vol.	volume

INTRODUCTION

111TH ANNIVERSARY OF BUDDHADASA BHIKKU

Bunchar Pongpanich

U Thong International Workshop on Defining Dvāravatī
30th August – 3rd September 2017
Bangkok, U Thong & Some Dvāravatī Sites in Western Thailand

This workshop, organised jointly by DASTA (Designated Area for Sustainable Tourism Administration), the Siam Society, the Piriya Krairiksh Foundation and BIA (Buddhadasa Indapanno Archives) [Figs.1–3], was initiated by Ian Glover of the Institute of Archaeology, University College London, whom first described the extensive Pre-Dvāravatī evidence found in Thailand and raised questions on the Pre-Dvāravatī gap. Accompanied by Anna Bennett, of the Conservation and Technical Services, Brussels and John Guy of The Metropolitan Museum of Art, New York, who were invited by DASTA through BIA to collaborate on the book *The Ancient History of U Thong: City of Gold*, published in 2017, greatly supported by Phuthorn Bhumadhon, founding director of the Discovery Museum Siam.

This workshop, with the simple objective of reviewing and searching for new knowledge relating to Dvāravatī, the earliest recognised proto-historic period of modern-day Thailand, welcomed many delegates from abroad, who study various issues, as well as other participants. Organized from 30th August through 3rd September 2017, the workshop was hosted at the BIA, the newly established Buddhadasa Indapanno Archives, on the lakeside of Chatuchak Park in Bangkok, with opening addresses by the honorable Sahawat Naenna, former Director of the Fine Arts Department of Thailand and a board member of DASTA, by Phuthorn Bhumadhon and by Ian Glover. Commemorating the 111th Anniversary of the Venerable Buddhadasa Bhikku, whom studied and published a pioneering work on the early peninsular history of Śrīvijaya in Chaiya, Surat Thani, and evidence of Buddhism with a special exhibition "Recently discovered Pre-Dvāravatī artefacts" [pages 144–146].

During the first two days of the workshop (the 30th-31st August, 2017), ten topics relating to Dvāravatī were presented [pages 147]. These included "*The Pre-Dvāravatī Gap*" by Ian Glover; "*The Fall of the Ancient Dvāravatī civilisation as mentioned in Khmer Inscription*" by U-Tain Wongsathit, Department of Oriental Languages, Silpakorn University; "*Making Sense of Dvāravatī in a Greater Southeast Asian World*" by John Guy, Florence and Herbert Irving Curator of the Arts of the South and Southeast Asian Art, The Metropolitan Museum of Art, New York; "*The Extent of Dvāravatī: How much can sema stones tell us?*" by Stephen Murphy, Asian Civilisation Museum, Singapore; "*The Traces of Dvāravatiī in Hariphunchai Kingdom*" by Benchawan Phonprasoet, curator of Hariphunchai National Museum; "*Old Mon inscriptions and the extent of Dvāravatī*" by Hunter I. Watson, National University of Singapore; "*Religion of Dvāravatī: The Art Historical Evidence*" by Piriya Krairiksh, Piriya Krairiksh Foundation, "*Phong Tuek Complexities*" by Wesley Clarke, The Castle Museum, Marietta, Ohio; Science, Technology & Economy of Dvāravatī: "*The role of the trade in precious metals*" by Anna Bennett, Director, Conservation and Technical Services, Centre for the Investigations of Works of Art; and "*Request for fine horses: Medieval Chinese tribute notes on Horse Usage in Dvāravatī and Southeast Asia*" by Lin Ying and Huang Jiaxin, Sun Yat-sen University, Guanzhou, China; as well as an address on "*New knowledge on Dvāravatī, the Earliest Proto Historic period of Thailand*" by Phuthorn Bhumadhon. The workshop continued with a full day (1st September, 2017) in Bangkok at Wat Suthat Thepwararam, where the great Dvāravatī stone relief slab on The Great Miracle of Lord Buddha from Nakhon Pathom is preserved behind the Great Śākyamuni Buddha statue [pages 148]. This was followed by a nice lunch on the Chao Phraya River at the Chakrabongse Villa and a walk with Ian Glover in the Pre-Dvāravatī and Dvāravatī galleries in the Bangkok National Museum [pages 148].

Then we spent two nights in Suan Tang, a proto-historic archaeological site in the Tha Chin River basin of Suphan Buri Province. The morning of September 2nd began with a walk around Khok Chang Din archaeological site [pages 149] with Supamas Duangsakul from the U Thong National Museum and the Fine Arts Department, Suphan Buri Office, and continued in the U Thong National Museum [pages 148] and other monuments and archaeological sites including a recently excavated site and a moulding workshop for Dvāravatī punched-coins. Then we enjoyed lunch and dinner with local residents.

The final day of the workshop, September 3rd, began early from U Thong in the Tha Chin-Mae Klong River basin, visiting the famous Ban Don Ta Phet excavation site with Ian Glover [pages 149], Phong Tuek complex with Wesley Clarke [pages 150], Nakhon Pathom National Museum [pages 150] before a farewell seafood dinner near the recently discovered Phnom Surin shipwreck near the mouth of the Tha Chin River [pages 151], downstream from U Thong ancient settlement.

This workshop brought not only knowledge, current research, new views and ideas, but also helped to strengthen friendships and future collaborations, domestically and internationally. Ian Glover and Anna Bennett cordially accepted our request to edit the preceding from that final day and continued until his last day in Sicily, April, 2018.

Gratitude is shown to all, but especially Anna Bennett for her devotion along with all colleagues on the success of the proceedings in eternal memory of our great and respected archaeologist of the Dvāravatī Gap, Ian C. Glover. Special thanks are given to Peter Skilling, as well as Hunter Watson, whom, even though he could not be present at the workshop, agreed to assist with compilation of contributions and in co-editing this volume.

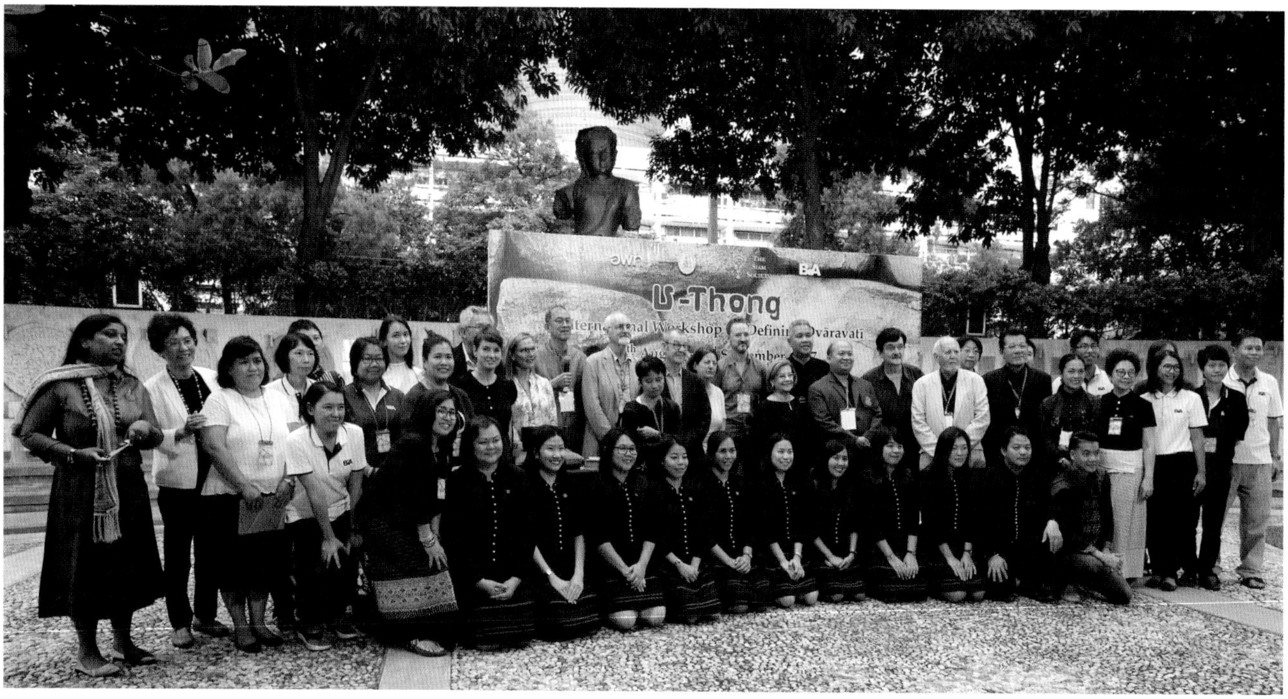

Fig.1 U Thong International Workshop on Defining Dvāravatī, 30th August – 3rd September 2017, organised jointly by DASTA (Designated Area for Sustainable Tourism Administration), the Siam Society, the Piriya Krairiksh Foundation and BIA (Buddhadasa Indapanno Archives).

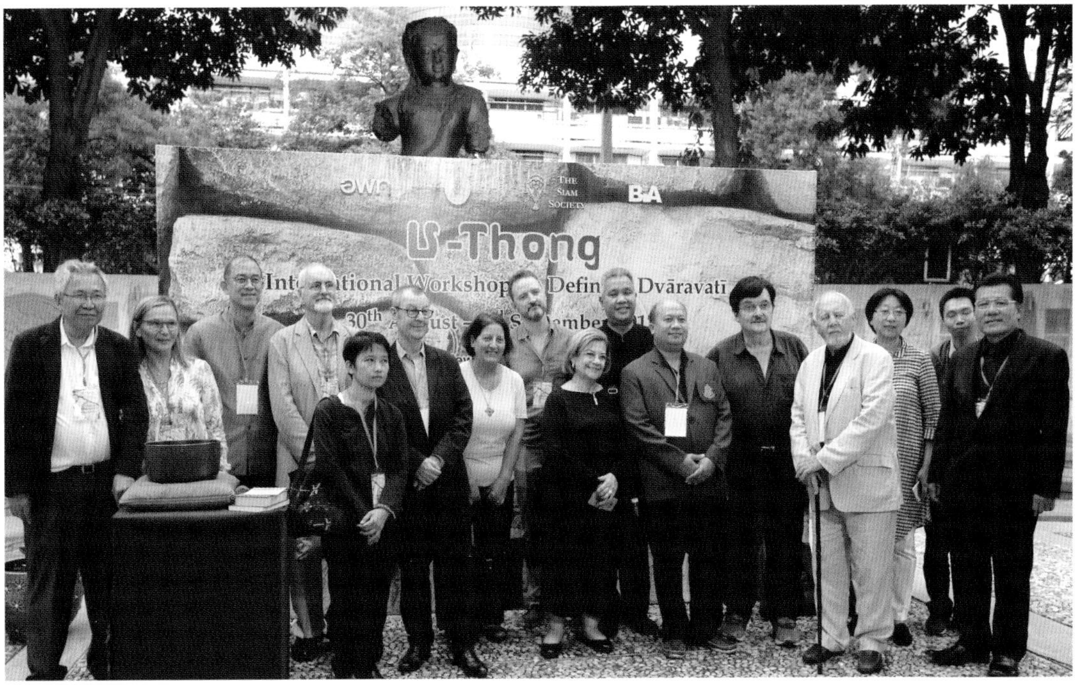

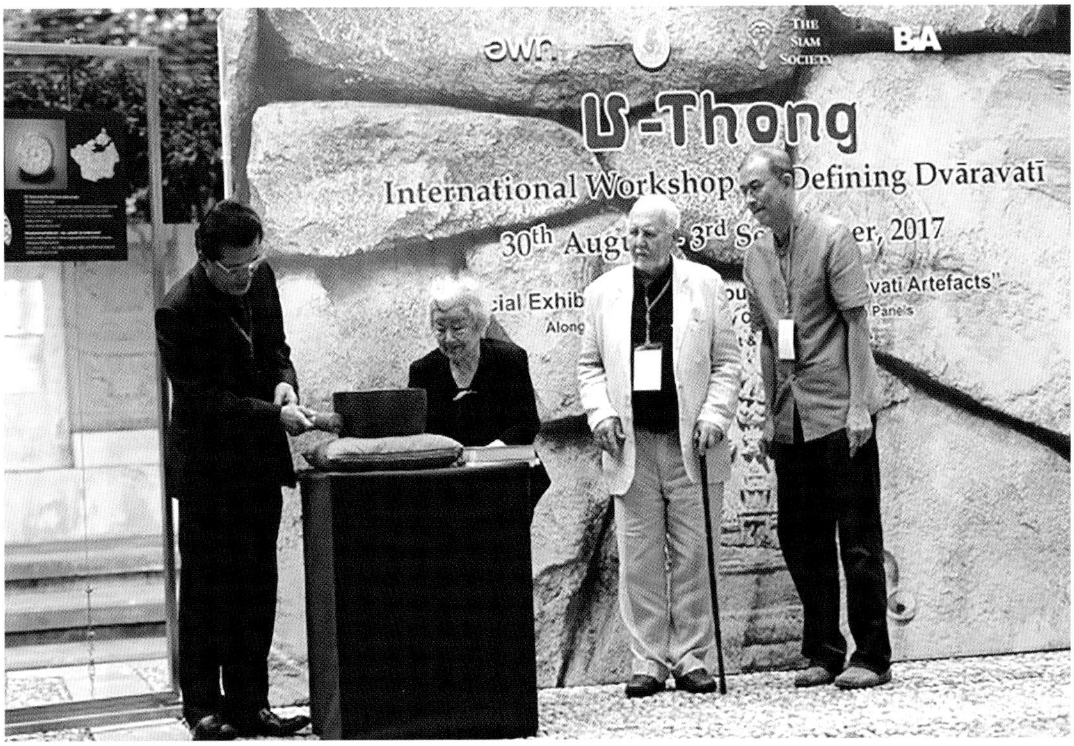

Fig.2 Opening ceremony with Phuthorn Bhumadhon, Anna Bennett, Bunchar Pongpanich, Wesley Clarke, Benchawan Phonprasoet, John Guy, Lia Genovese, Stephen Murphy, Mom Bongkojpriya Yugala, Taweebhong Wichaidit, U-tain Wongsathit, a volunteer at Bangkok National Museum, Ian Glover, Lin Ying, Huang Jiaxin and Sahawat Naenna.
Fig.3 Opening addresses by the honorable Sahawat Naenna, former Director of the FAD of Thailand and board member of DASTA, Yupa Bovornratanarak, Ian Glover and Bunchar Pongpanich.

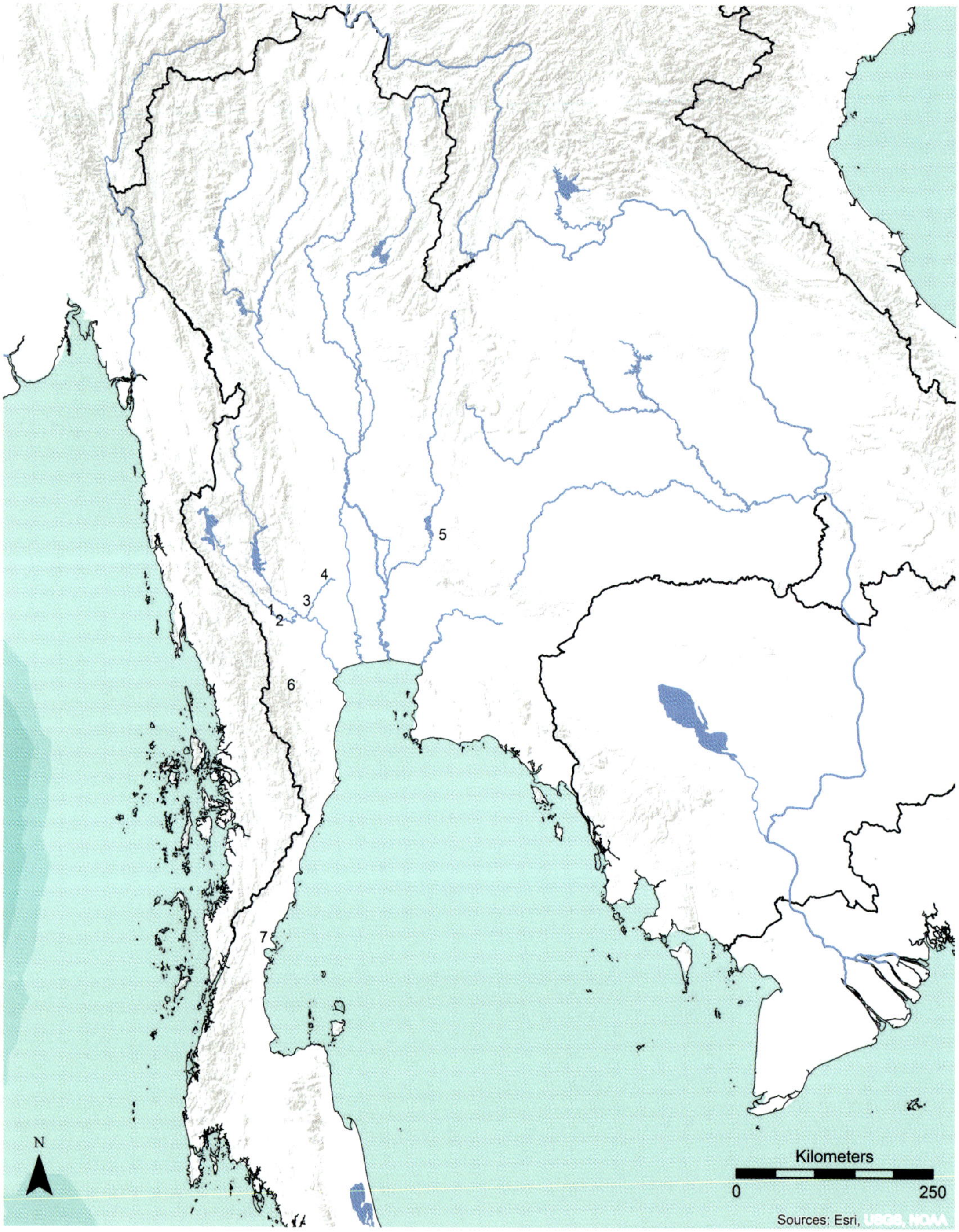

1. Prasat Mueang Sing
2. Ban Kao
3. Ban Don Ta Phet
4. U Thong
5. Ban Pong Manao
6. Khao Chamuk
7. Khao Sam Kaeo

Fig.1 Map showing locations mentioned in the text (map by Hunter Watson).
All photographs belong to the author unless otherwise stated.

THE PRE-DVĀRAVATĪ GAP

Ian C. Glover

Ban Don Ta Phet: A late prehistoric precursor to U Thong and the Dvāravatī Culture

The term 'Pre-Dvāravatī Gap'[1] arose after our excavations at Ban Don Ta Phet (BDTP) [Fig.1] in the 1980s when I was struck by the contrast between the objects excavated at the site – bronzes, iron tools and weapons, low fired pottery vessels, glass and stone beads – and the materials excavated at the Tha Muang site by Watson and Loofs in the 1960s, some of which I had seen in London, and the Dvāravatī culture collections in the U Thong and Nakhon Pathom museums and in the National Museum in Bangkok. I realised that there was a break in the record of the material culture that needed further consideration.

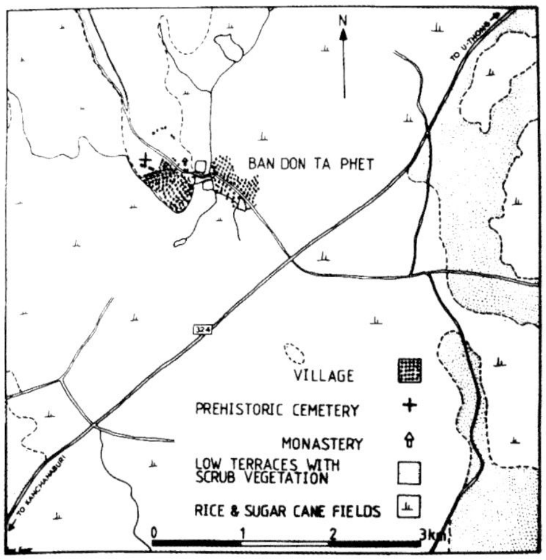

Fig.2 Map of Ban Don Ta Phet village. The archaeological site is denoted by a +.

Location, discovery and the initial excavations[2]

The archaeological site of BDTP [Fig.2] lies on the southern edge of the village bearing the same name in Phanom Tuan District, Kanchanaburi Province, some 25 km south of U Thong, 8 km north of the district centre of Phanom Tuan and 1.5 km west of Route 324 which leads towards Kanchanaburi. According to local residents, the area where BDTP is located used to be a expansive rice field and villagers from neighbouring districts travelled to work in the area. Over time an increase in population led to the establishment of a new village. A wide variety of glass beads were found on the ground throughout the area. The villagers paid little attention to these glass beads, fearing that bringing them home could invite misfortune to them, their families, and their livestock.

Archaeological evidence was first found on 25th September 1975 when students of the Wat Salawanaram School found a number of artefacts when they dug postholes to erect a fence west of the school building. After reporting this to the head of the National Museum U Thong, the school principal at that time, Krim Sooksamai, noted that the students had found more than a hundred interesting objects including spearheads, axes, arrowheads and many bronze artefacts, as well as beads made from glass and semi-precious stone. These artefacts were kept at the temple, in the school, and in the District Office. Later, the FAD asked local residents to stop further excavation and all the finds were transferred to the Bangkok National Museum for conservation. The first excavation was begun by the FAD on the 4th November 1975 and the second season was resumed in May 1976, led by Chin You-Di (Chin You–Di 1976). Four distinct stratigraphic layers were identified, but the few bones and funerary goods were unearthed only in the lower third layer, and Chin You-Di concluded that this was a cemetery site rather than a habitation area. Objects discovered included finely made bronze bowls, anklets and bracelets, semi-precious stone and glass ear ornaments, earthernware pottery, many iron tools, a single human skeleton, and a few rice grains. Chin You-Di suggested that the ancient occupants were Iron Age farmers who raised cows and buffaloes to plough their lands. This assumption relied on images of a male cow with a calf on fragmented bronze artefacts. Aside from farming, they also hunted using arrows, lances and spears and they fished with barbed hooks and harpoons. Carpentry was practiced as evident from axes and chisels. Spindle-whorls and fragments of cloth showed that weaving was known. Low-fired earthenware vessels were used in everyday life.

1 Earlier and in several publications I referred to 'The Dvāravatī Gap'; (Barram and Glover 2008 and Glover 2010). At the September 2017 seminar at the BIA in Bangkok the better title 'The Pre-Dvāravatī Gap' was adopted.
2 Chin You Di, 1976, Ban Don Ta Phet 1975-76: Excavation Report, Thai FAD, translated and later abbreviated by Khun Oraphan Chaivorarat, and Glover.

Apart from the single burial, only fragmentary skeletal remains were found, suggesting that these were secondary burials. Three groups of buried finds were thought to be of different families. Female burials were recognised by spindle-whorls, bracelets, anklets, and beads, whereas male burials were recognized by chisels, arrowheads, spearheads, and axes. The finds including a bronze goose and peacock figurine indicate association with Indian culture. According to Brahmin tradition, the *haṃsa* (goose) is Brahma's mount and the peacock is the mount for Śiva's son. In 1976, Chin You-Di suggested a date for the material to the Iron Age, approximately 2000–1700 years ago. Radiocarbon dates from excavations in 1981-82 and 1984-85 placed the site earlier, to the late centuries BCE.

Subsequent work on the excavated materials

During the 1976 excavations, Warangkhana Rajpitek, a student conservator from Bangkok, came to work on the unusual and delicate bronzes which had been excavated, and she continued this work at the Institute of Archaeology, University College London (Rajpitek and Seeley 1979; Rajpitek 1979). The present author was involved in supervising Warangkhana in London, and realising that more excavation was needed at this important site applied for permission from the Thai authorities. Encouraged by Chin You-Di, excavation resumed in December 1980 [Fig.3] with a team of Thai and British students and colleagues; work continued both at the site and on the excavated materials through to February 1985 (Glover 1983, 1990) [Figs. 4–32].

Subsequent work at Ban Don Ta Phet

A team from the Suphan Buri Office of the FAD conducted another excavation at the site in 2000 and recovered a similar range of materials. Some of these are on display in the small museum at Ban Kao (Wasan 2001). BDTP is not the only site that has yielded comparable material and the bronze bowls are almost identical to those found together with tin ingots at the tin mining sites at Khao Jamook in Chombeung District, Ratcha Buri province, 120 km southwest of U Thong and close to the Myanmar border (Bennett and Glover 1992; Glover and Bennett 2012) and to finds from Ban Ta Po, 7 km from Pasat Meung Sing which is also close to the Myanmar border (visited by Bennett 2016) and to three complete and one broken bowl found at Khao Sam Kaeo, a coastal settlement and production site in Chumphon province on the southeast coast of the Thai-Malay peninsular, which is contemporary or slightly later than Ban Don Ta Phet. Mention must also be made of the small excavation along the Khwae Noi River at Prasat Mueang Sing which has been preserved *in situ* as an exhibition but not published. Another site, that of Ban Pong Manao in Chai Badan District, Lop Buri Province has been well excavated by a joint community project with Silpakorn University and a good museum exhibition was built close to the site.

The Dvāravatī Culture

Dvāravatī is seen as the first historic culture in Thailand and has traditionally been dated by art-historical means and some Chinese textual reference to between the seventh and eleventh centuries CE, which is nearly one thousand years after the deposits at the archaeological site of BDTP Despite our knowledge of the distribution of sites thought to be related to 'Dvāravatī' there are few indigenous inscriptions associated with Dvāravatī. The only useful written information regarding the culture comes from a few brief references in Chinese historical records. Brown (1996: xxi) noted that "it is quite impossible to piece together a coherent diachronic cultural history for the region in the period prior to the political unification of present-day Thailand."

What lay in hundreds of years between the deposits excavated at BDTP and the emergence of the Dvāravatī culture remains something of a mystery although recent excavation at U Thong, Nakhon Pathom and elsewhere in west-central Thailand have extended Dvāravatī back to around the fourth or fifth century CE (Saritpong et al. 2011). However, Dvāravatī material culture provides a marked contrast to that of the late prehistoric Iron Age and is characterised by brick-built *stūpas* and other Buddhist and Hindu religious structures, as well as walled and moated enclosures. Iron tools are rare, and although hard stone beads are abundant, they suffer a marked decline in the manufacturing standard (Bellina (2003). The few burials reported at Phong Tuek (Clarke 2009) are not securely related to, or for certain, contemporary with the Dvāravatī monuments. So, was there a gap in the occupation of western Thailand? Is this an unlikely scenario or are there many, yet undiscovered, sites awaiting recognition and investigation?

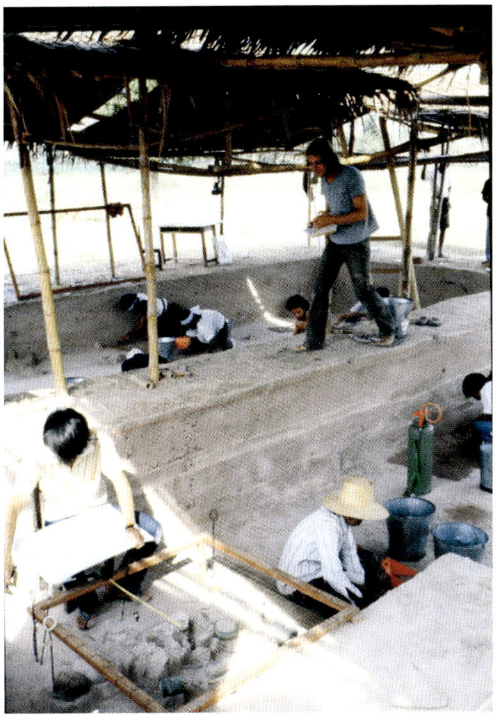

4

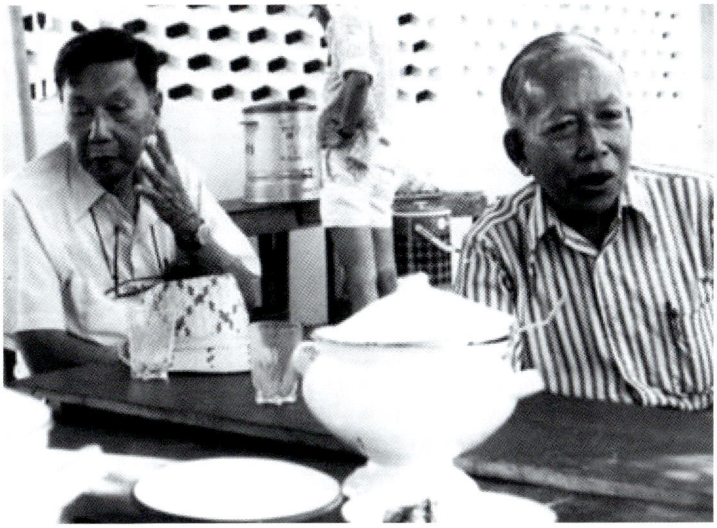

3

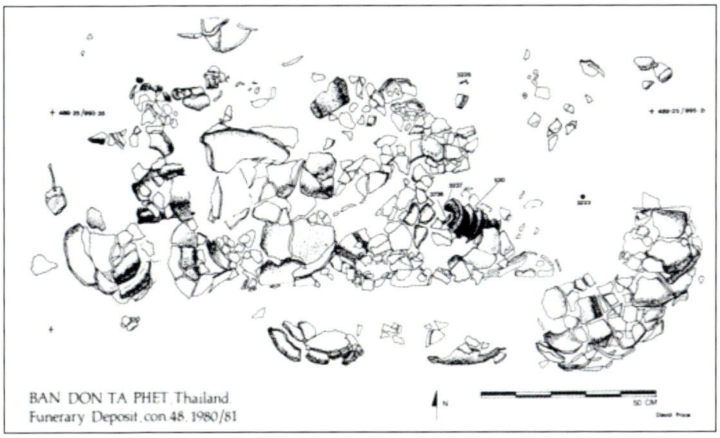

6

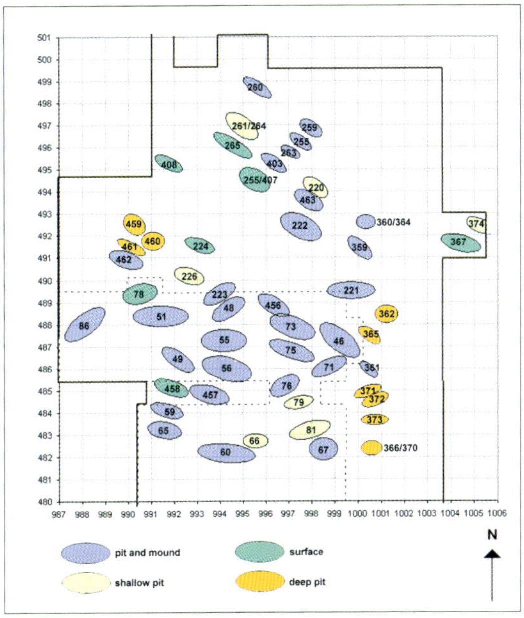

5

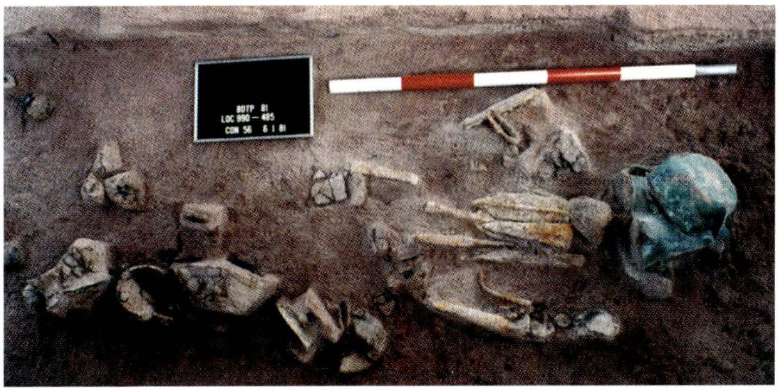

7

Fig.3 Sood Sangvichien and Chin You-di came to visit the 1981 excavation season in January 1981 (Glover 2017).
Fig.4 Excavations at BDTP in 1981. Burial context lay between 0.60–1.00 metre below the existing surface which had been much altered by the creation of a playing-field for the school.
Fig.5 Locations of burials from the joint British-Thai excavations in 1981 and 1985. The image is from the thesis by Moira Woods (2002).
Fig.6 Drawing of burial 'Context 48' at BDTP. In the 1980–81 season, all burial contexts were drawn to a 1:10 scale using a frame marked with 10 cm intervals. In 1983–84, the burial contexts were photographed from a vertical tower which, although saved time, proved to be less successful because of problems with light and shadow.
Fig.7 Photograph of burial 'Context 56'. Iron spears, were ritually killed by bending the blade prior to burial were studied by Anna Bennett (2013a) are similar in shape to spearheads from the Samon Valley, Myanmar (Bennett 2013b).

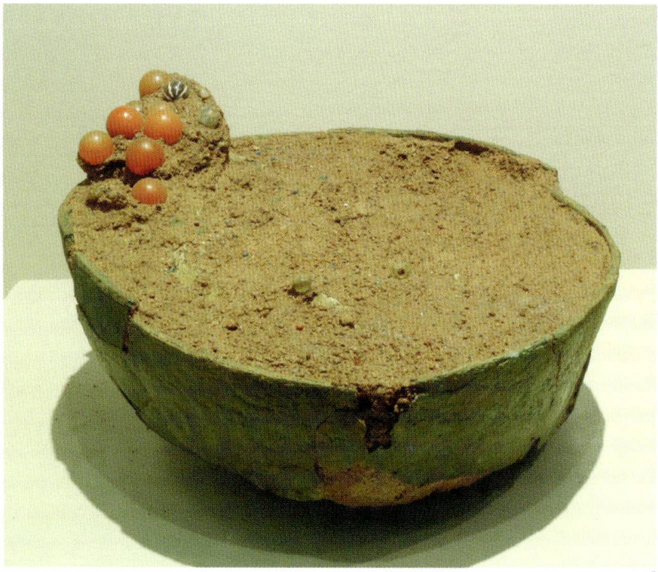

8

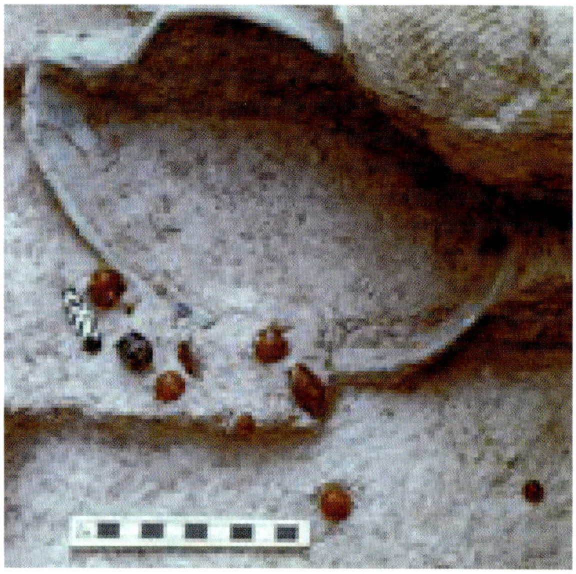

9

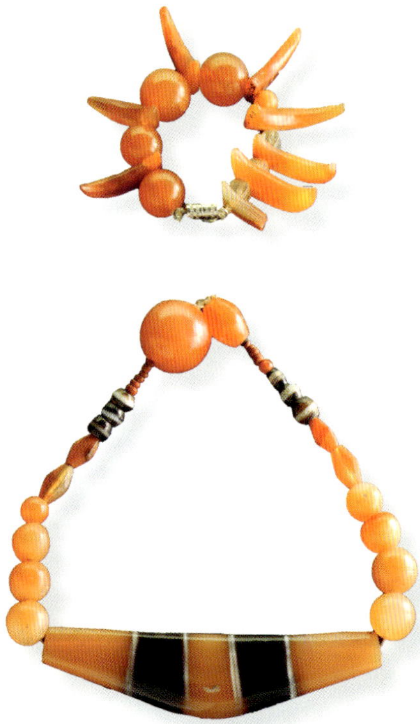

10

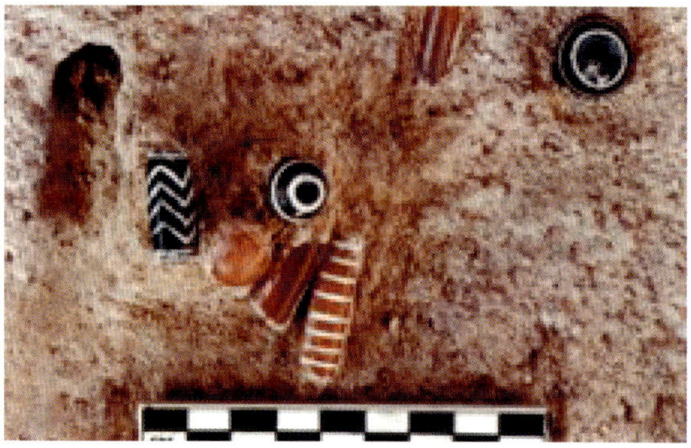

11

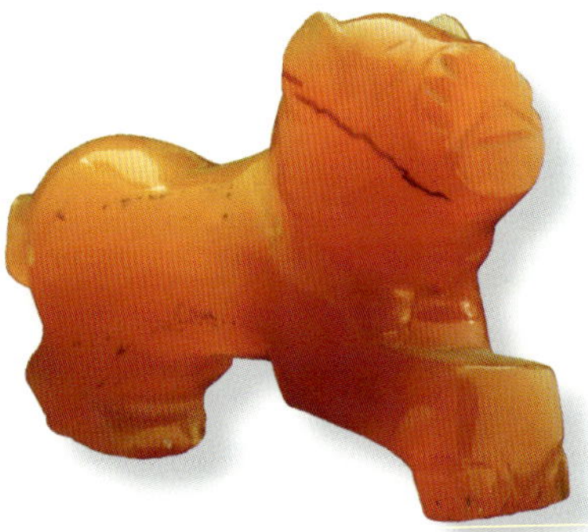

12

Fig.8 Details of BDTP burial 'Context 130' with agate and carnelian beads and a deliberately damaged bronze bowl, 1985.
Fig.9 Etched agate, carnelian and glass beads *in situ* in 'Context 130'.
Fig.10 Etched Beads, found at BDTP, Bangkok National Museum (Courtesy of SuthiRatana Foundation Bangkok).
Fig.11 Etched agate, carnelian and glass beads in situ.
Fig.12 Lion carnelian bead, found at BDTP, Bangkok National Museum (Courtesy of SuthiRatana Foundation Bangkok).

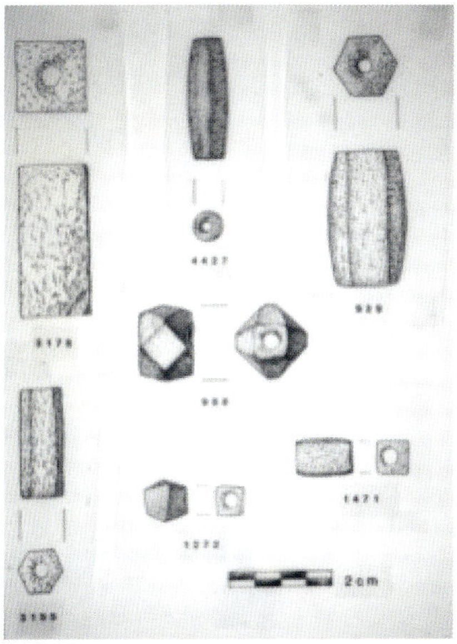

13

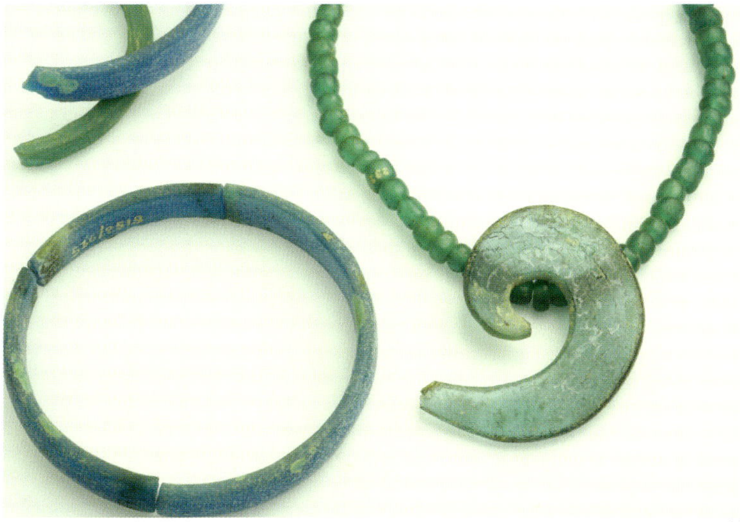

16

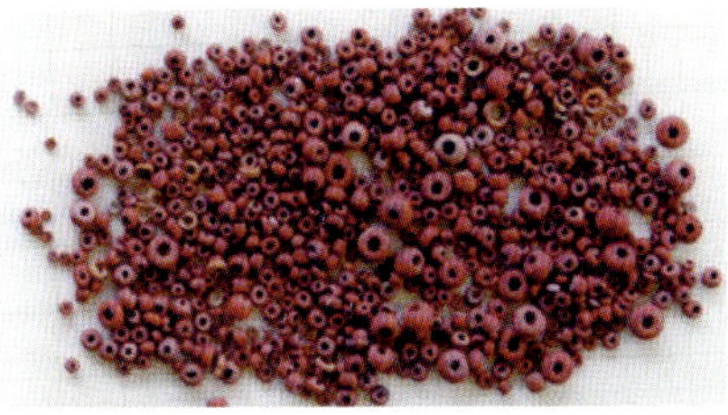

14

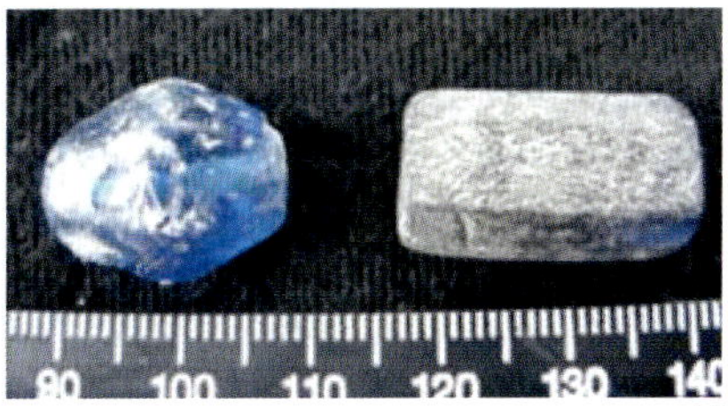

15

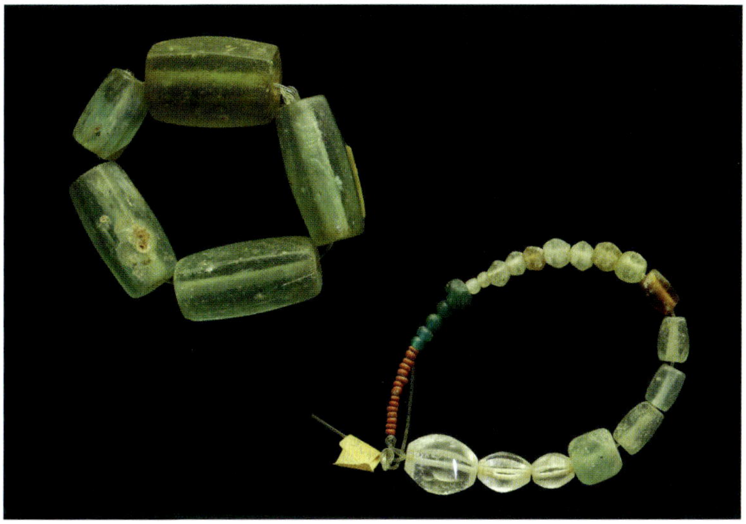

17

Fig.13 Illustration showing a variety of the 3,000 glass beads excavated at BDTP.
Fig.14 Some were Indo-Pacific types, much as these typical small red mutisalah beads.
Figs.15 Other beads were clear or translucent lapidary-worked potash glass beads rarely found elsewhere, leading to the suggestion that the glass was locally made rather than imported from India, as had previously be assumed. Glass compositions were studied by Kishor Basa (1991) and were re-analysed in more detail by Lankton and Dubussieux (2006).
Figs.16–17 Blue glass artefacts from BDTP, Bangkok National Museum (Courtesy of SuthiRatana Foundation Bangkok).

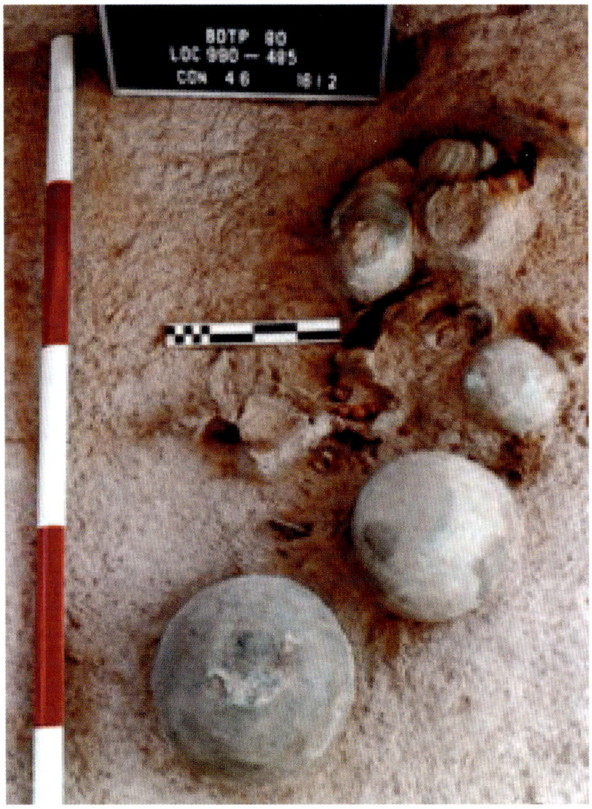

18

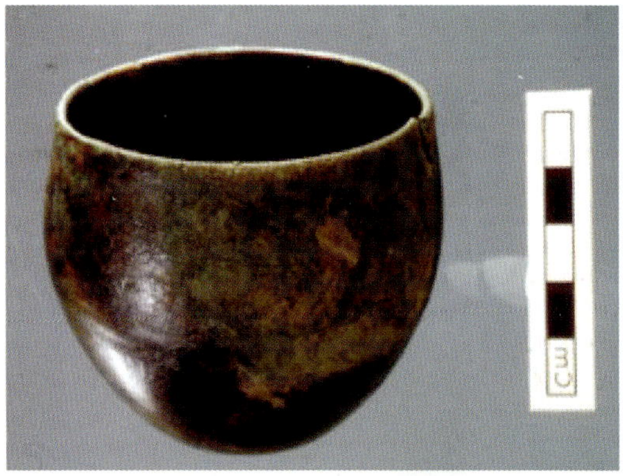

19

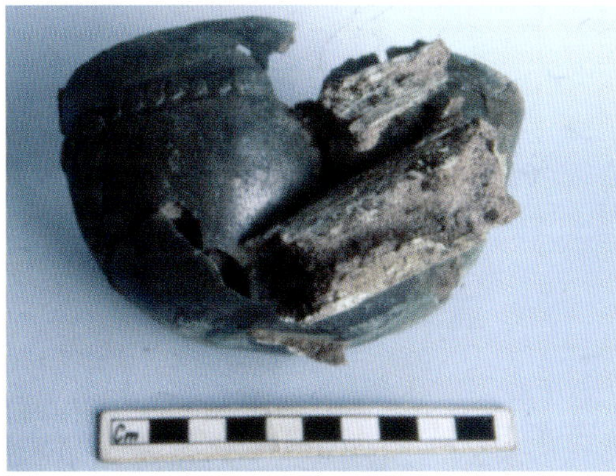

20

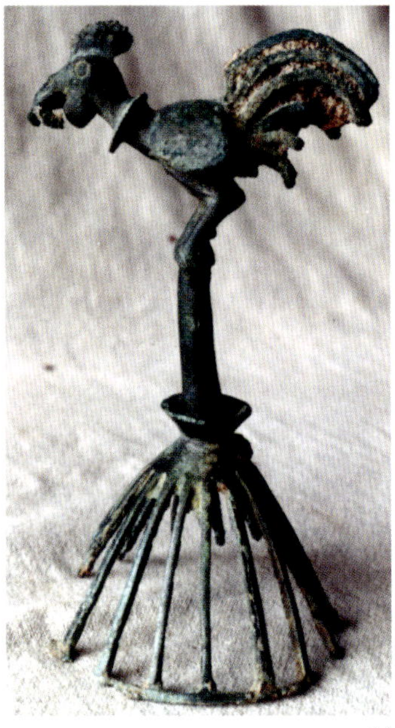

21

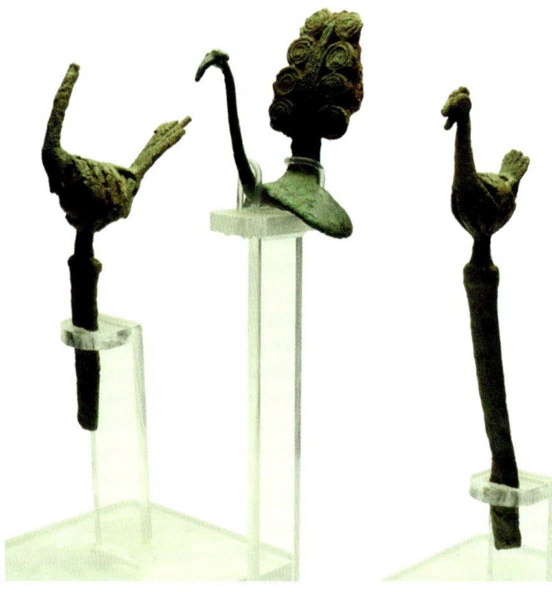

22

Fig.18 Amongst the more richly furnished burial groups, 'Context 46' was unusual for the number of bronze bowls, beads and this figurine of a fighting cock standing on a cage [Figs. 21]. BDTP, Bangkok National Museum.
Fig.19 Bronze artefacts were the focus of a joint article and two dissertations by Warangkhana Rajpitak (1979).
Fig.20 A bronze bowl after conservation. Unlike most of the bone from the site which no longer survived, a small piece of human bone has been preserved on the side of this bowl due to the high concentration of copper salts.
Figs. 21–22 Fighting cock standing on a cage and animal figurines cast in bronze, BDTP, Bangkok National Museum.

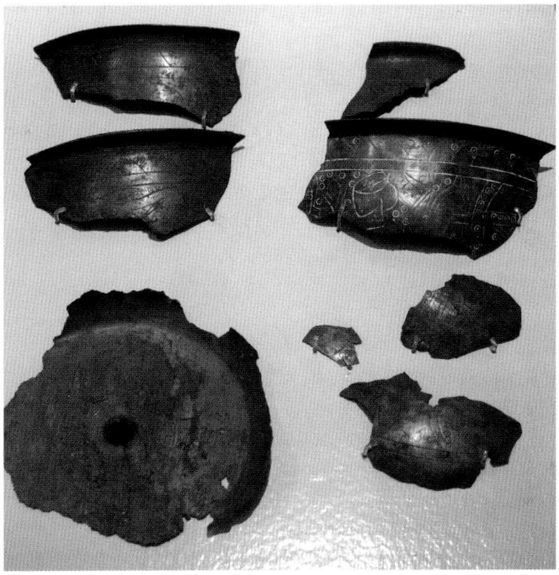

23

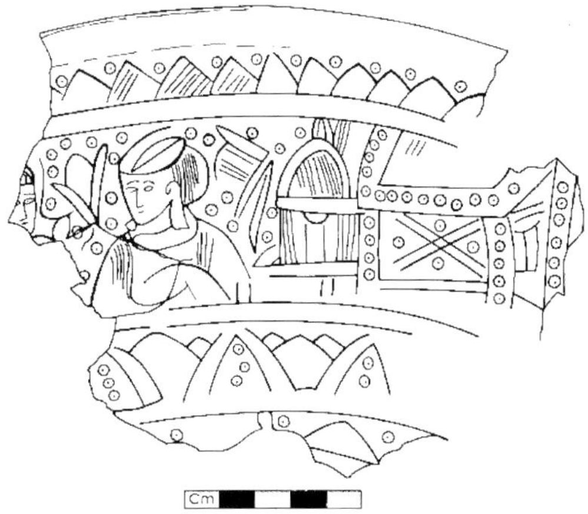

24

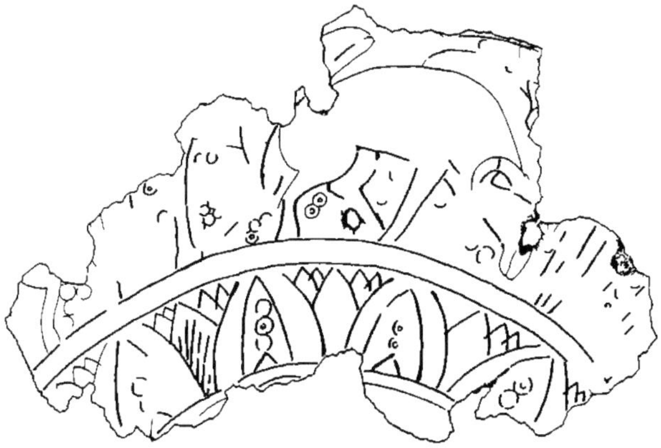

25

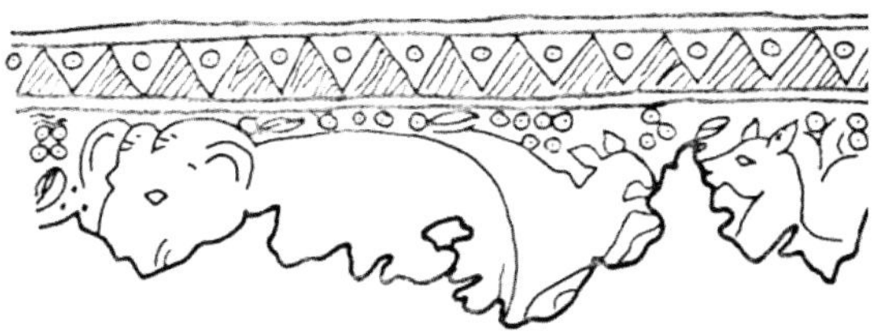

26

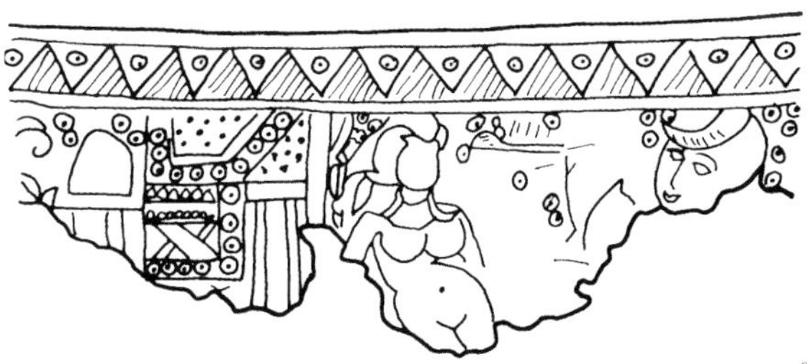

27

Figs.23–25 Decorated high-tin bronze bowls from BDTP, excavated in 1976. *Fig. 24* showing a wooden house, a woman, and on the far left a man's face, and *Fig.25* showing sheep or goats grazing above a stylized lotus flower.
Figs.26–27 Decorated high-tin bronze bowls from Khao Chamuk archaeological site, showing an elephant followed by a deer and a woman leaning against a wooden building. The hatched design below the rim of the bowls is very similar to the one in *Fig.24* (Bennett and Glover 1992; Glover and Bennett 2012).

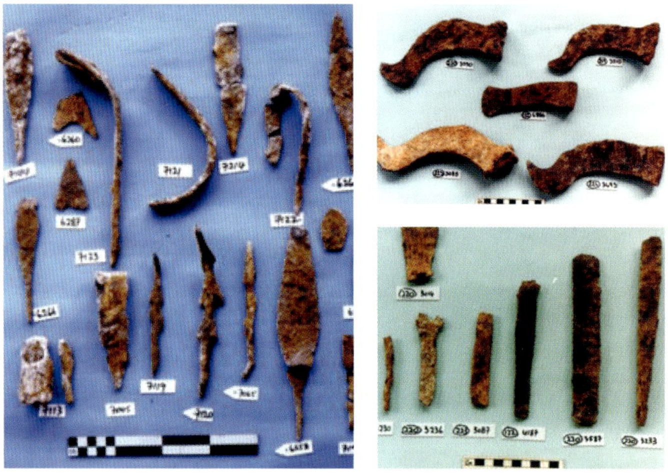

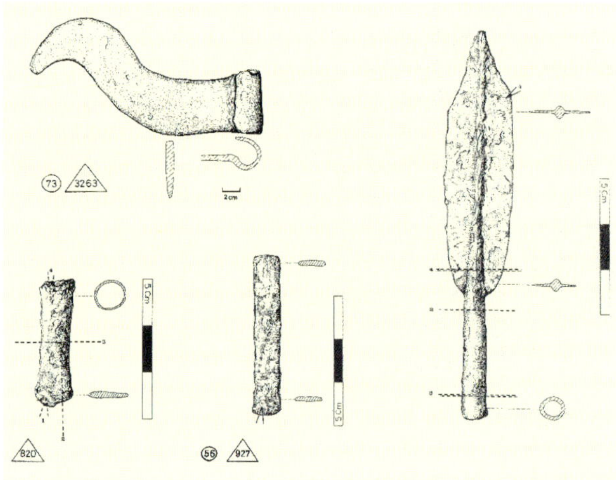

28/29

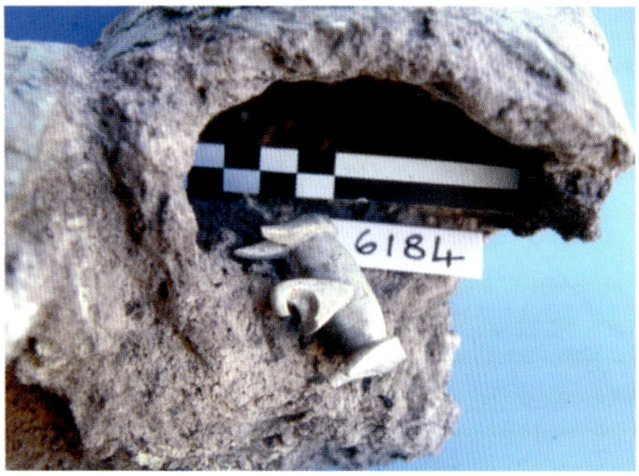

30

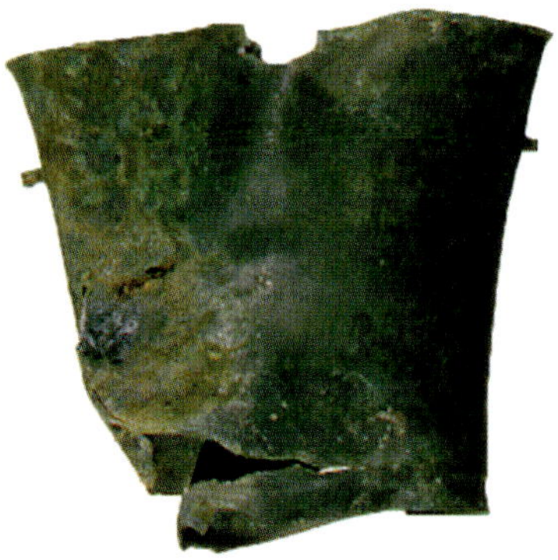

31

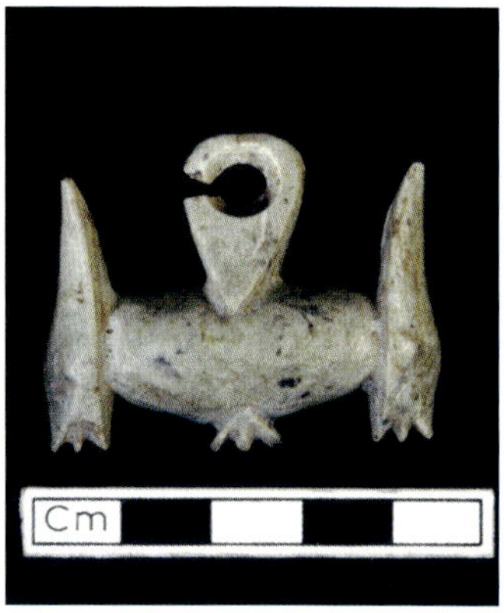

32

Figs.28a-c–29 Over 1,000 iron tools and weapons were excavated, more than from any reported prehistoric site in Thailand, and were studied by Bennett (1982). Some, such as the socketed billhooks, were identical to those found at Khao Sam Kaeo archaeological site and a few other late prehistoric sites in western Thailand (Bennett 2017). These were later recognised by Indian colleagues to be analogous to wooden floor mounted knives still in common use in Bengal and Orissa for slicing fish and vegetables (Bennett 2015).

Figs.30–31 A single two-headed nephrite ear pendant found inside a bronze bowl, typical of the Sa Huynh culture of the central coast of Vietnam, was excavated at BDTP in 1985. These artefacts were also traded north to the Dong Son sites of Northern Vietnam and east to the Philippines and Taiwan. The jade is thought to originate only in Taiwan. National Museum, Bangkok.

Fig.32 This bronze situla was excavated at BDTP, from burial 56 in 1980/81, and is regarded as a Dong Son import coming from South China or Northern Vietnam. It has a ring base with flaring straight sides, two strap handles and a shallow incised fishbone design in a band around the upper section. It was deliberately crushed before burial. ht. 20.5 cm, rim d. 21.7 cm. Analysis showed that it was cast with thick walls in a high lead low-tin bronze, with a composition of between 7.2–10.6% tin and 44.5–68% copper with up to 22% lead (Bennett 2017).

Acknowledgements

Many colleagues and students, both Thai and English, helped to excavate BDTP archaeological site and conserve the fragile finds. Several continued to study material back in the United Kingdom. I particularly want to thank the following: Brian Alvey, Kishor Basa, Anna Bennett, Ho Chui Mei, Lucy Clarke, Anne Farrer, Mark Johnson, Somchai Na Nakhon Phanom, Narawat Kamnounket, Warangkhana Rajpitek, Linda Mitchell, Lucy Wiliams, Tim Williams, Moira Woods, Rasmi Shoocongdej and 17 undergraduate students from Silpakorn University, Bangkok, Djie Dewbangkerd (camp manager) and Daeng (the chef).

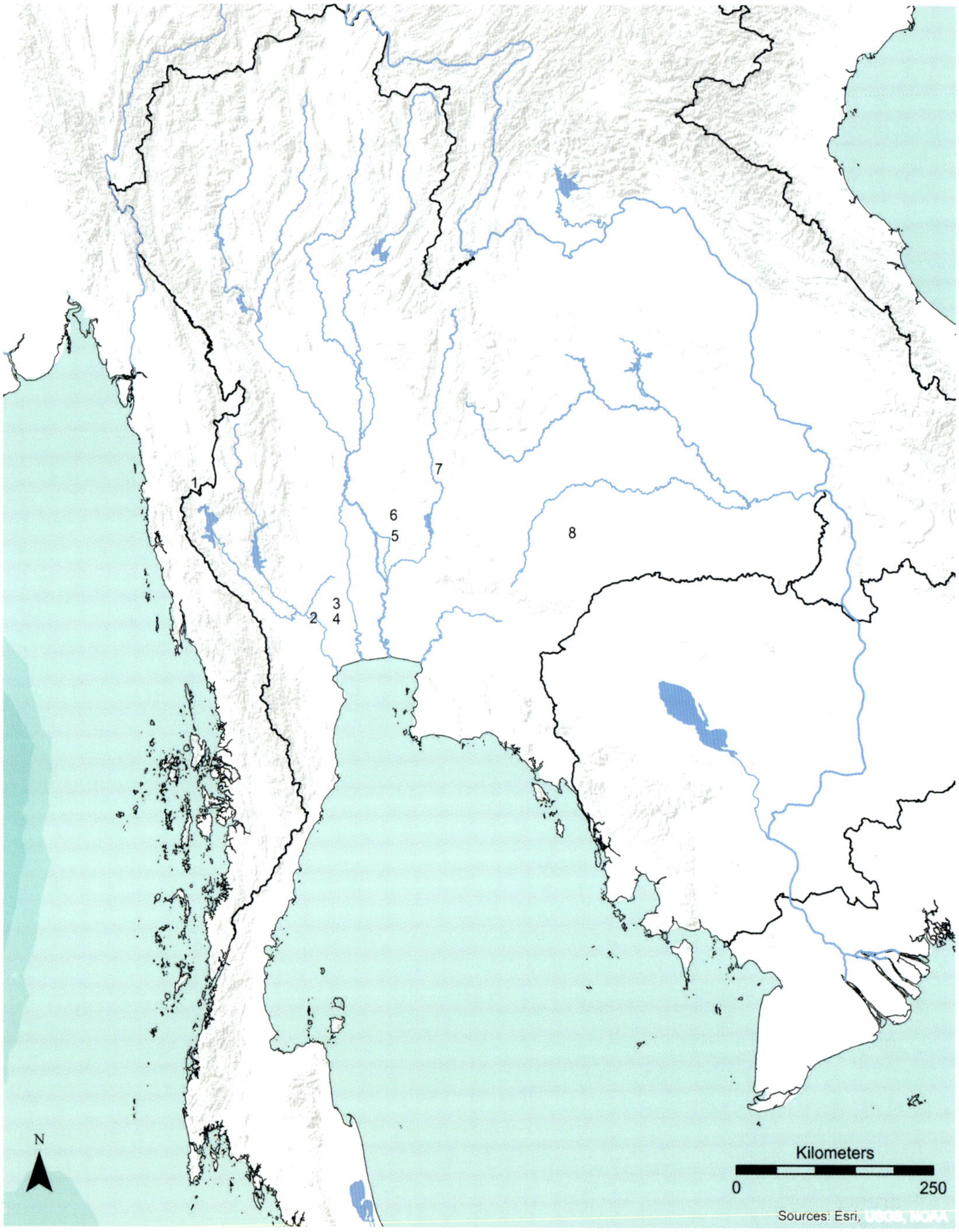

1. Three Pagodas Pass
2. Phong Tuek
3. Nakhon Pathom
4. Noen Phra
5. Lop Buri
6. Promthin Tai
7. Si Thep
8. Mueang Phet

Fig. 1 Map showing locations mentioned in the text (map by Hunter Watson).
All photographs belong to the author unless otherwise stated.

DVĀRAVATĪ FROM THE BOTTOM UP

Wesley Clarke

If we study a system at an inappropriate scale, we may not detect its actual dynamics and patterns but may instead identify patterns that are artifacts of scale. Because we are clever at devising explanations of what we see, we may think we understand the system when we have not even observed it correctly (Wiens 1989: 390).

We need to assess the archaeological evidence on its own terms in its full variety without being beholden to the models and vocabulary of the past (White 2017: 69).

Introduction

The concept of an early historic phenomenon labelled "Dvāravatī" in the region of central Thailand has been extant for over 130 years, yet uncertainty remains about the socio-political organization, subsistence strategies, geographical extent, and temporal range of this cultural entity. Indeed, even the application of the label "Dvāravatī" to an early historic presence in the region of central Thailand remains a debatable idea, since the term was used broadly across time and geography (Revire 2011: 205-206; 2015; 2016). This general incertitude is often attributed to the early and continuing focus on monumental architecture and a sculptural style as principle representatives of the Dvāravatī social phenomenon (Gupta 2003: 392-393; Glover 2010: 84; Brown 2017: 42). Initial archaeological explorations were focused on architectural locations, including the work of Cœdès and Manfredi at Phong Tuek ("P'ong Tuk" -- 1928a, 1928b), Quaritch Wales at Phong Tuek (1936; 1937a), Dupont's brief visit to Noen Phra in 1937, and his more extensive investigations in the vicinity of Nakhon Pathom in 1939 (1959) [Fig.1]. Dupont's seminal analysis of Dvāravatī material culture (1959) also focused on a relative chronology of Dvāravatī ritual art.[1]

This "art historical" emphasis, it is said, impeded efforts to discern the Dvāravatī phenomenon holistically, including attention to a developmental period that likely preceded the appearance of monumental works, and to non-elite aspects of Dvāravatī occupations. Items of monumental sculpture often have little or no functional or locational context recorded (Woodward 2005: 54; Stark 2006: 21.4) and represent a relatively small proportion of the potential material record for the early historic period in central Thailand. In tandem with this problematical material bias, Dvāravatī studies have also relied on extrapolation from a few external and internal documents (e.g. Chinese records, medallion inscriptions) that channelled explanatory emphasis toward external social catalysts, much of this subsumed under the moniker of "Indianisation" (Stark 2006: 21.2, 21.9, 21.18).

The circumstances resulting in the current gaps in our knowledge of Dvāravatī, however, are perhaps not as straightforward as the cited "art historical" explanation. As Robert Brown has recently observed, contemporary art historians are in agreement with archaeologists regarding the problems with an emphasis on architecture and sculpture, while also pointing out that much of the earlier discussion of Dvāravatī by all parties occurred within a dearth of material data (Brown 2017: 42–43). Given these informational limitations, Western, Indian, and Southeast Asian scholars (e.g. archaeologists, antiquarians, art historians, historians, epigraphers, etc.) shared a proclivity to observe and assess the Dvāravatī phenomenon from a "top-down" scale of conceptualization that has influenced the trajectories of Dvāravatī studies to the present day (Miksic 1995: 56; Gupta 2003: 392-393; Stark 2006: 21.4, 21.6; Hennequin 2010: 30; Brown 2017: 42), including the earliest enunciators of the Dvāravatī phenomenon (Fournereau 1895; Damrong Rajanubhab (1973 [1926]); Cœdès 1928a, 1928b, 1929; Quaritch Wales 1936, 1937b, 1966, 1969; Dupont 1959) who focused on ritual art and architecture at a few sites.

1 The problematical nature of the term "art" is acknowledged, which in its Western meanings has little to do with the social and religious functions of aestheticized objects in an early historic Southeast Asian context.

Scales of observation

The scale at which archaeological observations are made is an important but often overlooked factor in determining the nature of the phenomena perceived (Clarke 1973; Hodder and Orton 1976; Dunnell and Dancey 1983; Desjeux 1996; Banning 2002; Burger and Todd 2006; Lock and Molyneaux 2006). "Scale" refers to the spatial and temporal constraints imposed on observation, and can be thought of as that level or segment of a system that is in focus during the act of observing (Burger and Todd 2006: 238; Desjeux 1996: 49-50). Scalar levels of observation can be described in a hierarchy proceeding vertically from a base at the local/small/detailed/micro/qualitative level of operation to an apex at the global/big/comprehensive/macro/quantitative, and each level may include distinct units operating in a heterarchical arrangement of coeval power-sharing (Desieux 1996: 45-50; Crumley 2007; Souvatzi 2007; Wynne-Jones and Kohring 2007: 6). Archaeological deposits are typically palimpsests formed over multiple time periods and at different scales of behaviour, and the substantial impact of scale on archaeological observation makes it a fundamental issue when programs of data-collection and analysis are formulated and executed.

By "top-down" we mean an approach to documentation and analysis that operates from a broad scale, observing a subject's so-called "big picture" units of organization and patterns of adaptation and change at the apical levels of a system (Canuto and Fash 2004: 49; White 2017: 67). This is a useful way to look at phenomena; by this approach over-arching themes and broadly shared elements can be identified and described, and these in turn can provide direction to explanatory hypotheses and the organization of research at other scalar levels of observation (Embree 1989: 31; Burger and Todd 2006: 235-236; Lock and Molyneaux 2006: 9; Peregrine 2017: 40). But difficulties arise when conceptualization is imposed largely or entirely from broad-scale observations without taking into account the localized details that present congruence and variation on the broad themes (Bintliff 2006). Different behavioural patterns are often observed in the same data universe at different levels of scale, and multiple segments or levels in a system should be taken into account when it is characterized (Bentley and Maschner 2003: 4; Molyneaux 2005: 113-114; Burger and Todd 2006: 236-237, 240; Lock and Molyneaux 2006: 7). When top-down characterization dominates, a process of "reverse-engineering" is required in which the regional, sub-regional, and local are made to fit the broader observations.[2]

Thus, for example, when George Cœdès broadly asserted, early in his examination of the Dvāravatī phenomenon, that it was a Buddhist kingdom, he set in motion a tendency to view Dvāravatī as one or several large Buddhist polities, even when some of the site-specific data might suggest otherwise (Cœdès 1928a, 1928b, 1968; Revire 2015, 2016). Indeed, as will be discussed below, the observations and interpretations of Dvāravatī's early enunciators occurred in the milieu of limited data noted by Robert Brown, and with a strong top-down viewpoint.

"Bottom-up" surveys include the documentation of archaeological patterns at local-through-subregional components through time, providing details of shared behaviour as well as local variations that are not apparent at broader scales of observation. It is at the local scale of observation where "problematic" data at odds with the generalized broad-scale patterns are likely to be observed (Stark 1993: 94, 100; Molyneaux 2005: 113–114); such variant information is equally important in understanding a cultural system, highlighting the locally favoured alternatives to practices that may have otherwise been predominant over a region (White 2017: 68). This "microscale" approach allows for the construction of models and paradigms using a broad base of field data that foregrounds core decision-making communities, addresses variability, and contextualizes networks of social interaction at multiple levels of scale (idem.: 69).

Joyce White has recently addressed the predominance of top-down conceptualization in Southeast Asian archaeology and its ramifications for the resulting paradigms that "privilege macroviews" (White 2017: 67). The distortions of this approach include the conflation of processes (e.g. linking the arrival of bronze technology with substantial changes in social organization), the glossing of evidence that does not fit the broad normative explanation, and over-generalizing from small samples (White 2017: 67–68; Stark 2015: 71). White implores Southeast Asian investigators to counter the long

2 "Local" is a term often used without reference to a sharp definition (Cherry 2004; Acri 2017). The term is used here at a basic level of meaning referring to a spatial-geographical sector, generally limited to an archaeological site, locality, or sub-region, rather than to placement in an indigenous-versus-exogamous dichotomy of cultural sourcing.

dominance of top-down, broad-scale conceptualization with ground-truthing at all scales of observation, starting at the local "microscale", contextualizing cultural processes in a way that will promote alternative interpretations and a robust examination of paradigms (White 2017: 67, 69). White believes that future progress in Southeast Asian archaeology depends on such a "bottom-up" approach that builds "from our data rather than match our data to a pre-existing template" (idem.: 67–69, 74).

Miriam Stark has repeatedly emphasized the need to develop information at all scales of observation in order to "refit" the extant descriptions of early historic social developments on mainland Southeast Asia to the archaeological record (Stark 1993, 2006, 2015, 2016). She observes that few regions of the Southeast Asian mainland have been surveyed and analysed with the comprehensive, multi-scalar approach necessary to observe early socio-political systems in detail, and even fundamental questions about the presence or absence of state-level polities and their operational systems lack sufficient information for assessment (Stark 2006: 21.16; 2016: 78; 2017: 261).

The uses of Dvāravatī conceptualization

All observations of phenomena, including patterns in the archaeological record, are impacted by the predispositions both personal and theoretical that the analyst brings to the act of observing (Desjeux 1996; Stark 1993: 96; Burger and Todd 2006: 252). The task is to recognize the agency of these biases and understand how they influence the perception, analysis, and comprehension of archaeological data (de Laguna 1957: 181; Stark 1993: 93). The early scholars of Dvāravatī brought various viewpoints to the task of describing and understanding this early historic phenomenon, and their initial conceptualizations have had a persistent influence on Dvāravatī studies (Hennequin 2010: 30). Cœdès described the top-down approach taken in early researches, while also revealing something of the agendas at work in these efforts. Coupling the beginning of Southeast Asia's historic period with "the arrival of high-caste Indians", Cœdès asserted that:

> The ancient history of South-East Asian countries can be approached from two sides, the Indian and the Chinese, or better still from both at the same time (Cœdès 1964: 2-3).

This initial approach using available external and indigenous texts, he explained, was necessary in order to meet the "urgent task" of creating a chronological framework for ordering events and art, even at the expense of "'economic and social questions" which, he said, could only be investigated after the establishment of a chronology and narrative of events (idem.: 2).

Cœdès found that the adoption of Indian culture during the first millennium, including in areas of Dvāravatī control, exhibited "a constant parallelism between the great spiritual currents in India and in South-East Asia", perhaps sustained by periodic infusions of Indian refugees (idem.: 5, 12–13). Socio-political developments in China were also, he proposed, a strong influence on "the vicissitudes of the history of South-East Asian countries" (idem.: 14). While Cœdès recognized the agency of indigenous civilizations in this acculturation process (idem.: 3), he predicted that the accumulating research would reveal a "deeper Indianization" of Southeast Asian populations than did the analysis favouring indigenous cultural preeminence (idem.: 3–4). For Cœdès, Southeast Asia in the first millennium consisted of "Hinduized States" with an elite culture "no different in its essence from that of the Dravidian countries of India herself" (ibid).

This description by Cœdès late in his career of the initial conceptual approach to early historic Southeast Asia is striking in its top-down approach. The imposition of an over-arching chronology for both events and art was viewed as the necessary first step, with "economic and social" data – "the way the people lived, their beliefs, the social and economic conditions prevailing" (idem.: 4) - to be fitted in subsequently. The chronological narrative was drawn largely from Indian and Chinese texts, which was deemed appropriate given the profound influences on Southeast Asian developments assigned to both of these cultural wellsprings, and given the proposed compliant nature of indigenous traditions (Mabbett 1977: 154, 157).

In general, then, this was an approach that exuded "high culture centrism" focusing on elite segments and external sources (Lukas 2003: 82), an approach grounded in the experience brought to Siam by French scholars, joined with the objectives of Siam's elite. Early, predominantly Western scholars involved in deciphering the region's early history (Étienne Aymonier, Lucien Fournereau, Étienne Edmond Lunet de Lajonquière, Louis Finot, and George Cœdès) came to Siam from research in

Cambodia, where they had studied Khmer civilization by way of monumental architecture, art, and inscriptions (Hennequin 2010: 2–11). Their initial objective in Siam was to locate additional Khmer sites, thus setting up a core-periphery orientation relating Siamese remains to a cultural centre in Cambodian Indochina (idem.: 3). It is also important to note the symbiotic relationship that existed between French and Siamese investigators, with the foreign scholars encountering sites and objects already "unearthed, restored, exhibited ... and somewhat interpreted" by the Siamese (Hennequin 2010: 1). Indeed, the Siamese had been systematically locating and in some cases restoring early Buddhist architecture, and unearthing objects, since the mid-nineteenth century, when Rama IV began the reclamation of Phra Pathom Chedi. This work by the Siamese provided "raw material" for the French scholars who recorded, analysed, and reported these discoveries internationally according to Western standards (idem.: 2; Bayly 2002: 287–288), including the use of archaeology to evaluate indigenous historiographical traditions (Cherry 2004).

Of particular importance is the religious orientation of the Siamese work, which focused on elucidating Buddhist practices and history. It is also the case, however, that under the influence of European examples, the Siamese elite sought to further "the spirit of a single people" and sense of nationhood, to document the Thai aristocracy's rise to power as a progressive historical development, discover among the country's sculptural and architectural remains "a distinctive style that would testify to the political ascendency of the Thai race", and generally assert a cultural equivalence with the West (Charnvit Kasetsiri 1979: 139–140, 161; Glover 1993: 47; Peleggi 2004: 133–142; Piriya Krairiksh 2012: 21; Bayly 2002). In these endeavours, the Siamese adopted the antiquarian approach's "thirst for ancient objects as distinct from the study of their original setting", largely eschewing the discernment of early historic social and utilitarian contexts (Peleggi 2004: 136, 139, 141–142).

Thus, when Cœdès conducted the first field work at a site attributed to Dvāravatī in 1927 (Phong Tuek – Fig. 1), and subsequently interpreted these findings as part of an initial description of a Dvāravatī entity, he did so in a conceptual milieu that foregrounded Buddhism, nationalism, monarchy, and foreign sources of civilization. The resulting broadly conceived chronology and art style, developed with Prince Damrong Rachanubab (Damrong Rachanubab 1919, 1928; Coedès 1928a; Hennequin 2010: 11), were derived from the accumulated material data and epigraphic sources, much of the former lacking robust social and functional context (Peleggi 2004: 134, 136, 149–150; Piriya Krairiksh 2012: 14–15). Cœdès (1925a: 152–154; 1926: 191–192) had from the start consistently viewed Dvāravatī as a Buddhist kingdom (as first proposed by Fournereau in 1895), represented in time and across geography by a Gupta-inspired art style (as intuitively recognized by the Siamese in the late nineteenth century, and briefly described by Lunet de Lajonquière in 1909). Additionally, the idea that this kingdom was inhabited by ethnic Mons had been postulated by Paul Pelliot in 1904 based on little or no direct evidence (Pelliot 1904: 230–231; Cœdès 1925b, 1929; Hennequin 2010: 8, 16). By the time Coedès arrived at Phong Tuek in 1927, then, a general top-down conceptualization of Dvāravatī was in hand, even before the first systematic excavations on a Dvāravatī site had commenced.

Another significant enunciator of the Dvāravatī phenomenon, and the second investigator of Phong Tuek, was H. G. Quaritch Wales (e.g. 1936, 1951, 1966, 1969). Quaritch Wales' visit to Phong Tuek was brief, and followed Cœdès by nine years, but the general view of Dvāravatī had not changed substantially, owing in large part to the lack of additional field work during the interim (Hennequin 2010: 16–17). Quaritch Wales arrived in Siam as Field Director of the Greater-India Research Committee, charged with "carrying out archaeological explorations in Greater India" on behalf of the Royal Asiatic Society, India Society, and School of Oriental Studies (Wales 1937a: 174; 1937b: 7). His over-arching paradigm for early historic Southeast Asia is clearly stated the following year, explaining that the "vigorous development of Indian culture in Indo-China and Java was due to the energy of waves of colonists" creating "a great Indian culture deep-rooted in an alien soil" (Wales 1937b: 115–116). In the region of Dvāravatī specifically, this imposition of "Buddhist Indian colonies" was pressed on "Thai people ... as yet in a very backward state of civilization" by Indianized Mons "swarming across the Three Pagodas Pass into Central Siam" (idem.: 121–122, 130).

Quaritch Wales was an early excavator of Dvāravatī sites including Phong Tuek (1936), Si Thep (1936), and Mueang Phet (1955; see also McNeill 1997), and published a summary overview of the "earliest kingdom of Siam" in 1969. He readily admitted that he approached the subject of early historic developments in Southeast Asia primarily through elite religious practices and art (Wales 1951: 17, 21, 26), and ascribed substantial agency to the impact of "native genius" in resisting and/or adapting outside influences (idem.: 18). In Dvāravatī territory specifically, however, he perceived a condition of "extreme acculturation" resulting in a "purely colonial imitative culture" where local genius had been eliminated as a significant factor (idem.: 12, 18, 23, 25, 47), in contrast to an "eastern zone" (Java, Champa, Cambodia) where Indianization was tempered by a robust local genius which ultimately reasserted local cultural sensibilities (idem.: 18–19).

Clearly both Cœdès and Quaritch Wales approached the initial conceptualization of Dvāravatī from the "Greater India" viewpoint shared with Indian nationalist scholars. South Asian intellectuals had been inspired by the work of Western (mostly French) scholars at monumental sites in Southeast Asia, particularly as characterized by the French Indologist Sylvian Levi (Bayly 2000: 600–601; 2004: 706–714). The Indian movement, manifested in the Greater India Society (founded 1926), extolled the "civilizing mission" by Indian colonists that transformed "barbaric" Southeast Asia through a relatively benevolent, non-martial process (Bayly 2000: 600–601; 2004: 713–719). Emphasis in this scenario was on the transfer of the elite social structures connected to religion and political organization, exemplified in monumental architecture and art (Bayly 2004: 713–714, 725–727; Gupta 2003: 392–393, 404).

Cœdès had "praised these Greater India polemicists for 'rediscovering' their heritage as a 'great colonizing people'" (Bayly 2000: 602). In the case of both Cœdès and Quaritch Wales, Dvāravatī was viewed as a product of and intermediary for the new ideas and practices emanating from South Asia. In the general context of modern colonial hegemony, framed in the diffusionist impulses of European analysis, and secure in the absence of detailed local field data that might suggest alternative explanations, the "Greater India" paradigm seemed to fit, no less so as the proposed dependency on outside sources of "civilization" also paralleled the colonialist project effected in Southeast Asia by the homelands of European scholars at work in the region (Bray and Glover 1987: 111; Glover 1993: 46–47; Bayly 2002: 291–293; Cherry 2004: 119–120).

The idea of cultural colonization across a vast "Greater India" has over time been adjusted to admit the equal or greater impact of "local agency" in the adaptation of Indic elements and practices (Bayly 2004); more recently, a critique has come forward of the local–cosmopolitan/indigenous-exogamous binary as an inadequate description of the complex transregional dynamics of enculturation, suggesting that this process is better characterized by Kulke's "cultural affinities" and Wolters' "shared cultural matrix", conditions where South and Southeast Asians were relatively equal participants in a cultural mileau shared by many groups and regions (Kulke 1990; Wolters 1982; Acri 2017). The salient point with regard to Dvāravatī studies is that the initial top-down characterizations presumed that this cultural entity was fundamentally dependent on South Asian sources for the elite social and material elements that were the focus of those studies. This presumption tended to stunt consideration of evidence that might have suggested a larger indigenous role in a multi-directional enculturation process, particularly as non-elite, bottom-up segments of the Dvāravatī record were almost entirely ignored for many decades.

Phong Tuek complexities[3]

In the history of Dvāravatī studies, the site of Phong Tuek ("P'ong Tuk") in Kanchanaburi Province, west-central Thailand [Fig.1], stands as one of the seminal resources in the initial conceptualization of this early historic entity. Phong Tuek was the first systematically excavated Dvāravatī site, and was long considered to be the earliest known Dvāravatī settlement (Briggs 1945: 99–100). One irony of this status is that Phong Tuek was only minimally sampled and reported. A re-evaluation of the original field work by George Cœdès and H. G. Quaritch Wales, including the latter's field notes, reveals

3 "Complexity" is another term frequently used by archaeologists without clarity regarding the meaning imputed. A formal body of theories and analyses has developed in recent decades under the rubric of "complexity science", however, that is now applied to many fields including archaeology (Holland 2014; Bentley and Mascher 2003). A basic tenet of complexity theory relating to the subject of this paper holds that elements at smaller scales interact to create different, "emergent" phenomena at larger scales, i.e. at each level of complexity, new properties appear, and "the whole is greater than the sum of its parts" (Bently and Maschner 2003: 1–7; Hodder 2012: 163; Kohler 2012). White (2017: 74) specifically connects this "emergent paradigm" with the bottom-up approach to research that she calls for in Southeast Asia, and it is this emergent quality of dynamic interaction among a social system's components that directly addresses transition and change in society (Crumley 2007: 33). In the present paper, however, the "complexities" briefly described for Phong Tuek are noted to illustrate the manner in which a top-down approach to the site tended to minimize and simplify site content; no attempt is made to substantially analyse the existing skewed data for Phong Tuek according to principles of complexity.

that not only were the reported site elements minimally documented, but some important elements were not disclosed (Clarke 2011, 2014, 2015). Indeed, the top-down predispositions that Cœdès and Quaritch Wales brought to Phong Tuek caused them to overlook, ignore, or misinterpret various site elements, apparently in an effort to fit the archaeological material to their overarching conceptualization of Dvāravatī. These shortcomings of the original excavation sampling and reporting now categorize the extant Phong Tuek data as a less useful record of the Dvāravatī phenomenon. Even so, the information from Phong Tuek exemplifies how the local site data was filtered by the top-down perspective of its investigators.

The general setting and characteristics of Phong Tuek have been provided in detail elsewhere (Clarke 2014, 2015). The rural hamlets of Phong Tuek reside at the westward bank of the Mae Klong River, situated at the interface of the Chao Phraya basin to the east and hilly-to-mountainous Tenasserim uplands to the west. The Mae Klong valley provides a north-south conduit between the Gulf of Thailand and its maritime connections, and Three Pagodas Pass and its connections to inland routes of communication and trade [Fig.1]. Phong Tuek therefore occupies a location intermediate to major environmental and cultural zones, and to routes of trans-regional interchange.

The architecture and artefacts recovered by the 1927 and 1936 investigations were interpreted by both Cœdès and Quaritch Wales to indicate "a city of the Buddhist kingdom located ... between Cambodia and Burma and provisionally referred to ... under the name Dvāravatī" (Cœdès 1928a: 208–209; Wales 1936: 42), a characterization made with minimal information on the site's content and organization, or even its general areal extent. Regarding this urban designation, the sites of many first millennium "urban centres" in central Thailand are marked by moats and/or walls (Quaritch Wales 1936: 46; Wheatley 1983: 203–208; Gallon 2013: 152–160), features conspicuously absent at Phong Tuek,[4] and it seems unlikely that "city" is the appropriate label for this settlement. Later, Quaritch Wales changed his characterization of Phong Tuek to that of "a town that was never more than 'a natural halting place for travelers," and "a way-station filling ... approximately the same function as [a] small market town" (Wales 1969: 63, 65). A categorization of Dvāravatī period settlements compiled by Matthew Gallon indicates that of 33 locations attributed to the Dvāravatī culture and having their general layout described, only three sites, including Phong Tuek, are non-moated (Gallon 2013: 152–160). The role of such sites in a Dvāravatī settlement hierarchy or heterarchy, however, remains uncertain.

The urban role within a kingdom initially ascribed to Phong Tuek by Cœdès and Quaritch Wales reflects the top-down paradigm to which they subscribed when they arrived at the site. Observing the broad geographical distribution of the Dvāravatī art style, Prince Damrong Rajanubhab (1973 [1926]) and Cœdès (1929) equated this phenomenon with a single Dvāravatī kingdom, or "royaume". This projection further described Dvāravatī territory as roughly equivalent to the modern borders of Siam. The characterization of Dvāravatī as a large unified polity has persisted throughout subsequent discussion of Dvāravatī socio-political organization (e.g. Quaritch Wales 1969; Lyons 1979), even as alternative possibilities have been introduced (Revire 2016).

Phong Tuek produced the first architectural remains systematically investigated as Dvāravatī features. Dupont's subsequent analysis of the Chedi Chula Prathon and Wat Phra Men structures, at the locality of Nakhon Pathom, revealed that they had developed in three stages of accretion, suggesting that chronological subdivisions existed within the life span of Dvāravatī, a possibility which however Dupont did not explore in detail (Hennequin 2010: 18). The 2008 re-evaluation of Phong Tuek recognized three discrete groups of architectural features with differing construction materials, and suggested this might reflect varying construction methods through time: a northern "San Chao/Banana Plantation" group combining laterite and brick construction materials; a central group of structures composed entirely of brick; and a southern "Ban Nai Ma" group composed of laterite-only (Clarke 2011: 173–174). Since brick-only fabric appears to be the earliest permanent construction type on mainland Southeast Asia (Stark et. al. 2006: 111), it is possible that the brick-only features represent an early construction phase at Phong Tuek, especially as this is where inhumation burials were found in proximity (see comments below); the discrete groups of laterite-only and laterite-and-brick construction might also have temporal associations. At least in Quaritch Wales' case, these three construction types were apparent but elicited

4 Chinese accounts of first millennium urban centres on mainland Southeast Asia, however, include settlements with wooden palisades (Guillon 1999: 76), a feature that would not be apparent on the modern land surface at Phong Tuek.

no recorded consideration as to what these differences might indicate regarding cultural changes through time. In general, neither Cœdès or Quaritch Wales discussed the possibility of occupational complexity through time at Phong Tuek to any significant degree, despite the long time span initially assigned by Cœdès (second to sixth centuries CE – 1928a: 207). Clarke (2014) has suggested that the inclusion of non-cremation interments in apparently Buddhist ritual contexts at Phong Tuek may represent the persistence of an indigenous tradition in the face of new ideologies from extra-local sources. Even so, it may also present a significant alteration in local mortuary behaviour, given the assertion by some observers that the dominant prehistoric mortuary pattern in Thailand was "residential burial", with graves placed around and under houses (MacDonald 1980; Adams and King 2011; White 2017: 66–67). The burial of some individuals with ritual architecture, then, may represent the persistence of certain indigenous elements of practice which, however, were occurring in a new functional context.

When Quaritch Wales excavated and reported these burials (1936, 1937b, 1937c, 1964), he wavered in their cultural attribution but ultimately assigned them to a pre-Dvāravatī occupation as much as 500 years older (1936: 47; 1937a: 89). The logic he used to arrive at this determination appears to have been faulty (Clarke 2014: 215–216), but the multi-component implication of Quaritch Wales' original interpretation was minimally discussed by him regarding any ramifications this might have for the history or functional content of the site. Likewise, Cœdès (1928a: 195, 197, 199) was aware of at least one inhumation burial found by local residents at the site in 1927, reportedly in close association with Dvāravatī artefacts, but no speculation was proffered regarding the potential ritual or functional implications of this discovery.

Perhaps no object associated with Phong Tuek more represents the expanded social complexity now documented for the site than the Viṣṇu image uncovered by road construction in the 1950s [Fig.2], and represents also the manner in which early conceptual trajectories set for Dvāravatī studies impacted subsequent thinking. This well-executed stone sculpture presents both unusual stylistic forms and a striking combination of elements derived from dispersed cultural sources (Lavy and Clarke 2015). Attributed to the seventh or eighth century CE, the syncretic style, perhaps representing a local sculptural tradition, and elements that appear to be derived from Arakan, Pre-Angkorian Cambodia, and the Cham civilization of Vietnam, reflect multiple scales of operation and provide "valuable testimony of a particularly intense period of interactions spanning mainland Southeast Asia" (idem.: 19).

When this figure was uncovered, it should have had a significant impact on both the interpretation of Phong Tuek's early historic record and the general discussion regarding trans-regional socio-political interaction during the Dvāravatī period. But it did not, and the reasons for this may have been established when Cœdès asserted that Phong Tuek was part of a Buddhist kingdom (1928a: 207), a top-down observation which ignored evidence uncovered at the site. Among the four architectural features excavated by Cœdès in 1927, one square laterite foundation identified by him as a "small temple" had a square pedestal at its centre (idem..: 198–199). In both the published drawing and photograph of this pedestal [Fig.3], a shallow channel is apparent extending from the mortised centre on one side, suggesting that this is a yonī or snānadroṇī type platform associated with Śaivite practices.[5] The implications of this feature for the presence of Hindu practices at Phong Tuek, however, were never acknowledged by Cœdès, nor by extension a place for Brahmanism in the initial description of a Dvāravatī kingdom.[6] This followed a long-established bias; Hindu objects had been depicted among early historic remains in Thailand since the late nineteenth century (Fournereau 1895, 1908), but were largely ignored in subsequent discussions, perhaps due to the Siamese focus on narrating the rise of a Buddhist civilization (Hennequin 2010: 5, 23). While the presence of Hindu objects and practices in Dvāravatī contexts has subsequently been recognized and discussed (e.g. Quaritch Wales 1969: 90; Srisakra Vallibhotoma 1986: 231–235; Brown 1996: 48, 51, 56–61; Ray 1997: 43; Phasook Indrawooth 1999 [2542 BE]: 233; Nandana Chutiwongs 2009: 59–60; etc.), the assertion that Dvāravatī was predominantly Buddhist has persisted to the point that recent internationally organized museum exhibitions still reflect this bias (Revire 2016: 393–394, 398). It seems likely that the early predilection to gloss the Hindu elements at Dvāravatī sites is also why the later discovery of a seventh or eighth century Viṣṇu image at Phong Tuek was essentially ignored in discussions of the site for over sixty years.

5 This pedestal, and the subject channel, are still visible at Phong Tuek.

6 Coedès did recognize that "Hindu cults" flourished for a time in the "Mon country" of lower Burma (1964: 7-8), but he did not expand this observation to include the Dvāravatī Mon civilization proposed for central Thailand.

The local specifics at Phong Tuek briefly reviewed here are mostly phenomena that Cœdès and Quaritch Wales chose to ignore or minimize. Conceiving Dvāravatī as an Indic-style Buddhist kingdom imposed on subservient local traditions, site-level observations were geared to fit the general paradigm. This established interpretive trajectories that influenced the observation and description of Dvāravatī sites for much of the twentieth century. In recent decades, a few sites have been added to the record for Dvāravatī and the field work has tended to address a broader set of questions about Dvāravatī social and material content (e.g. Phasook Indrawooth 1983; Phasook Indrawooth et al. 1991; Mudar 1999; Phattharaphong Kaongoen 2002 [2545 BE]; Saritpong Khunsong et al. 2011; Gallon 2013, 2014; Thanik Lertcharnrit 2014), reflecting a shift toward bottom-up research (Stark 2017: 260). Thanik Lertcharnrit's long-term excavations at Promthin Tai, a smaller semicircular moated site in Lop Buri Province [Fig.1], is a good example of research that is establishing details in archaeological context for a Dvāravatī occupational sequence (2005, 2006, 2009, 2010, 2011, 2014; Thanik Lertcharnrit and Carter 2010). A few systematic regional surveys examining a wide range of occupational types through time are also developing a more holistic view of the early historic period in Thailand (e.g. the Lop Buri Regional Archaeological Project – Respoli, Ciarla and Pigott 2013; and the Phon Songkhram Archaeological Survey in the upper Mun River Valley of northeast Thailand – Evans et al. 2016). Even so, details regarding the internal arrangement, material content, and socio-temporal range of all types of Dvāravatī settlement are still inadequately documented.

Conclusions

After more than 130 years of study in Thailand, the term "Dvāravatī" remains problematical regarding it social meaning, temporal placement, and geographical distribution (Miksic and Goh 2017: 248–249). This is largely due to the "top-down" approach to data selection and analysis utilized from the beginning of Dvāravatī research and field studies, which retarded a more holistic approach to the Dvāravatī phenomenon. The initial conceptualization of Dvāravatī as an "Indianized" Mon Buddhist kingdom has persisted in publications and museum exhibits, even as alternative concepts have been proposed and debated, and at the present level of documentation it may be best to regard Dvāravatī as an "archaeological complex" of uncertain social structure and political reach (idem.: 249). Both top-down and bottom-up approaches are useful for discerning patterns in the archaeological record. The challenge is not to eschew one approach in favour of another, but to integrate differing scales of observation, recognizing their distinctive vantage points within the Dvāravatī archaeological record. It has been argued here that the top-down conceptualization of an early historic Dvāravatī entity resulted in a skewed view of these early historic developments that can only be rectified with a conscious shift toward bottom-up, empirical data collection at multiple scales of observation and analysis. A multi-scalar perspective is likely to produce new and varying models of Dvāravatī socio-political organization, leading to a more detailed and reliable understanding of the Dvāravatī phenomenon. The resulting insights may surprise us. For example, what if the originally asserted Dvāravatī kingdom was instead a series of relatively unstable principalities, with socio-political continuity to be found mostly at the level of local communities (Stark 2006: 21.13–21.14, 21.16, 21.48; Acri 2017: 24)? Indeed, what if the monumental architecture found at a place like Phong Tuek was not so much a representation of centralized control but rather an expression of relatively stable local institutions (Indorf, Gudur and Clarke 2014; Souvatzi 2007)? Old and new postulates for the socio-economic structure of Dvāravatī across time and geography can only be evaluated with data that includes much more local and regional information, developed from the ground up. The resulting multi-scalar record for Dvāravatī, reconciling top-down themes with bottom-up variability, is likely to present a view of early historic social structures and processes that is much more dynamic than our current portrayals.

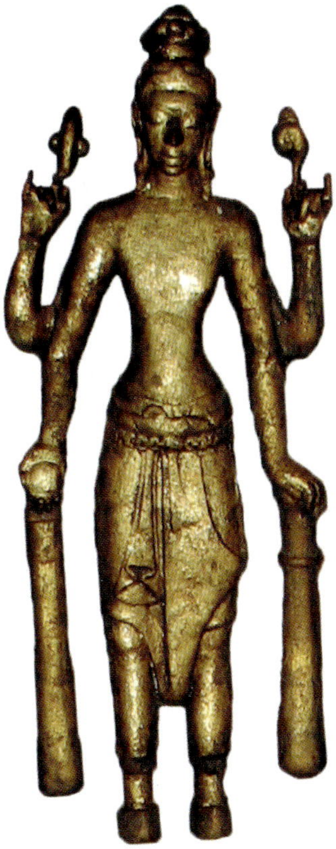

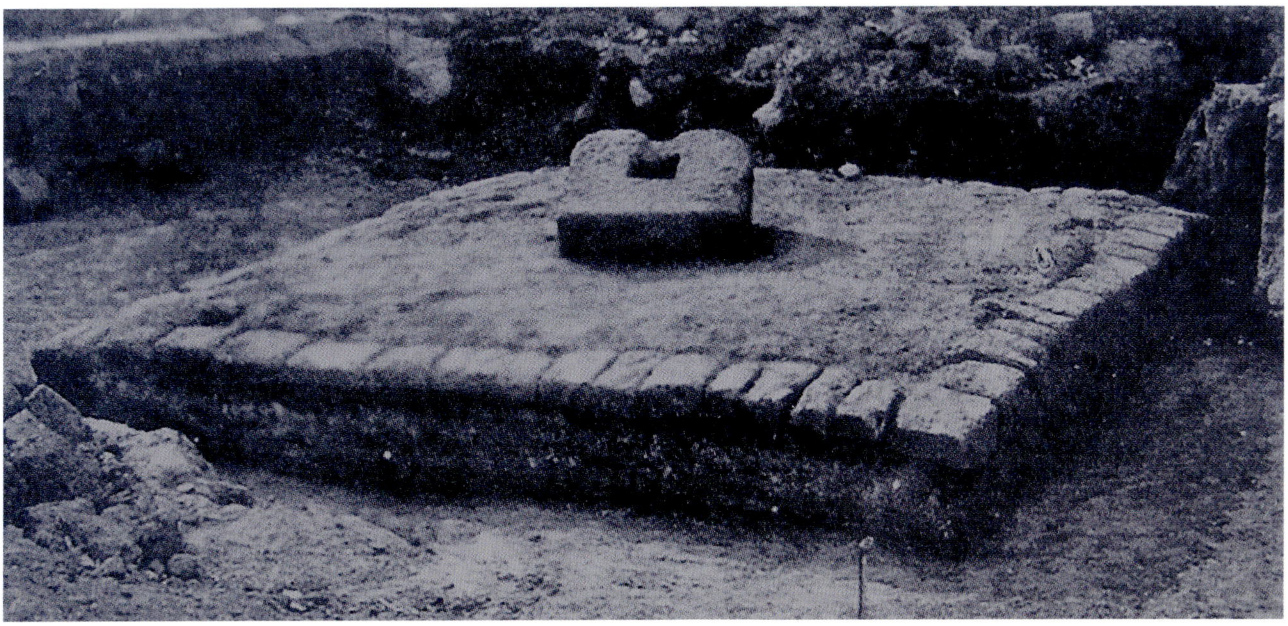

Fig.2 Viṣṇu image found and reconstructed at Phong Tuek in the 1950s.
Fig.3 Excavated laterite shrine foundation, "Ban Nai Ma" location, with pedestal at centre showing a channel cut across the upper side from the central mortise hole (Cœdès 1928b: 3).

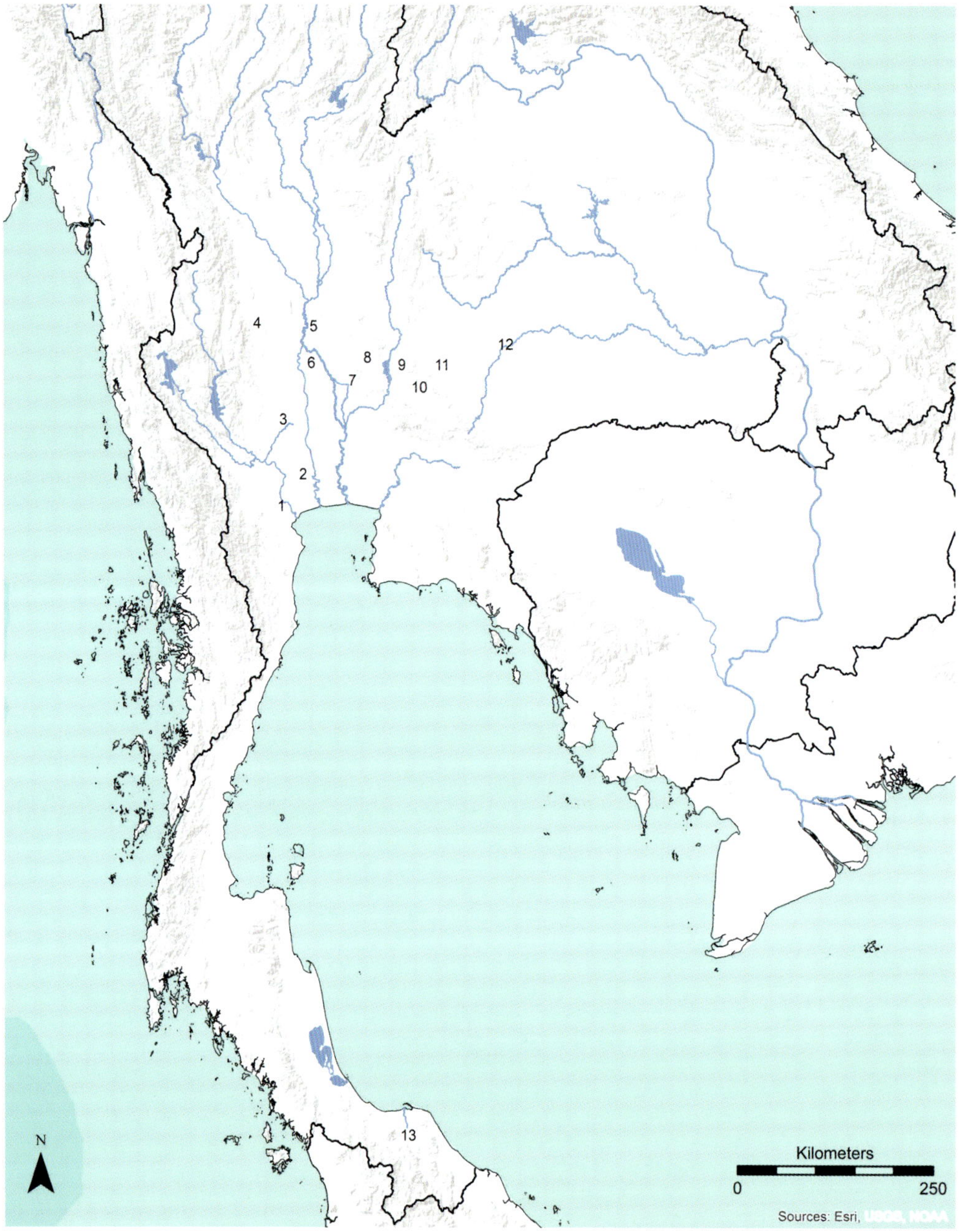

1. Khu Bua
2. Nakhon Pathom
3. U Thong, Khok Chang Din
4. Lan Sak
5. Khok Mai Den
6. Sankhaburi
7. Lop Buri
8. Dong Maroom
9. Sap Champa
10. Wat Chantuek
11. Mueang Sema
12. Phimai
13. Yarang

Fig 1 Map showing locations mentioned in the text (map by Hunter Watson).
All photographs belong to the author unless otherwise stated.

NEW KNOWLEDGE ON DVĀRAVATĪ

THE EARLIEST PROTO-HISTORIC PERIOD OF THAILAND

Phuthorn Bhumadhon

This paper is dedicated to Ian Glover who was my teacher and close colleague. Since I first met him at Ban Don Ta Phet, we kept in contact until the year he passed away, a connection of more than 40 years. I have always been very impressed by his behavior and he was a real archaeologist's idol; he loved to teach, he loved to work, he offered support and encouragement to numerous young archaeologists, he was always eager to learn things, and he remained young at heart.

Introduction

There are two main points I would like to consider in this paper. First, "Dvāravatī " became known in Thailand's academic circle in 1928. Since then, it has been accepted that there was a Dvāravatī culture as well as an art style under the same name. The centre of the Dvāravatī culture was believed to have been situated on the Central Plain while Dvāravatī-style art was scattered in every region of the country. This gives an arguable impression that any area where Dvāravatī art is discovered is regarded as Dvāravatī territory. In fact, there are a number of debates/questions about this ancient land which remain inconclusive. It is necessary to raise some examples of ongoing debates here for consideration. Second, this paper will focus on new knowledge about this ancient civilization which has emerged in the past years.

Existing knowledge

There is a need both to review existing knowledge about this ancient civilization and to examine some aspects of new knowledge.

1. With regard to existing or old knowledge, it is worth considering whether the use of the term Dvāravatī, both as a historical period and an art style, is appropriate. Since 1977, Piriya Krairiksh in his book, "Art styles in Thailand: A Selection from National Museums and An Essay in Conceptualization" proposed that Dvāravatī was a political unit with an ambiguous history. In his opinion, calling the art found in every part of Thailand "Dvāravatī" gave rise to the misleading impression that it was a land with vast influence. Instead, Piriya suggested that we substitute the term "Dvāravatī style" by "Mon style" art. However, after some 40 years, his suggestion has never been seriously considered.

2. We continue to identify Dvāravatī as an entity that lasted five or six centuries; the FAD identifies the sixth century as the beginning of the civilization and the tenth century as its end, attributing all artifacts from that era to Dvāravatī. The question of why such a conclusion was reached and the explanation behind it remains unresolved. Is the said period still valid?

3. Most information about Dvāravatī history comes from the interpretation of artefacts and evidence from excavated archeological sites of between the sixth and the tenth century. Intense excavation work on Dvāravatī sites, which had been very active with the help of the École française d'Extrême-Orient, started to fade in the late 1960s. Since then, most of the sites, some with special characteristics, have been heavily looted and/or destroyed [Fig.2]. They have lost their importance as a study area that could have enabled the replenishing of our knowledge of this historical civilization. Lop Buri is one such extraordinary site which shows a continuity of human settlement from the prehistoric age, through the Dvāravatī period and subsequent periods up until the present day. It is a pity that the state has failed to protect and preserve its heritage, and has neglected to thoroughly study the area and in order to complete our knowledge. Why is this the case?

4.There is little access to information held by the government, concerning excavation reports, translation of inscriptions and of recently found artefacts. Nor is there information forthcoming from private owners of objects that were looted and traded. Such difficult access to source material has resulted in a dependence based on and confined to old knowledge. The question is: how can we overcome this obstacle?

5. We should investigate the extent of diplomatic, trade and cultural relations between the Dvāravatī state and areas in the northeastern part of Asia, which is now China, Korea and Japan. In their studies on ancient glass beads, Bunchar Pongpanich and James Langton have tried to establish links between the two regions (Lankton: 2019: 68–77; Pongpanich 2109: 251–54). At the same time, Piriya Krairiksh has been focusing his research on the expansion of the Sukhavati School of Buddhism from China to the Dvāravatī state.

6. There may be links between the Dvāravatī state and the northwestern part of India. Piriya Krairiksh has found that the decorative stucco at Chula Pathon Chedi in Nakhon Pathom was inspired by stories in popular Sanskrit language Buddhist folk tales from northwestern India. Those who study Dvāravatī should investigate this important evidence.

New Evidence

The need to focus on new evidence that has emerged in the past years is paramount. Newly found materials either excavated or looted from archaeological sites over the past years include the following examples:

1. A number of artefacts inscribed with Sanskrit "Dvāravatī" have been found [Figs. 3–6]. A silver coin from the Kok Chang Din archaeological site, U Thong, with a Sanskrit inscription reads "Śrī Dvāravatī Īśvara Puṇya" and on the other side are images of cow and a calf [Fig.3]. Two other silver coins, which can be dated to around the sixth to seventh century, found at Sankaburi, Chai Nat Province [Fig.4-5], have a similar inscription and image. Another inscription in Sanskrit, written as *Dvāravatī Pateḥ*, which means a Dvāravatī ruler, was found on a lotus shaped base of a Buddha image at Wat Chantuek, in Pak Chong District, Nakhon Ratchasima Province, now kept at the Phimai National Museum, and can be dated palaeographically to the sixth century [Fig.6].

2. Discovery of an inscription [Fig.7] in Cambodia which mentions the invasion of "the western land", believed to be Dvāravatī, by the Khmer army under King Sūryavarman I (r.1006-1050). The invasion is believed to be the cause of the fall of the Dvāravatī culture and this information seems to correspond to the archaeological evidence in Lop Buri Province (U-tain, this volume).

3. Some newly-found artifacts in non-typical forms carry significant implications. Many of these have been discovered in new areas, including Lan Sak District, Uthai Thani Province[Fig.1]. Such spectacular finds include the head of a Buddha image [Fig.8], and terracotta figures in the form of humans and animals [Figs.9a–f]. These artefacts are similar to objects found in Bengal, India, and this evidence should trigger questions as to how, and to what extent, they might relate to the artefacts in the Dvāravatī cultural areas.

Another interesting question concerns the route that links Dvāravatī on the Central Plain of Thailand to the outside world. It is highly likely that the transpeninsular route on the upper part of Southeast Asia began from the Mawlawying Gulf to the Chao Phraya River Basin and the Mun-Chi River Basin, before reaching the sea at the Tonkin Gulf [Fig.1].

Some archaeological objects including Buddha images and remnants of *dharmacakra*, etc., that belong to the typical Dvāravatī style of art on the Central Plain were found in Nakhon Ratchasima Province, especially in the area of Mueang Sema, Sung Noen District, and further to the east [Figs.10–11]. Archaeological objects, which include stucco motifs in the form of a seated Buddha, which is widely found in the Cham area and might be decorative parts of a religious site, were excavated from a lesser known site in U Thong, Suphan Buri Province [Figs.12a–b].

Foreign objects, many of which can be dated before or contemporary with Dvāravatī, including a ladle or musical instrument [Fig.13a–b] and bronze cups [Fig.14a–b] from the Dian culture in Yunnan have been found by looters in Lop Buri Province. Numerous religious sculptures presumably made in the Chinese Sui-Tang dynasties have also found been in many areas [Fig.15].

For those interested in the Buddha's preaching which was widespread in the Dvāravatī period, in addition to the well-known "Ye Dhamma" stanza that was discovered in 1977, there are new finds which feature other episodes of the Buddha preaching including his first speech after attainment or enlightenment, the Triple Gems and the Four Noble Truths. Most of these new finds were discovered in the Pattani River Basin [Fig.1] and include part of a Pāli inscription on terracotta which highlights the Triple Gems as a way to end suffering. Dated to the seventh century, it was discovered in U Thong [Fig.1] and is now on display at the U Thong National Museum [Fig.16]. An octagonal pillar found at Sap Champa in Lop Buri Province contains an inscription in Pāli that features the Lord Buddha's first sermon after attaining enlightenment and now on display at the Somdet Phra Narai National Museum [Fig.17]. *Stūpa* foundations and votive tablets with inscriptions have been found in Yarang District, Pattani Province [Fig.18–19a–c].

Recommendations

Thailand should have a research and study centre on Dvāravatī. The proposed centre should pursue new research and link it to existing knowledge in order to create a complete picture of this ancient culture, both in terms of its history and its art form. This should be the responsibility of the Fine Arts Department or Silpakorn University and participants of this seminar may also contribute to the establishment of such a centre. There is a need to review and verify existing knowledge. For instance, this should include the period when Dvāravatī came into existence and when it came to an end.

The Fine Arts Department, by law, is an authorized agency responsible for the protection of archaeological sites. It is obliged to perform its duty vigorously and efficiently to protect Dvāravatī sites which are most clearly demarcated by a wall or moat [Figs.20 a–d]. The FAD should preserve this evidence before the areas are completely ruined. Some areas like Kok Mai Den in Nakhon Sawan Province; Sap Champa and Dong Maroom in Lop Buri Provice and Ku Bua in Ratchaburi Province remain in good condition and can still be protected and preserved as study sites.

Conclusion

It should be noted that the knowledge of Dvāravatī involves the principle of universality: Dvāravatī settlements were universal in that they comprised people from different races, including Mon, Khmer, Thai and ethnic groups such as the Karen. Moreover, Dvāravatī culture also followed the universal principle of freedom of choice with regard to religion. The evidence shows that people in this cultural area practiced different sects of Buddhism, Hinayana or Mahayana, as well as Hinduism. Dvāravatī universality is also reflected in the location of its cultural area which was on the international trade route. People from India, China, and Persia visited the area to not only trade, but to worship a religion and engage in cultural activities. In summary Dvāravatī was a universal cultural area of the world where different groups of people settled nearly 2000 years ago. Their settlement patterns could provide an example for us to learn how to coexist with others.

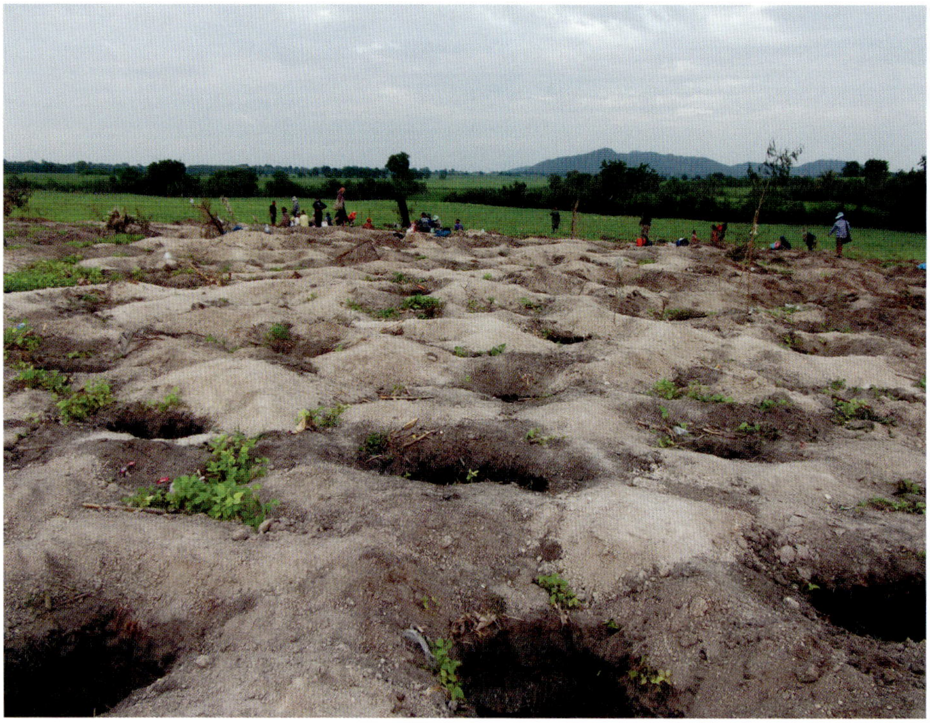

Fig.2. Looting at the archeological site of Ban Chon Mueang in Lop Buri Province. With weak law enforcement on the part of the state, looters can get into any archeological site to search for artefacts.

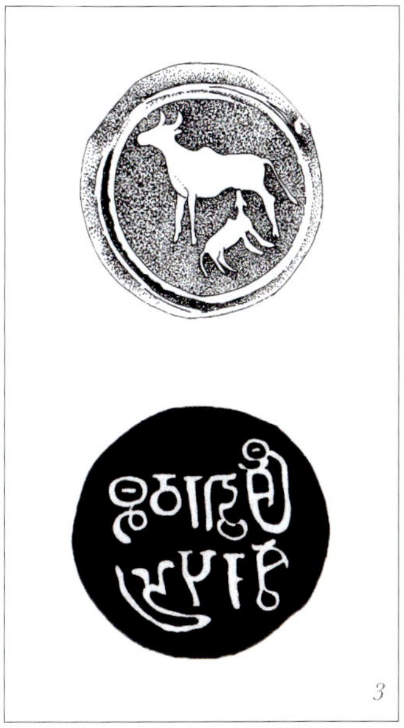

3

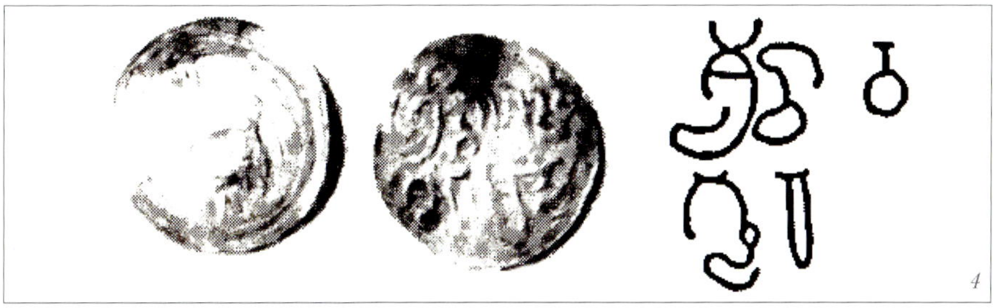

4

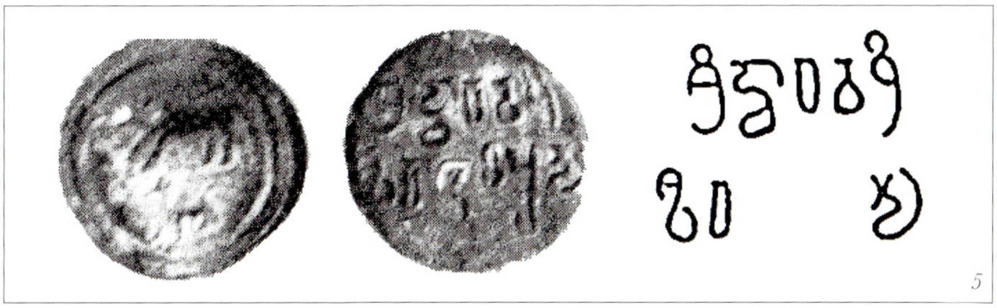

5

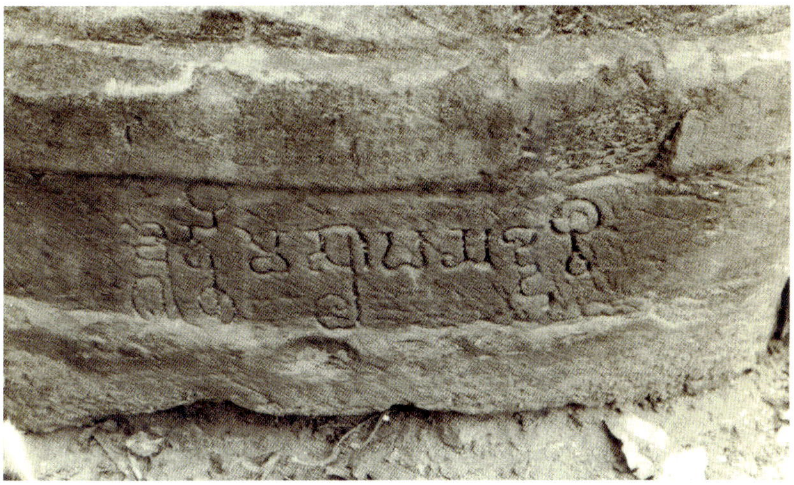

6

7

Fig 3. Illustration of a silver coin from the Kok Chang Din archeological site, U Thong. On one side there is inscription in Sanskrit which reads "Śrī Dvāravatī Īśvara Puṇya". On the other side of the coin, there are images of cow and a calf (FAD 2002).
Fig 4. Illustration of a silver coin, which can be dated palaeographically to around the seventh century, from Sanka Buri, Chai Nat Province. The coin is engraved in Sanskrit with "Śrī Dvāravatī Īśvara Puṇya". Images of a cow and a calf are on the other side.
Fig 5. Silver coin, dated palaeographically to around sixth to seventh century, from Sanka Buri, Chai Nat Province. The coin, is engraved with Sanskrit language, "*Sri Dvāravatī Dhevi Savarapunya.*" Images of mother cow and a calf are on the other side of the coin.
Fig 6. Inscription in Sanskrit, *Dvāravatī Pateḥ*, which means a Dvāravatī ruler, was found on a lotus shaped base of a Buddha image at Wat Chantuek, in Pak Chong District, Nakhon Ratchasima Province, now kept at the Phimai National Museum, and can be dated palaeographically to the sixth century.
Fig 7. The Sūryavarman I inscription in Khmer and Sanskrit now on display at the National Museum of Cambodia, in Phnom Penh, mentions the assignment of officials to rule the land in the west in which the Ramans or the Mons resided. The said area means the Central Plain of modern-day Thailand. Photo courtesy of Ian Glover.

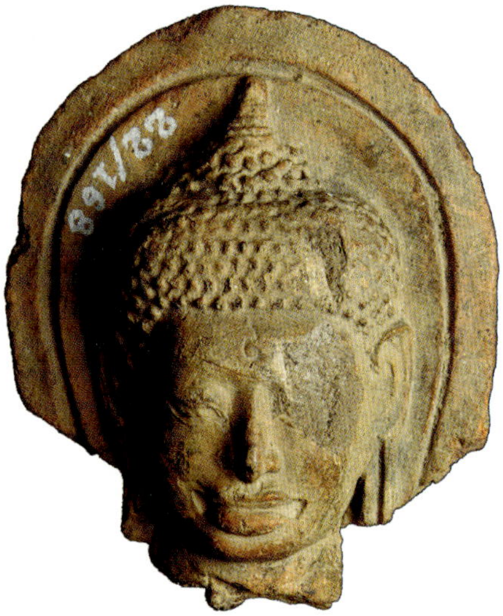

8

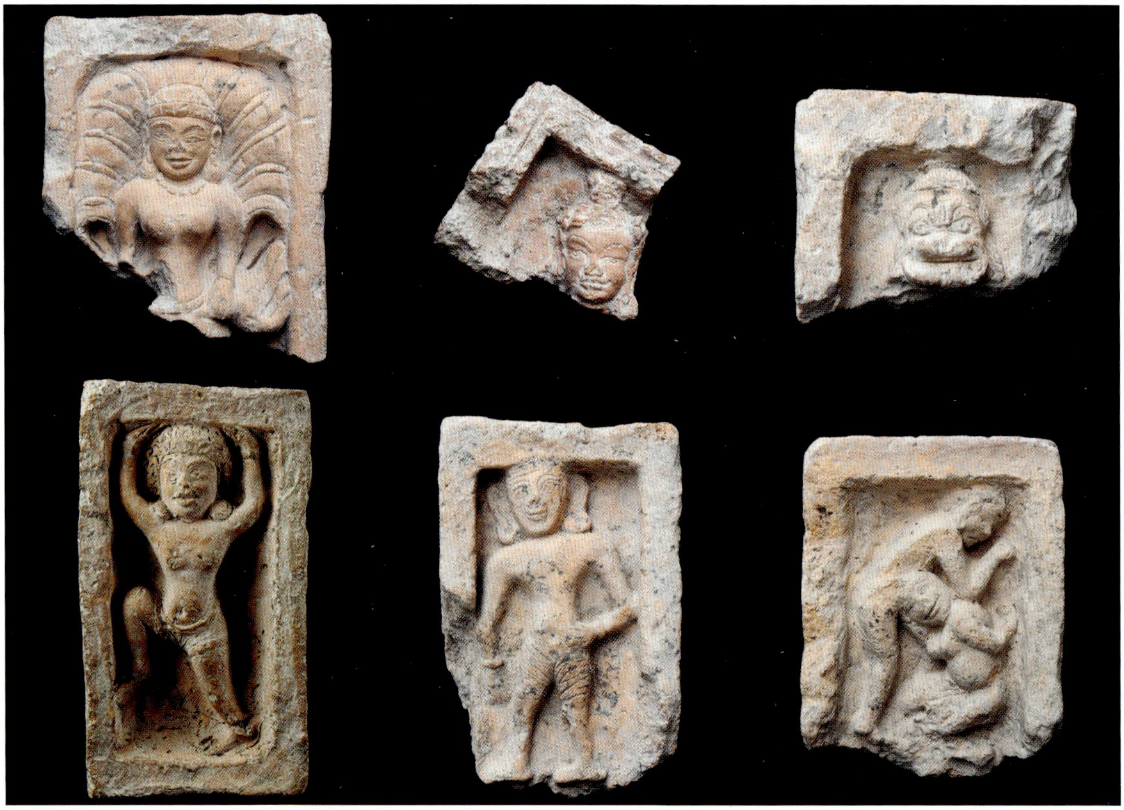

9a–f

Fig 8. An image of the head of the Buddha discovered in Lan Sak District, Uthai Thani Province near to the Thai-Myanmar border.
Figs. 9a–f. Terracotta items in the form of a person and a lion discovered in Lan Sak District, Uthai Thani Province near to the Thai-Myanmar border which are similar to Paharpur Vihara, Bangladesh. These are in the National Museums in Lampun, Lop Buri and Bangko respectively.

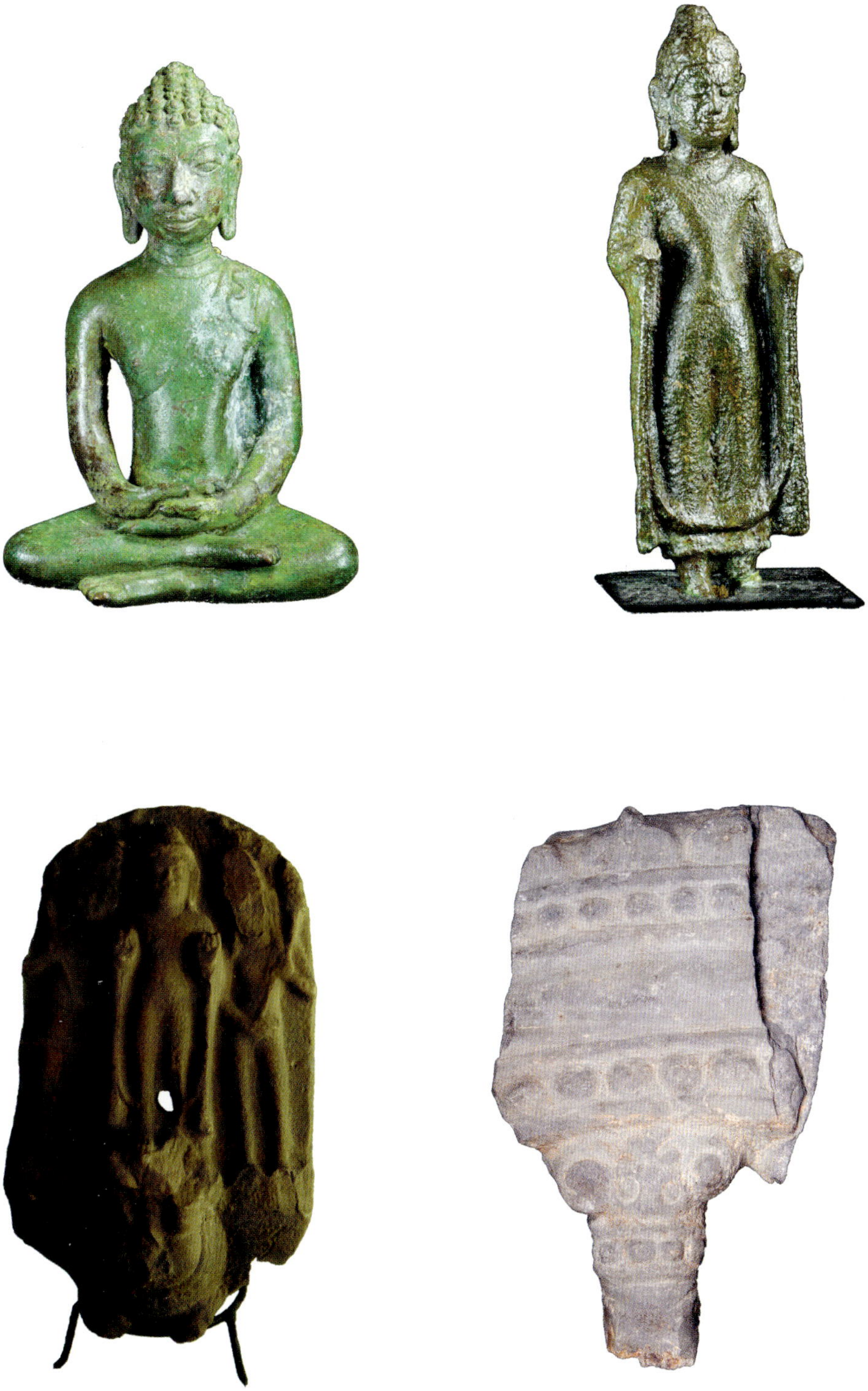

Figs. 10a–d. Buddha images and *dharmacakra* found in Nakhon Ratchasima, now at the Phimai National Museum.

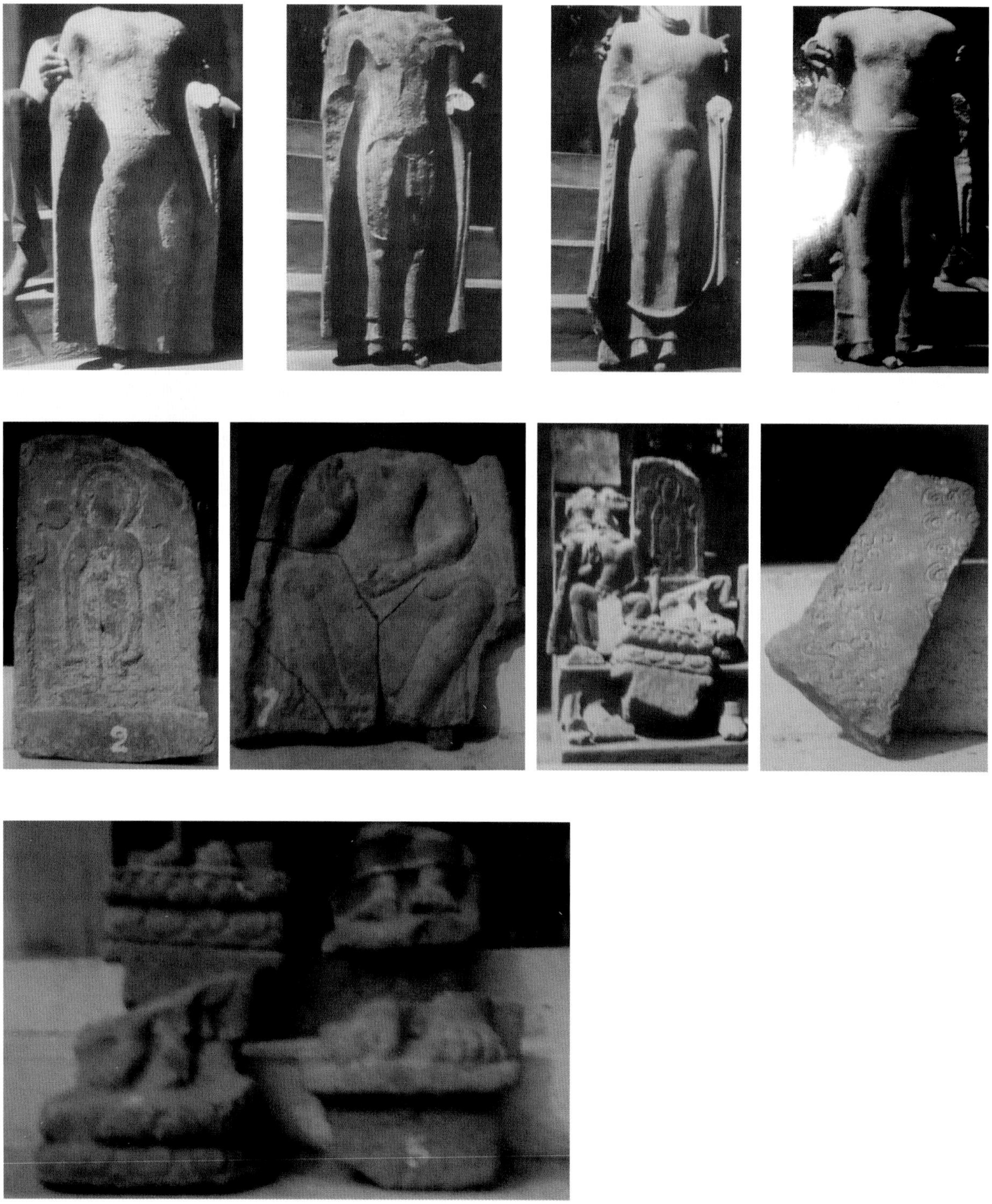

Fig.11a–i. Some sculptures that were found in Mueang Sema, Sung Noen District, Nakhon Ratchasima Provinc, in 1975 (An archive item from the National Archive Office, FAD).

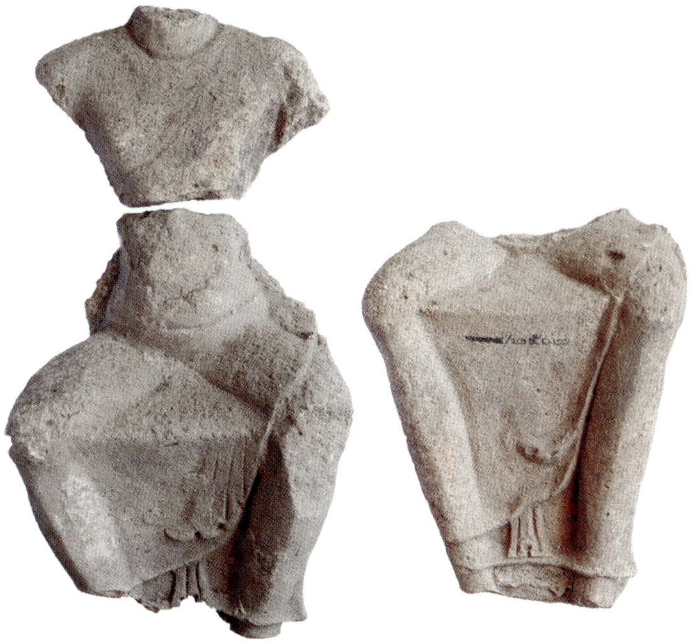

12a–b

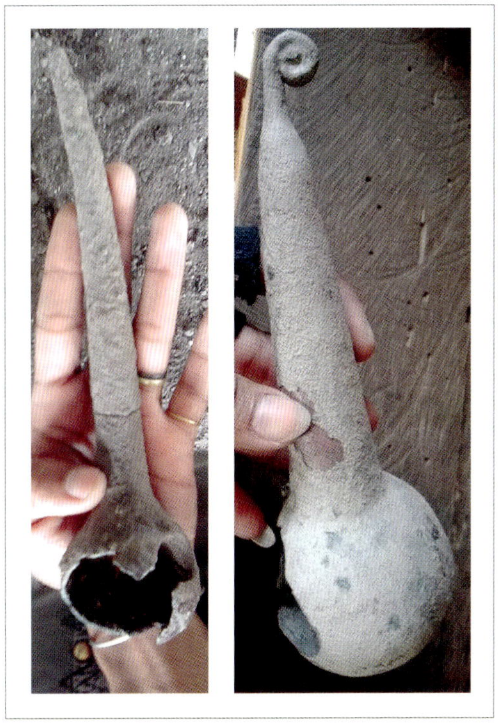

13a–b

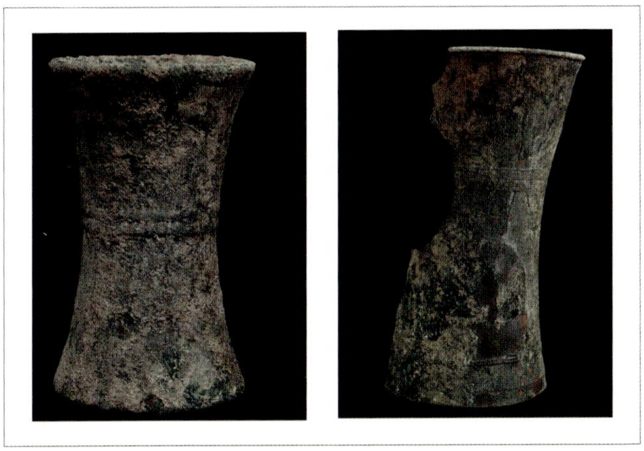

14a–b

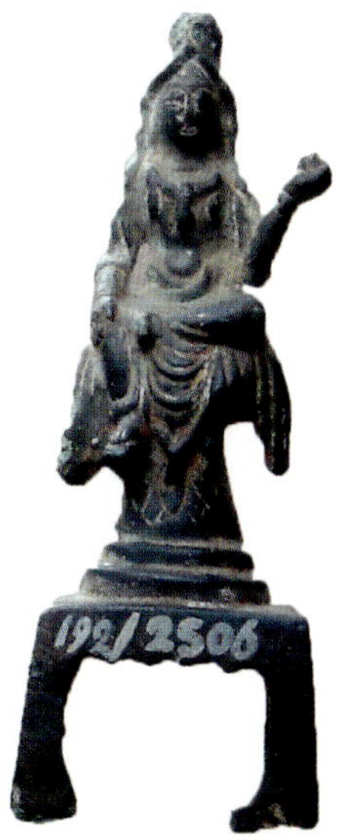

15

Fig.12a–b. Stucco motif in the form of a seated Buddha might be a decorative part of a religious building. Now on display at the U Thong National Museum in Suphan Buri Province.

Figs.13a–b. Ladle or musical instrument in the shape of a gourd from the Dian culture, in Yunnan, from c. the third century BCE to the first century CE, found by looters in Lop Buri Province.

Figs. 14a–b. Bronze cups from the Dian culture in Yunnan which were found by looters in Lop Buri Province.

Fig.15 A sculpture of a bodhisattva, dated around Sui (581-618 A.D.) - early Tang dynasty (618-907), found in Phra Prom District, Nakhon Si Thammarat Province, now on display at the Bangkok National Museum.

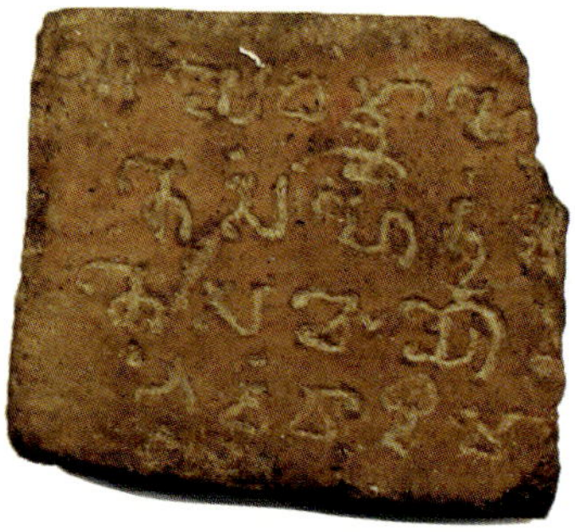

16

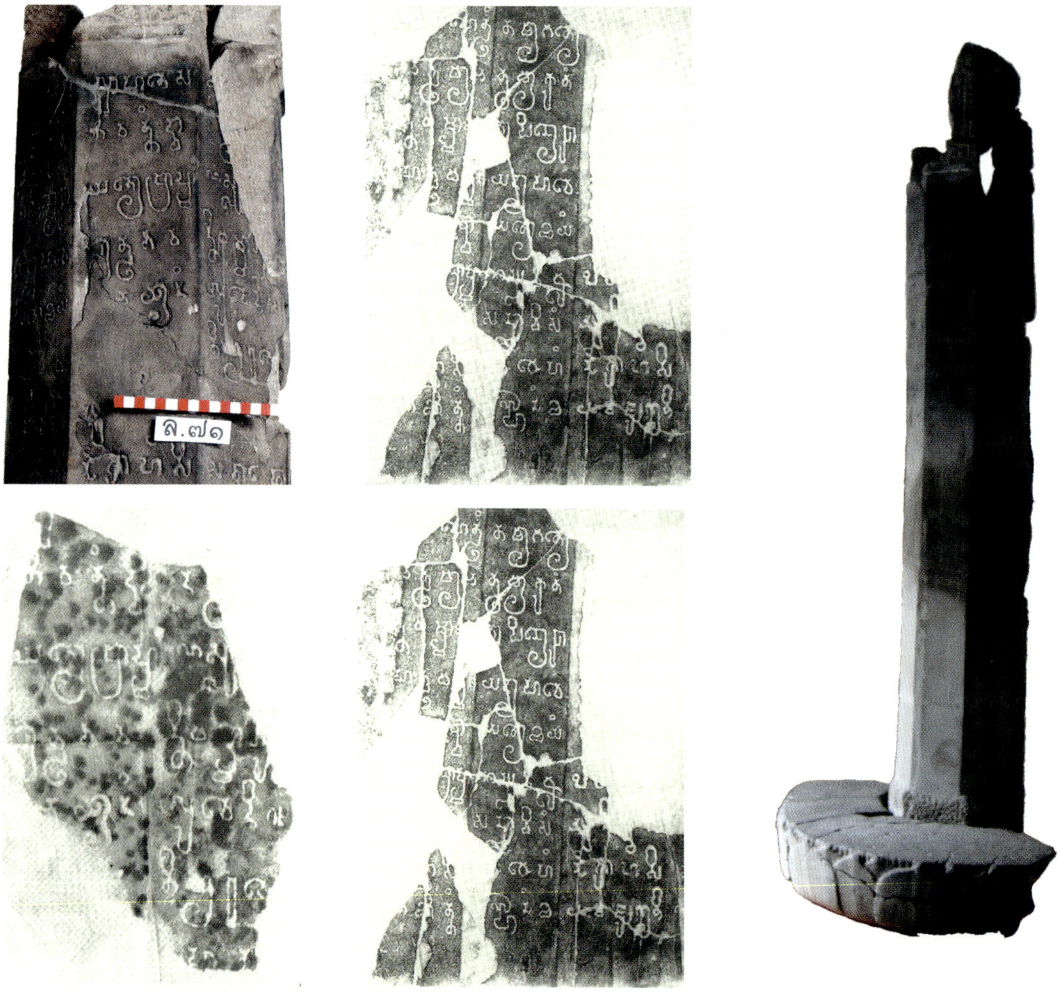

17a–e

Fig.16. Part of a Pāli inscription which highlights the Triple Gems as a way to end suffering. The terracotta piece, dated palaeographically to around the seventh century, was discovered at U Thong, and is now on display at the U Thong National Museum.
Fig.17a–e. An octagonal pillar found at Sap Champa, Lop Buri Province, bearing an inscription in Pāli that features the Lord Buddha's first sermon after attaining enlightenment, now on display at the Somdet Phra Narai National Museum.

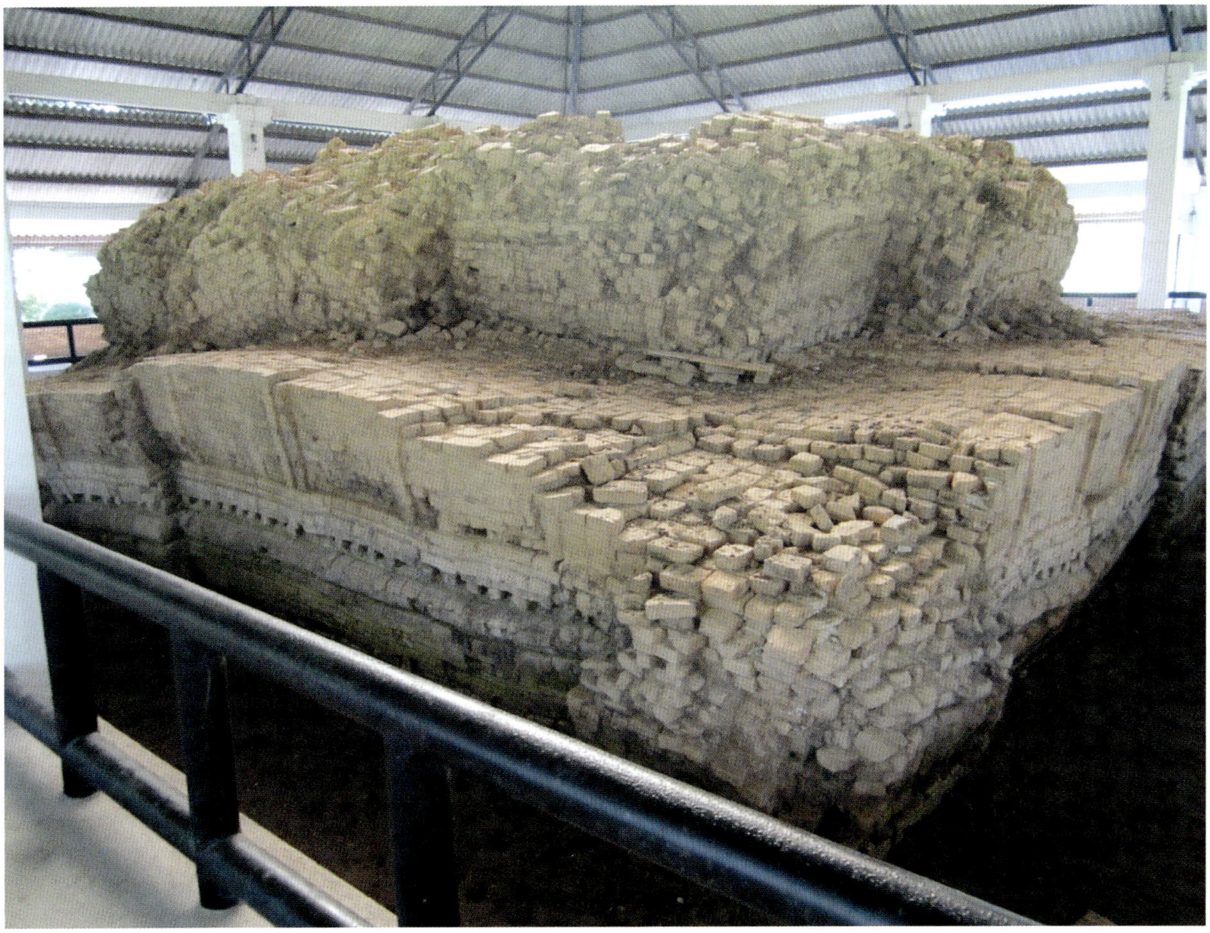

18

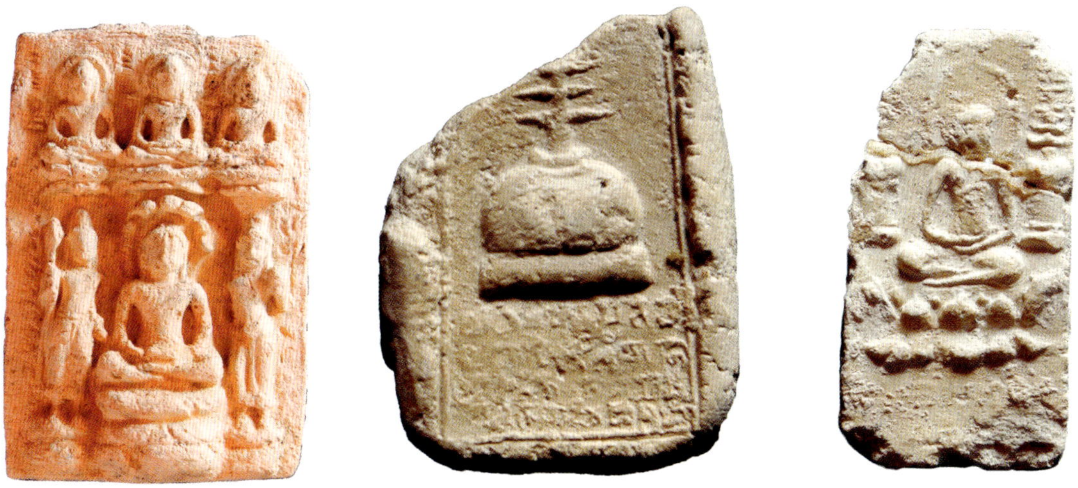

19a-c

Fig.18. Foundation of a *stūpa*.
Fig.19a–c. Votive tablets and an inscription found in Yarang District, Pattani Province.

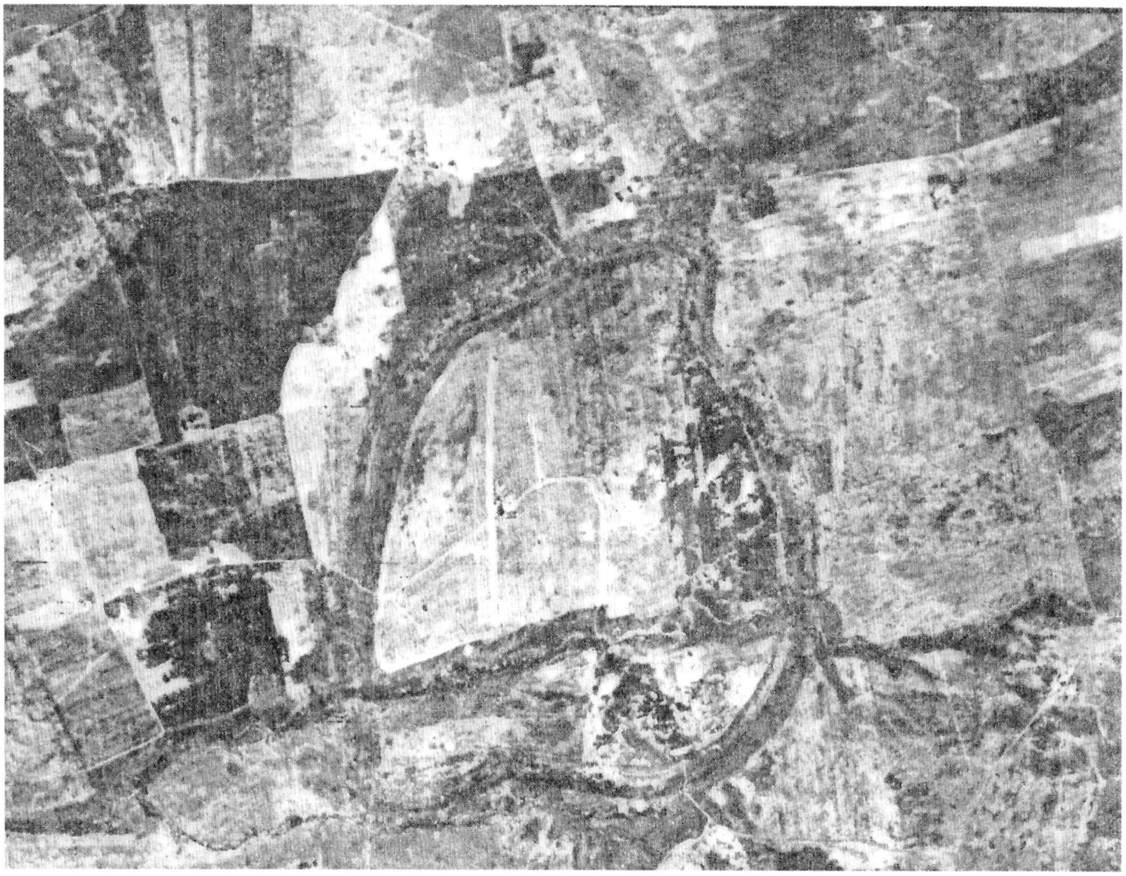

Fig 20a Aerial photograph showing the Dvāravatī site of Sab Champa, Lop Buri Province, clearly demarcated by a wall or moat.

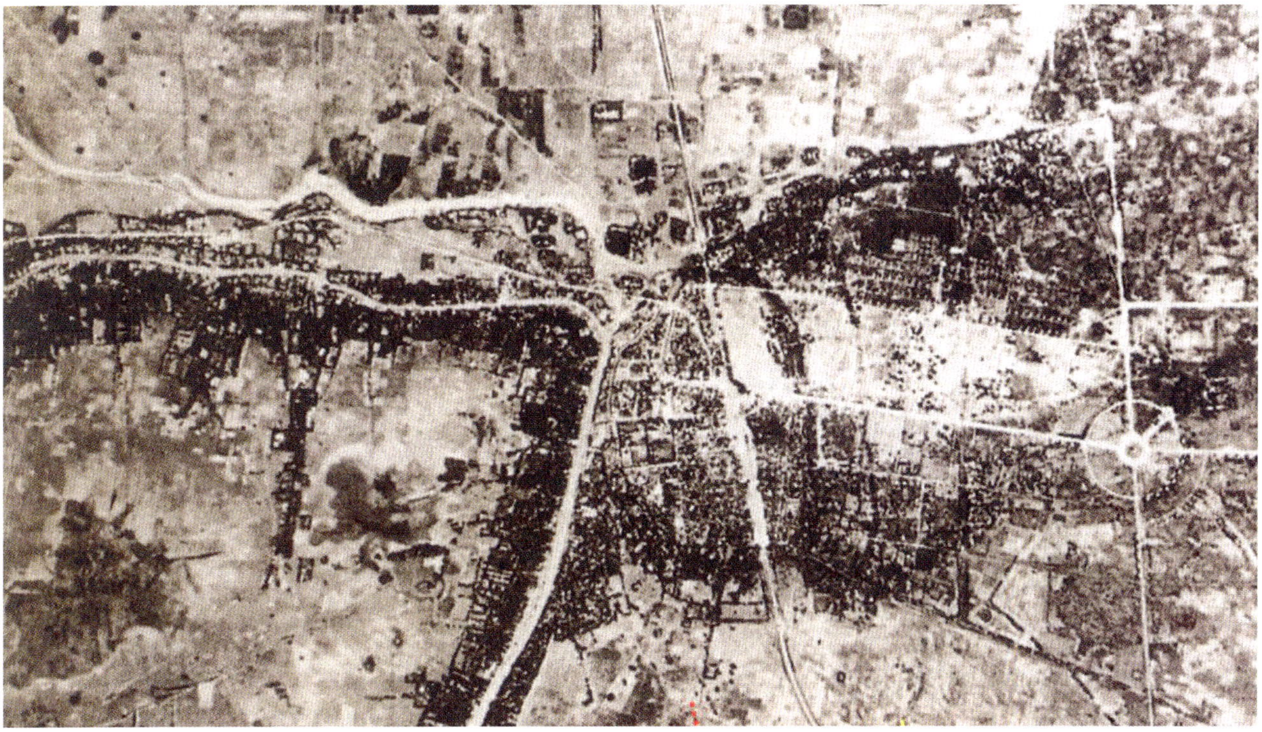

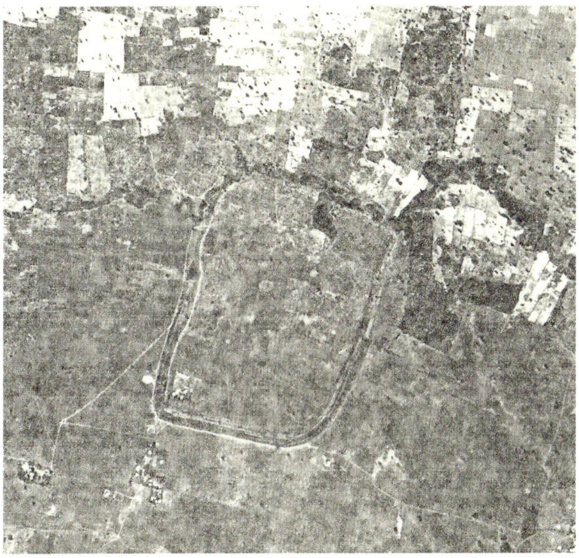

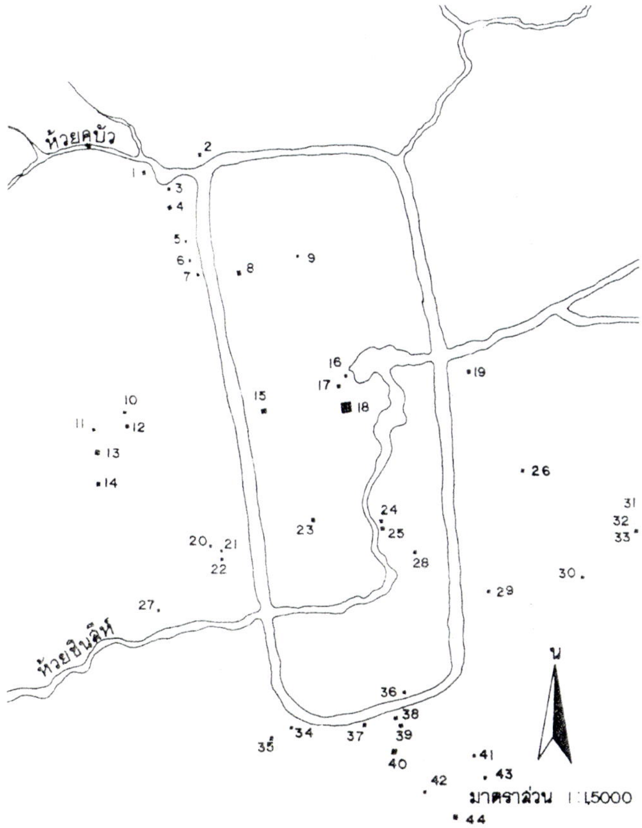

Fig.20b-d Aerial photographs of the Dvāravatī sites of Lop Buri and Dong Marum, Lop Buri Province and a map of Ku Bua, Ratchaburi Province. The sites are clearly demarcated by a wall or moat.

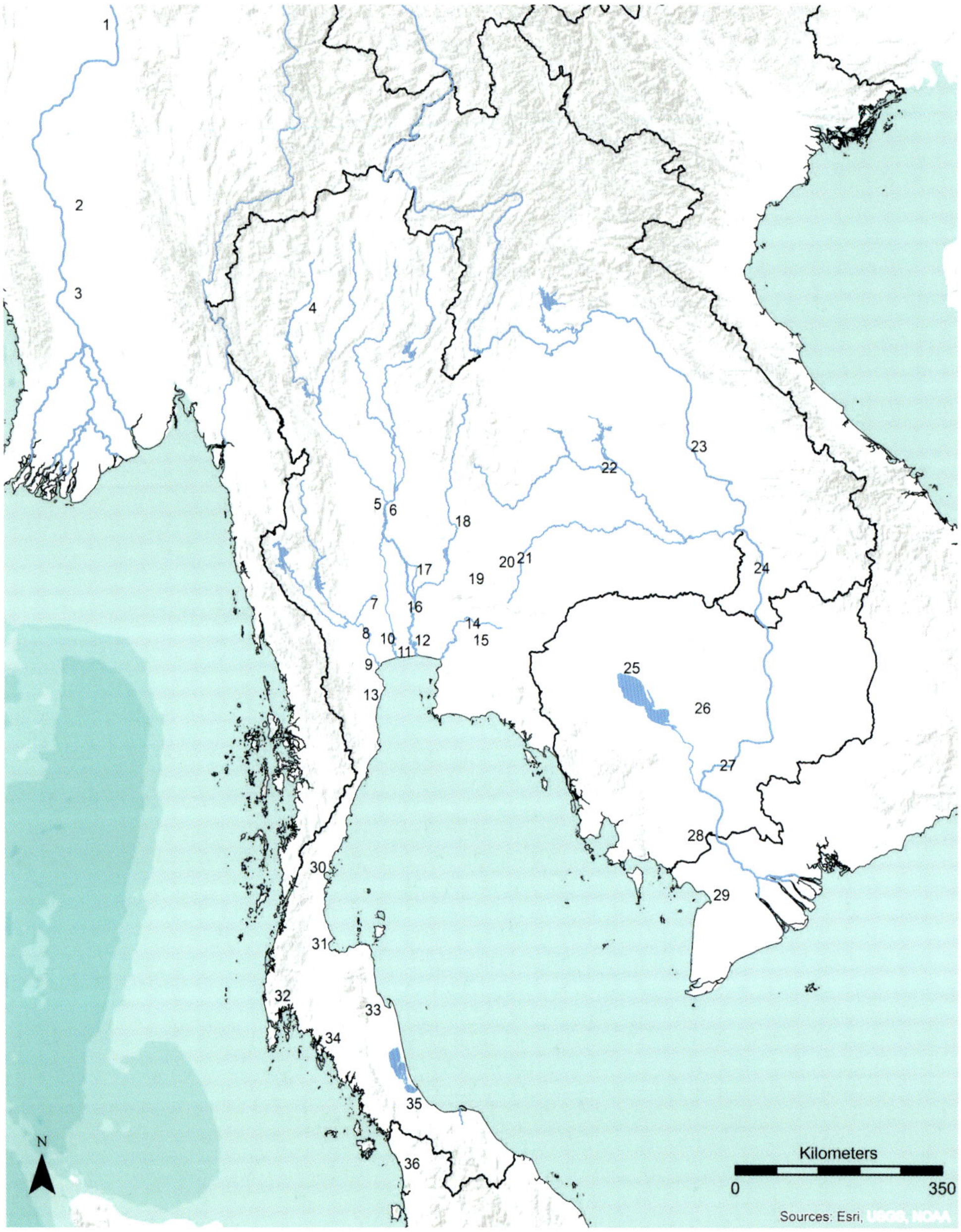

1. Halin
2. Beikthano
3. Sri Ksetra
4. Hariphunchai
5. Thap Chumphon
6. Nakhon Sawan
7. U Thong
8. Phong Tuek
9. Khu Bua
10. Nakhon Pathom, Huai Chorake
11. Phanom Surin shipwreck
12. Bangkok
13. Phetchaburi
14. Prachin Buri
15. Si Mahaphot
16. Ayuthaya
17. Lop Buri
18. Si Thep
19. Wat Chantheuk
20. Mueang Sema
21. Nakhon Ratchasima
22. Fa Daet Song Yang
23. Savannakhet
24. Wat Phu, Champasak
25. Angkor
26. Sambor Prei Kuk
27. Kampong Cham
28. Angkor Borei
29. Oc Eo
30. Chumphon, Khao Sam Kaeo
31. Chaiya
32. Takua Pa
33. Nakhon Si Thammarat
34. Wat Khlong Thom
35. Wat Khao Noi
36. Kedah

Fig.1 Map showing locations mentioned in the text (map by Hunter Watson).
All photographs belong to the author unless otherwise stated.

MAKING SENSE OF DVĀRAVATĪ

John Guy

Introduction

The first millennium landscape of lowland Southeast Asia is punctuated by numerous fortified and moated urban settlements which signal two significant historical developments, early urbanization and the beginnings of state formation. These urban centres, known in Thai as *mueang*, to the Burmese as *main*, the Khmer usually as *pura*, and the Malays as *negari*, represented the power-bases of local rulers who increasingly assumed the trappings of Indic culture, expressed in the writing of their spoken languages in Indic scripts, the adoption of Sanskrit for ritual use, and the worship of Brahmanical and Buddhist deities.[1] These were independent centres of localized rule, their peripheries porous and overlapping with other polities. They were likely far more numerous than the surviving sites dispersed across lowland Southeast Asia would suggest. There must have been many smaller units of which no archaeological traces remain; the Pre-Angkorian inscriptional corpus records thirty such *pura* in Chenla territories alone, where recognized chieftains resided (Vickery 1998: 327).[2] The Sanskrit terms *nagara* and *maṇḍala* can usefully be applied to these localized political units.[3] Archaeological footprints can be traced from the great Pyu cities of Beikthano, Halin and Śrī Kṣetra in central Myanmar, across Thailand to Cambodia and southern Laos. However, by far the greatest concentration of traceable fortified moated urban centres is in central and northeast Thailand. Of these, amongst the oldest and largest, akin to the Pyu cities to its west, are Nakhon Pathom in central Thailand and U Thong, to the north in Suphan Buri Province.

The ancient urban centre of U Thong was distinguished by earthwork walls and a large moat connected to the nearby Suphan (Tha Chin) River, a distributary of the Chao Phraya River. Nakhon Pathom was similarly served by the Tha Chin River, providing ready riverine access to the Gulf of Thailand. The Tha Chin River enters the Gulf of Thailand in Samut Sakhon Province, where a newly discovered shipwreck, identified as an Arab dhow and likely of Persian origin, was excavated in 2013-2015 (Guy 2017a). This demonstrates that these first millennium settlements in central Thailand had ready riverine access to the international trade goods circulating at this time. That this trade was active prior to the Dvāravatī period is witnessed by the discovery in U Thong of a third century Roman coin witnessing a wider spectrum of long-distance goods circulating (Borrell 2008). Others Roman coins, and intaglio seals of both Indian and Mediterranean origin, are known from the early entrepôt of Oc Eo, in the Mekong delta, dating to the second to third centuries (Malleret 1959–1963). The oldest *stūpa* at U Thong, Phra Paton, likely owes its foundation to the early first millennium, and belongs to the first wave of monumental *stūpa* building, at sites which extended from U Thong to Nakhon Pathom and south to Chaiya and Nakhon Si Thammarat. Although U Thong boasts a number of Sanskrit inscriptions, it has, to date, yielded only one confirmed Mon inscription, recently recorded on a portable clay sealing (see Watson & Skilling, this volume), no *in situ* stone inscriptions in Mon are known there. Rather, Mon inscriptions are more closely associated with Nakhon Pathom Province, appearing on stone associated with religious architecture, especially of Nakhon Pathom *mueang* itself (Skilling 2009). A number of terracotta model *stūpa*, such as found at Nakhon Pathom and at Thap Chumphon, Nakhon Sawan Province, typically carry a Pāli *ye dharma* verse (Skilling 2003: 100; see also Skilling 2015; Watson 2018).

Defining Dvāravatī

The dominant political entity in early historical central Thailand, still largely undefined, is that of Dvāravatī (Baptiste and Zephir 2009; Glover 2010). This political unit had its ethnicity established, as best we can tell, by the use of the Mon language, though undoubtedly its populations were rather more heterogeneous. Though its elites adopted the trappings of Brahmanical culture as a means to consolidating

1 See Sanskrit Studies Centre 2003 for papers on the presence of Sanskrit in first millennium Southeast Asia. For the sculptural record, see Krairiksh 2012, Guy 2014.
2 For an important discussion of pre-Angkorian political organization, see Vickery 1998, Chapter 8.
3 Oliver Wolters' application of the Indian *maṇḍala* concept (1982) has been widely adopted in studies of historical political process in Southeast Asia; the notion of the ungoverned, of regions beyond frontiers, has been explored by Scott 2009.

political authority, they also supported monastic Buddhism, sometimes on a grand scale, on occasions marshalling state-like resources of manpower and money. This is witnessed most spectacularly by the suite of four monumental limestone enthroned Buddhas, each 3.75 m. in height, that are believed to have originally graced the cardinal directions of the *stūpa* at Wat Phra Men, Nakhon Pathom (Revere 2014). All heavily reconstructed, they nonetheless may be assumed to have resembled that depicted on the *stambha* base panel recovered at Wat Sat, Nakhon Pathom [Fig.2]. Supplemented by great throne-back settings and with Wheel-of-the-Law bearing pillars (*dharmacakrastambha*) in the courtyard [Fig.3], these constituted some of the most majestic assemblages of Buddhist imagery of their day. Such ensembles could only have been organized with centralized support, even if funding was pluralistic (Guy 2014: 204–205, 212–215). The wider populations appear to have integrated Buddhism early into their local belief systems. The proliferation of small-scale bronze icons - and no doubt perishable images that no longer extant - of the Buddha in the later first millennium can be taken to reflect this wider patronage base, including monastic [Fig.4]. These icons are the public face of Dvāravatī (Baptiste and Zephir 2009; Guy 2014). Whether they are the product of a discrete political entity, or merely a shared cultural milieu, are questions to be addressed.

The Sanskrit word Dvāravatī means "gated," and can be taken to refer to an urban centre with a gated wall. Traces of such a wall are best preserved at the moated Pyu city of Śrī Kṣetra in lower central Myanmar (Stargardt 1990). Its earliest appearance is in the Sanskrit epic the *Mahābhārata*, referencing the ancient Indian city of Dvārakā, the capital of the Anarta kingdom.[4] In Thailand, Buddhist imagery on sacred boundary markers (*sema*) and diminutive clay sealings provide vivid depictions of what these walled and gated cities once looked like, depicted as settings for the telling of Jātaka Tales [Fig.5] (Guy 1989: Pl.10). They depict high walls, seemingly with capping stones, punctured with gated multi-storied guard towers encompassing open pavilions with peaked and cusped rooflines, much resembling traditional Thai wood architecture. This tradition was preserved into later periods in regions of Mon concentration, such as Lamphun in northern Thailand, where the essential elements of the Dvāravatī-style gated settlement persisted into the twelfth century [Fig.6].

Two silver coin-like medallions were discovered in 1943 within the moated city of Nakhon Pathom, beneath the foundations of a now destroyed small *stūpa* associated with Wat Phra Paton [Fig.7].[5] They have proved to be the 'Rosetta Stone' of Mon history, linking the Mon cultural sphere to the name Dvāravatī, only previously known in Chinese transliterations. The medallions display, on the observe, a cow and calf or a flowering vase (*pūrṇaghaṭa*) and, on the reverse, a Sanskrit text first read by George Cœdès as śrīdvāravatīśvarapuṇya, "meritorious deed of the ruler of Dvāravatī" (Cœdès 1963; Boeles 1964: 100–102). This has proved to be the first archaeological context in which the name Dvāravatī can be understood to identify a kingdom. We have no secure way of determining where the lord(s) of Dvāravatī's capital was located, but it is a reasonable assumption that U Thong or Nakhon Pathom, or both, may have fulfilled this role at different times. Cœdès assigned the inscription paleographically to the seventh century.

A number of further finds of these medallions have been reported, including in 1997 the important Khok Chang Din hoard at U Thong, excavated at what proved to be a Brahmanical sanctuary, complete with *liṅgas* and ponds for ritual bathing, southwest of the moat. In the foundations of one of these Brahmanical sanctuaries (Site 7), a small terracotta pedestal jar was recovered containing nine silver medallions, three of which bore the same inscription as that first reported in 1943 [Fig.8]. The context of these discoveries, both within the basements of sanctuaries, strongly suggests they served as foundation deposits. It is tempting to suggest therefore that the medallions were conceived as auspicious tokens, and that their presence in both a Brahmanical and Buddhist setting was a conscious act of sanctification of each site. Peter Skilling's reading of the Sanskrit śrīdvāravatīśvarapuṇya as "merit of the glorious lord of Dvāravatī" or "merit of the lord of glorious Dvāravatī" suggests a prevailing overlordship, be it symbolic or actual (Skilling 2003: 94–95). The distribution of these inscribed Dvāravatī medallions may well serve as a useful indicator of the extent of Dvāravatī suzerainty, just as the location of Aśokan inscriptions and pillars are our best barometer of the extent of the Mauryan Empire in third century BCE India. Certainly, a shared cultural milieu is one of the defining indicators of the period (Brown 1996).

4 The earliest sections have been assigned to 400 BCE; it assumed the form known today by around 400 CE.

5 The site of Huai Chorake was recorded by Pierre Dupont during his 1939-1940 campaign at Phra Paton; Dupont 1959.

Linked through connecting trade routes that generated wealth beyond their agrarian bases, these *mueang* likely formed confederations, loose alliances of shared interests which still allowed each chieftain-ruler local autonomy whilst subscribing to wider interests. Shared language, kinship alliances and economic interdependence were probably all forces which drew these *mueang* into some form of political federation. Were some *mueang* in a tributary relationship to others? The mid-seventh century Sanskrit inscription of a ruler at U Thong, named as Śrī Harṣavarman, suggests so.

The Śrī Harṣavarman copper plate inscription (K.964), found within the ancient settlement area, names a local ruler who came to power through "regular succession," that is, he was not a usurper [Fig.9]. He asserts his Khmer lineage, identifying himself as the grandson of "King Śrī Īśānavarman," and expresses loyalty to him through religious gift-giving (*dana*). The inscription states in part:

> Sri Harsavarman, grandson of the king Sri Isanavarman, who had spread the mass of his glory, obtained the throne of lions through regular succession. He got [inherited] the fortunate Amratakaevara [*linga*, Shiva's authority under which he ruled] a palanquin adorned with jewels, with a parasol, dancers, and musical instruments. And then, he gave Sri Isanevara [Isanavarman] a *kośa*, comprising poetical compositions as well as songs, dances (Cœdès' translation (1958), cited in Brown 1996: 49–50)

The ruler speaks of securing "the throne of lions," and the ubiquitous presence of lion imagery at Dvāravatī sites confirms this allusion to kingship. The principal gift was a *kośa*, typically understood as a precious metal sheath cover for a Śiva *liṅga* [Fig.10] (Guy 2000). References to *kośa* are rare in Khmer-culture Sanskrit language inscriptions, unlike Cham epigraphy, where they are frequently mentioned as royal *dana*, the earliest dated occurrence being in the Hoa Lai temple inscription of 778 CE.[6] This is a reminder that whilst Buddhism was widely practiced in the Mon territories, the ruling elite principally followed Brahmanism. Both Śaiva and Vaiṣṇava imagery found at U Thong confirm this. Copper plate inscriptions typically served as legal documents, especially property deeds, and were widespread in India by the sixth to seventh century, but are rarely encountered in Southeast Asia, with the notable exception of Java. In recording that he sent lavish gifts for adorning a *liṅga* to his grandfather, King Śrī Īśānavarman, almost certainly Īśānavarman I of Chenla (dates uncertain; active c.627–637 CE), he is honouring his Khmer lineage (Vickery 1998: 22). It seems unlikely then that the political entity named Dvāravatī on silver medallions and found in sanctuary foundations at U Thong could have existed there at that point in time. If it had, it would in all probability have been named in Śrī Harṣavarman's inscription. However, the first recorded Chinese source to acknowledge embassy exchange with a political entity named Dvāravatī occurred in 638 (Jiu Tang shu, Wade 2014: 27), confirming that some region, presumably other than U Thong, used that name in the second quarter of the seventh century.

This moment may signal a diminishing political dependence on Chenla and a realignment with other Mon *mueang* in central Thailand, especially the largest of all, Nakhon Pathom. This moated urban centre, twice the area of U Thong, and located some 80 km. southeast of U Thong, controlled river access to the Gulf of Thailand. With the growing economic importance of long-distance trade, an alliance between U Thong and Nakhon Pathom, and encompassing Phong Tuek, Kamphaeng Saen and Khu Bua, seemed credible and advantageous. This was likely the political configuration of Dvāravatī in the seventh and eighth centuries and probably beyond.

In central Thailand, this name appears in Chinese sources from the second quarter of the seventh century as "Duheluobodi" (and variants of that name), and was described as a 'country' that observed Buddhism. The Chinese sources locate it quite precisely in geographic terms, east of central Myanmar (Śrī Ksetra), "before" Cambodia (Īśānapura, i.e. Sambor Prei Kuk) (Li 1996: 110). Another contemporary Chinese source, the *Jiu Tang shu* (History of Early Tang), locates Dvārapatī by naming its contiguous polities, namely to the south Pan-pan [Thai peninsula], to the north Jia-luo-she-fo [unknown], to the east Zhen-la [Cambodia] and, to the west, the Great Sea.[7] A survey of the distribution of the epigraphic evidence places it securely in the lower Mae Nam Chao Phraya River system (Skilling 2003).

The entity Dvāravatī was largely Mon speaking, as far as can be judged from the inscriptional record, and seems

6 None have ever been recovered outside Cham territories; see Guy 2018. For the Hoa Lai inscription, see Griffiths and Southworth 2011.

7 *Jiu Tang shu* was compiled in the tenth century, see Wade 2014: 27-28.

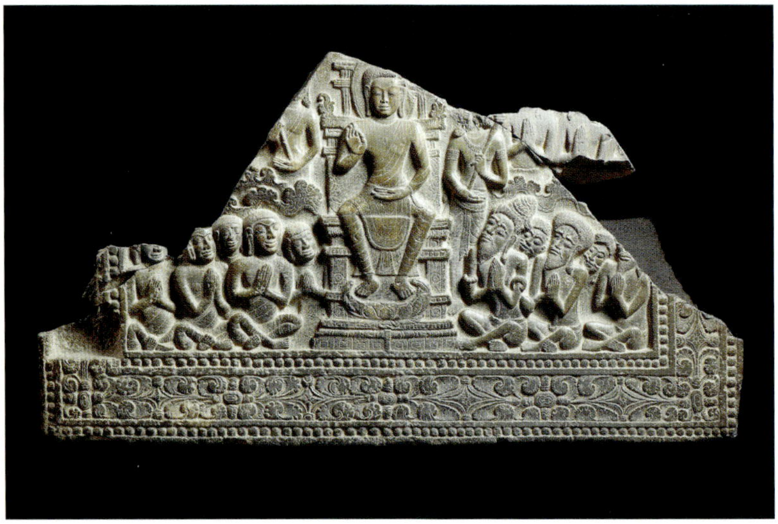

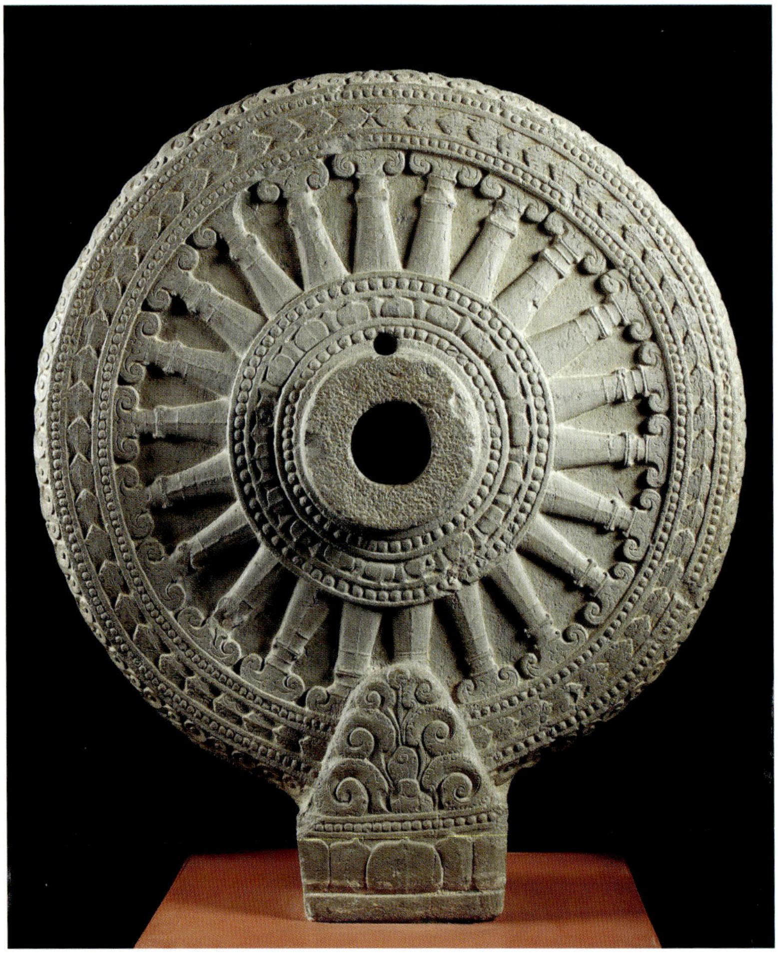

Fig.2. Base socket for a Wheel of the Law pillar (*dharmacakrastambha*). Recovered from Wat Sai, Nakhon Pathom, seventh to eighth century. Limestone, h.60 cm, w.111 cm. Phra Pathom Chedi National Museum, Nakhon Pathom, courtesy of FAD.
Fig.3 Dharmacakra ('Wheel of the Law'). Found at Phra Pathom Chedi, Nakhon Pathom, Central Thailand, seventh to eighth century. Sandstone, d.97 cm. Phra Pathom Chedi National Museum, Nakhon Pathom, courtesy of FAD.

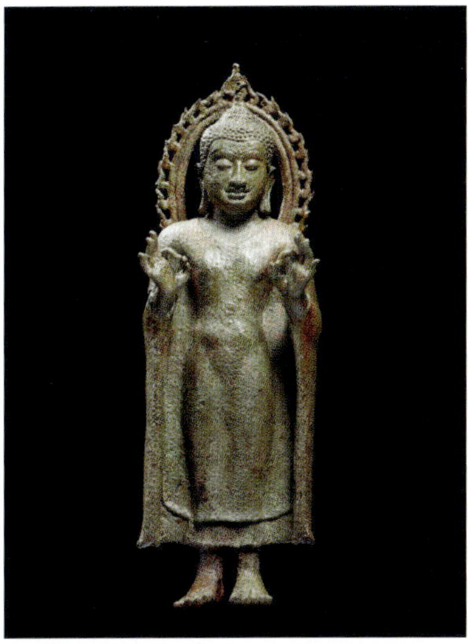

4

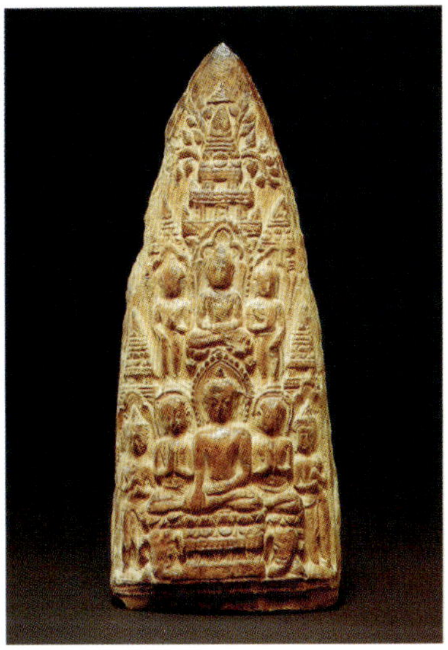

6

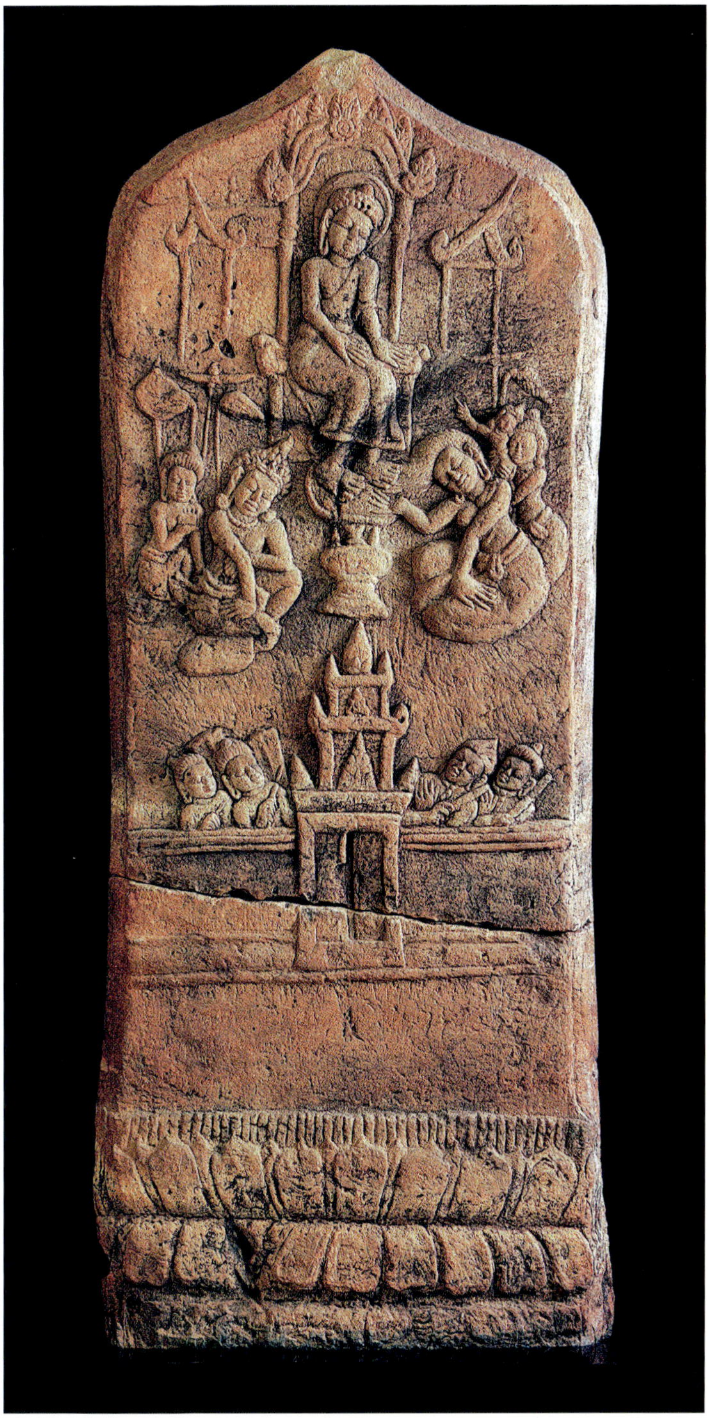

7

Fig.4 Buddha Preaching, hands in *vitarkamudra*. Excavated at U Thong (Site 11), Suphan Buri, in 1963. Copper alloy, h.32 cm. National Museum U Thong, Suphan Buri, courtesy of FAD.
Fig.5 Sema, sacred boundary stone, depicting a Mon fortified city with tower gatehouse. Scene of the Buddha's return to Kapilavastu, his princely home, being venerated at his wife's palace. From Mueang Fa Daet Song Yang, Kalasin, northeast Thailand. Sandstone, h.204 cm. Khon Kaen National Museum. Photograph courtesy of River Books.
Fig.6 Seal moulding depicting the Buddha attaining enlightenment in a Mon architectural setting, the foliage above evoking the Bodhi tree at Bodhgaya. Hariphunchai, Lamphun, northern Thailand, c. twelfth century. Terracotta, h. 17.7 cm. Private Collection, London.

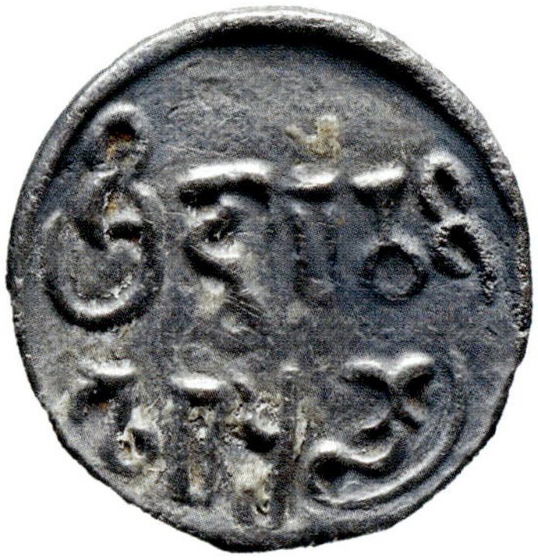

7

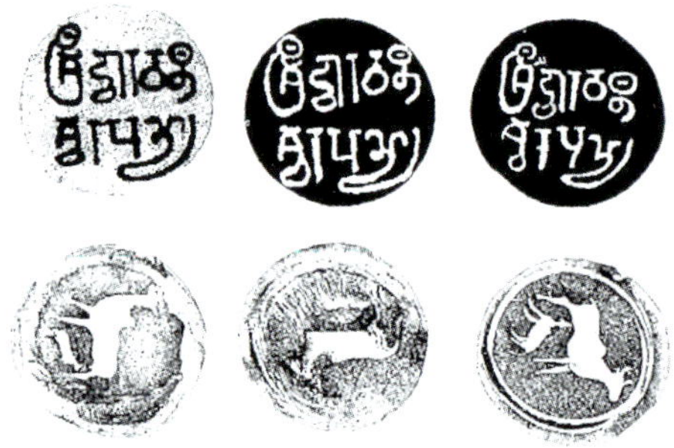

8

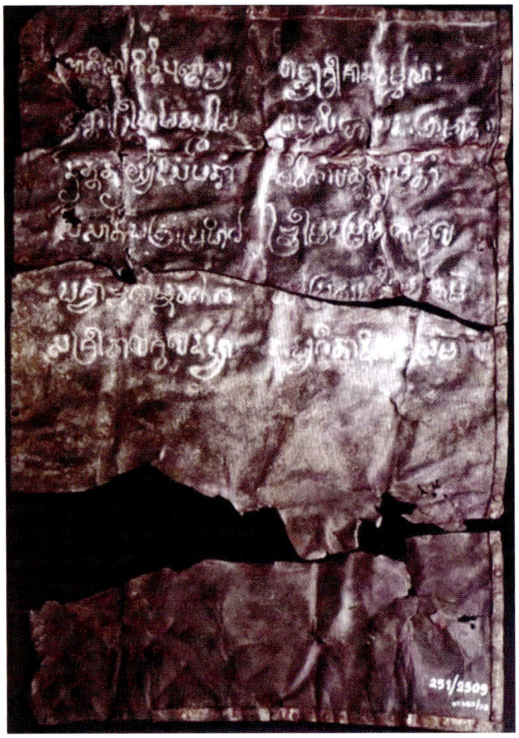

9

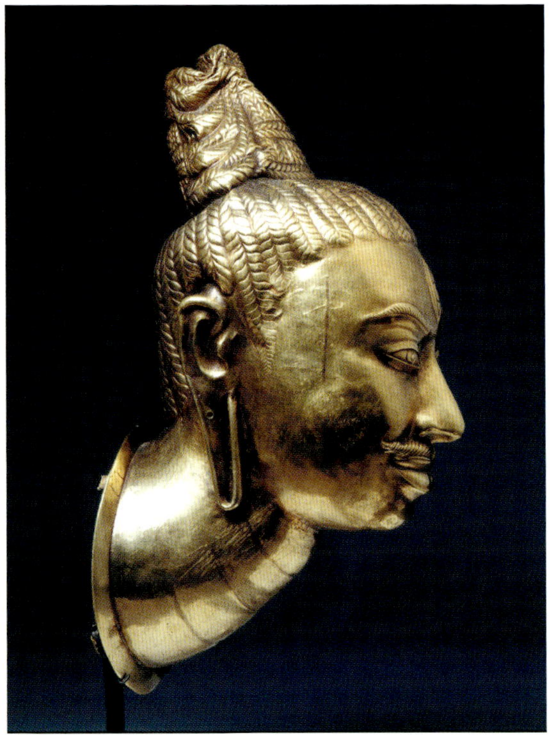

10

Fig.7 Medallion inscribed */śrīdvāravatīśvarapuṇya/*, "meritorious deed of the ruler of Dvāravatī", found in 1943 near Wat Phra Paton, Nakhon Pathom. Seventh to eighth century. Silver, d.1.7 cm. Phra Pathom Chedi National Museum, Nakhon Pathom. Photograph courtesy of River Books.
Fig.8 Three "ruler of Dvāravatī" inscribed silver medallions, excavated in 1997 in the foundations of a Brahmanical sanctuary at Khok Chang Din (Site 7), southwest of the moat at U Thong. Seventh to eighth century. Silver, d.1.7 cm. National Museum U Thong, Suphan Buri. Line drawings courtesy of FAD.
Fig.9 Śrī Harṣavarman copper plate inscription (K.964), found within the ancient city of U Thong, Suphan Buri Province. Mid-7th century. Copper. U Thong National Museum, Suphan Buri. Courtesy of the FAD.
Fig.10 Liṅga kośa. Repoussé and modelled head of Śiva, originally riveted to a silver sheath for covering a stone liṅga during worship. Champa, central Vietnam, c. eighth to tenth century. Electrum, h.28 cm. Private Collection, Europe.

to have spanned from the seventh to tenth centuries (Nai Pan Hla 1991). Envoys were received from this polity at the Tang court in the second quarter of the seventh century, in 638, 640 and 649 (*Jiu Tang shu*, Wade 2014: 27). This flurry of diplomatic activity suggests this is a moment of political efflorescence for Dvāravatī. It may simply reflect the political ambitions of one of the regional polities that had risen to prominence, perhaps only for a generation under a highly effective ruler. The *Xin Tang shu* (*New History of the Tang*) records that the country was reputed for its fine rhinoceros horn, no doubt a favoured tribute item with such delegations.[8] The Chinese pilgrim Yijing's (635–713) account of his India pilgrimage included brief descriptions, probably based on hearsay rather than direct experience, of a number of Southeast Asian kingdoms he 'encountered' on his homeward journey in 688-689 (Li 2000: 120).[9]

As a polity name only known in these Chinese sources, Dvāravatī was first verified archaeologically with Cœdès' reading of this name in royal titles on coin-like medallions of the period [Fig.7] (Cœdès 1963). Subsequently, at least one Sanskrit inscription, on religious imagery, confirms the presence of the name in association with elite patronage. The base of a Buddha image, found at Nakhon Ratchasima, is inscribed "daughter of the lord of Dvāravatī ... the queen set up the image .. this is of Tathagata [Buddha]'. This is the first unequivocal confirmation of what the seventh and eighth century archaeological landscape tells us, that we are witnessing elite patronage – dare we call it 'state patronage'? – of large stone and brick edifices, most notably Buddha imagery and *dharmacakrastamba* in the context of monastic complexes.

The earliest historical references to the region are to be found in Indian Sanskrit and Pāli sources describing the perils of merchants' sea journeys to the lands of gold. India's earliest vision of the lands of Southeast Asia was as a source of gold, hence the naming of the region as Suvarṇabhūmi (Land of Gold) and Suvarṇadvipa (Island of Gold) by Indian writers. Historians have long sought to find this El Dorado, failing to grasp the generalized sense in which the term was used by these early Indian commentators. It was undoubtedly many places, and one place, the zone encompassed by mainland and peninsular Southeast Asia. Nonetheless, a fourth century Buddhist source, the *Suparaga Jātaka*, recounts a merchant's sea voyage from Broach, western India, to "both ports" of Suvarṇabhūmi, named as Laṅkasobha and Katahadvipa (Skilling 1992). These have convincingly been identified as Laṅkasukha (likely Pattani) and Kedah, known entrepôts on either side of the Malay Peninsula. This phrase, however, might be better understood as "two ports (of many)"; undoubtedly other ports of Suvarṇabhūmi were similarly known to the early Indian geographers, such as Thaton in lower Myanmar.

Important new evidence began to emerge in 2013 which situates the ports of mainland Southeast Asia in a wider maritime landscape in the latter half of the first millennium. The chance discovery of a trading ship in the delta zone of the Tha Chin River in Samut Sakhon Province, Gulf of Thailand, named the Phanom Surin shipwreck, has expanded our understanding of central Thailand's international connectivity in the late eighth to early ninth century (Nareerat Preecharpeechacupt 2014 [in Thai]; Guy 2017a). The ship architecture identifies it as belonging to the Arab dhow tradition of shipbuilding, and traces of residual cargo indicate a trading network that connected the Gulf of Thailand to both China and the Persian Gulf [Fig.11] (Guy 2017: Figs.6–9; 2003). This vessel provides the first recorded evidence of a West Asian trading vessel in Thailand, and only the second confirmed find in Southeast Asia (Guy 2006; Krahl and Guy 2011).

Uniquely, in the archaeology of Southeast Asia, it has provided the first recorded discovery of Persian Gulf 'torpedo jars', one of which is inscribed with a proper name – presumably of the owner of the jar – in Pahlavi, Middle Iranian, the script and language of the Sasanians (Guy 2017b) [Figs.12, 13].[10] Furthermore, the name form indicates the identity of the person as a Zoroastrian (Guy 2019: 156–57). The importance of this discovery cannot be overstated. This is the first archaeological evidence to securely establish the presence of West Asian merchants in the Dvāravatī zone, and that a Pahlavi-speaking Iranian belonging to the Zoroastrian community formed a part of the mercantile community. Depictions of presumed Iranian-Sogdian merchants have long been known from the excavated terracotta décor of Buddhist *stūpa* at a number of Mon Buddhist monuments, most notably at Khu Bua Site 40, [Fig.14] and at Nakhon Pathom, most compellingly in the so-called 'graffiti brick' from Chula Pathon *stūpa*, which had a portrait sketch of

---

8 *Xin Tang Shu*, in Wade 2014. The Asian rhinoceros was well known in medieval Southeast Asia, and is depicted in a relief scene at the Bayon temple, Angkor Thom.

9 Yijing's pilgrimage to India lasted from 671 to 689.

10 For a date Gulf context for the Chinese ceramics, see Whitehouse 1973.

a western foreigner incised into the wet brick clay sometime in the eighth century [Fig.15] (Guy 2014: 40, Cat. No.11). Such foreign merchants were undoubtedly active at the major Mon urban centres. Traces of Persian Gulf turquoise glazed earthenware ceramics, a reliable barometer of West Asian networks, have been reported from a number of mainland sites: most numerous are coastal locations, extending along the Cham coastline to Vietnam and southern China, but they have also appeared at such interior centres as U Thong, Si Mahaphot (Prachin Buri Province) and Angkor (Glover 2002). Whilst the presence of Persian Gulf ceramics does not of itself prove the presence of West Asian traders, they certainly confirm their commercial connections and networks. Whilst the merchants aboard the Phanom Surin vessel were likely most immediately engaged in commerce with Nakhon Pathom and neighbouring centres such as Khu Bua and Phetchaburi, they could also have engaged in longer distance trade, direct or indirect, with a number of urban centres in the interior, including U Thong, Lop Buri, Si Thep and Prachin Buri. On the peninsula, Nakhon Si Thammarat was a major early urban centre with strong cultural ties to the Dvāravatī zone.

Recent archaeology has revealed the emergence of exceptional levels of social organisation and technical innovation occurring between the third and sixth centuries CE (Higham 2002: 2). Western imports, principally Indian, were already present in the first to third century, a defining indicator of sustained commercial exchange between these regions (Borrell 2008).[11] Spectacularly large-scale stone sculptures signal the existence of substantial Brahmanical shrines, few of which survive beyond foundation traces. The standing Gaṇeśa and Viṣṇu images from Si Mahaphot, the Si Thep Viṣṇu (National Museum, Bangkok), Skanda (Chantrakasem National Museum, Ayutthaya) and Ardhanārīśvara (Ubon Ratchathani National Museum) all bear witness to important cult icons belonging to now largely untraced shrines (Piriya Krairiksh 2012). They necessitated elite patronage sustained over long periods, and are our most secure indicators of the central role that imported religious systems had assumed in the public expression of power among the rulers of mainland Southeast Asian *mueangs*. A large-scale terracotta *chandrasala* (blind window) antefix belonging to an early Śiva shrine at U Thong is one of the earliest architectural remains of what must have been numerous Brahmanical shrines, typically of fired brick, at U Thong. Assigned to the second half of the fifth century, it is in the form of an elliptical window framing a bust of Śiva, shown with his ascetic's hair drawn up in a top knot and wearing large circular earplugs [Fig.15]. Another Śaiva shrine antefix was recovered in the peninsular at Wat Khao Noi, Songkhla, witnessing the pervasiveness of early Hindu temples now largely lost to us.

Clay merchant sealings, the majority of which bear Hindu imagery and stamped, in the first instance at least, from imported Indian metal moulds, are a further indication of the penetration of a Brahmanical world view on mainland Southeast Asia in the later first millennium. As tokens of trade and exchange, these sealings chronicle spatially the movement of people as well as goods, and underscore the importance of commercial interfacing between *mueangs*. Such seal impressions may have served as a form of promissory note.[12] Moulded clay figures of Brahmanical gods found in Mon territories further support the notion of a presence of traders of Indian origin and/or descent. Gaja-Laksmi, Hariti and Kubera are the most widely represented and may all be understood as propitious deities associated with the pursuit of wealth, cults attractive to merchant communities [Fig.16] (Guy 2014: 164-65).[13] They were primarily produced from fired clay moulds as well as metal dies, as was the practise in India at this time, and their ready replication no doubt served to build allegiances to these cults amongst trader communities, expatriate and local alike. Examples of these are most prolifically recorded from Lop Buri, Suphan Buri and Nakhon Sawan Provinces.

These appropriated religious systems travelled deep into the interior of mainland Southeast Asia, emulated it would seem in even the smallest polities. The discovery in 2008 of a cache of silver and gold religious images and utensils at Nong Hua Thong, Savannakhet Province, Laos, bears witness to this. The site is a fortified riverine settlement on the Xe Bang Fey, a tributary of the Mekong, in southern Laos, with riverine links to such major Khmer centre as Champasak and further south, to Sambor Prei Kuk on the Mekong.[14] The hoard consists principally of religious imagery, and includes a standing eagle-form which from the context can be

11 Thai-French excavations in Chumphon Province in Peninsula Thailand have provided new evidence of contact back from at least the third century BCE, see Bellina 2017.

12 See Guy 2014, pp.165-65 for further discussion of the role of sealings, and Ghosh and Ghosh 2011 for a wider context.

13 See also Ghosh and Ghosh 2011.

14 The hoard is stored in a bank by the provincial government and not accessible for study. See Lorrillard 2010-2011.

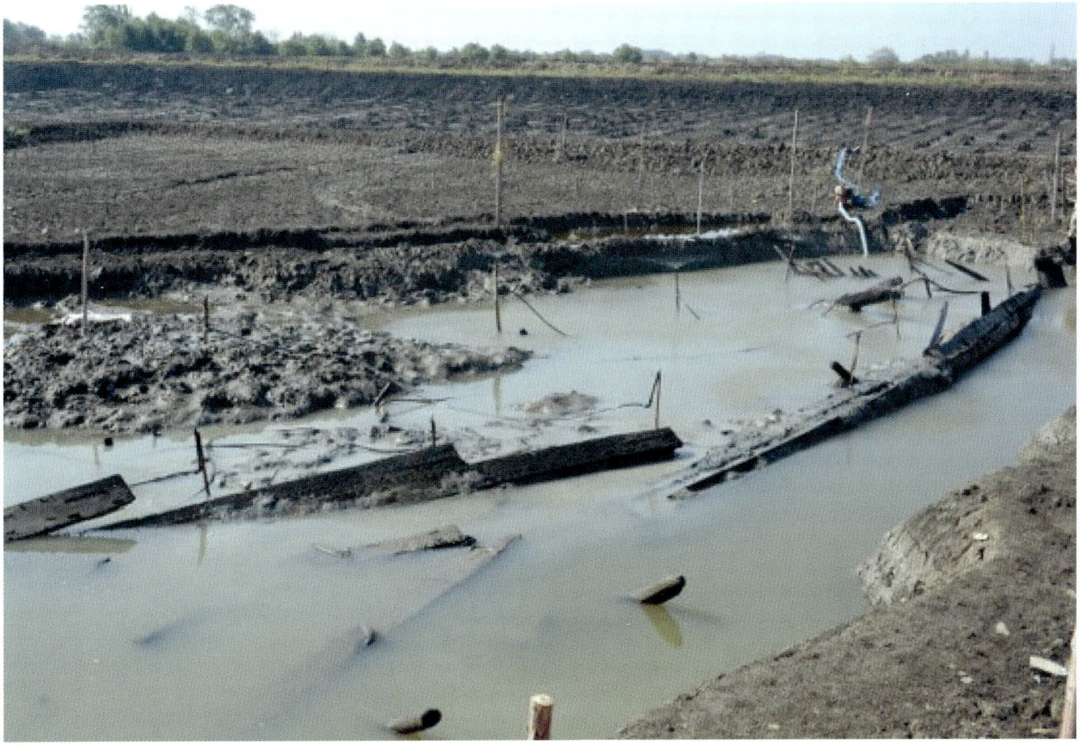

11

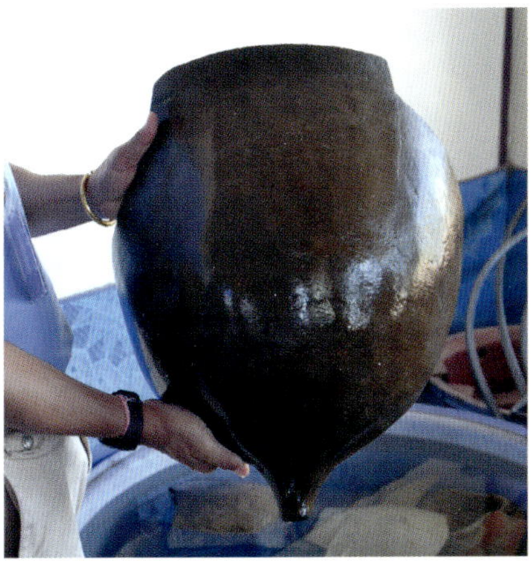

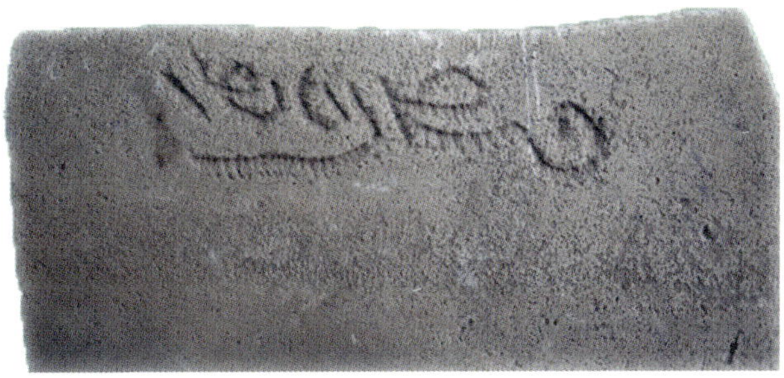

12 *13*

Fig.11 The Phanom Surin shipwreck excavation, 2014, Samut Sakhon Province, Gulf of Thailand. Photograph Bangkok Post, courtesy of FAD

Fig.12 'Torpedo' storage jar, Phanom Surin shipwreck excavation, 2014, Samut Sakhon Province, Gulf of Thailand. Persian Gulf, 8th century earthenware. Photograph John Guy with permission of FAD.

Fig.13 Inscribed ceramic fragment written in regular Pahlavi language and script, reading Yazd-bōzēd, a proper name presumably identifying ownership. Phanom Surin shipwreck excavation, 2014, Samut Sakhon Province, Gulf of Thailand. Persian Gulf, eighth century earthenware. Photograph John Guy with permission of FAD.

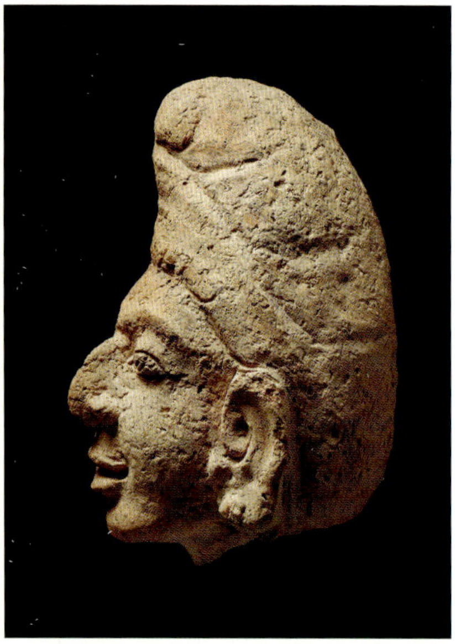

14

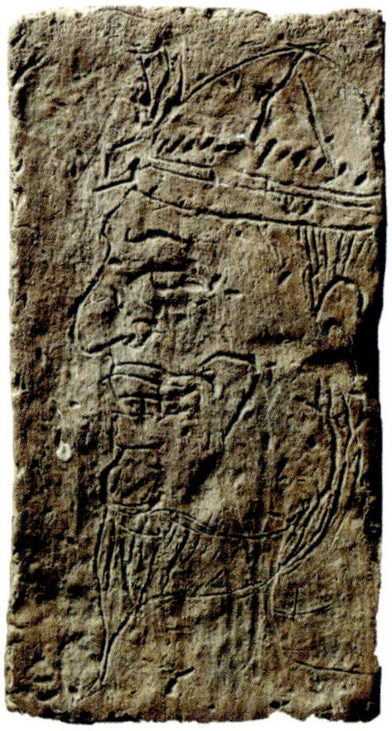

15

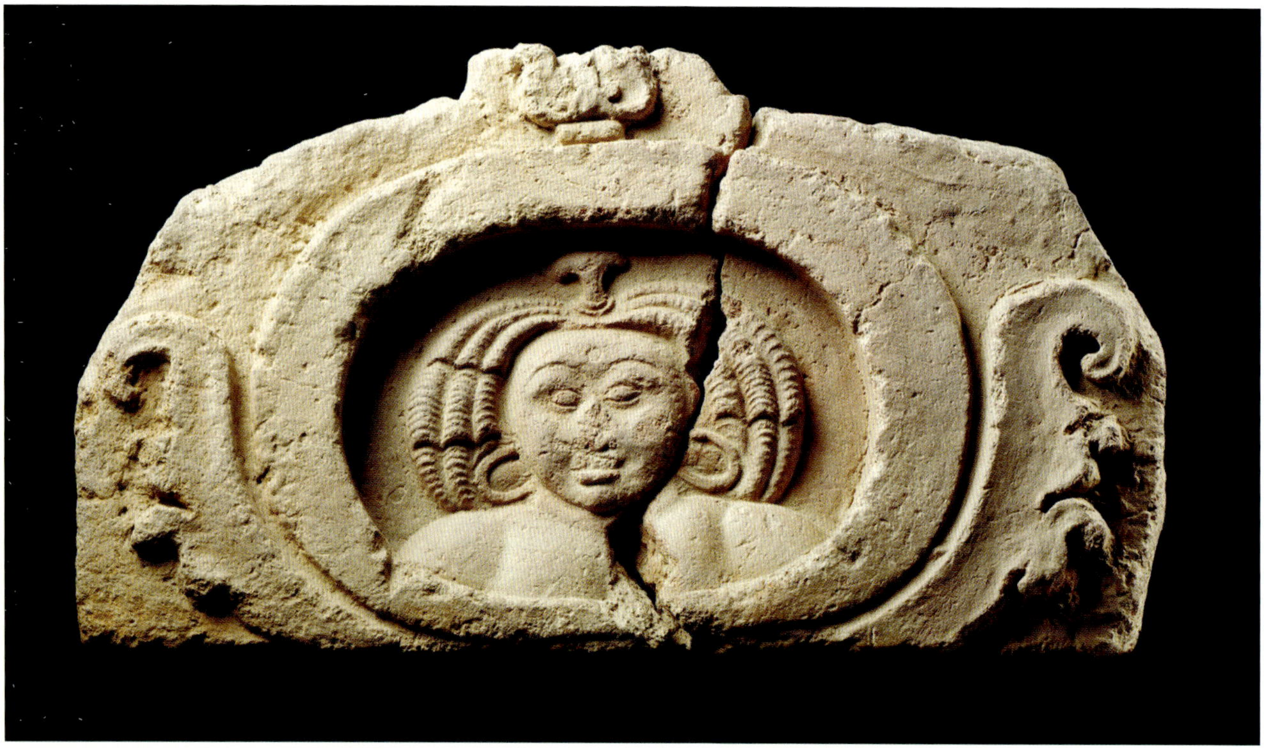

16

Fig.14 West Asian merchant depicted in décor of *stūpa* site 40, Khu Bua, Ratchaburi Province. Terracotta, ht. 23 cm. National Museum, Bangkok, courtesy of FAD, Thailand.
Fig.15 Graffiti-brick depicting a West Asian merchant, recovered from Chula Pathon *stūpa*, Nakhon Pathom. Terracotta, ht. 27 cm. Phra Pathom Chedi National Museum, Nakhon Pathom, courtesy of the FAD, Thailand.
Fig.16 Architectural antefix depicting Shiva in an ornamental window (chandrasala). Found Wat Satavas, Ban No Lao, U Thong, ca. sixth century. Terracotta, 39 cm. U Thong National Museum, Suphanburi, courtesy of the FAD, Thailand.

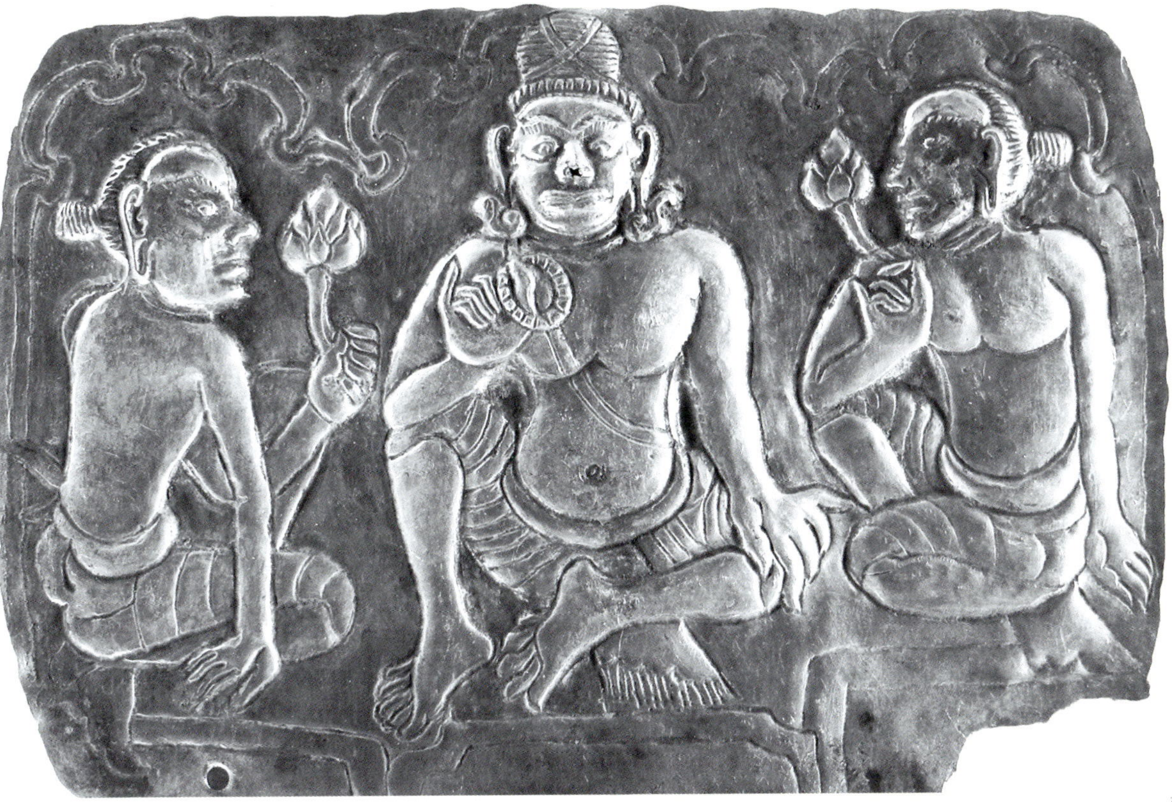

17

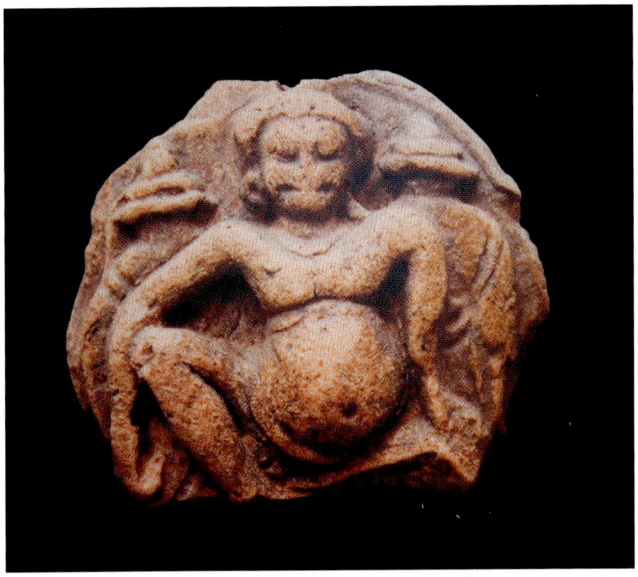

18

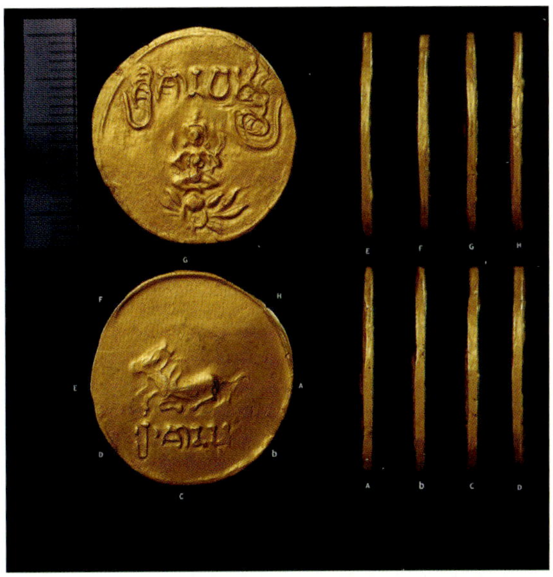

19

Fig.17 Kubera, Brahmanical guardian of treasures, seated in royal ease, flanked by money jars, sixth to seventh century. Moulded clay, ht. 6 cm. Wat Chan Sen collection. Chan Sen, Nakhon Sawan Province.
Fig.18 Plaque depicting a deity, possibly Kubera, and devotees offering lotus, ninth to tenth century. Repoussé silver alloy. Found in 2008 at Xe Bang Fey, Nong Hua Thong, Savannakhet Province, southern Laos. Courtesy of the Ministry of Information and Culture, Laos.
Fig.19 Medallion reportedly found at Angkor Borei, Takeo Province, southern Cambodia. Inscribed *Isanavarman* on obverse, and *Isanapura* on reverse, linking it to Sambor Prei Kuk, early seventh century. National Bank of Cambodia, Phnom Penh. Courtesy of Kontomroy-Jean Philippe Delpal.

accepted as a Garuda. The cluster, which includes coarse silver vessels in the late Tang style, broadly spans the eighth to tenth centuries. One silver repoussé plaque depicts a seated male figure with the braided hair of an ascetic and holding a rosary (*mala*), flanked by two male devotees offering lotus [Fig.18]. The iconography is inadequate to determine a secure identification, but the Brahmanical god of wealth Kubera is a strong contender.

But not all elite religious patronage was Brahmanical, as a newly re-read inscription on a sandstone base supporting a Buddha image from Wat Chantuk, Nakhon Ratchasima (Korat) makes clear: "daughter of the Lord of Dvāravatī ... the queen set up the image ... of the Tathagata [Buddha]" (Skilling 2003: 96-97). Peter Skilling's assembly of this fragmentary and still incomplete Sanskrit inscription in cursive southern Brāhmī script is highly important on a number of counts: first, it is the first stone inscription to name Dvāravatī; secondly, it confirms the patronage as royal, and third, that the donor was a queen (and a "daughter of the Lord of Dvāravatī"). Female patronage of early Buddhist art in India is well attested from the Kushaṇ Era, first to third century CE; the Wat Chantuek inscription is amongst the earliest confirmations that such practices were followed in mainland Southeast Asia, even when the male members of the royal households observed Brahmanical practices.[15] Further, the reading of the Wat Chantuek inscription extends the geographical reach of the Dvāravatī zone significantly in the northeast of Thailand.

The medallions issued by the king(s?) of Dvāravatī are very similar conceptually to those issued by the Pyu monarchs of Śrī Kṣetra, central Myanmar, and most strikingly, to a recently published gold medallion reportedly found at Angkor Borei, southern Cambodia [Fig.19] (Griffiths 2014: 57, fig.45). Remarkably, this latter medallion has a cursive inscription on the obverse with the name 'Īśānavarman' above a yogic figure on a lotus, and on the reverse a seated humped bull with the name 'Īśānapura,' linking it to the early seventh century ruler of Sambor Prei Kuk. The ruler's name-bull ensign combination is evocative of the "ruler of Dvāravatī" medallions [Figs.7–8]. The religious centre at Sambor Prei Kuk (Īśānapura) has a *maṇḍapa*, at Prasat Yeai Poeun (Sanctuary S2) which, according to its inscription, housed a silver bull (*Vrsabda*) dedicated to the cult of Śiva (Bhattacharya 1961: 88). The in-situ pedestal indicates that this would have approximated life size, akin to the only surviving metal example, found in Kandal Province in 1983 [Fig.20].[16] If this gold medallion refers to Īśānavarman I, then it corresponds with, or perhaps immediately predates, the "ruler of Dvāravatī" medallions. Given the familial connections between the Chenla ruling household and that of U Thong in the early decades of the seventh century, as claimed in the Harṣavarman copper plate, these similarities would seem unlikely to be coincidental.

Silver Pyu issues typically have combinations of auspicious Indic symbols, including the throne-stool (*bhadrapiṭha*), *śrivatsa* symbol of good fortune, a rising sun burst (*svastika*) and a conch (*śaṅkha*) (Guy 2014, Cat. No.36 A, B). Both the Mon and Pyu coins-medallions were likely issued for the same purpose. We can only speculate as to their intended function, but were probably commemorative tokens in the first instance. However, judging by their wide distribution in the mainland, they may over time have assumed a degree of legitimacy as a means of exchange. Pyu silver and gold 'coins' have been recovered widely in the Pyu territories in central Myanmar, with concentrations at the royal cities of Śrī Kṣetra and Halin (Mahlo 2012). They also circulated widely, as finds at U Thong and in the Funan entrepôt of Oc Eo in the Mekong delta witness (Malleret 1959-1963).

Southeast Asia has long been celebrated in Indian literature as an abundant source of gold, reflecting the passage of Indian traders drawn to Suvarṇabhumi since antiquity. The discovery of an Indian goldsmith's touchstone at one of the earliest identified entrepôts of peninsular Thailand confirms the pattern. It was found in the vicinity of a tidal stream marked by Wat Khlong Thom, in Krabi Province, a site which has proved rich in long distance trade goods. The stone is inscribed in Tamil-Brahmi script of the third or fourth century CE: *Perumpatan kal* ("[This] is the [touch] stone of Perumpatan"), *patan* or *pattan* meaning goldsmith (Shanmugan 1996).[17] This is the earliest known Southern Brāhmī inscription in Southeast Asia and clear evidence that Indian merchants ventured early to the region to secure gold.

On the western side of isthmus region of the Thai peninsula, at Takua Pa, traces of gold workings were noted at a site associated with an Indian trading community (Lamb 1964: 76-86). Both substantial Hindu sculptures and a lengthy Tamil inscription dated to the ninth century survive. The stele commemorates the donation of a tank

15 Female patrons, both nuns and laywomen, feature prominently in the early commissioning of Buddha images; for an inscriptional survey in Kushaṇ-Era Mathura, see Schopen 1997. 248-50.

16 This silver alloy Śiva bull is now under worship at the Silver Pagoda Monastery, Royal Palace, Phnom Penh.

17 See also Karashima 2002.

named in honour of the Pallava monarch Nandivarman II (r.826-50) and identifies the patrons as a community of merchant's resident there under the protection of a garrison of soldiers (mercenaries) (Sastri 1949). The donors identify themselves as members of the Manigramam (Manikkiramam), a prominent Indian merchant guild known from inscriptions in the Deccan and Kerala (Abraham 1988: 29-33). The antiquity of Takua Pa as an Indian entrepôt is suggested by its likely identification with the 'Takkola' of the *Milinda Panha*, a Pāli Buddhist commentary text likely dating from the early centuries CE. Another Pāli source, the non-canonical *Mahā Niddesa*, which is unlikely to date later than the first century BCE, names a distant port as 'Tamali', which has been linked to Tambraliṅga on the east coast of the Thai Isthmus, that is, a region that could include Chaiya and Chumphon, both districts that have yielded extensive evidence of Indian trade contact from the early centuries BCE, including the recent find of a Mauryan-period Indian ringstone, the first such object ever discovered outside northern India [Fig.21] (Bennett 2017: Figs.2.36–2.39; 2019: 95–105]. Much debate has surrounded the purpose of these objects, but jewellery moulds remain the most credible explanation.[18] The merchant guild identified in the Takua Pa inscription, the Maniggraman, operated within a consortium of guilds better known as the Ayyavole-ainurruvar, and would have included gold and jewellery merchants, and as witnessed by the Krabi touchstone, goldsmiths as well. At Khao Sam Kaeo in Chumphon Province, east coast, evidence has recently been discovered for the processing and working of gold, and the re-fabrication of glass, as recorded at Takua Pa, on the west coast (Lamb 1964; Bellina 2017). The activities of these Indian traders and artisans, documented throughout the first millennium, may have been the catalyst for the commercial scale extraction of alluvial gold from the river systems of peninsula and island Southeast Asia.

The Chinese commentators on Dvāravatī

Written sources for the early history of state formation in Southeast Asia are overwhelmingly Chinese, and principally of two kinds: official histories that have sections recording foreign tribute missions, and private diary accounts, the earliest of which are exclusively those of pilgrim monks journeying through Southern Asia. Coins first issued by the Tang emperor Gaozu in 621 have been found in peninsular Thailand around Chaiya, underscoring an early level of commercial activity between the regions bordering the Nanhai (Southern Sea) (Piriya 2012: 32, Pl.1.3).[19] Around this same time, the remarkable Chinese monk Xuanzang, who incidentally never visited mainland Southeast Asia during his seventeen years of Indian pilgrim travels (629 to 645), provided one of the first descriptions of these territories. He was undoubtedly repeating no longer extant sources when he wrote:

> Northeast of there [the country of Samataṭa in Bengal] in the valley beside the great sea is the country of Śrī Kṣetra; further to the southeast of the great sea is the country of Kāmalaṅka [possibly Langkasuka on the Thai peninsula]; further to the east is the country of Dvārapatī; further to the east is the country of Īśānapura [Sambor Prei Kuk]; further to the east is the country of Mahācampā [Champa, known to the Chinese as Linyi] (Li Rongxi 1996: 302).

Xuanzang's description was repeated verbatim fifty years later by another pilgrim-monk, Yijing (635–713), excepting that he added the following observations on the significance of these Southeast Asian polities for the Buddhist diaspora:

> All these countries greatly venerate the Triple Gems. There are many men who observe the precepts, and the ascetic practice of alms-begging is the custom of the monks in these countries (Li 2000: 12).

Unlike Xuanzang, who journeyed both to and from India via Central Asia, Yijing embarked from the southern Chinese port of Guangzhou, aboard a Persian merchant ship in 671, and journeyed via the Nanhai to peninsular Southeast Asia. He resided in both Srivijaya and the Malay Peninsula, likely including Kedah, for some months, to study Sanskrit in preparation for embarking to India. He displays limited knowledge of 'Dvarapati,' only referring to it as a source of medicinal cardamom (Li 2000: 120). But an anecdote recorded by Yijing tells us much about this seventh century polity and its connectivity through trade to a greater world of religions and ideas. He recounts meeting a monk after his return to China in 645 called Master Da-cheng-deng, whose Chinese parents had taken him to Dvāravatī when he was a youth. Their purpose is

18 I am grateful to Ian Glover for first drawing this object my attention; published Bennett 2017. For the distribution of finds of ringstones in India, see Gupta 1980; Srivastava 2008 and for those in western museums and private collections Bennett 2019.

19 See also Wade 2014.

not stated, but we may assume that they were merchants; others at this time must have made similar journeys with small gilt bronze Buddhist images for sale, as vividly witnessed by the Kampong Cham hoard discovered in 2006 [Fig.22] (Jett 2010). During the family's sojourn there, the son became a monk, remaining in Dvāravatī territory whilst his parents returned home. Only some years later did he finally return to China, accompanying a Chinese envoy named Tan Xu (Li 2000). Yijing's account makes clear that monastic Buddhism was flourishing in seventh century central Thailand, and that it enjoyed active contact with China as well as India. Further evidence of Chinese monks active in Central Thailand appeared in the form of three clay sealing recovered during excavations at the Khlang Nai *stūpa* site, Si Thep, each inscribed on the reverse into the wet clay at manufacture with the name of a Chinese monk, Wenxiang, likely in the eighth century when this monastery and associated *stūpa* were constructed.[20]

As archaeological investigations continue to progress in mainland Southeast Asia, the sheer scale and social complexity of the early polities are becoming clearer to us. Aerial photographic surveys conducted across Thailand during World War II first signaled to the field archaeologist what was not always immediately self-evident on the ground, namely the scale and complexity of these first millennium urban settlements, marked by massive earthwork ramparts and moated perimeters, and their relationship to the wider topography and river systems.

What remains a challenge is investigating those early centres of urbanization that have remained under continuous habitation to the present day. Both Nakhon Pathom and U Thong are ancient cities where modern habitation seriously inhibits archaeological investigation. As the two greatest polities active during the period that can be directly associated archaeologically with a culture that called itself 'Dvāravatī,' the opportunities for advancing the scientific study of this culture remains somewhat circumscribed. The urban centre of Angkor Borei in southern Cambodia, likely the premier city of Funan, remains significantly populated and presents similar, if less extreme, issues for the archaeologist. This contrasts with several of the other principal centres of first millennium urbanization in the region, which were abandoned in antiquity or given over to light agricultural activity and village settlement. Champasak (Wat Phu) in southern Laos, Sambor Prei Kuk (Īśānapura) in central Cambodia, and Śrī Kṣetra in central Myanmar, are instances where significant later urbanization did not occur, leaving the archaeological landscape largely undisturbed and accessible to modern researchers. These three ancient sites are now recognized amongst some of the oldest urban centres in early Southeast Asia, of a significant size by any mid-first-millennium global measure.

Beyond the epigraphic record and historical commentators, frustratingly fleeting as they are, is the archaeological footprint. The polities we recognize as sharing a "Dvāravatī culture" are territories that displays all the hallmarks of mid-first millennium urbanized centres built on the twin economic drivers of a rich agrarian base and connectivity of river systems to long distance trade. A shared material culture provides an identity, and the architectural and sculptural record provides important insights.[21] Indeed, the religious imagery is often our best window onto the world of beliefs and religious practices of the people whose written records are scant as those of Dvāravatī.

Whilst U Thong and Nakhon Pathom were premier polities, at their peak in the seventh and eighth centuries, they were not without their rivals. Khu Bua, a short river journey from Nakhon Pathom in Ratchaburi Province, was a major Buddhist centre, Phong Tuek in Kanchanaburi Province marked the borderlands to Pyu territories west, whilst to the east Si Thep was a powerful regional presence, as was Mueang Sema in the northeast, and Si Mahaphot in eastern Prachin Buri Province. Each of these great moated and fortified centres of later first millennium Thailand represented a nodal point on the political landscape. Was the king of Dvāravatī "one king to rule them all"; almost certainly not. But that the silver medallions of this ruler(s) were ritually deposited in sacred foundations at both U Thong and Nakhon Pathom raises the possibility that the authority of that royal house, at some point, touched both cities. Whether this was concurrently, or sequentially, remains an open the question. The nature of the relationship between these polities is not well understood. Shared material culture indicates a predominantly Buddhist culture with an overarching Brahmanical elite, in dynamic relationship, fueled by a level of political and economic integration unprecedented in early Southeast Asia.

20 First published in a FAD report in 1994; see Brown 1996: 37.

21 Brown 1996 was innovative in this regard, building on a tradition established by a number of French scholars, most notably Pierre Dupont and Mireille Bénisti, and on the archaeology of Subhadradis Diskul and Helmut Loofs. See also Guy 1999; 2014.

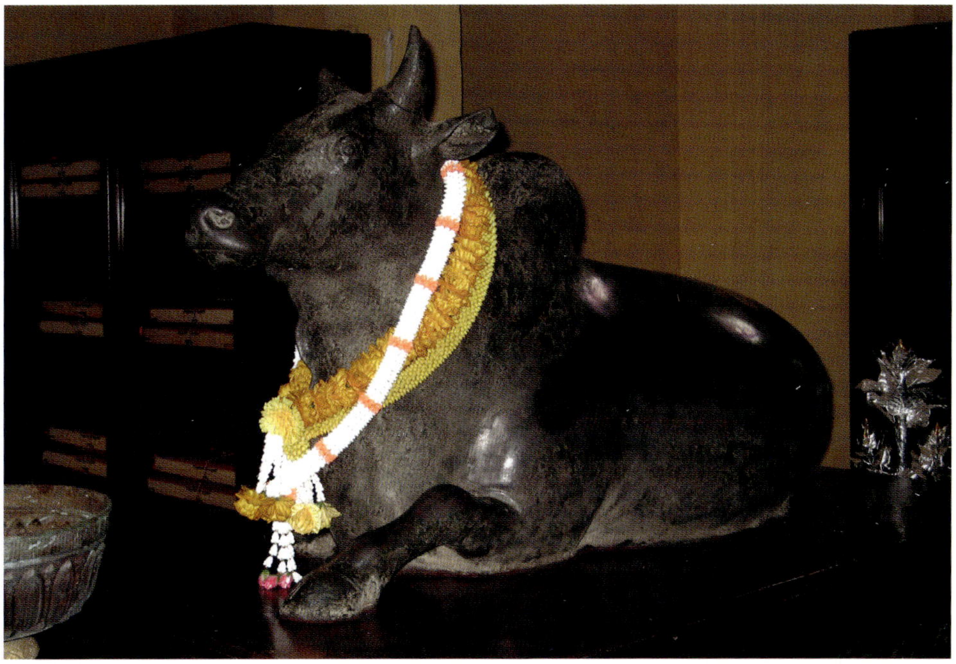

20

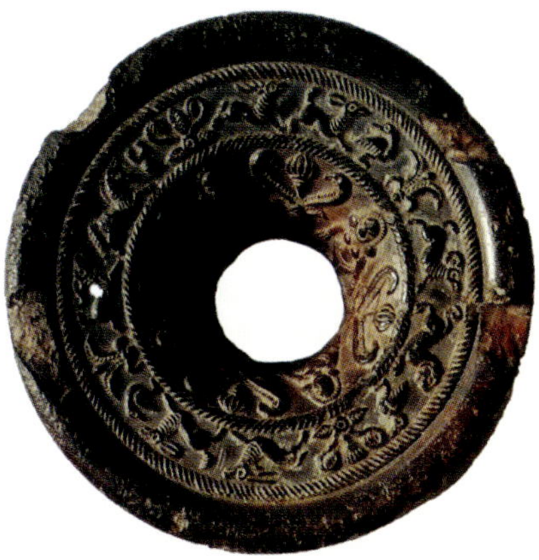

21

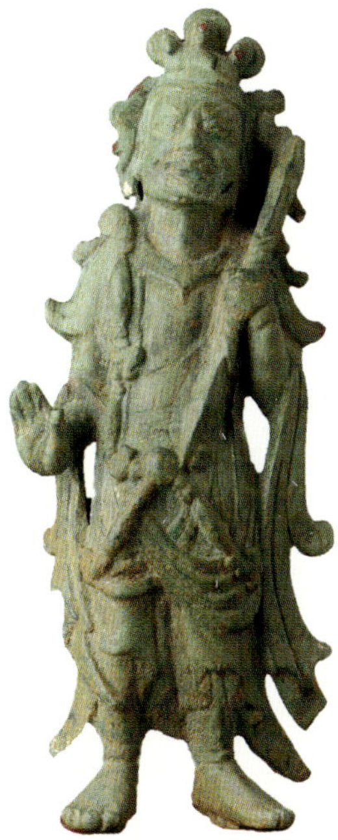

22

Fig.20 Siva's bull (*Vrsabda*). Angkorian period. Found in 1983 at the Tuol Kuhea temple site, Kandal Province, southern Cambodia. Currently at the Silver Pagoda, Royal Palace, Phnom Penh. Silver alloy, l.1.3 m. Photo John Guy.

Fig.21 Ringstone, carved with animal and floral designs. Recovered from a riverbed, Khao Sam Kaeo, Thai Peninsula. Mauryan period, ca. third to second century BCE, northern India. Sandstone, diam. 5.8 cm. SuthiRatana Foundation, Bangkok (Bennett 2019).

Fig.22. Guardian deity with vajra. Sui or Tang dynasty, China, late sixth to seventh century. Found as part of a hoard of bronze icons in Kampong Cham Province, Cambodia in 2006. Bronze with traces of gilding, h.15 cm. National Museum of Cambodia, Phnom Penh.

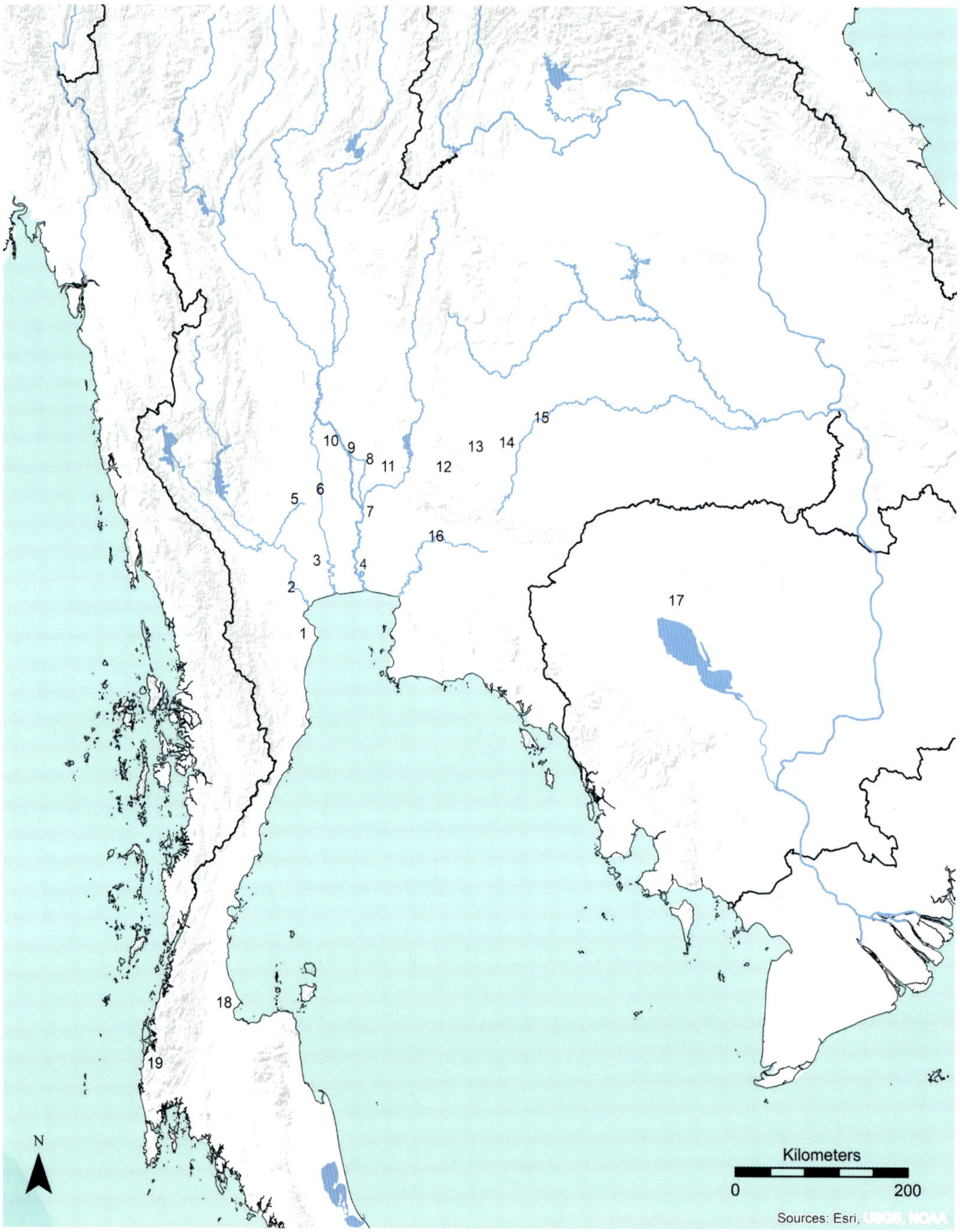

1. Phetchaburi
2. Ratchaburi
3. Nakhon Pathom, Huai Charoke
4. Bangkok
5. U Thong,
6. Khok Chang Din, Phu Hang Nak
7. Suphan Buri
8. Ayuthaya
9. Lop Buri
10. Sing Buri
11. Khu Mueang
12. Tham Phothisat
13. Wat Chantheuk
14. Bo Ika
15. Nakhon Ratchasima
16. Phimai
17. Prachin Buri
18. Angkor
19. Chaiya
20. Takua Pa

Fig.1 Map showing locations mentioned in the text (map by Hunter Watson).
All photographs belong to the author unless otherwise stated.

DVĀRAVATĪ IN INSCRIPTIONS AND MANUSCRIPTS

Peter Skilling (Bhadra Rujirathat)

Introduction

I dedicate this article to the late Ian Glover. One of my first visits to U Thong was on a study tour organized by the Siam Society and guided by Ian. As Ian and I walked together along a dirt track in the ancient city, Ian bent down, picked up a fragment of a broken stone quern from the dust and stubble—a typical artefact of Dvāravatī culture—and handed it to me. His practised eyes had spotted an antiquity where my own, much younger, had seen nothing. Herein lies a parable: intellectually, Ian observed many things that other scholars did not notice, and the combination of his generous spirit, his sustained vision, and his quenchless curiosity inspired many of us in the field—the dust and stubble of this antique land—for many decades. Ian, you are missed.

This chapter is an essay at a historiography of the primary sources for the Indic-language name Dvāravatī. By primary sources, I mean inscriptions and texts in Sanskrit and Thai. I do not include sources in Chinese or in the languages of neighbouring Southeast Asian cultures: these are beyond my scope and they deserve specialized studies in their own right. I also cannot go into the historiography of the term in fields such as art history, in which the term Dvāravatī art was already used by 1924 for objects from sites in the northwest corner of the Gulf of Siam, including Prachinburi, Lop Buri, Phra Pathom, Ratchaburi, as well as Chaiya in the South. In the words of George Cœdès,

> "On a provisoirement attribué ces sculptures à l'Art de Dvārāvatī, nom d'un royaume que les historiens chinois placent vers le VIIe siècle de notre ère entre la Birmanie et le Cambodge, situation et date qui correspondent bien au lieu d'origine et ainsi que je vais essayer de montrer, a l'ancienneté probable de ces objets."[1]

The French scholar described the items that he illustrated in plates II to VI (all of Buddhas) as 'Art de Dvārāvatī' and used the term in his notes on other objects. Prince Damrong Rajanuphab used 'Dvāravatī period' (สมัยทวารวดี) for a phase in the history of the Buddhist art in Siam in his *Tamnan phra phutthachedi* ·ตำนานพระพุทธเจดีย์, first published in 1926.[2] In this system, Thai art begins with that of Dvāravatī.

The category 'Dvāravatī art' was unquestioned until Piriya Krairiksh challenged the existing system of periodization of Thai art, notably in his book, *Art Styles in Thailand*, published in 1977 (Piriya 1977). I agree with many, even most, of Piriya's points in his criticism of the term, but I do not find his proposal to replace 'Dvāravatī' with 'Mon style' appealing or realistic. It replaces one blanket term with another. Piriya's suggestion that "with our present knowledge, it is preferable to call each style by the name of the site from which a particular work of art is found, such as the Nakhon Pathom style and the Lop Buri style in central Thailand, the Sung Noen style in Nakhon Ratchasima Province", etc., is conceptually a step in the right direction—but it brings its own problems, not the least being the large number of artefacts from Thailand that float without provenance in the oceans of the illegal antique market or that find their homes in collections and museums abroad. More recent classifications that attempt to cover the art of Southeast Asia as a whole—in which Dvāravatī would belong to a broad 'classic period'—lose or obfuscate geographical, cultural, and temporal specificities and are not satisfactory (Miksic and Goh 2017: 12-14). More restrictive systems that apply to specific regions are preferable, for example that used for Cambodia by Coe and Evans: Early farmers, Early kingdoms, Classic, and Post-classic (Coe and Evans 2018: 9). These categories may well overlap with similar periodizations in other areas but they do not impose themselves on them. At any rate, I have pointed out before that whether we use the term Dvāravatī to mean a state or a kingdom, or a period of Thai history, or an art style, without defining our terms—and often mixing the various meanings together—this only breeds confusion. If we do use the term Dvārāvatī, we need to state clearly what we mean by it (Skilling 2003: 100-102).

1 One has provisionally attributed these sculptures to the 'Art of Dvāravatī', the name of a kingdom which Chinese historians place between Burma and Cambodia, the location and date of which correspond well to the place of origin, and, as I will attempt to demonstrate, to the antiquity of these objects.

2 I have consulted the edition published by Matichon in 2002 [2545 BE]. For an English translation, see *Monuments of the Buddha in Siam* (1973) pp. 9–11.

The discovery of Indian-language sources for the name Dvāravatī has been a slow process. George Cœdès gave a summary of the evidence for the name Dvāravatī that was available up to the publication of his *Les états hindouisés d'Indochine et d'Indonésie*, first published in 1948 and reprinted in 1989.[3] He gave more or less the same information in the English translation, *The Indianized States of Southeast Asia* (Cœdès 1996: 86-87). His longer articles, "Découverte numismatique au Siam intéressant le royaume de Dvāravatī" and "A la recherche du royaume de Dvāravatī" give masterful accounts. This chapter is divided into four parts: The Wat Chantheuk inscription; Inscribed medallions; Dvāravatī in the titles of Siamese capitals; and Concluding questions on what this all means.

The most recent discovery at the time of writing was the Wat Chantheuk inscription, published in 1989. In 2019, however, excavations at Wat Phra Ngam, Nakhon Pathom, recovered a stone slab engraved in ornate Dvāravatī-period Southeast Asian Brahmi. The inscription, said to be in Pali or Sanskrit and to mention 'Dvāravatī', has not yet been made public. The FAD will publish this important epigraph in due course.

The first silver medals were published in 1963. A comprehensive study of the use of the name Dvāravatī in the titles of Siamese capitals and in Thai literature was published in 1939. The luminaries who have played key roles in this prolonged quest include Prince Dhani Nivat, Prince Damrong Rajanubhab, and several generations of Thai epigraphists and Sanskritists, and the European scholars George Cœdès, Claude Jacques, and J.J. Boeles. All of these also studied the material remains of Dvāravatī, along with others from H. Quaritch Wales up to Ian Glover and those who follow in his footsteps.

The Wat Chantheuk Sanskrit 'Dvāravatī' inscription (NM 4; K. 1009)

Wat Chantheuk is a temple in Chantheuk Subdistrict, Pak Chong District, Nakhon Ratchasima Province (วัดจันทึก ต.จันทึก, อ.ปากช่องม จ.นครราชสีมา). It lies along the ancient route from the Central Plains to the Khorat Plateau, a route marked by prehistoric and historical period sites including the famous cave Tham Phothisat (ถ้ำโพธิสัตว์) with its large and magnificent reliefs. Wat Chantheuk is about 50 km from Wat Dhammachakra Semaram (วัดธมมจักรเสมาราม), which lies about 30 km from the city of Nakhon Ratchasima (โคราช). At Wat Dhammchakra Semaram there is a large stone reclining Buddha from the seventh to eight centuries that remains under worship. The area was formerly known as 'Old Khorat' (Mueang Khorat Kao เมืองโคราชเก่า) and several early inscriptions were recovered there, including the Bo Ika inscription (see below). There are several Khmer period monuments in the area.

Today Wat Chantheuk is an ordinary Thai temple with a raised teaching hall (*sala kan parian* ศาลาการเปรียญ) and some residences. There are no indications that the history of the site goes back to at least the second half of the first millennium. The only antiquity in evidence is kept behind bars in the *sala*: a four-sided stone pillar that is carved with Buddhist reliefs from a later period (eleventh to twelfth centuries?) when Khmer culture was predominant. But earlier antiquities that were found before 1965 suggest that there must have been an active ceremonial and religious centre in the vicinity of Wat Chantheuk in the seventh to the eighth centuries. No structural remains are known to survive, but, after all, the area has never been excavated. That this was a significant site is shown by the fact that fragments of at least four large stone Buddha images were recovered from the temple grounds. By any standards these statues are huge, as large as, or larger than, any of the standing stone Buddhas from central Siam. Beyond this, an exceptionally large stone image base bears a Sanskrit inscription that attests to a marriage alliance between the local ruler and the ruler of Dvāravatī. Regrettably, there do not seem to be any accounts or records of when, where, by whom, or how the artefacts were uncovered. This inscription is the subject of this section.

The Wat Chantheuk inscription is engraved on the large circular red sandstone base of an image of the Buddha (so far untraced). The base [Fig.2], now displayed in the Phimai National Museum (พิพิธภัณฑสถานแห่งชาติ พิมาย), is broken into six pieces; it measures approximately 223 cm in circumference or 104 cm in diameter. At the centre is an open square meant to receive the tenon of an image.[4] The inscription [Fig.3] is engraved in Sanskrit in Southeast Asian Brāhmī letters (the so-called 'Pallava script') on a band running below a ring of down-turned lotus petals. Both petals and band run around the entire base, but only about one third of the total circumference of the band was inscribed. The base was presented to the museum

3 Cœdès, *Les états hindouisés d'Indochine et d'Indonésie:* I have had access only to the 1989 edition and the English translation.

4 The pieces of the base bear inventory numbers 26/2/2508 to 26/6/2508 and 26/17/2508.

by a past abbot of Wat Chantheuk at an uncertain date, which must have been before 1965, when the pieces were assigned inventory numbers. There do not appear to be any records of the previous history of the pedestal apart from some photographs. In *Corpus des inscriptions du pays khmers, Inscriptions préangkoriennes nommant un roi* [Corpus of the Inscriptions of the Khmer Lands: Preangkorian inscriptions that mention a king], French savant Claude Jacques (1929–2012) published a photograph of the base [Fig.4] with an estampage of two sections of the inscription (EFEO estampage no. 1221).[5] The base is photographed in the outdoors; I am not certain, but I suspect that it is was photographed in the compound of Wat Chantheuk.

In Thailand, the Wat Chantheuk inscription has been read and published in two stages.

1) The fragment called 'Fragment C' in this article was discovered first and was registered by the National Library as N.M. 14 (น.ม.๑๔) It bears a single and incomplete line. This was published in Thai for the first time in 1986 in *Inscriptions of Thailand*,[6] but the reading was not entirely correct and, because of the fragmentary condition, the interpretation was incorrect. Claude Jacques had already published the same fragment in 1969 in the *Bulletin de l'École française d'Extrême-Orient* (Jacques 1969), with a better reading but, as we shall soon see, his interpretation of the missing image as the goddess Śrī is untenable.

2) On January 5, 1989, a team from the Faculty of Oriental Languages, Department of Archaeology, Silpakorn University, (*ภาคภาษาตะวันออก คณะโบราณคดี มหาวิทยาลัยศิลปกร)* identified another piece of the inscription. This is the fragment (here called 'Fragment B') that contains the name 'Dvāravatī'.[7] The two pieces were published together by Kannika Wimonkasem (กรรณิการ์ วิมลเกษม) and Chirapat Prapandvidya (จิรพัฒน์ ประพันธ์วิทยา) in 1999 (Kannika and Chirapat 1999 [2542 BE]), with new readings and translations that are substantially correct. The two parts of the inscription have recently been published in the second edition of *Inscriptions in Thailand* with the previous readings and reasonable reproductions of the estampages.[8] Unfortunately, the inscription does not give any date; Kannika and Chirapat assigned a date of *circa* twelfth century BE (CE 550–650) on the basis of palæography. Jacques dated the inscription to the sixth century CE. These estimates seem reasonable. The inscription, spread over three of the six fragments of the base, remains incomplete. [Figs.8–9] Reading from the left, the first fragment, here called 'Fragment A', is badly damaged and the few broken letters cannot be read except that there appear to be a double *daṇḍa*, which should indicate the opening of a verse or a sentence.[9] The beginning of Fragment B is lost owing to a break in the stone, as is the middle of Fragment C.[10] As it stands, the inscription may be tentatively read as an *anuṣṭubh* verse or *śloka*:

Fragment A | | unreadable
Fragment B ... *-tava*[11] *sutā dvāravatīpateḥ*
Fragment C *mūrttim asthāpayad devī ... -īn tāthāgatīm imām* | |

(Arranged as a verse: 'x' represents one lost syllable)
x x x x x *-tava / sutā dvāravatī pateḥ /*
mūrttim asthāpayad devī / x *-īn tāthāgatīm imām* | |

The incomplete word that opens line *D* should be an adjectival form modifying *mūrtti*, 'image'. The nature of the image is already stated by the adjectival form *tāthāgatīm*, 'of the Tathāgata', that is, of the Buddha. A possible, and even likely, solution is the adjective *śailīn*, 'made of stone', which states the material from which the 'image of the Tathāgata' is made.[12] This gives us:

x x x x x *-tava / sutā dvāravatī pateḥ /*
mūrttim asthāpayad devī / [śail]*īn tāthāgatīm imām* | |

... daughter of the Lord of Dvāravatī ... the queen set up this [stone] image of the Tathāgata.[13]

5 Jacquesn (n.d.) *Corpus des inscriptions du pays khmers*. Planches. Tome 1, pp. 203–205, with pls. 74[a] and 74[b].

6 *Inscriptions in Thailand* I (National Library 1986a), pp. 144–46; the fragment, measuring 80 x 16 x 33 cm, was read by Cha-ame Kaewglai ชะเอม แก้วคล้าย.

7 This piece bears the inventory number 26/17/2508.

8 *Inscriptions in Thailand*, second edition, Vol. 1 (National Library 1986a) pp. 71–73. It is regrettable that the wrong reading and interpretation of Fragment C as published in the first edition have been retained and the improved version of Kannika and Chirapat has been ignored. For Fragment B, the editors follow Kannika and Chirapat's transcription and reading.

9 A *daṇḍa* ('stroke, bar') is a straight vertical line used in Indian and cognate writing systems as a stop. Double *daṇḍas* are often (but inconsistently) used to open or close significant units of writing in both prose and verse.

10 Fragment A = 26/2/2508; Fragment B = 26/17/2508; Fragment C = 26/5/2508.

11 The *-ta*, quite clear, is the subscript component of a conjunct consonant. This means that the syllable was long.

12 I thank Diwakar Acharya for this suggestion (Lumbini, February, 2013).

13 Claude Jacques restores the inscription to *mūrttim asthāpayad devī – [śr]īn tāthāgatīṃ imam*. He understood this to be a pedestal for an image of the goddess Śri 'adoptée en l'occurrence par les bouddhistes' ('adopted on this occasion by the Buddhists') and translated the fragmentary inscription as 'La princesse a fait installer cette statue de Śrī, qui est adepte du Tathāgata' ('the princess had this statue of Śrī, who was an adept of the Tathāgata, installed').

In addition to the six fragments of the lotus base, the Phimai National Museum received thirteen red sandstone sculptural fragments from Wat Chantheuk [Figs.5–7] (Skilling 2003: 97–99, illustrations 30–32).[14] Initial hopes that it might be possible to reconstruct the Buddha mentioned in the inscription were dashed when it was found that the fragments come from three or even four images, none of which is complete. Three fragments come from the chest and head of a massive image.[15] The face has not survived; the head has the long ears and thick curls typical of Southeast Asian statues of the period. Another two pieces belong to the legs and lower robe of a smaller image.[16] Four pieces belong to another massive image, from the waist to the ankles,17 while two pieces belong to the torso and upper legs of a different, smaller image.18 A large tapering tenon supporting a square base with a pair of feet broken at the ankles appears to belong to the inscribed lotus base into which it is now set [Figs. 2–9].19

The fragments belong to what is usually called the Dvāravatī style. I hope that further study of their stylistic features will clarify their relation to images recovered from neighbouring sites such as Sung Noen (สูงเนิน) This may enable scholars to determine the features of the regional style and to go beyond the practice of painting everything with the broad brush of Dvāravatī.[20]

Even in its incomplete state, the inscription tells us that the image of the Buddha was set up by a queen, a daughter of the ruler of Dvāravatī (Cœdès 1961:5). This is the first stone inscription that uses the name Dvāravatī to be discovered to date. It adds to the numismatic and literary evidence for the name Dvāravatī. In general, royal or court inscriptions of the early period were composed in Sanskrit, the prestige language of the 'Sanskrit cosmopolis'. In some cases, bilingual inscriptions—Sanskrit plus a vernacular—were produced. In these courtly or 'secular' environments, the decision to use Sanskrit was independent of the canonical language preferences of the Buddhist schools or *nikāyas*. The inscriptions are simply Sanskrit compositions produced by a Sanskritic culture. *Comparisons: A Sanskrit lotus base inscription from Lop Buri (LB 5; K 577)*[21]. The Wat Chantheuk inscription is not the only example of a standing image with a royal donative record` inscribed in Sanskrit on its base, and we may compare it formally with a Sanskrit inscription from Lop Buri.[22] On 28 June 2467/1924, Luang Boribal Buribhand (Puan Inthuwong) หลวงบริบาลบุรีภัณฑ์ (ป่วน อินทุวงศ์) recovered a large stone statue of a standing Buddha from a low earthen mound in the northeastern corner of the perimeter wall of Wat Mahathat, Lop Buri (Wat Mahādhātu วัดมหาธาตุ ลพบุรี). Excavations conducted there uncovered the basement of a building of which the superstructure had completely disappeared. It is not certain, however, that this was the statue's original location.[23]

The damaged and headless statue, now displayed in the Somdet Phra Narai National Museum, Lop Buri, is made of grey sandstone [Figs.10]. The arms and hands are broken off; possibly the image stood with the hands raised and held at the same level by the chest, a common posture in the art of the area and period.[24] The Buddha stands on a double lotus base with a tenon that extends 0.56 m below the base. The statue measures 1.6 m in height, including the base. A Sanskrit quatrain in *śloka* metre is engraved in two lines at the front on the upturned lotus petals [Figs.11a–b]:

> *taṅgurajjanādhipatinā śāmbukeśvarasūnunā*
> *nāyakenārjjaveneyaṃ sthāpitā pratimā muneḥ* | |

Nāyaka Ārjava, chief of the people of Taṅgura and son of the Lord of Śāmbuka, has erected this image of the Sage [*muni*, the Buddha, Śākyamuni]. In his *Receuil des inscriptions du Siam, deuxième partie*, published in 1929, George Cœdès noted that in this inscription the toponyms Taṅgur and Śāmbuka were met with for the

14 See Skilling 2003, 'Dvāravatī: Recent Revelations and Research', pp. 97–99 and illustrations 30–32.
15 Inventory numbers 26/13/2508, 26/14/2508, and 26/15/2508.
16 Inventory numbers 26/13/2508 and 26/12/2508. Note that the number '13' is duplicated, assigned to two fragments from different images, and that one number is missing from this account.
17 Inventory numbers 26/7/2508, 26/8/2508, 26/10/2508, and 26/18/2508.
18 Inventory numbers 26/9/2508 and 26/11/2508.
19 Inventory numbers 26/1/2508.
20 See Piriya's remarks about 'Sung Noen style', above, p. 2.

21 *Chareuk boran runraek*, pp. 59–61; *Inscriptions in Thailand* vol. 1, 1st edition (National Library 1986a) pp. 229–231; *Inscriptions in Thailand* Vol. 1, 2nd edition, (National Library 2016a) pp. 316–318, reproduces the information of the earlier edition.
22 Cœdès, *Recueil des inscriptions du Siam* II (second edition, 1961), p. 5. The design and conception of the statue and its base are quite different to those of Wat Chantheuk. In the case of the latter, the base is a separate, independent unit, with a hole into which the tenon of the statue would have been inserted. The Lop Buri image is made from a single stone.
23 Cœdès, p. 4, "Les fouilles exécutées en cet endroit ont révélé le soubassement d'un édicule dont la superstructure a complètement disparu. Il n'est d'ailleurs nullement certain que la statue ait été primitivement placée en cet endroit."
24 See for example Piriya, *The Roots of Thai Art*, figs. 1.22, 1.38, 1.82–85, 1. 88–90 (noting that the author's identification of these figures with Amitābha is not supported by any evidence).

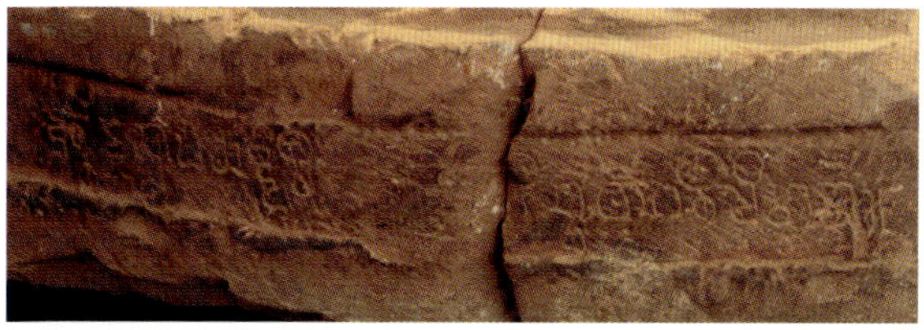

3

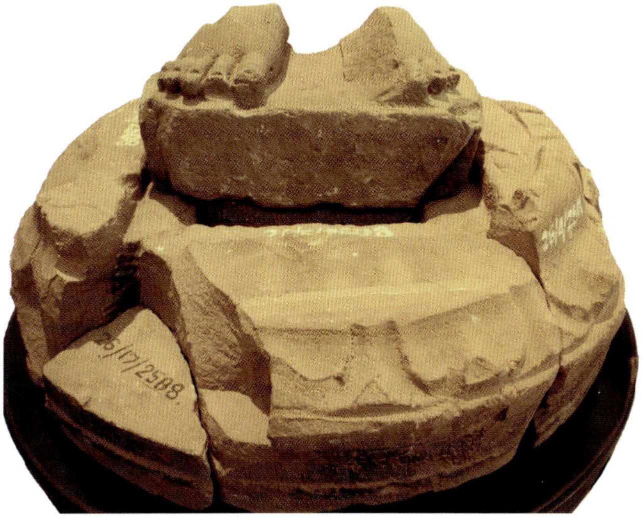

2

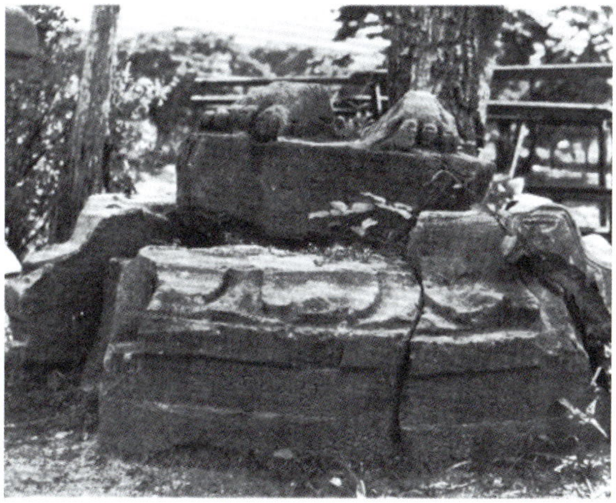

4

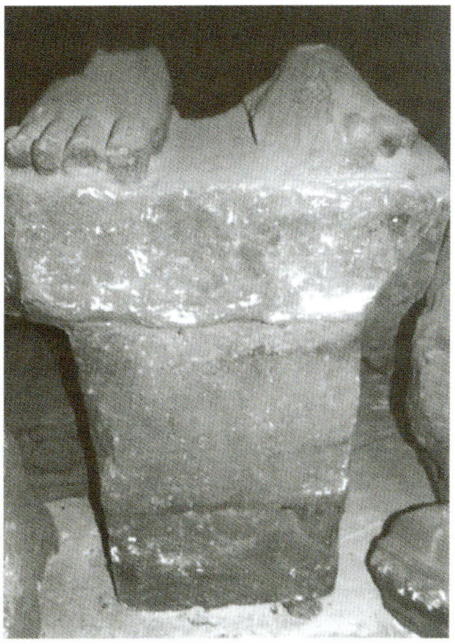

5

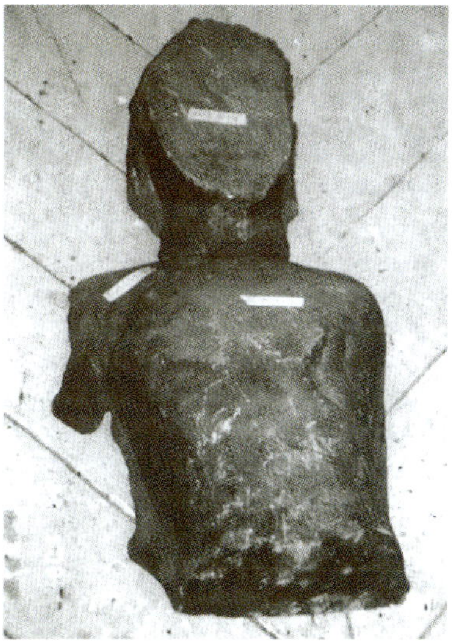

6

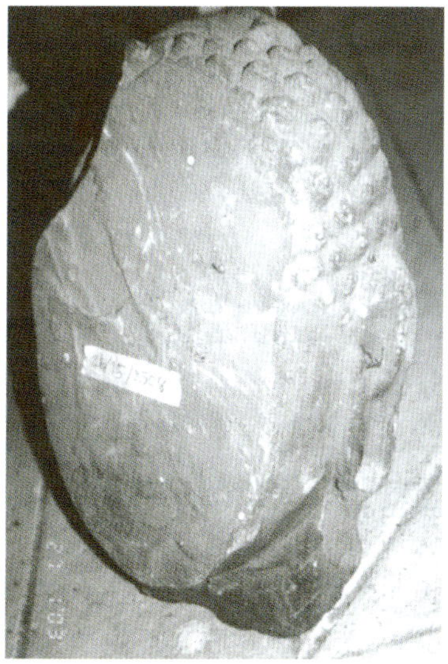

7

Fig.2 The Wat Chanteuk inscription is engraved on the large circular red sandstone base of an image of a standing Buddha.
Fig.3 Inscription engraved in Sanskrit in Southeast Asian Brāhmī letters.
Fig.4 Base photographed in the outdoors, presumably at Wat Chanteuk in Pak Chong District, Nakhon Ratchasima Province.
Fig.5 Broken torso of a Buddha image from Wat Chanteuk. Phimai National Museum.
Fig.6 Damaged head of Buddha image from Wat Chanteuk. Phimai National Museum.
Fig.7 Tenon and base of image of a standing Buddha from Wat Chanteuk. Phimai National Museum.

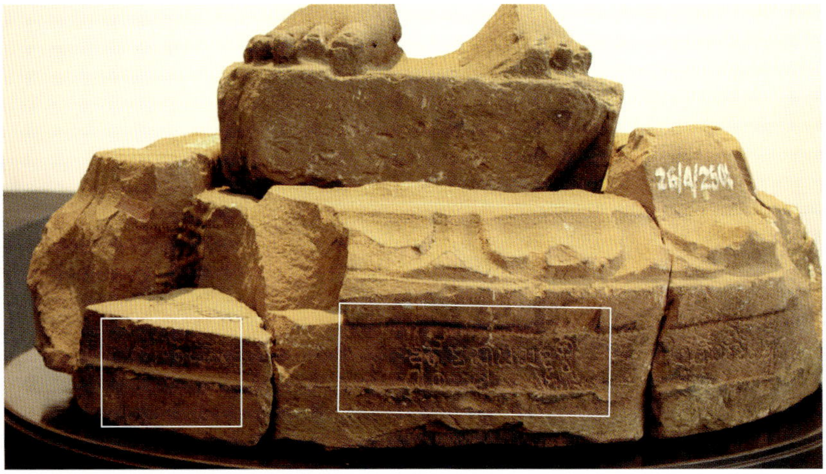

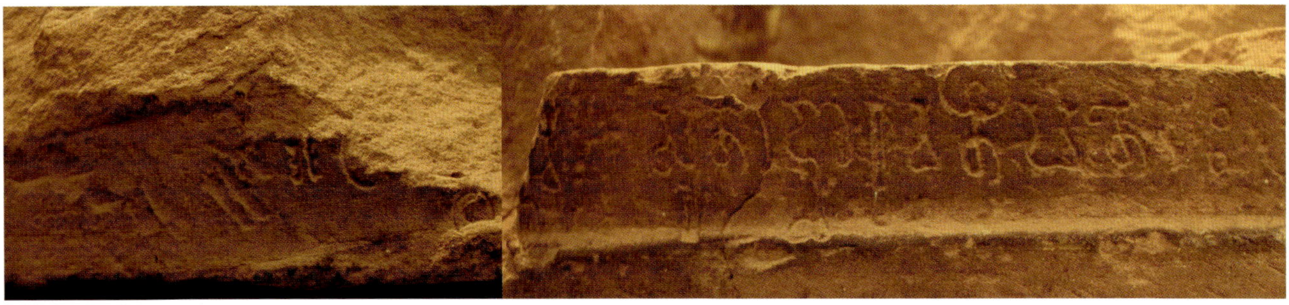

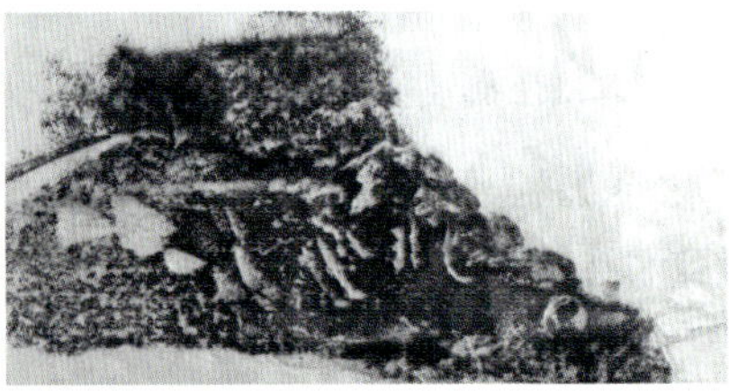

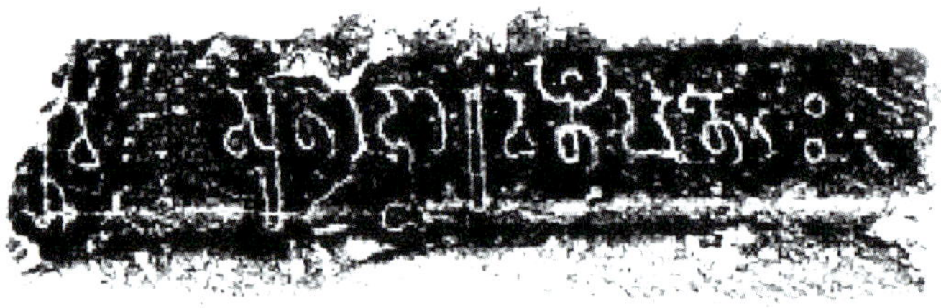

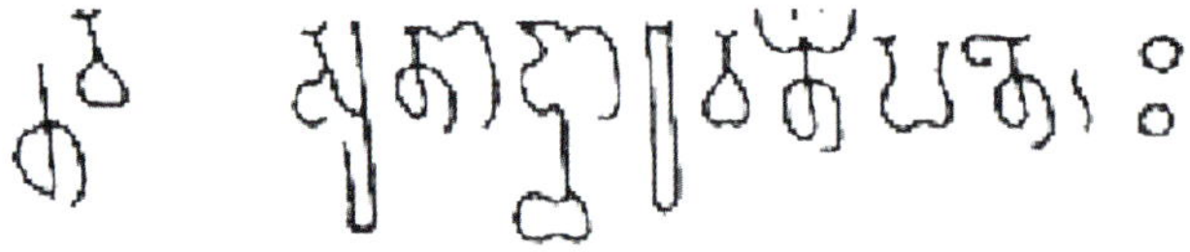

| | unreadable

. . . . . -*tava* / *sutā dvāravatī pateḥ* /

... daughter of the Lord of Dvāravatī

Fig 8 Sections of the Wat Chanteuk inscription.

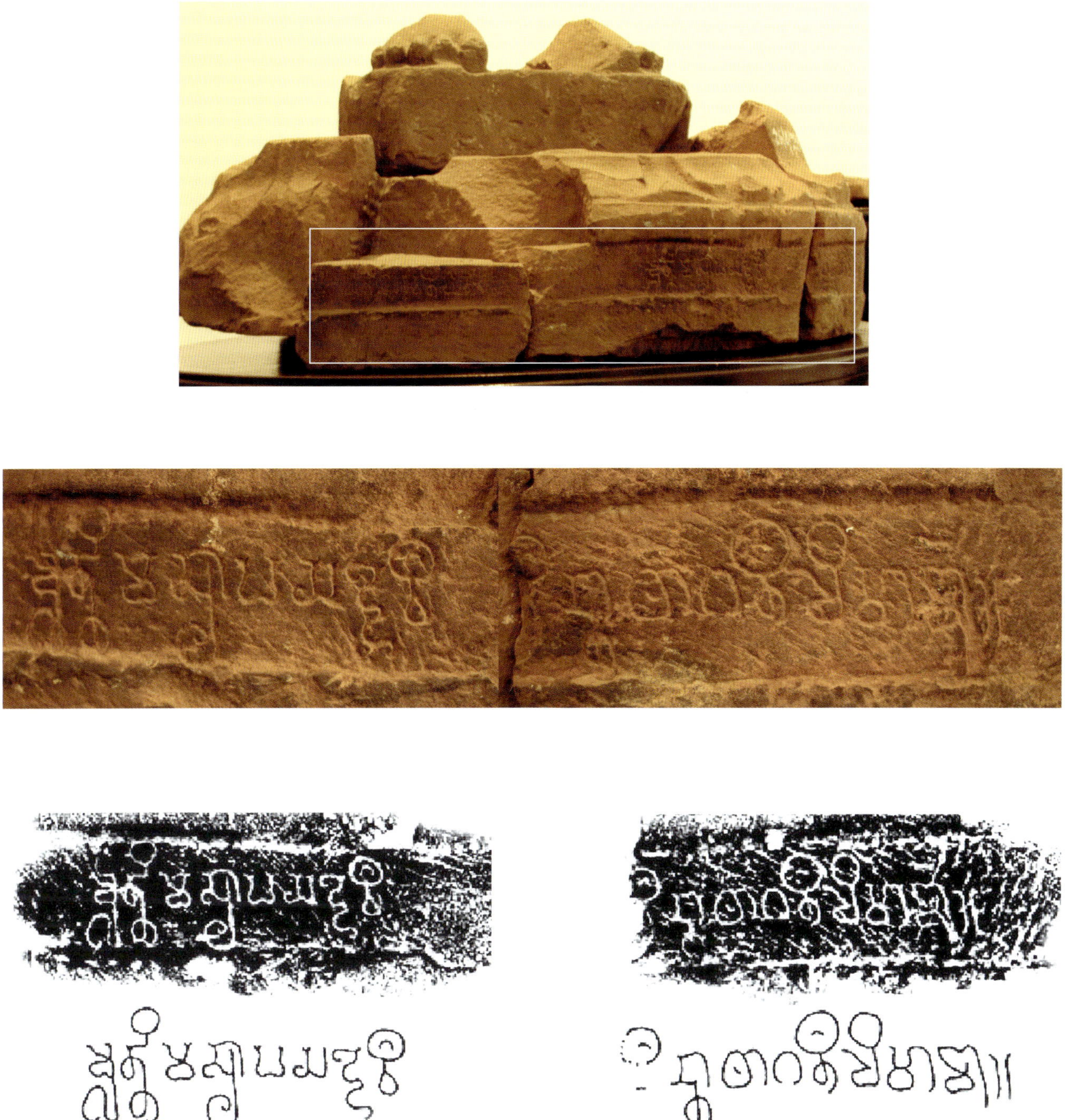

mūrttim asthāpayad devī / [śail]*īn tāthāgatīm imām* | |

... the queen set up this [stone] image of the Tathāgata.

Fig.9 Sections of the Wat Chanteuk inscription.

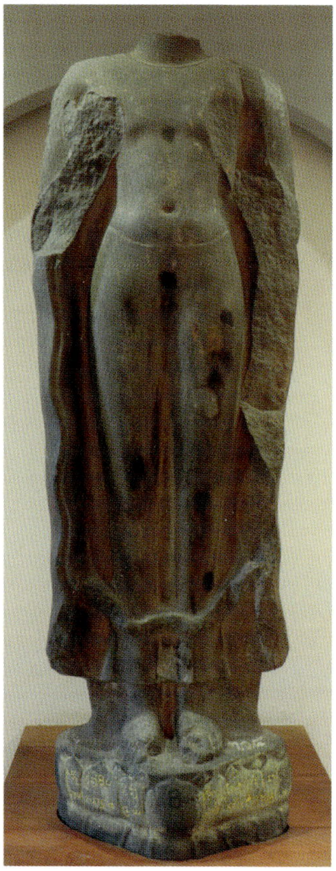

10

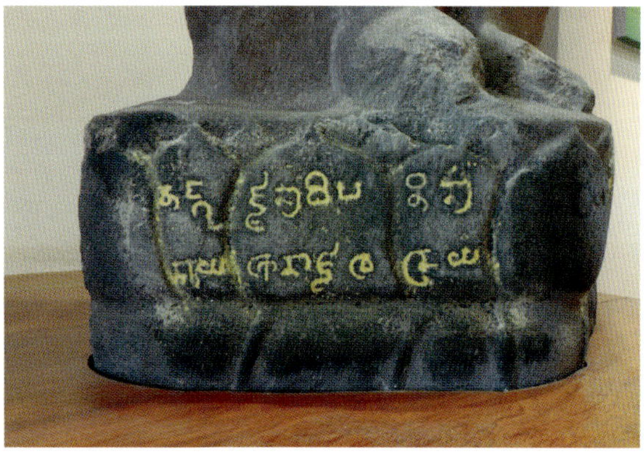

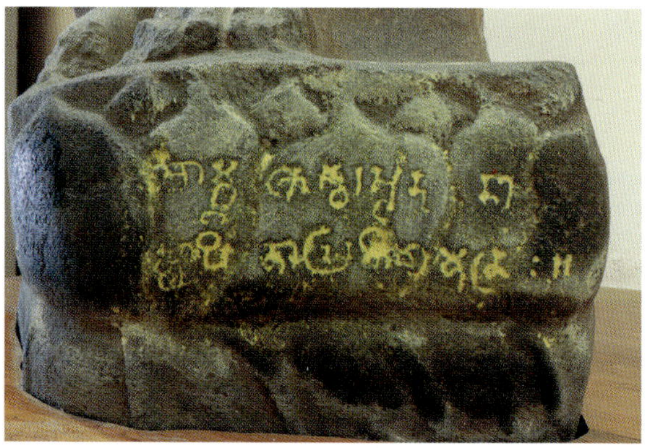

taṅgurajjanādhipatinā
śāmbukeśvarasūnunā

nāyakenārjjaveneyaṃ
sthāpitā pratimā muneḥ | |

11a–b

Nāyaka Ārjava, chief of the people of Taṅgura and son of the Lord of Śāmbuka, has erected this image of the Sage [*muni*, the Buddha, Śākyamuni].

Fig 10 Standing Buddha, made of grey sandstone. The arms and hands are broken off; possibly the image stood with the hands raised and held at the same level by the chest, a common posture in the art of the area and period. The Buddha stands on a double lotus base with a tenon that extends 0.56 m below the base. The statue measures 1.6 m in height, including the base.
Fig 11 A Sanskrit quatrain in *śloka* metre is engraved in two lines at the front on the upturned lotus petals. Somdet Phra Narai National Museum, Lop Buri.

first time, and that they remained to be identified. He remarked that Taṅgur recalled by its form the Naṅgur of the Tamil inscription from Khao Phra Narai in Takua Pa เขาพระนารายณ์ ตะกั่วป่า (Cœdès 1929: 32-33, Pl.XII; Boeles 1986), which dates to the ninth century. Takua Pa lies on the west coast of the Thai-Malay peninsula, about 900 km south of Lop Buri. The meaning of Taṅgur is not clear, and the inscription is the record of a foreign guild written in Tamil for Tamils. The Lop Buri and Takua Pa inscriptions are geographically and culturally far apart: I find it difficult to envisage any significant connection between the two names.

For the second toponym, Cœdès referred to Śambūkapaṭṭana in line 116 of the twelfth century inscription of Phreah Khan of Angkor (พระขรรค์ นครวัด, K. 908) (Cœdès 1992). This is a long Sanskrit eulogy (179 lines covering four faces) of King Jayavarman VII and a record of his meritorious foundations, amounting to an inventory of deities erected and consecrated during his reign. Verses 113 to 120 enumerate some of the twenty-three deities. Verses 116 to 117a refer to Lavodayapura, Svarṇapura, Śamvūkapaṭṭana, Jayarājapurī, Śrī Jayasiṃhapurī, and Śrī Jayavajrapurī, a string of cities corresponding to modern Lop Buri, Suphan Buri, Ratchaburi, Sing Buri, and Phetchaburi in lower central Siam [Fig.1]. The only city that cannot be identified is the very one that interests us, Śamvūkapaṭṭana. Lop Buri belongs to the cluster of cities mentioned, and a connection between the Śāmbūka of LB 5 from Lop Buri and the Śamvūkapaṭṭana of K908 from Cambodia is probable.

Cœdès writes further that:

> The titles *nāyaka* and *adhipati* are interesting. One knows from Ma Tuan-lin [馬端臨Ma Duan-lin] that in the kingdom of Ch'ih-t'u [赤土Chi tu)] they designated provincial functionaries. 'Each town in Ch'ih-t'u is placed under the authority of two main officials called *na-ya-kia* [那邪迦*nayejia*] and *po-ti* [鉢帝*bo di*]' (*Méridionaux* p. 469). The exact location of Ch'ih-t'u or 'the Land of the Red Earth' which evidently corresponds to the Raktamṛttika of the Kedah inscription, is not known with any certainty. It was located in any case in the Malay peninsula, and its civilization would have been analogous to that of the kingdom of Dvāravatī, to which I believe it possible to attribute the inscribed statue. Here, the founder of this statue had the two titles *nāyaka* and *(adhi)pati*, or more precisely, he had the title or rank of *nāyaka* and performed the function of *pati* of the land of Taṅgur.[25]

For Chih-tu we can now benefit from the chapter "The Red-Earth Land" in Paul Wheatley's *Golden Khersonese* (Wheatley 1980: 26-36). Wheatley's masterful study was first published in 1961; naturally enough, there have been new archaeological discoveries since then and these necessarily call for some revisions and reconceptualizations. Regarding the Raktamṛttika of the Buddhagupta stele, in the early 1960s clay monastic sealings of the "Raktamṛttika Mahāvihāra" were found in excavation in West Bengal and published in 1968 (Das 1968: 56-59, Pls. I and IA (1), III (14); Skilling 2003: 21-25). This matches information recorded by Xuanzang about a *saṃghārāma* named Lo-to-wei(mo)-chi-sang-kia-lam [絡多末知僧伽藍 Luo duo mo zhi Seng jia lan], a transcription which corresponds to Raktamṛttika-saṃghārāma, situated beside the capital city of Kie-lo-na-su-fa-la-na [羯羅拏蘇伐剌那Jie luo na su fa la na, Karṇasuvarṇa] in eastern India (Li Rongxi 1995: 109-110; 1996: 303-305). It is nearly certain, then, that Buddhagupta Mahānāvika came from Raktamṛttika in Bengal.[26] If such is the case, then Chih-tu, the 'Red-Earth Land', of the Chinese sources may well translate a local, vernacular name for a site on the Thai-Malay peninsula rather than a Sanskrit toponym. Sanskrit 'Raktamṛttika' means 'red clay'; in Chinese both 泥 *ni* and 土 *tu* mean 'earth' and 'clay' and there is a compound form 泥土 *ni tu* meaning 'earth' / 'clay'. Xuanzang's book gives a note with reference to the eastern Indian monastery saying that 絡多末知 Luo duo mo zhi means 赤泥 *chi ni*, red clay.

---

25 Cœdès 1961, Receuil 2, p. 5 : 'Les titres de *nāyaka* et *adhipati* sont intéressants. On sait par Ma-tuoan-lin, qu'ils désignaient dans le royaume de Tch'e-t'ou des functionnaires provinciaux. « Chaque ville de Tch'e-t'ou est placée sous l'autorité de deux mandarins principaux appelés *na-ya-kia* et *po-ti* » (*Méridionaux* p. 469). L'emplacement exact de Tch'e-t'ou ou « Pays de la Terre Rouge, » qui corresponde vraisemblement au Raktamṛttika de l'inscription de Kĕdah, n'est pas connu d'une façon certaine. Il se trouvait en tout cas sur la Péninsule Malaise et sa civilisation devait être analogue à celle du royaume de Dvāravatī, auquel j'ai cru pouvoir rapporter la statue inscrite. Ici, le fondateur de cette statue cumulait les deux titres de *nāyaka* et de *(adhi)pati*, ou plus exactement il avait le titre ou le grade de *nāyaka* et remplissait la function de *pati* du pays du Taṅgur.'

26 The inscription reads, in part, *mahānāvikabuddhaguptasya raktamṛttika-vās*[*tavyasya*]. The ending in -*vāstavya* is frequent in Indian inscriptions and usually means 'resident of'. See Skilling (2015) 'An Untraced Buddhist Verse Inscription', p. 25.

Terminology

As for *pati* and *adhipati*: these are rather widely used terms for 'ruler'. The Wat Chantheuk inscription uses *pati*, and the Lop Buri inscription uses *adhipati*. The term *adhipati* is used in an inscription from Ayuthaya dated to 937 CE, *śrī-cānāśādhipati* (K. 949, see below). The terms are used in India, for example in the copper plate grant of Devapāla from Nalanda, which refers to 'Mahārāja Śrī Bālaputradeva, overlord of Suvarṇadvīpa'—Suvarṇṇadvīpādhipati (Sastri 1923-1924: 92-102). Another term for ruler is īśvara, used on the silver Dvāravatī medallions and in the Sanskrit inscription from Bo Ika (śrī-cānāśā-īśvara: see below).

Inscribed medallions: Śrī-dvāravatī-īśvara-puṇya

One of the first scholars to reconstitute the Chinese name Tuoluobodi (陀羅缽地) to Dvāravatī was Samuel Beal (1825–1889), in the course of his translation of Xuanzang's record of his travels in the eighth century.[27] That Dvāravatī was the correct equivalent became widely accepted.[28] Prior to the publication of the second fragment of the Wat Chantheuk inscription in 1989, the only Sanskrit epigraphic evidence for Dvāravatī was that stamped on silver medals or medallions from central Siam. The first Thai-language publication of the inscribed Dvāravatī medallions, by Chalerm Yongboonkerd, appeared in the journal *Sam Thahan*.[29] Chalerm first discusses Chinese references to Dvāravatī and the work of French scholars. He then writes that he began to encounter a lot of silver coins when he was preparing a book on Thai coins and that he had the chance to see two silver coins. They were not fully round, and measured about 1.2 to 1.5 cm in diameter. One side of some bore a conch (*śaṅkha*), of others a full pot (*pūrṇaghaṭa*, *pūrṇakalaśa*), of others a cow looking back to the right at her calf or a cow looking back to the left at her calf (*savacchadheṇu*). The other side had writing in Sanskrit in the Pallava script. He goes on to give some information about the discovery as he heard it from both the person who had found the coins and the owner (unfortunately he does not name or identify either of them). The finder told Chalerm that he had dug the coins up in an earthenware pot (หม้อทะนน) in the foundations of a *chedi* in Noen Hin, Nakhon Pathom Province more than ten years earlier; but the owner said that his own forebears had dug the coins up in an orchard in Noen Hin.[30] Whatever the case, Chalerm sent photos to George Cœdès through the Siam Society in Bangkok. Like Cœdès, Chalerm states that he thinks the artefacts are not coins but rather mementoes of merit of the kings of Dvāravatī. Chalerm's article contains photos of both faces of the two coins.

Chalerm's story links up to the first English report, published in the *Journal of the Siam Society* for September, 1963, by J.J. Boeles, at that time director of the Siam Society Research Center. There are some discrepancies. As Boeles tells it,

> During World War II, in 1943, two small medals of very pure silver have been found under a chedi at Huay Chorakay (Crocodile Stream), Tambol Nern Hin, Changvat Nakorn Pathom, inside a small earthenware jar together with more medals of that type as well as other medals of the conch shell type. The medals of the conch shell type have since been lost. The Huay Chorakay crosses the road from Bangkok to Nakorn Pathom, under a bridge, reached after having passed the monument Wat Phra Paton. The site of Nern Hin (or Nön Hin) is mentioned by Dupont. The diameter of these two circular coins is 2 cm.; both coins are in the possession of Nai Yongboonkerd.

27 Beal, *Si-Yu-Ki: Buddhist Records of the Western World*, II, p. 200. Beal writes 'the kingdom of Dvârapati (To-lo-po-ti)' in the text, and in footnote 33, he notes that 'Dwâravatî is the classic name for the town and district of Sandowê, but in Burmese history it is also applied to Siam', referring to Phayre, *History of Burma*, p. 32. Phayre's *History* was published in 1883, and his speculations about the names mentioned by Xuanzang are mostly wide of the mark. Sandoway was indeed called Dvāravatī, but at a later period (or, at least, I have never heard of any evidence for the early period), and at any rate Phayre thought that 'Siam would agree with the directions indicated by the Chinese pilgrim'. In his *Mémoires sur les contrées occidentales*, Tome second, p. 83, Stanislas Julien has '*To-lo-po-ti* (Dârapati?)'.

28 For a bibliographical history of the use of the term by historians see Cœdès (1964) *'A la recherche du royaume de Dvāravatī'*, pp. 58–60, and idem (1963), 'Découverte numismatique au Siam intéressant le royaume de Dvāravatī'.

29 The reference is in Boeles (1964) *'The King of Śrī Dvāravatī'*, p. 114, n. 26. I am grateful to Aoun Thongchai Likhitphonsawan for sending a copy of this hard to find source at short notice, which hopped to me like a white rabbit drawn from a magician's hat.

30 Chalerm (1964) p. 42,
เนื่องจากการเรียบเรียงหนังสือกษาปณ์ไทยของข้าพเจ้าเมื่อเร็วๆ นี้ ข้าพเจ้ามีโอกาสได้พบเหรียญเงินโบราณจำนวนหนึ่ง รูปลักษณะไม่กลมทีเดียวนัก มีเส้นผ่าศูนย์กลาง ๑.๒ – ๑.๕ ซ.ม. ด้านหนึ่งของบางเหรียญเป็นรูปปูรณฆฏ หรือ ปูรณกลศ บางเหรียญเป็นรูปวัวตัวเมียหันหน้าไปทางขวากับลูกอ่อน และบางเหรียญเป็นรูปวัวตัวเมียหันหน้าไปทางซ้าย กับลูกอ่อนอีกด้านหนึ่งเป็นอักษรสันสกฤตครั้งราชวงศ์ปัลลวะ ผู้ที่ขุดได้ แจ้งแก่ข้าพเจ้าว่า ขุดได้พร้อมกับเหรียญเงินตราสังข์อยู่ในหม้อทะนนใต้ฐานเจดีย์ที่ตำบลเนินหิน จังหวัดนครปฐม เมื่อสิบกว่าปีมาแล้ว แต่ก็มีผู้ที่มีเหรียญเหล่านี้อยู่ในความครอบครองแจ้งกับข้าพเจ้าด้วยเหมือนกันว่า บรรพบุรุษของเขาขุดได้ในที่สวนตำบลเนินหิน จังหวัดนครปฐม.

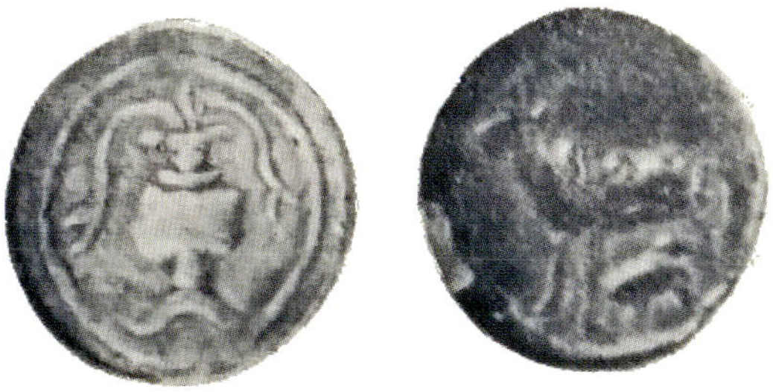

12

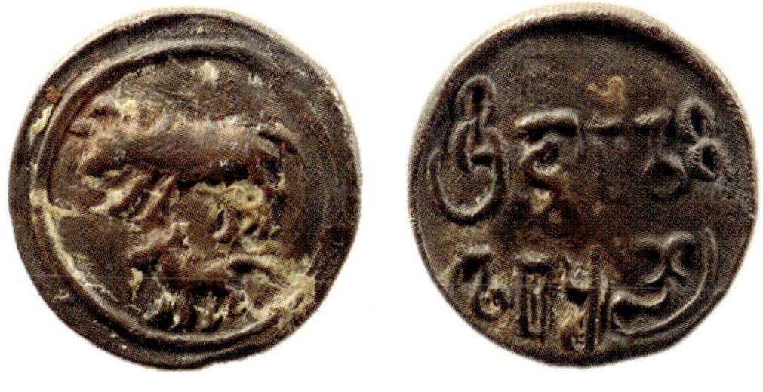

14

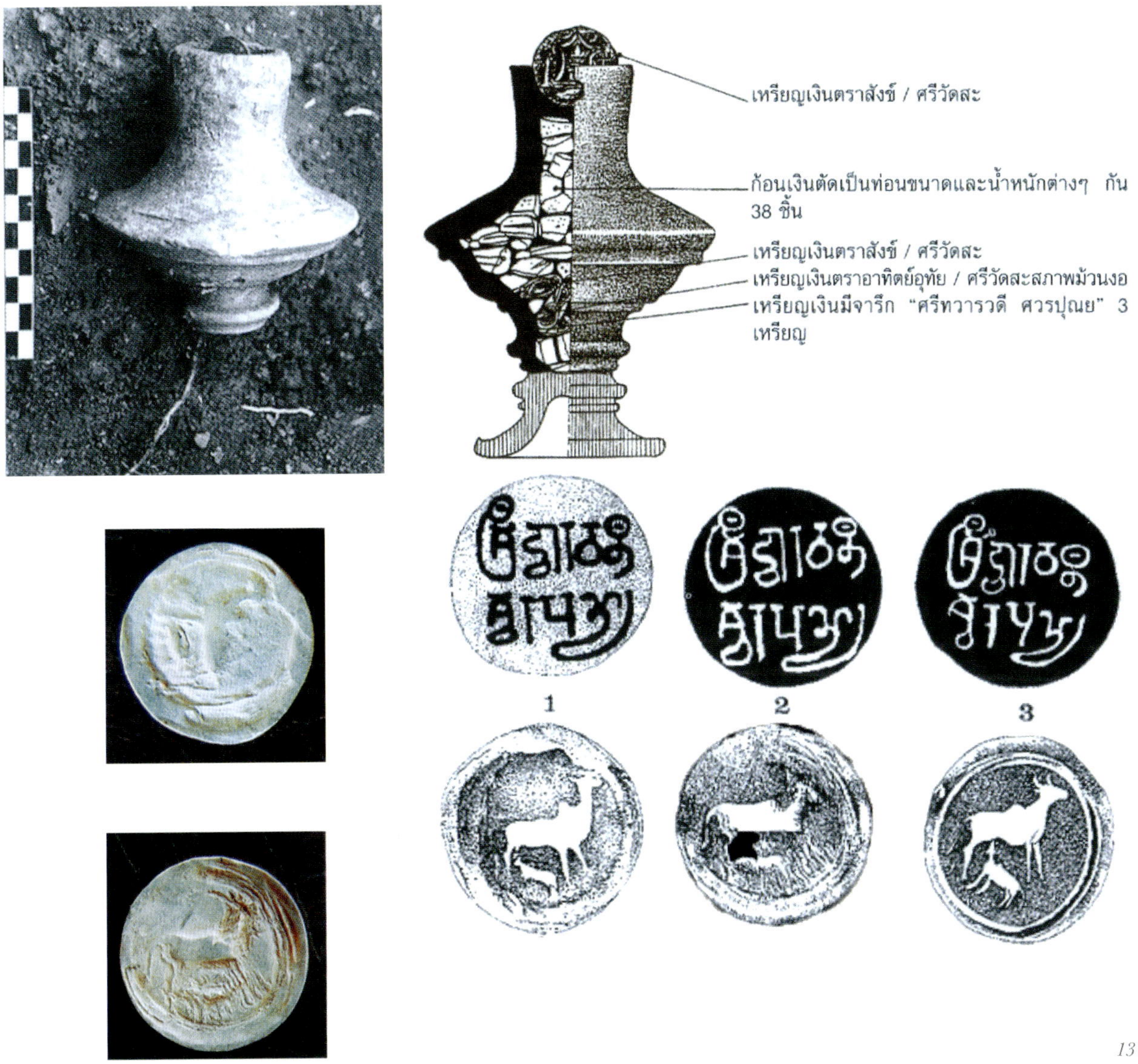

13

Fig.12 Verso of inscribed Dvāravatī medals.
Fig.13 Earthenware vessel filled with coins and medallions. Khok Chang Din, U Thong.
Fig.14 Dvāravatī medallion.

The site of "Nern Hin" is mentioned by Dupont: 'une terasse en briques, N'on Hin, n'a pas encore fait l'objet d'un relevé; une apsara en stuc y a été trouvé'.[31] The report that the medals were found with a hoard of coins in an earthenware pot agrees with other attested cases, for example at Khok Chang Din and at Phu Hang Nak at U Thong.

French savant Cœdès saw the significance of the coins immediately, and wrote, 'this numismatic discovery confirmed the exactitude of the restitution of the toponynm from the Chinese transliterations' (Cœdès 1963; 1964: 10; 1989: 145, No. 5). Since then, other inscribed Dvāravatī medallions have been found. There are several different models, depending on the auspicious symbol on the verso; the important thing is that all of them proclaim, in Sanskrit written in Southeast Asian Brāhmī, 'the religious merit of the glorious Lord of Dvāravatī'. As Cœdès pointed out, these are not coins, but tokens of merit, to be ritually installed in the foundations of (mostly religious?) structures (Cœdès 1963: 290). In a sense, the locations where they have been found map the reach of the king of Dvāravatī's merit. For this reason, it is especially unfortunate that many of them belong to private collections and have no provenance.

Robert Wicks gives a good summary of early central Siamese coinage with examples of a range of medals and coins (Wicks 1992: 157-163). Ronachai and Mihailovs give excellent pictures of inscribed Dvāravatī medals and a concise summary. They treat the artefacts as coins but also write that 'it is possible that they were medals rather than coins'. They remark that 'the alloy for these series is quite uniform and is over 98% silver with the remaining element being copper ... Only silver strikes are known to exist'. They note the existence of 'counterfeit fantasy types' and illustrate two modern counterfeits with a genuine piece (left) for comparison (pl.A31). It is unfortunate that the transcription and translation of the legend are both wrong (Ronachai and Mihailovs 2002: 49-51, Pl.A29-A32).

A series of inscribed Dvāravatī medallions has been published in the second edition of *Inscriptions in Thailand*.

1) Nth 8 / นฐ 8. From Nakhon Pathom, reported in a translation by Prince Subhadradis Diskul of *L'art de Dvāravatī* by Jean Boisselier, who refers to Georges Cœdès (*Nityasar Silpakar* 11.5, January 2513). Now in the Bangkok National Museum, (pp. 152–154).

2) Nth 18 / นฐ18. From Noen Hin, Huai Chorakhe Subdistrict, Mueang District, Nakhon Pathom Province (เนินหิน ต.ห้วยจรเข้ อ.เมือง จ.นครปฐม). At present with Phaiboon Phuangsamli (pp. 155–157).[32]

3) Sph 20 / สพ 20. Three inscribed medallions from Khok Chang Din, Chorakhe Sam Phan Subdistrict, U Thong District, Suphan Buri Province (คอกช้างดิน ต.จระเข้สามพัน อ.อู่ทอง จ.สุพรรณบุรี). Now in the U Thong National Museum (pp. 158–160) (FAD 2545).

4) Lb 20 / ลบ 20. From Ban Khu Mueang, In Buri District, Sing Buri Province (บ้านคูเมือง อ.อินทร์บุรี จ.สิงห์บุรี). Now kept in the Department of Archaeology, Silpakorn University, Bangkok (pp. 161–163).

The medals bear the same text:

śrī-dvāravatī-īśvara-puṇya
Merit of the glorious Lord of Dvāravatī.[33]

The phrase has often been broken up as: *śrī-dvāravatī-śvara-puṇya*. However, there is no such word as *śvara*, and the phrase is composed from *dvāravatī* + *īśvara*. According to Sanskrit *sandhi* rules, the two long '*ī*' join together but remain a long '*ī*', which is what we see here: dvāravatīśvara.

There remains, however, the question of whether the phrase was written as a Sanskritic sentence or as a prestige title. According to the rules of Sanskrit syntax, a nominal compound should finish with a case-ending, which, in this case, would be *puṇyaṃ*. All of the medallions are the same, with no case ending. It remains an open question as to whether those who conceived of the medal intended to write in proper Sanskrit, whether they felt that for a medal the string of words was sufficient, or whether they wrote it as Old Mon, which would not require any case ending.

31 Dupont (1959) *L'Archéologie mône de Dvāravatī*, p.2 0. Also mentioned on p. 65 and indicated on the Carte archéologique de Nakhon-pathom as Nern-Hin.

32 According to the second edition of *Inscriptions in Thailand*, it is published there for the first time. It is said that there is no evidence as to when it was discovered; it was sent to Term Mitem to read in 2004.

33 The *śrī* can also be read with Dvāravatī : Lord of glorious Dvāravatī, which strikes me as less likely. In any case, *śrī* is an adjective that is not a fixed part of the toponym, which is Dvāravatī and not Śrīdvāravatī. The same holds for Cānāśa: it is Cānāśa or Cānāśapura, not Śrīcānāśa.

Other Dvāravatīs

An inscription from Thvār Kdei or Thvār Prambei in Cambodia uses the term Dvāravatī twice. It is engraved on the abutments (*piédroit*); the southern abutment has 13 lines in Sanskrit and 6 lines in Khmer, while the north abutment has 39 lines in Khmer (Cœdès 1954: 132-139). The north abutment refers to the village of Dvāravatī twice: a royal grant of the village (l1.7) and the setting up of a *liṅga* named Śrī Cāmpeśvara there (l.13). It is likely that this refers to a place in the area, in Cambodia, and is not related to the Dvāravatī of central Siam (Aymonier 1900: 444-446; Lunet de Lajonquière 1902: 263).

Stone images: An inscription from Nagarjunakonda (EIAD 54)

A Sanskrit inscription from Nagarjunakonda in south India refers to the installation of a stone Buddha statue during the twenty-fourth regnal year of Ehuvala Chāntamūla, that is, approximately between 250–300 CE.[34] A translation reads:

> Success! In the twenty-fourth year of Great King Śrī-Ehavalacāntamūla of the Ikṣvākus, in the fourth fortnight of the rainy season, on the fifth day. In Śrīparvata, in Vijayapurī, in the monk's cell (*pariveṇa*) of the Great Queen, Kumāranandin—guild's chief (*śreṣṭhin*) from Syandakaparvata, son of Īśvarabhatta of the Bamakīyas, who originates from the °Iru...-family—together with (his) wife, the guild's-chief-wife, and (his) son Īśvarabharttin and the remaining group of his kinsmen and relatives established this stone image of the Bhagavant,[35] the foremost of all beings, who has perfected all qualities, the Complete Perfect Buddha, the Buddha, for the well-being and happiness of himself and all beings. And on this there is a stanza: By the merit accumulated having made this pious gift, may this world attain *nirvāṇa*.

The inscription is engraved on a sculpted stone panel [Fig.15] that was discovered *in situ* at Site 106 during the 1956–57 season, above a long frieze (h.50 × w.252 × d.17 cm) that bears representations of the four main events of the life of the Buddha carved in deep relief and flanked by pairs of *mithunā*. The inscription is written in Southern Brāhmī script in a single line (h.3.5 × w.241 cm) above the frieze. [Figs. 17, 18] The interpretation poses some difficulties. What is the *śailamayī pratimā?* The word *pratimā* is usually used for a sacred image (a Buddha, a Tīrthaṅkar, or a deity) that a donor has set up (*pratiṣṭhāpitā*) for worship. But here we have not a free-standing statue, but a long narrative frieze that is 2.5 meters in length, illustrating four major events in the career of Śākyamuni, set between pairs of *mithunās*. The stone with its rondels are not simply decorative and I understand them to be supports for devotion and inspiration rather than images for ritualistic cult or worship (*pūjā*). Can such a frieze be a *pratimā?* I believe that this is the only example of a set of narratives being described as a *pratimā* known so far, but perhaps it lies within the realms of possibility. The epigraphic records of Buddhism, and Indian sculpture, are fragmentary and incomplete. We know so little.

R. Subrahmanyam mentions the inscription as follows: it 'says that "an image made of stone" (*śailamayī pratimā*) was installed. The common word used for an image is simply *pratimā*, and the specific reference to a *śailamayī pratimā* in the present inscription possibly indicates that the stone image replaced a previous one made of wood or stucco. On this occasion, then, the present inscription would have been carved on the flat vacant strip of the broad pedestal. The reliefs on the inscribed slab, however, should not be considered dated in spite of the inscription's date.' To me, this is not very convincing in this case and even more so in the case of the Wat Chantheuk image.

Dvāravatī in the titles of Siamese capital cities

The most comprehensive article on Dvāravatī in Thai written sources remains the seminal article published by Prince Dhani Niwat in the *Journal of the Siam Society* in 1939 (1969). Dvāravatī is one element of the name of the Siamese capital Ayuthaya as given in the preambles to three sections of the *Three Seals Law Code* (*Kotmai tra sam duang*) [Figs. 18, 19, 20]: The Law on Witnesses (1350), Royal Legislation (1351), and the Law on Ordeal by Water or Fire (1355).[36] In all of these preambles, the

34 The inscription was noticed in *Indian Archaeology 1956–57 – A Review*, p. 36, with a photograph of the inscribed sculpture stone (pl. LVIIA). The inscription was first described and edited by D.C. Sircar as 'Inscription of the time of Ehuvala Chāntamūla, Year 24', published as no. 4 in his 'More Inscriptions from Nagarjunakonda', pp. 11–13. It was re-edited as EIAD 54 by Arlo Griffiths and Vincent Tournier, with contributions by Stefan Baums and Ingo Strauch, from the published estampage and their own photographic documentation, after an autopsy of the stone. It is now on display at the Nagarjunakonda Museum (acc. No. 13).

35 Saṁmyaksambuddhasya buddha[s] a ◊ śailamayī ◊pratimā ◊ pratiṣṭhāpit[ā].

36 The translations of the titles are from Baker and Pasuk, *The Palace Law of Ayutthaya and the Thammasat*, Table 1, pp. 4–5. The dates are as given by

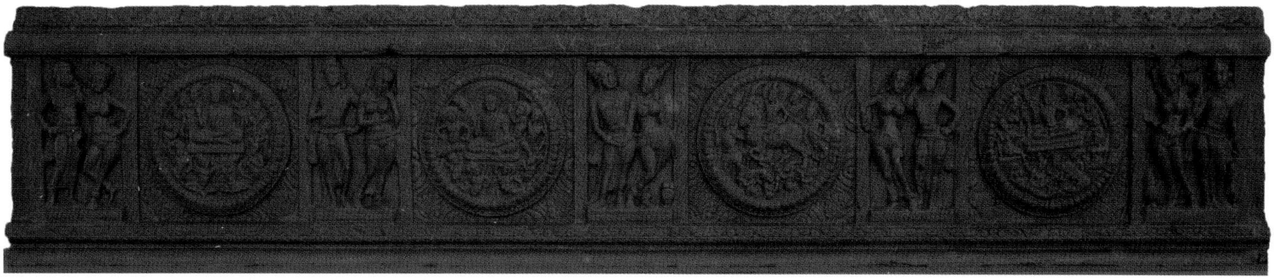

15

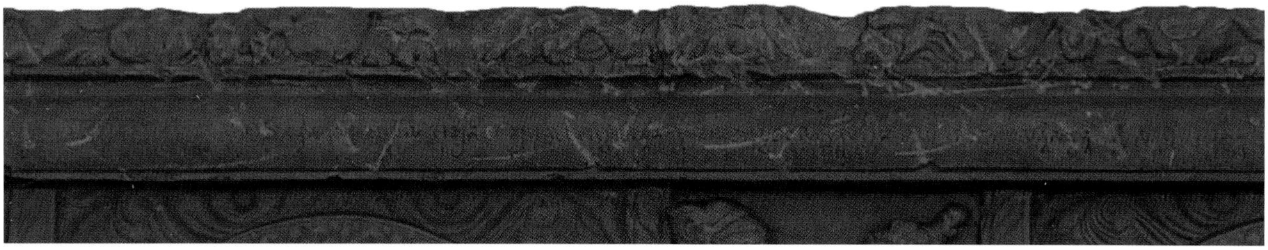

16

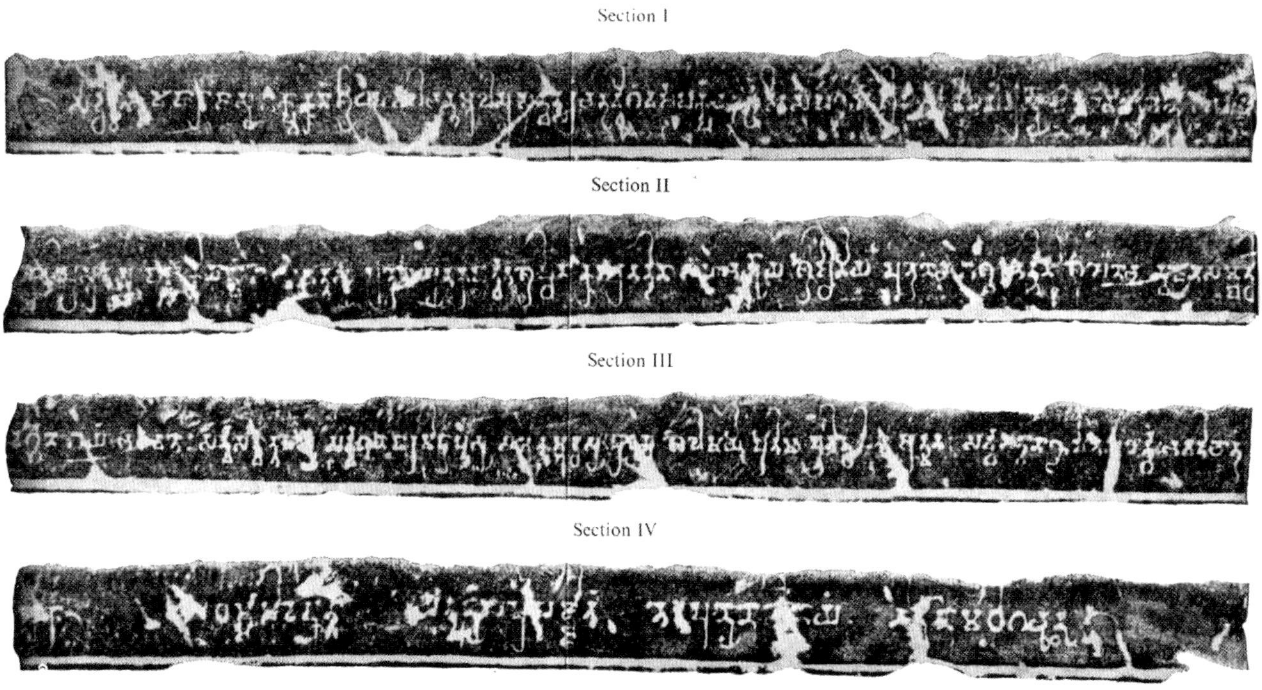

17

Figs.15–16 Inscribed sculpted stone panel, Site 106, Nagarjunakonda, Andhra Pradesh, India.
Fig.17 Inscription, sculpted stone panel, Nagarjunakonda, Andhra Pradesh, India.

name of the capital is *Krung-deb -dvāravatī-śrī-ayudhyā-mahātilakabhaba-nabaratana-rājadhānī-purīramya* (กรุงเทพ ทวารวดี ศรีอยุทธยามหาดิลกภพ นพรัตนราชธาณีบูรีรมย์) / *Krung thep thawarawadi si ayuthaya mahadilokaphop nopharat ratchathaniburirom.*[37] Prince Dhani Nivat notes that two other sections of the Three Seals Law Code use only 'Si Ayudhya', while the remaining sections had no occasion to refer to the name of the capital at all. He also notes how various literary works in Pāli (*Ratanabimbavaṃsa*, 1429 and *Jinakālamālinī*, about 1516) and the Thai poem *Yuan Phai* (latter half of the fifteenth century) use forms of Ayuthaya without mention of Dvāravatī. This is also the case with the Dānsai inscription, dated 1560, which refers to the capital as *Phra-mahānagara-śrī-ayodhyā-mahātilakabhaba-naba-ratana* (พระมหานครศรีอยุทธยามหาดิลกภพนพรัตน์) / *Phra Mahanakhon Sri Ayodhyā Mahādilokaphob Noparat /.*[38]

There are other examples of pairing of the name Dvāravatī with Ayuthaya. One is an official letter from the Governor of Tenasserim to the Danish court, dated 1620 CE, which refers to *Krung-deb-mahānagara-dvāravatī-śrī-ayudhya* (กรุงเทพมหานครทวารวดีศรีอยุทธยา) / *Krung thep mahanakhon thawarawadi si ayuthaya.*[39] Another document is a treaty between Siam and the Netherlands dated Śaka era 1026 (1664 CE).[40] [Fig.21]. A Thai version of this treaty, concluded in Ayuthaya, was discovered by J.J. Boeles in the Arsip Nasional Republik Indonesia (National Archives of Indonesia) in Jakarta. He states that the treaty gives the name of the old capital several times and invariably as *Krung-deva-mahānagara-pavara-dvāravatī-śrī-ayuddhyā* (กรุงเทพมหานครบวรทวารวดีศรีอยุทธยา) / *Krung thep phra mahanakhon bowon thawarawadi si ayuthaya.* A letter written in Pāli to the court of Kandy in Sri Lanka in 1757 has *deva-mahānagara-pavara-dvāravatī-siri-ayuddhyā-mahātilakabhaba-nabaratana-rājadhānī-puriramya* (Suphaphan 1988: 193; Filliozat 1997: 99.8). Somdet Phra Phonarat in his *Royal Chronicle* composed at Wat Phra Chetuphon (Wat Pho), Bangkok, [Fig.22] refers to the ancient capital as *Krung-deb-mahānagara-pavara-dvārāvatī-śrī-ayuddyā-mahātilakabhaba-nabaratana-rājadhāṇīpūrīramya* (กรุงเทพมหานครบวรทวารวดี ศรีอยุทธยา มหาดิลกภพนพรัตนราชธาณีบูรีรมย์) / *Krung thep mahanakhon bowon thawarawadi si ayuthaya mahadilokaphop nopharat ratchathani burirom* (Phonarat 2015: 9). He compares it to the name of the Ayuthaya of Phra Ram Narai Awatan (Phra Rāma-nārāya-avatāra). Another example is an inscription (K.1213) set up by Chaophraya Bodindecha (เจ้าพระยาบดินทรเดชา) Sing Singhaseni (สิงห์ สิงหเสนี), (1777–1849) in Cambodia in 1842 [Fig.22]. Now at Wat Buddhaghosārma (วัดพุทธโฆษาจาราม), it is the only known Thai-language inscription in Phnom Penh. At the beginning (lines 1–5), the record states that Chaophraya Bodin was ordered by His Royal Majesty the King of Krungthep Mahanakhon to march overland from Krung Thep Thawarawadi Si Ayutthaya Mahadilokaphop Nopharat Ratchathani Burirom Udom Ratchamahasathan to Cambodia (ยกพหยาตาราออกจากกรุงเทพทวารวดีศรีอยุทธยามหาดิลกภพนพรัตนราชธาณีบูรีรมอุดมราชมหาราชสถาน) (Skilling with Santi, forthcoming). A large number, seemingly the majority, of official and literary works of the Ayuthaya and Bangkok periods call the capital either Ayuthaya or Krung Ratanakosin. Prince Dhani Nivat notes that some literary works refer to Dvāravatī in various forms, both alone and in combinations.[41]

> Dvārabati, *Anirudh khamchan*;
> Krung-thep-dvāravatī-mahātilaka, *Bunnowād*;
> Dvāravatī, *Kham phak ramakian*;
> Dvāravat-śrī-ayudhayeśa (khet syām), *Sanphasith khamchan*;
> Krung dvāravati-śrī, *Sudhanū khamchand.*

Are the literary allusions to Dvāravatī and Ayuthaya the products of historiographic thought or historical memory? Or they are intended to evoke the glories of an imagined past, like references to Albion or Camelot in English writing? These are topics for reflection and discussion. In sum, Dvāravatī was seen as the forerunner of Ayuthaya and the name resonated in later imaginations of the capital city. This seems to have begun with the very foundation of Ayuthaya by Prince U Thong, although there is no contemporary evidence. The earliest evidence might be the Three Seals Law Code, but the dating of the documents is contested because the received versions were copied and revised in the First Reign.

Prince Dhani Niwat, 'The City of Thawarawadi Sri Ayudhya', p. 32, but the texts all give 1166. For the Three Seals Law Code and its contents, see Baker and Pasuk, *The Palace Law of Ayutthaya and the Thammasat*, Introduction, with tables, p. 4.

37 *Phra aiyakan laksana phayan* [*Phra-ayākār-lakṣaṇa-bhañāṇ*] in *Kotmai tra sam duang chabab ratchabanditayasathan*, Ratchabanditayasathan [Royal Institute], Bangkok, 2550 [2007], vol. 1, pp. 593 (facsimile), 620.8 (transcription); *Phra ratchabanyat* [*Phra-rājapaññati*] in idem, vol. 1, pp. 1031 (facsimile), 1059.8 (transcription); *Laksanaphisut* [*Lakṣaṇa-bīsūd*] in idem, vol. 2, pp. 77 (facsimile), 97.10 (transcription).

38 Finot (1915) 'Notes d'épigraphie'.

39 Letter 1 in Prince Dhani Nivat 'Early Trade Relations'. Tenasserim is a port on the west coast of the Thai-Malay peninsula, at that time under Ayuthaya, later taken by Burma and eventually incorporated into British Burma.

40 Boeles, 'The King of Śrī Dvāravatī', p. 112, No. 11. This appears to be 'the 1664 Treaty', the Dutch version of which is discussed in ten Brummelhuis, *Merchant, Courtier and Diplomat*, pp. 38–40.

41 Prince Dhani Nivat, 'The City of Thawarawadi Sri Ayudhya', pp. 55–56. For my own notes on 'Dvāravatī and the literary imagination' see Skilling (2003) 'Dvāravatī: Recent Revelations and Research', pp. 102–104.

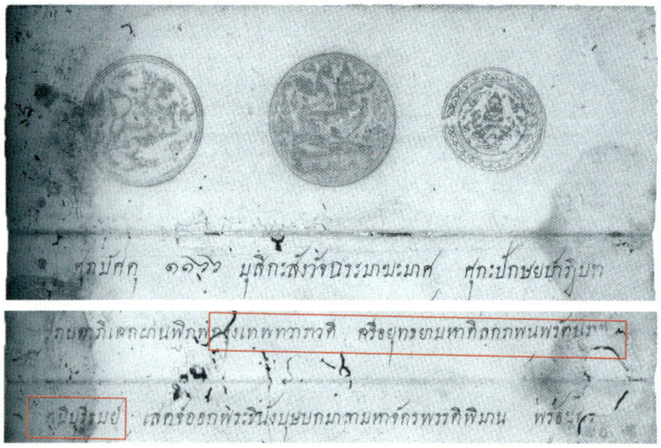

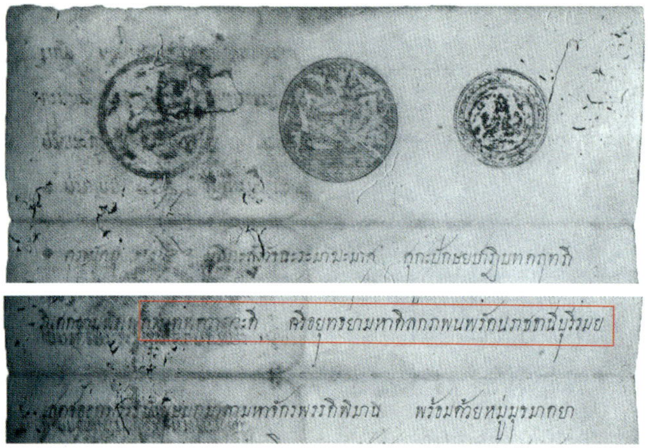

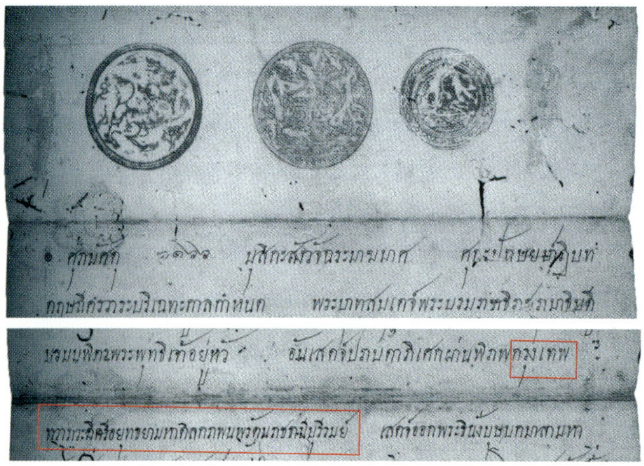

18–20

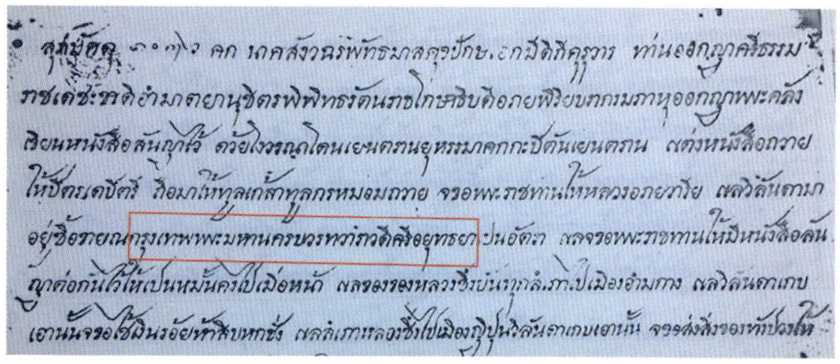

21

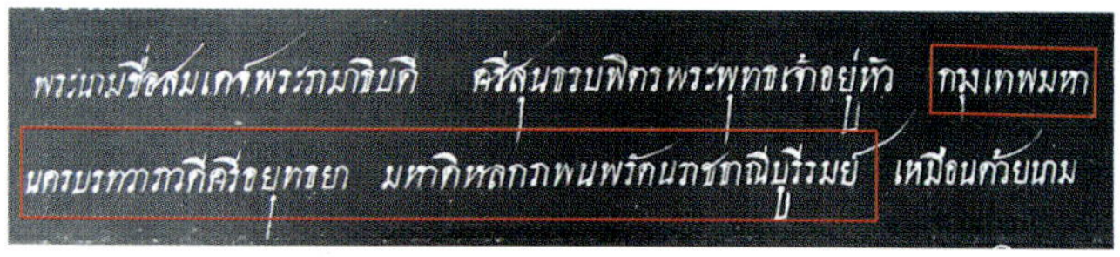

22

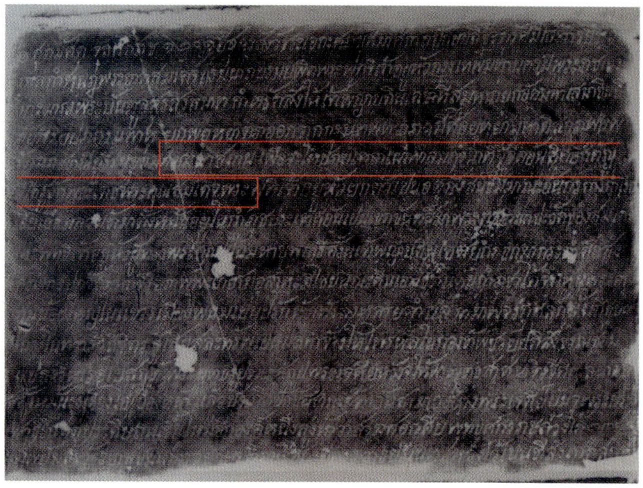

23

Figs.18–20 Three Seals Law Code, preamble.
Fig.21 Excerpt from the 1664 treaty between Siam and the VOC of the Netherlands.
Fig.22 Royal Chronicle of Somdet Phra Phonarat composed at Wat Phra Chetuphon (Wat Pho), Bangkok, refers to the ancient capital as *Krung-deb-mahānagara-pavara-dvārāvatī-śrī-ayuddyā-mahātilakabhaba-nabaratana-rājadhāṇīpūrīramya.*
Fig.23 Inscription of Chaophraya Bodindecha, Phnom Penh.

The Dvāravatī inscriptions: What do they tell us?

What does the Wat Chantheuk inscription tell us about Dvāravatī? It tells us that a daughter of the ruler of Dvāravatī married a king and became his queen, and that she set up an immense stone image of the Tathāgata. If merit is measured in terms of prestige, then her deed was very meritorious and very prestigious. That is about all. The damaged state of the pedestal is unfortunate, but whether it could have told us more, for example the name of the king or his kingdom, is doubtful. Since only a few letters are lost at the beginning of the first *pada* not many words could be missing.

I make the assumption that Wat Chantheuk is the original site of the image and its base, because of its size and because of the large statues that are associated with it. They are not easily portable. The queen's inscription describes her as the daughter of the ruler of Dvāravatī; from this I conclude that the site of the inscription, the vicinity of the present-day Wat Chantheuk, could not itself have been located *in* or within the bounds of Dvāravatī—it could only have been in another kingdom, another realm or land. That is, the inscription does not extend the frontiers of Dvāravatī up to old Khorat. Rather, it shows that, in another, neighbouring and friendly kingdom, the ruler took as queen a royal daughter of the Dvāravatī line. This would be a marriage alliance, a marriage of family politics.

What kingdom was this? We do not know. Might it have been Cānāśa, a polity that is referred to in the Bo Ika (บ่อ อีกา) inscription?[42] The toponym Cānāśa is known from only two inscriptions: the Bo Ika inscription and an inscription found at Ayuthaya, dated to the year 937, that mentions a line of princes of Cānāśapura.[43] Cānāśa or Cānāśapura is not mentioned in any literary sources; it is a mystery that cannot be solved by speculation. More material evidence and, especially, more epigraphic evidence is needed.
This is the 'early kingdoms period' of Thai history.[44] A conglomerate of kingdoms that were defined and framed by their ecologies and landscapes flourished in the area of modern Thailand. But history has left us no details, no maps. As I have said in previous work, I do not accept the Dvāravatī writ large of previous scholarship, and regard rather that conglomerates, clusters, of states and kingdoms, with shifting alliances, developed in the Chao Phraya Basin and the neighbouring plains. The large and distinctive images found at Chantheuk and Sung Noen suggest that the area was one of these centres of power and wealth and that it merits further excavation and archaeological and historical exploration.

Acknowledgements

Many people have helped me during the long years during which Dvāravatī has remained a passion. I sincerely thank them all. I thank the staff of the Siam Society and of any number of museums and institutions in Thailand and worldwide. For this article, it is my pleasure to express my special gratitude to Saerji, Diwakar Acharya, Dhiravat Na Pombejra, Santi Pakdeekham, Monika Zin, Pairot Singbun, Bunchar Pongphanit, Thongchai Likhitphonsawan, and Trent Walker. I thank Prapod Assavavirulhakarn for spirited conversations that began somewhere in the last decades of the last century and still continue. I am grateful to the Fragile Palm Leaves team under the Henry Ginsberg Fund—Somneuk Hongprayoon, Phongsathorn (Peun) Buakhampan, and Laksana (Kung) Janechang, for their dedicated and tireless work in making estampages, taking photographs of inscriptions, artefacts, and sites, and keeping track of it all. I thank the Phimai National Museum, the Somdet Phra Narai National Musuem, the National Museums of Thailand, and the Fine Arts Department of Thailand for facilitating access to the artefacts in their collections. I am deeply grateful for the support of the Khyentse Foundation and the Henry Ginsberg Fund without which the collection of materials for this article would not have been possible, and I thank the Buddhadasa Indapañño Archives and all of those who have worked so enthusiatically to bring this book together as a tribute to the culture of Dvāravatī and its long-time friend, Ian Glover.

42 For Bo Ika see K 400 in Cœdès (1954), *Inscriptions du Cambodge* VI, pp. 83–85 ; no. 118 in *Prachum silachareuk* IV, pp. 221–224. In this inscription there is a short '*a*' in the first syllable. In the Ayuthaya inscription both the *a*'s are long.

43 K 949: Cœdès (1996) 'Une nouvelle inscription d'Ayuthya' ; *Prachum silachareuk* IV, no. 117, pp. 216–220; Coedès, *Indianized States of Southeast Asia*, p. 122. Old Korat was on the old trade routes and on the route taken by the Ayuthaya armies when they marched to the Korat plateau : it is possible that the inscription was removed to Ayutthaya at some point.

44 See for example Coe and Evans, *Angkor and the Khmer Civilization*, Chapter 5.

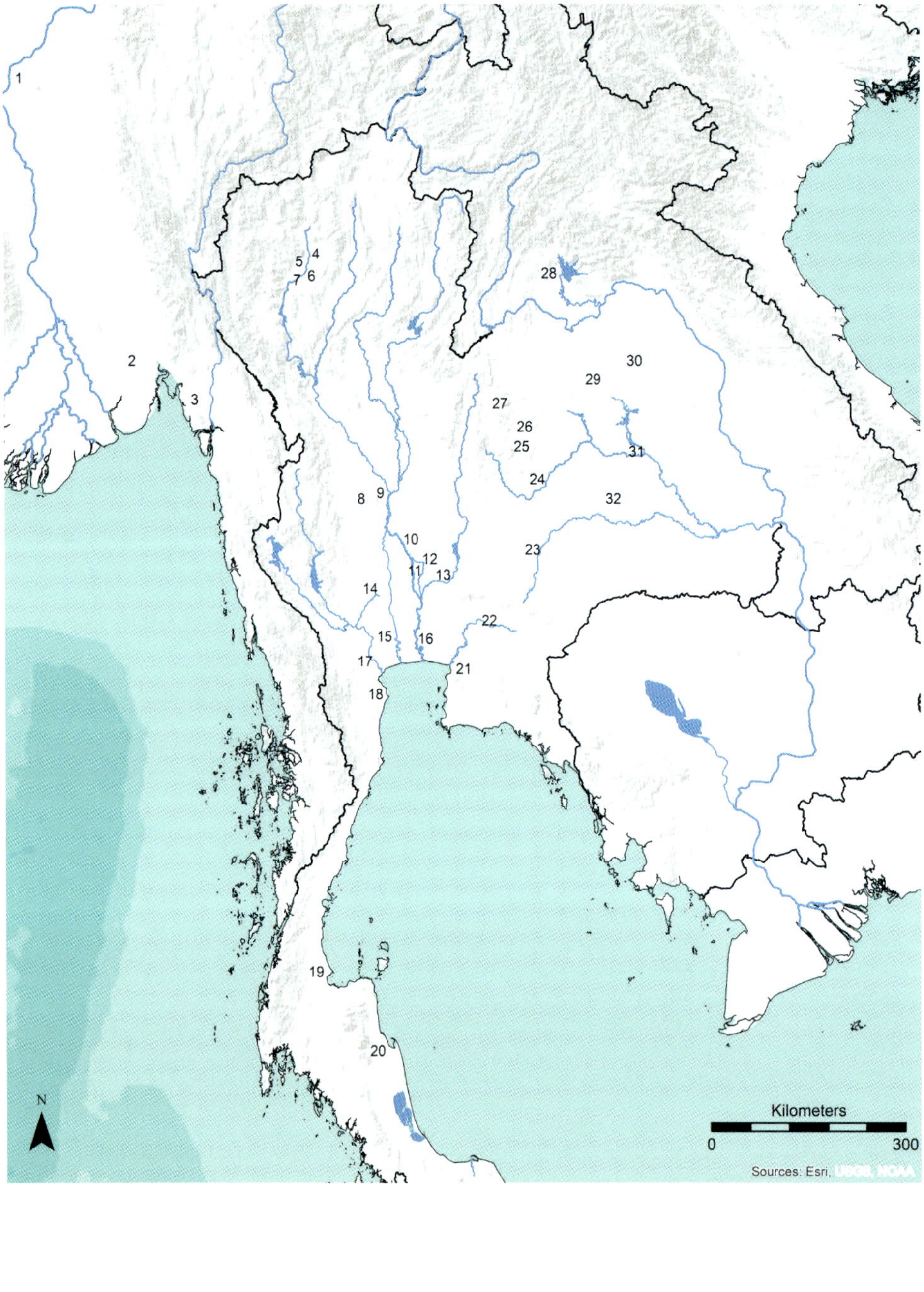

1. Bagan
2. Pegu
3. Thaton
4. Wiang Kum Kam
5. Wiang Mano
6. Hariphunchai (Lamphun)
7. Wiang Tho
8. Bueng Khok Chang
9. Thap Chumphon
10. Chan Sen
11. Wat Khoi
12. Lop Buri
13. Khao Wong Cave
14. U Thong
15. Nakhon Pathom
16. Bangkok
17. Ratchaburi, Khao Ngu Hermit Cave, Khu Bua
18. Phetchaburi
19. Chaiya
20. Nakhon Si Thammarat
21. Phra Rot
22. Prachin Buri
23. Nakhon Ratchasima
24. Ban Kut Ngong, Ban Khon Sawan
25. Kaset Sombun
26. Chum Phae
27. Dong Klo
28. Ban Thalat, Vientiane
29. Wat Don Kaeo
30. Ban Phan Na
31. Fa Daet Song Yang
32. Na Dun

Fig 1 Map showing all locations mentioned in text (map by Hunter Watson).
All photographs belong to the author unless otherwise stated.

OLD MON INSCRIPTIONS AND THE EXTENT OF DVĀRAVATĪ

Hunter Ian Watson

Introduction

In Thailand, Old Mon inscriptions have been discovered in the central, northeastern, and northern regions. Some scholars argue that Old Mon inscriptions are also in southern Thailand, but the author disagrees that any inscriptions discovered in the south thus far are composed in Old Mon. The inscriptions found in different regions of Thailand are homogenous neither in type of artifact nor in style of writing, and they date to different periods. Most Old Mon inscriptions in Thailand have been found in central and northeastern Thailand and tend to be relatively short in content, often only a few lines in length, and tend to give very little historical information. Old Mon is the only local language inscribed on artefacts found in central Thailand dating to the earliest centuries of writing in the region, leading some scholars to argue that Dvāravatī was a Mon culture with a Mon-speaking population. However, these assumptions could be misleading, because they are based on limited evidence and fail to consider the ethno-linguistic complexity of the past. This paper will discuss some of these problems by considering Old Mon inscriptions found in Thailand.

This paper presents Old Mon inscriptions found in Thailand and considers implications for the extent of Dvāravatī based on epigraphic evidence. A century ago, scholars began studying inscriptions in the region. Inscriptions from the earliest period of Siam's history were mostly composed in Sanskrit, Pāli, and Old Mon; thus, it was proposed the population of Dvāravatī was Mon (Cœdès 1925; 1928; 1966). But this theory proves problematic, as we must consider not only the presence or absence of languages but also the volume of evidence available. This paper will show that Old Mon inscriptions in Thailand are more numerous and widely distributed than was previously known, indicating the extent of the geographical area in which epigraphic Old Mon has been attested. Nevertheless, it is notable that there have been relatively few Old Mon inscriptions discovered among ancient sites on the Central Plain, often thought to be the core of Dvāravatī. I argue the idea that the Dvāravatī population was ethnically Mon and primarily spoke the Old Mon language was a presumption made without sufficient evidence. Considering only a few inscriptions, this hypothesis was never strongly grounded and it failed to consider the other ethno-linguistic groups. While Old Mon inscriptions provide evidence that Old Mon was indeed used at the time of Dvāravatī, the evidence available is not enough to conclude definitively that Dvāravatī was a homogenous Mon society in the ethno-linguistic sense. This is not to suggest that Old Mon was not an important language, neither is it to say that the ancient population might not have spoken Old Mon, but the idea of Dvāravatī being 'Mon' might be an over-simplification which misleads and fails to recognize the complexity of ethno-linguistic diversity at the time. I believe Dvāravatī was more likely composed of a variety of ethnic groups, and that tentatively there is a lack of evidence to determine the local vernacular.

The material in this paper is drawn from my MA thesis on Old Mon epigraphy (Watson 2013 [2556 BE]). I conducted a survey of Old Mon inscriptions in Thailand to study the development of word spellings, translating inscriptions relying on Harry Shorto's *A Dictionary of the Mon Inscriptions from the Sixth to Sixteenth Centuries* (1971). Several Old Mon inscriptions were last studied decades ago and numerous more have been discovered, some of which have been studied while others have not. To date, I have registered over one hundred Old Mon inscriptions in Thailand. Some are large steles with numerous lines of texts while others are short, such as clumps of clay bearing stamps or seals with only a few words, providing little in the sense of historical information but which are useful as an indicator of the geographical spread of Old Mon.

This paper is divided into two parts. First, I explain the evolution of the argument equating Dvāravatī with Mon. Then, I provide an overview of Old Mon inscriptions in Thailand, describing the types of artifacts and the locations where they were found. In the summary, I will discuss the problem with considering the population of Dvāravatī as being ethnically Mon. For a map of locations, see Fig.1; for a map of distribution of inscriptions, see Fig.2.

Dvāravatī and Mon ethnicity

In this section I describe the circumstances which led scholars to label the ancient culture of Siam as Dvāravatī and why the population came to be considered as Mon. Early scholars of Siam did not account for the Mons and did not recognize the Old Mon language among the earliest inscriptions found. Pierre Lefèvre-Pontalis (1897: 74) wrote about the advancement of Thai speaking populations into the Chao Phraya River Valley, describing only the Thai and Khmer with no mention of the Mon. The first Old Mon inscription from Siam studied in a published report was the standing Buddha image from Wat Khoi [Fig.3]. Étienne Aymonier (1901: 82) described the script style as being Cambodian, but he was uncertain about the language of composition. Étienne Lunet de Lajonquière (1907: 322) first described the octagonal pillar from Lop Buri, stating the script was Cambodian but not reporting which language was inscribed.

The first references to Dvāravatī were actually made prior to this. Samuel Beal (1884: 200) proposed that the name *Duo-luo-po-ti*, in ancient Chinese texts, could be transliterated as "Dvârapati". Paul Pelliot (1904: 223, 231) suggested that Dvāravatī was an ancient polity "probably Mon or Khmer" in the region of Lop Buri. George Cœdès (1925: 16) supported this proposition, showing the Lop Buri octagonal pillar was written in Mon and arguing that Lavo (Lop Buri) had been "a center of Mon civilization". Cœdès further suggested the founders of Haripuñjaya, if not of "pure Mon race", were Mon in language and civilization.

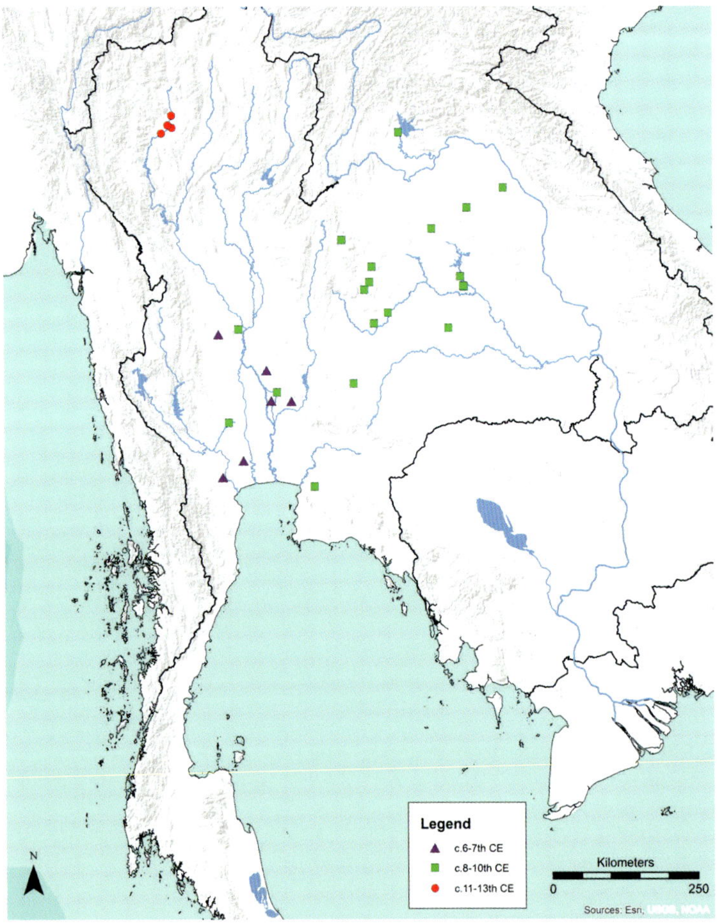

Fig.2 Spatial distribution of Old Mon inscriptions found in Thailand (map by Hunter Watson).

After the connection between the Mon and Dvāravatī was proposed, the idea gained momentum. Cœdès (1928: 20–23) cited that Lunet de Lajonquière labelled the archaeological remains from Nakhon Pathom to Prachin Buri as the "Hindu non-Cambodian Group", but based on analysis of more recently discovered art, Cœdès proposed labelling it the "Art of Dvāravatī", which he thought could be attributed to the Mon. Cœdès' theory was developed together with Prince Damrong Rajanubhab, who also studied the art and history of Siam. The concept of Dvāravatī as an art style was proposed by Prince Damrong in 1926, and Cœdès promoted this in a publication in 1928 (Piriya Krairiksh 2012: 14). Stephen Murphy (2016: 374) states that after this it became "entrenched in the scholarship of both Thai and international scholarship alike." The development of the National Museum of Thailand was a collaborative effort between Cœdès and Damrong, classifying the art and archaeology of Siam into periods (Hennequin 2010: 11–14; Peleggi 2013: 1539–1540). From then, early art was understood as belonging to "Dvāravatī", a Mon polity encompassing most of modern Thailand.

The idea was endorsed by others. Reginald Le May (1938: 15, 21) argued that "during the second half of the first millennium... the dominating people inhabiting Central Siam were of the Môn race..." Lawrence Briggs (1945: 98–99) stated that "Dvāravatī was originally a Mon kingdom..." Pierre Dupont published a book entitled *L'archéologie Mône de Dvāravatī*, in which he claimed the Mons were "a group of populations" around the Chao Phraya River from the sixth-eleventh century and at Lamphun from the eighth-thirteenth century, but he admits ignorance of whether the "intermediary" or "peripheral" regions were Mon (Dupont 1959: 1). Erik Seidenfaden (1951) further labelled some sites on the Khorat Plateau as being Mon.

The name Dvāravatī was confirmed after discovery of silver medallions inscribed with [Śrī Dvāravatī]. Jan Jetso Boeles (1964: 101–103) published an article presenting two inscribed silver coins from Nakhon Pathom, with a reading offered by Cœdès as [śrīdvāravatīśvarapuṇya], meaning "meritorious work of the king of Śrī Dvāravatī." Cœdès (1966: 113–114) followed with an article affirming his earlier theory, stating the population of Dvāravatī were indeed Mon and that they spoke the Mon language. But some scholars began to recognize the problem of objectively identifying the population of Dvāravatī in this manner. Quaritch Wales (1969: 17–18) stated he never questioned that "the Môns formed the ruling caste in Dvāravatī", but also said that "Môn-Khmer, Thai, etc. are distinctions based on linguistic and associated cultural grounds, and I have now long realized that the cultural problems with which we are concerned are likely to be solved in terms of culture not of race." Clearly, he still concurred that at least the upper class of Dvāravatī were Mon, but he drew a distinction between race and culture which was not prevalent in the work of earlier scholars.

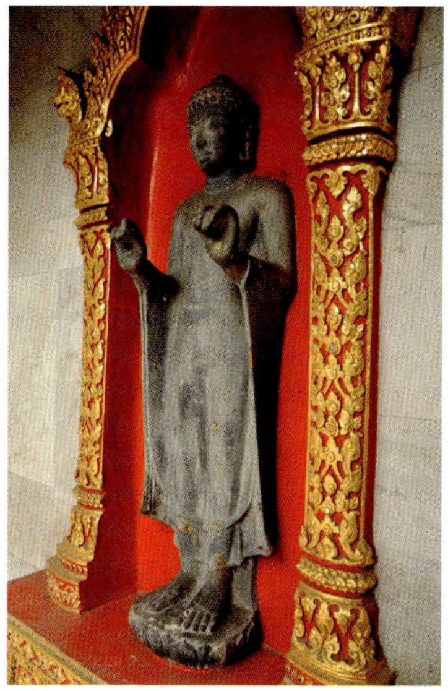

Fig.3 Standing Buddha image from Wat Khoi.

Aside from the matter of ethnicity and language, other issues regarding Dvāravatī are debated. One is how the term 'Dvāravatī' came to be used differently by various fields of scholarship. Dvāravatī has been considered a kingdom, a culture, an ethno-linguistic group, a style of art, a political or ceremonial center, or perhaps some combination of these (Glover 2010; Piriya Krairiksh 2012 [2555 BE]; Murphy 2013; 2016; Revire 2016; Skilling 2003). Murphy (2016: 375) points to the problem surrounding the definition of Dvāravatī where the artistic style was first developed, after which the historical period was drawn, suggesting this is restrictive as it pre-defines the period and ignores recent archaeological evidence which indicates different dates. Barram and Glover (2008: 175, 181) explain that the traditional dating of Dvāravatī is around 600–1000 CE, but based on archaeological evidence they argue to push this date back two centuries. Regarding the labeling of art, some scholars have attempted to reconcile this, such as Piriya Krairiksh, who suggested using the term "Mon art" rather than "Dvāravatī art", but Robert Brown (1996: xxiii–xxiv) warns against the problems of using ethnic or linguistic terms to label art styles.

Another complex issue regards the geographical extent that can be considered Dvāravatī. Karen Mudar (1999: 1, 7) did a study of moated settlements on the Central Plain from the sixth-ninth century, suggesting there was a "single regional economic system" which shared a common material culture. Based on the sizes and distribution of moated sites, she proposed a division of regions and the sites which were arguably regional centers, with Nakhon Pathom as the primary center. Murphy describes how archaeologists identified a material culture which spread from the Central Plain to the Khorat Plateau and the peninsular region to the south. The distribution of Dvāravatī style art led some scholars to make claims for the political boundaries of Dvāravatī, but this seems unjustified as the extent of its material culture would have been wider than its political control (Murphy 2016: 372, 378). Not everyone agrees these regions were necessarily under administrative control of the Central Plain. Regarding the connection between populations on the Central Plain and the Khorat Plateau, Wales (1969: 112) suggests that the Khorat Plateau was isolated geographically from the Central Plain, so it seems logical that cultures in these regions would have developed separately. Peter Skilling (2003: 101) likewise expresses doubt that the administrative power of Dvāravatī extended beyond the Central Plain.

The Haripuñjaya culture is considered by some to be related to Dvāravatī culturally and perhaps even politically. Haripuñjaya is today the town of Lamphun, located on the Ping River in the Chiang Mai-Lamphun Basin. According to Thai chronicles, Haripuñjaya was founded by the local population and a princess from Lavo was invited to rule (Rawi 2014 [2557 BE]: 132–136, 143–144). Sarasawadee Ongsakul (2000 [2543 BE]: 35–36) argues this marked the shift from tribal communities to a complex society, being the first development of this kind in northern Siam. Sarasawadee (2009 [2552 BE]: 67) explains the Ping River Valley developed more quickly than other areas of northern Thailand because of easy access from the Central Plain via the Ping River, and because the region is a wide river basin with fertile soil, suitable for urbanization. Before the founding of Haripuñjaya, village level society already existed, but when Haripuñjaya was established the area received cultural influence from outside the region (Ibid: 78–80). Sarasawadee (2000 [2542 BE]: 41) argues this brought the changes needed to move the developing society to a state level.

Haripuñjaya lasted several centuries. During the early phase it seems to have been related to Dvāravatī, but with time the two diverged culturally. Sarasawadee (2009 [2552 BE]: 71–73) divides the art and architecture of Haripuñjaya into two periods, being from the eighth-tenth and eleventh-thirteenth century. She describes how the earlier art shows similarities with that of Dvāravatī but in the later period it became unique to Haripuñjaya, also exhibiting influence from Burma and India. Based on excavations conducted at Lamphun, Khomsi Saenchit (2009 [2552 BE]: 495) argues the archaeological record indicates three periods, with the earliest beginning around the seventh century. Charles Higham and Rachanie Thosarat also argue for three periods. They explain there was an Iron Age presence in this region and describe evidence of Dvāravatī style ceramics which can be dated to between 570–760 CE. They argue the second phase continued to show similarities with the Dvāravatī style, as well as influence from Burma, while the third phase shows influence from Khmer and Chinese ceramics, with samples radiocarbon dated to the thirteenth century (Higham and Thosarat 2012: 236–237).

Another point which merits discussion is southern Thailand and supposed connections with Dvāravatī and the Mon. This is likely due in part to the fact that some scholars have argued that Old Mon inscriptions were found at Nakhon Si Thammarat, a claim with which I disagree and will return to in the following section. The site of Khu Bua, in Ratchaburi Province, is considered to have been a part of Dvāravatī. In Petchaburi Province, there are supposedly no large moated sites resembling the style of Dvāravatī, although artifacts were discovered which indicate that this area was likely on the periphery of the Dvāravatī culture (FAD 2000 [2543 BE]: 22). However, the Kra Isthmus further south seems to have been less closely associated with Dvāravatī. In Surat Thani Province, there is some evidence of Dvāravatī style art, including a broken *dharmacakra* as well as a standing Buddha statue (FAD 2002 [2545 BE]: 40–41). But some suggest this region was more closely tied to Śrī Vijaya (Wannasarn 2013: 3; FAD 2002 [2545 BE]: 42). Janice Stargardt (2001: 312) states that from the sixth to ninth century this region did share connections with the culture in Central Thailand, but later developed stronger ties with what is now Indonesia. Thus, there is still debate about the peninsular region of modern Thailand. But epigraphic evidence does not support the theory of it being in the sphere of Dvāravatī culture.

Old Mon inscriptions in Thailand

In this section I will describe findings relating to Old Mon epigraphy in Thailand. Numerous Old Mon inscriptions have been found in Thailand and Myanmar, and a few in Laos. Formerly, Shorto (1971: ix–x) divided the Mon inscriptions into five groups, being in central and northern Thailand as well as in Myanmar at Thaton, Bagan, and Pegu. But, with the discovery of Mon inscriptions in northeastern Thailand and central Laos, it became possible to establish a sixth group (Diffloth 1984: 56–57; Bauer 1987–1988: 159). Thus, Old Mon inscriptions in Thailand can be divided into three groups. Although most of these are undated, they can be dated approximately by palaeographic comparison with dated inscriptions. From the first period, around the sixth to seventh centuries, Old Mon inscriptions have been found on the Central Plain, written in the commonly labelled 'Pallava' script (Watson 2013 [2556 BE]: 5). It has been noted that usage of the label 'Pallava' is problematic (Griffiths 2014: 54; Griffiths & Lammerts 2015: 989–990), but here it is used for convention. From the second period, around the eighth to tenth centuries, Old Mon inscriptions have been found on the Khorat Plateau and the Central Plain, written in the 'Post-Pallava' script. From the third period, around the eleventh to thirteenth centuries, Old Mon inscriptions have been found in northern Thailand, written in the 'Old Mon' script (Watson 2013 [2556 BE]: 5).

From the first period, a small number of Old Mon inscriptions have been found. The standing Buddha statue with a one-line inscription on the base was reportedly from Wat Khoi, Lop Buri Province (Aymonier 1901: 82; Cœdès 1925: 186; 1929: 15; Kongkaew 1986c [2529 BE]: 34–37). This location is now technically in Sing Buri Province due to a shift in the provincial borders. Aymonier (1901: 82) reported that about 20 lines were also inscribed on the back of the statue, including a number which he suggested might have been 1031. If true, this would probably correspond with the year 1109 CE, which does not seem realistic due to the script style being much older. Unfortunately, this statue has been imbedded into the wall at Wat Benchamabophit in Bangkok, so it is impossible to confirm these details.

Three short inscriptions were found at Bueng Kok Chang archaeological site, Uthai Thani Province. Two were reported as Old Mon and one as Sanskrit (Phuthorn & Somchai 1981: 41–47; Kongkaew 1986b: 129–131; 1986c: 48–56). But I argue only one is Old Mon (Watson 2013: 56). At Nakhon Pathom, one Old Mon inscription has been discovered (Cœdès 1952: 149–150; Dupont 1959: 16; Wiraprachak 1986c: 31–33) [Fig.4]. The stone is broken along four edges and inscribed on two faces in reversed directions, so if one side is upright the opposite side appears upside down, indicating it was not likely intended as a standing stele. In Saraburi Province, a three-line message is inscribed at the mouth of Narai Cave [Fig.5]. Dating palaeographically to around the sixth century, it records a procession to the cave, presumably for a religious ceremony. This inscription has been studied a number of times (Phuthorn & Somchai 1981: 53; Kongkaew 1986c: 45; Bauer 1991b: 64; Pan Hla 1988–1989: 85; Watson 2013: 52–53). Another short inscription is at Tham Ruesi Cave in Ratchaburi Province, thought by some to be Sanskrit (Kongkaew 1986b: 68) [Fig.6]. But I believe it to be Old Mon, a view proposed by Cœdès (1929: 33). Old Mon inscriptions from the first period have also been found on clay artifacts. Clumps of clay with impressed seals were found at Chansen archaeological site, Nakhon Sawan Province, three of which were reportedly inscribed in Old Mon (Phuthorn & Somchai 1981: 85–90). After inspecting all three, I believe only one is Old Mon (Watson 2013 [2556 BE]: 56) [Fig.7].

From the second period, Old Mon inscriptions have been identified on the Central Plain and the Khorat Plateau. The octagonal stone pillar found at Lop Buri bears four messages, dating to about the eighth century (Cœdès 1925: 186–187; Cœdès 1929: 17–19; Halliday & Blagden 1930: 83–85; Kongkaew 1986c [2529 BE]: 60–66; Watson 2013 [2556 BE]: 58–63). In Chon Buri Province, one clay tablet with an impressed Buddha image bears a short message etched into the back. Furthermore, numerous clay artifacts, often referred to as miniature *stūpas*, are today scattered around museums and temples across central Thailand. Several are inscribed in Pāli and Old Mon with the same message [Fig.8]. A few of these have been studied (Kongkaew 1986b [2529 BE]: 35; 1986c [2529 BE]: 98; Bauer 1991b: 65; Kannika and Phongkasem 1999 [2542 BE]: 143–149; Watson 2013 [2556 BE]: 64–65, 85–86; Revire 2014: 245–246).

Recently, I conducted a comprehensive study of this group of artifacts (Watson 2018). Due to close similarities in the artifacts and the inscriptions, it is possible to conclude that these were created at the same time and place, being at the Tap Chumphon archaeological site, Nakhon Sawan Province. Recently, a clay tablet inscribed in Old Mon was discovered at U Thong, in Suphan Buri Province (Hunter and Skilling, this volume).

Old Mon inscriptions have been identified on the Khorat Plateau in northeastern Thailand and central Laos. An inscribed standing Buddha image was discovered in Nakhon Ratchasima Province (Revire 2014: 246). Most Old Mon inscriptions in this region are on *sema* stones, or Buddhist boundary markers. *Sema* stones are found across the plateau, but only some are inscribed, the messages often being short, recording meritorious deeds and names of donors. Several of these have been studied (Bauer 1991a; Uraisi 1988). Many of the *sema* stones inscribed in Old Mon originated from areas around the provinces of Chaiyaphum and Kalasin. In Chaiyaphum Province, inscribed *sema* stones have been found at Ban Kut Ngong village, [Fig.9] at Khon Sawan District, and at Kaset Sombun District, as well as in nearby Chum Phae District, Khon Kaen Province [Fig.10]. In Kalasin Province, another group of *sema* stones inscribed in Old Mon has been found. One bears the date 693, likely corresponding with 771 CE (Watson 2013 [2556 BE]: 68–69).[Fig.11]. Other inscribed *sema* stones have been identified in Udon Thani Province and Sakon Nakhon Province. In Vientiane Province of Laos, one Old Mon inscription was discovered several decades ago (Guillon 1974: 340–344). More recently, additional Old Mon inscriptions have been reported (Lorrillard 2014: 56), and I have seen photographs of yet other inscriptions which are likewise written in Old Mon. Recently, Old Mon inscriptions have also been discovered in Phetchabun Province; thus, the geographic area of Old Mon inscriptions on the plateau continues to increase.

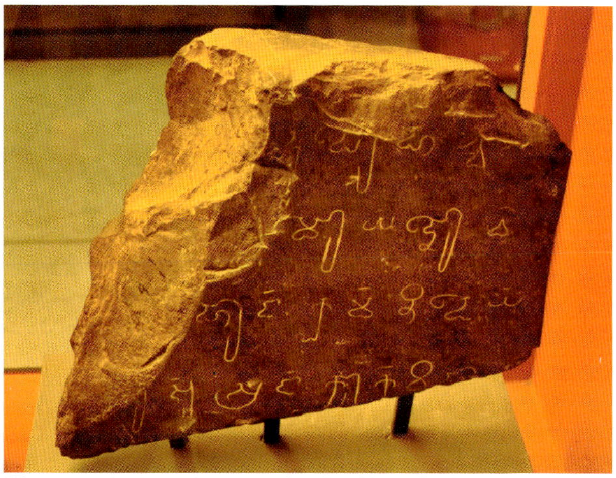

Fig.4 Inscription discovered at Nakhon Pathom Province.

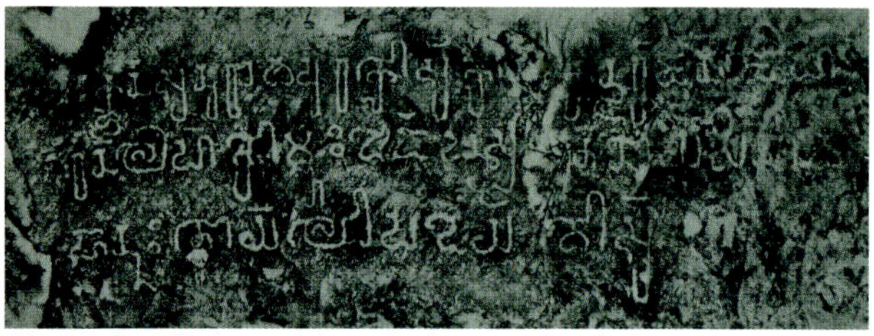

Fig.5 Ink rubbing of inscription at Narai Cave, Wat Khao Wong in Saraburi Province.

Fig.6 Ink rubbing of inscription at Ruesi Cave in Ratchaburi Province.

There have also been clay tablets inscribed in Old Mon found on the Khorat Plateau, in the provinces of Maha Sarakham and Kalasin, with stylistic differences between locations. Readings have been published for some of the clay tablets found in Maha Sarakham Province [Fig.12] (Champa 1981: 63–66; Prasan, Champa and Thoem 1981: 51–55; Kongkaew 1986c [2529 BE]: 77–84; Bauer 1991a: 66; Uraisi 1988: 197–199). I have translated a few more recently discovered tablets (Watson 2013 [2556 BE]: 86–87). Several bear writing in red ink, a feature not identified elsewhere. These also have Old Khmer words, a feature identified in other inscriptions from the same period. Moreover, six tablets with impressed Buddha images inscribed in Old Mon were found at Fa Daet Song Yang archaeological site, Kalasin Province (Prasan and Cham 1968: 108–111; Kongkaew 1986c [2529 BE]: 85–89, 90–94; Bauer 1991a: 66; Watson 2013 [2556 BE]: 65–67). Unfortunately, I have been unable to locate these tablets, and museum staff were likewise perplexed about their current whereabouts.

From the third period, Old Mon inscriptions have been found only in northern Thailand, associated with the Haripuñjaya culture, which is often viewed as being a distinct period and culture not necessarily directly tied to Dvāravatī. These inscriptions are written in the Old Mon script, which appears similar to the script style found in Myamnar. Kannika Wimonkasem (1999 [2542 BE]: 305) argues that the script style of Haripuñjaya developed

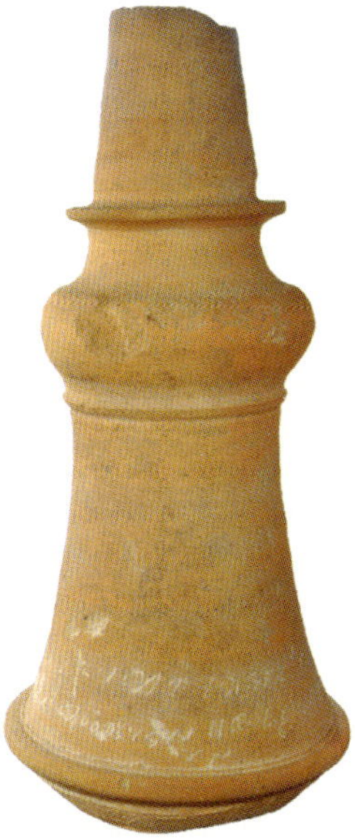

7

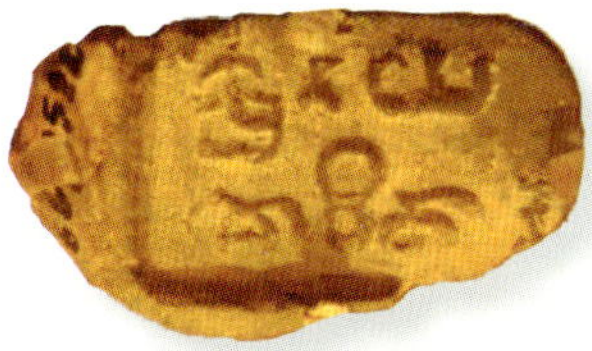

8

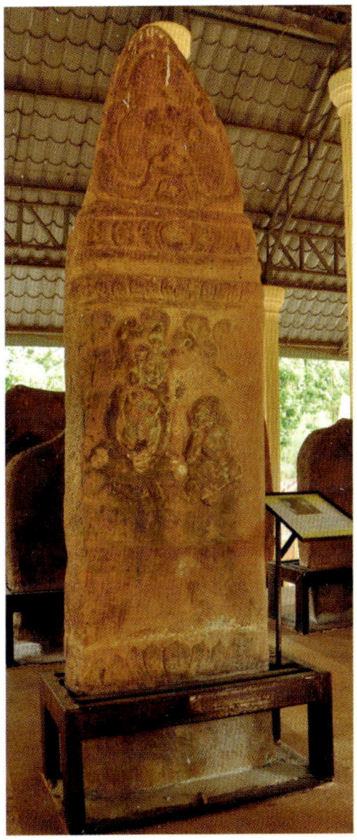

9

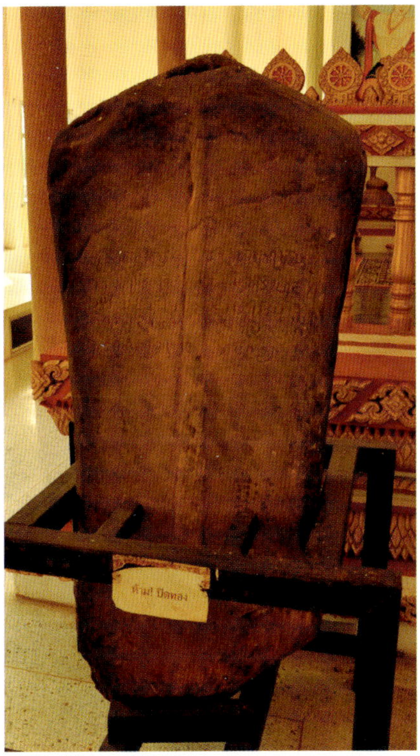

10

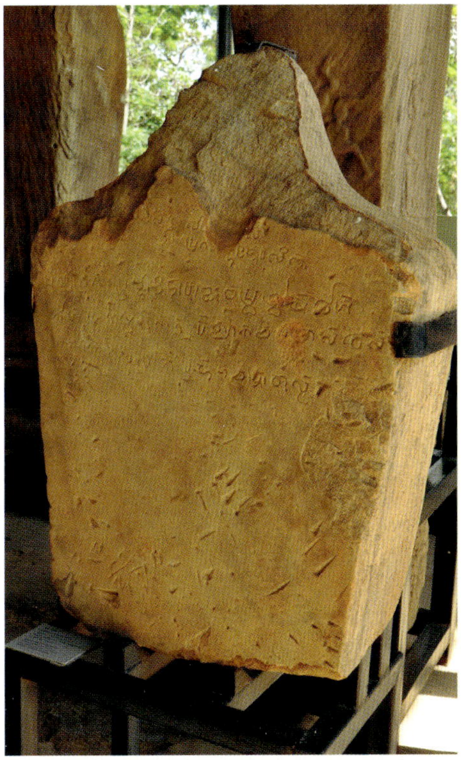

11

Fig.7 Inscribed clay miniature - from Tap Chumphon, Nakhon Sawan Province.
Fig.8 Inscribed clay sealing from Chansen, Nakhon Sawan Province.
Fig.9 Inscribed *sema* stone from Ban Kut Ngong, Chaiyaphum Province.
Fig.10 Inscribed *sema* stone from Wat Non Sila, Khon Kaen Province.
Fig.11 Inscription from Kalasin Province.

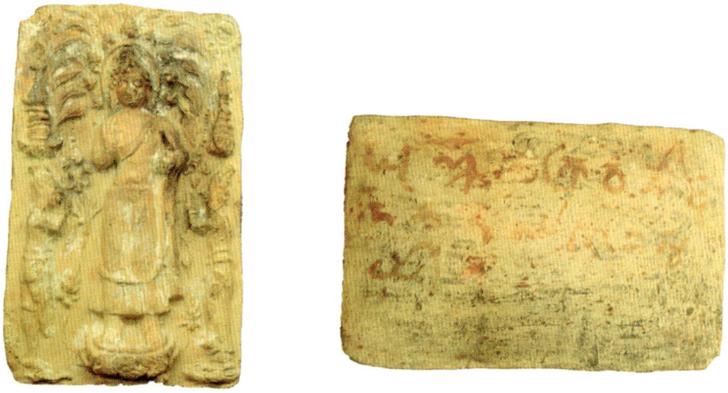

12

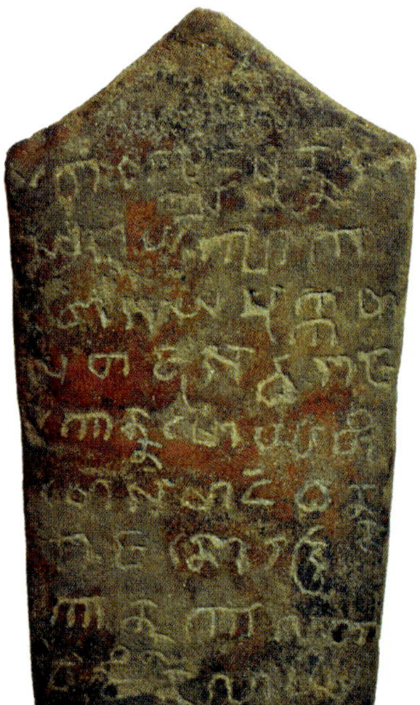

13

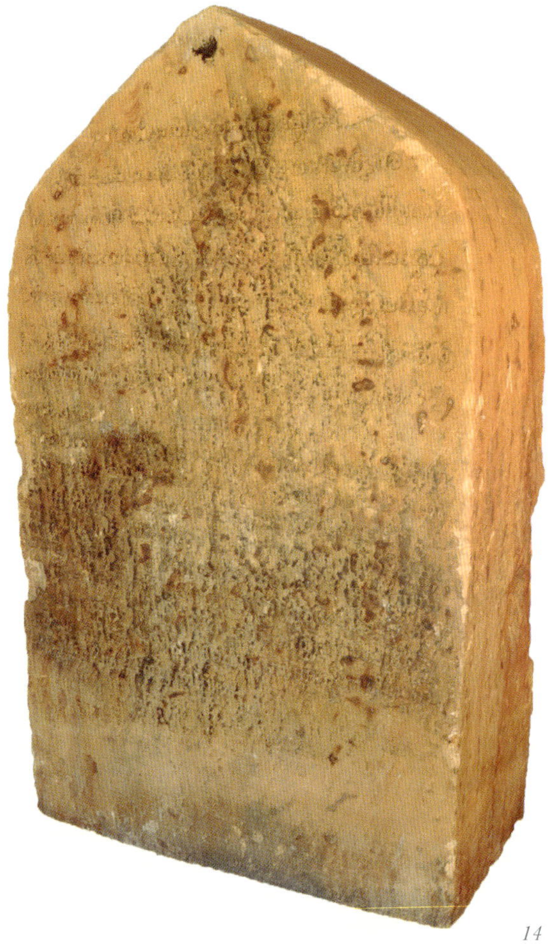

14

Figs.12a-b Clay tablet with red ink inscription from Maha Sarakham Province.
[Photograph courtesy of Khon Kaen National Museum]
Fig.13 Inscription from Wiang Mano, Chiang Mai Province.
Fig.14 Inscription from Lamphun Province.

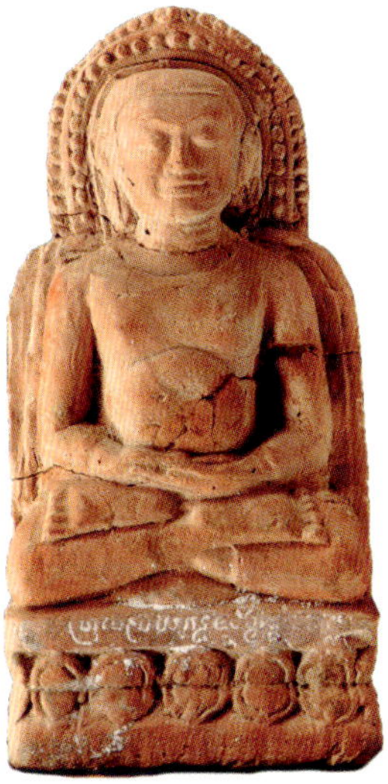

15

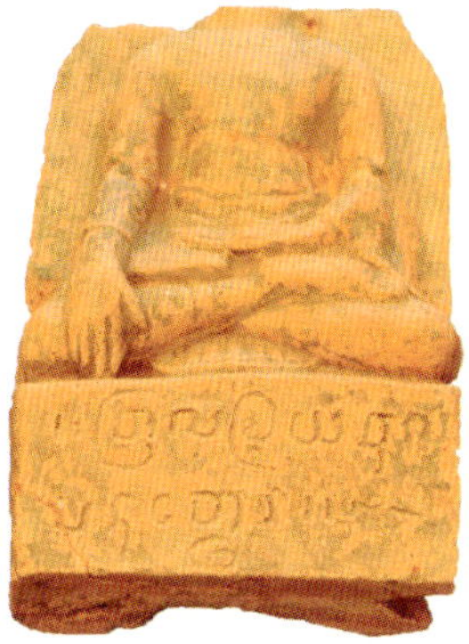

16

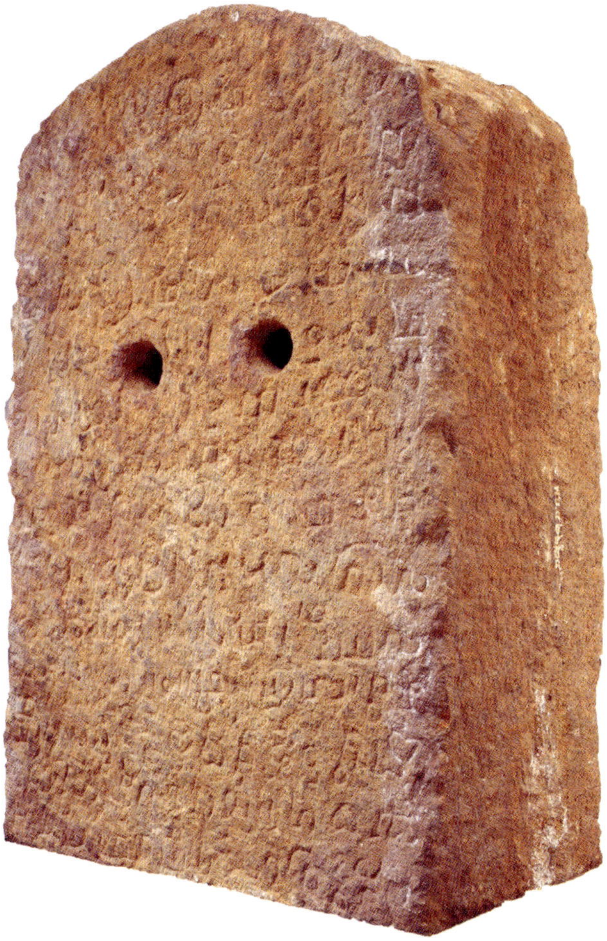

17

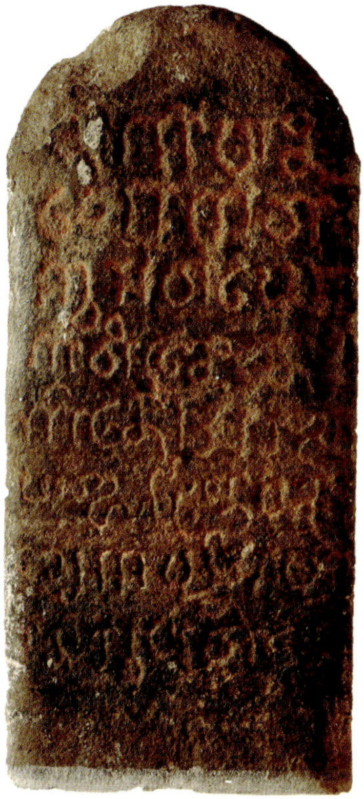

18

Fig.15 Inscribed clay tablet from Chiang Mai Province.
Fig.16 Inscribed clay tablet from Lamphun Province.
Fig.17 Inscription from Wiang Tho, Chiang Mai Province.
Fig.18 Inscription from Nakhon Si Thammarat Province (arguably not Old Mon).

from the Dvāravatī style script. Seven large steles were found at Lamphun [Fig.14]. Some of these have been published (Cœdès 1925: 189–195; Halliday & Blagden 1930: 87–105; Champa, Thoem and Khongdecha 1977 [2520 BE]: 91–118), but I argue for different translations on some of them (Watson 2013 [2556 BE]: 88–110). While Old Mon inscriptions on the Central Plain and the Khorat Plateau tend to be short, those in northern Thailand are longer, having more content and detail, including names of people and places, items donated to temples, records of construction projects, an account of an earthquake and subsequent renovations, and description of a sacred ceremony involving the interment of palm-leaf manuscripts and an umbrella with floral designs in a "cave", which might be interpreted as a man-made structure.

One inscription in Old Mon was discovered at the Wiang Mano archaeological site [Fig.13]. Griswold and Prasert (1971: 156) have studied this inscription, although I proposed a slightly different translation (Watson 2013 [2556 BE]: 110–111). I argue that one word thought to be a personal name should be interpreted as a place name, possibly the ancient name of Wiang Mano. Another inscription was found at the Wiang Tho archaeological site [Fig.17]. It is not very legible, but I believe it also bears two place names. Several clay tablets with Old Mon inscriptions were found at Wiang Kum Kam archaeological site, Chiang Mai Province [Fig.15]. These are similar in shape and style, all having one line of text which is slightly different on each artifact and which appears to be names of monks (Bauer 1991b: 61; Watson 2013 [2556 BE]: 112–113). Another clay tablet was discovered at Lamphun, but it is stylistically different from the Wiang Kum Kam tablets [Fig.16].

Returning to the topic of southern Thailand, two inscriptions from Nakhon Si Thammarat Province were proposed as being written in Old Mon. Consequently, other publications have repeated this claim (for example, see FAD, n.d: 18, 24). This stimulated the idea that Old Mon usage extended down the Malay Peninsula. But after some consideration, I disagree, arguing that neither of these are inscribed in Old Mon. Regarding the first, Cœdès (1929: 55) offered a reading, dating it to the fifth to sixth century, but neither offered a translation nor proposed the language inscribed. Kongkaew and Champa proposed it to be Old Mon (Kongkaew and Champa 1984 [2527BE]: 86–88; Kongkaew 1986a [2529 BE]: 12–14; 1986 [2529 BE] c: 38, 41). But I was unable to read it as Old Mon, concluding it must be a different language. Other scholars have debated the language inscribed. Wannasarn Noonsuk (2013: 59) explains that Preecha Noonsuk examined this inscription with Rohana Dheera and again with Kamaleswar Bhattacharya, claiming it is Sanskrit and dating it to the sixth to seventh century. Prapod Assavavirulhakarn and Peter Skilling (2006–2007: 17–21) also studied this inscription, suggesting it is Prakrit and dating it to the eighth to ninth century.

Regarding another inscription from Nakhon Si Thammarat, [Fig.18] Cha-em and Champa suggest it is a mixture of Mon and Burmese, dating to the thirteenth century (Champa 1980 [2523 BE]: 94; Cha-em and Champa 1986 [2529 BE]: 112). Kongkaew (1986a: 19) argued it was Old Mon, showing influence from Haripuñjaya. However, I was unable to translate it into Old Mon using Shorto's dictionary (1971) and questioned the language of composition. Wannasarn (2013: 59) has proposed it to be Tamil and Sanskrit. At present it seems the language of composition for both inscriptions is still debated, but I am unconvinced that either are Old Mon. Therefore, I argue there have not yet been any Old Mon inscriptions found in southern Thailand; thus, any claim for Old Mon in southern Thailand based on epigraphic evidence should be called into question.

Summary

The number and distribution of Old Mon inscriptions throughout Thailand provides a glimpse of the temporal and geographic spread in usage of the Old Mon language; however, the spread of Old Mon inscriptions is not necessarily indicative of the spatial spread of the Dvāravatī culture. Over one hundred artifacts inscribed in Old Mon have been discovered in central, northeastern, and northern Thailand which can be dated palaeographically to about the sixth to thirteenth century. On the Central Plain, Old Mon inscriptions are generally sporadic, with few at any single location, and these are relatively short in length. On the Khorat Plateau, in some cases numerous inscriptions have been found at a single location, but these are for the most part short in length. In northern Thailand, a group of large, lengthy Old Mon inscriptions have been found at Lamphun and related sites in the Chiang Mai-Lamphun Basin.

The question, then, is what amount of epigraphic

evidence is required to make claims about the ethnicity, or even the vernacular, of an ancient population. By comparison, the ancient Khmer population produced many lengthy inscriptions, providing strong evidence for the usage of Old Khmer. Although Old Mon is the only local language represented in epigraphs from the earliest period of Siamese history, many sites considered integral to Dvāravatī have yielded only a few, short donative inscriptions written in Old Mon. From Nakhon Pathom, often considered the capital, only a single Old Mon inscription has been found. From U Thong, another important location, only a single inscribed clay tablet has been recovered (Watson and Skilling, this volume). From the area around Khu Bua, Ratchaburi Province, only one cave inscription has been identified.

Inscriptions in Old Mon have been found over a relatively wide area of the Central Plain, which by the second period went as far north as Nakhon Sawan and as far east as Chon Buri. Nevertheless, even this evidence is sparse. The discovery of a single inscribed tablet may indicate that the language was present, but it must be realized that such an artifact is produced by a single person and cannot be taken to represent the local populous as a whole. Also, many of these small artifacts can be easily transported, so the place of discovery might not have been the place of production. Scholars have noted the language of the Nyah Kur people, a minority in Thailand, is similar to epigraphic Old Mon. Gérald Diffloth (1984: 11) suggested Nyah Kur was a "sister-language" of modern Mon which likewise developed from Old Mon. Diffloth states Old Mon is the "lone candidate" for a vernacular language of the population of Dvāravatī, but argues that a lack of inscriptions in Thai or Khmer does not imply that those groups might not have also been part of the ancient society (Ibid.: 5).

Other scholars have contested the traditional view. Dhida Saraya (1999: 8) suggests that Dvāravatī was centered in the Chao Phraya River Valley, but expresses uncertainty over the capital city, the extent of authority, and the ethnicity of the population. Phasook Indrawooth (1999: 182) argues that the discovery of Old Mon inscriptions does not necessitate that the local population were Mon. She explains that evidence based on language alone is insufficient to be able to claim the ethnicity of the population, and consideration must also be paid to other aspects of their culture. Murphy (2016: 374) points out that having a "common material culture does not necessarily imply a common or homogenous ethnic group." He states that Old Mon was only used in religious epigraphy and may not have been the dominant vernacular. David Wyatt (2001: 3–7) suggests that past cultures should not be defined in ethnic terms, explaining Dvāravatī had a "multicultural quality that tended to make it different from neighbouring areas that were more culturally homogenous." Wyatt attributes this to two causes, the first being that "the Central Plain was a multiethnic region" and the second that Siam was located at a crossroads of both land and sea, leading foreigners to pass through, bringing new things and ideas. Wyatt says ancient Siam was a singular entity only by virtue of spatial proximity, but that it was more multicultural and multilinguistic than neighboring regions. He emphasizes that the usage of Old Mon does not mean the population was ethnically Mon.

I agree that an ancient Mon-Khmer language was used by a portion of the population. But it is difficult to claim it was the local vernacular, and based on current knowledge we are unable to make definitive claims about the ethnicity of Dvāravatī. Old Mon may have been the vernacular of the ruling class or the ecclesiastic community, but that does not necessitate that all members of society were Mon or that other ethno-linguistic groups did not co-exist. Perhaps it would be preferable not to equate the population of Dvāravatī with any particular ethno-linguistic group.

In conclusion, the geographic distribution of Old Mon inscriptions can thus be interpreted in different ways. In one respect, it does give a spatial distribution of artifacts which seem to have some relation to the culture of Dvāravatī. But this does not necessarily entail that every location where Old Mon inscriptions have been discovered was either controlled by or related to Dvāravatī. Although this does not prove anything definitely, it does provide additional information which can be considered when evaluating other evidence for the cultural development of the region.

Acknowledgements

I would like to thank John Miksic, Bruce Lockhart, Patrick McCormick, and Nicolas Revire for commenting on drafts of this paper. I would also like to thank the various museums, temples, and private collectors who allowed me to photograph artifacts.

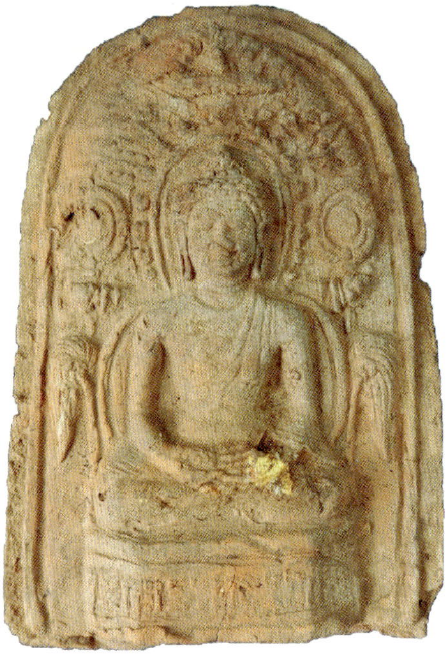

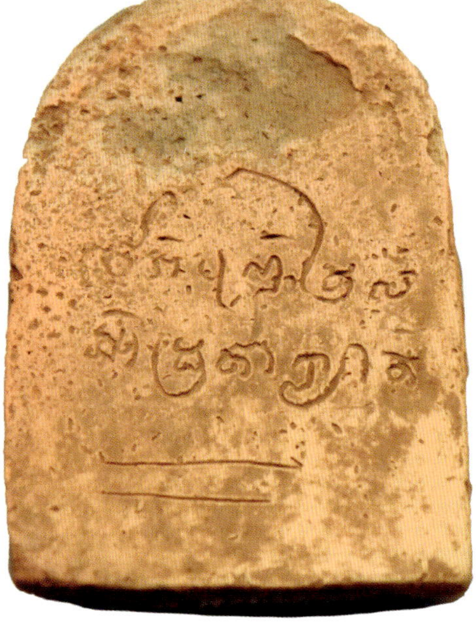

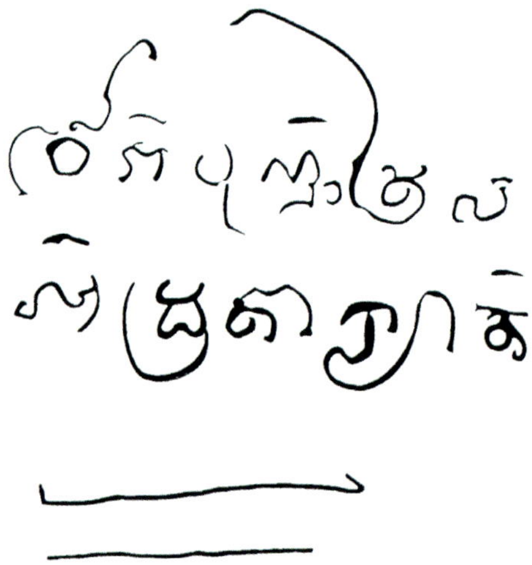

Figs. 1-3 Inscribed clay tablet from Phu Hang Nak, U Thong, Suphan Buri Province. Excavations in 2016 by the FAD Office 2 Suphan Buri. Courtesy of the FAD. and a drawing by Hunter Ian Watson.

A CLAY TABLET FROM U THONG INSCRIBED IN OLD MON

Hunter Ian Watson and Peter Skilling (Bhadra Rujirathat)

Phu Hang Nak Site No. 2 is an archaeological site on a hill to the west of the ancient settlement of U Thong. The ruined remains of multiple brick chedi are located on the hilltop. Excavations in 2016 by the FAD Office 2 Suphan Buri unearthed clay sherds, bricks, and fragments of terracotta Buddha images (FAD 2018 [2561 BE]). Especially interesting is the discovery of three lidded clay vessels in which sacred or consecrated objects were installed. One lidded vessel contained 48 stamped terracotta tablets, one image of a seated Buddha made of bronze, one gold foil, three silver Dvāravatī period coins, and one silver foil. The 48 clay tablets bear stamped images of the Buddha (Prachya 2018 [2561 BE]). The second lidded vessel contained 50 stamped terracotta tablets, one lead piece depicting a bodhisattva or a deity, two small lead pieces depicting a female with hands raised in homage, and other items including fragments of gold leaf. The vessel had been damaged by the roots of trees. The third lidded vessel contained 41 clay tablets, one silver Dvāravatī coin, and fragments of gold leaf.

A total of 139 clay tablets were recovered, all of which bear identical impressions of a Buddha seated in meditation on a throne, flanked by regalia and under a parasol. Only one tablet is inscribed [Figs 1-3], bearing a short donative inscription on the reverse. The inscription is written in the Old Mon language. Although undated, it can be dated approximately to the seventh century CE on palaeographic comparison with other inscriptions. Some of the letters appear similar to script styles from the eighth or even the ninth century, but this tablet is likely earlier due to the archaic appearance of the letter [m]. The message is clearly written, with the letters etched deeply, although there are some stray marks and scratches which could distract from the reading. The inscription was created by incising into the clay tablet using a stylus prior to the tablet being fired.

The tablet is described by Prachya Rungsaengthong in an article explaining the discovery at Phu Hang Nak Site No. 2. The inscribed message was studied by Kongkaew Veeraprajak. Although no transcription is provided, an interpretation is given in Thai as "This merit (is of) King Maratā (the builder of) the Buddha image" (Prachya 2017 [2560 BE]: 28–29). This interpretation given by Kongkaew is plausibly correct. The present article will further analyze the inscribed message by providing a full transcription, describing the unique features of the inscription, and explaining possible variant translations.

I propose the following transliteration for the inscribed message:

Line 1	vau^{a}' puñ' trala-
Line 2	^{a}' mra tā kyāt'
Line 3	=

In this transcription, the symbol [^{a}] represents the letter [a] when used as a final consonant, and ['] represents the *virāma* symbol, used to denote a final consonant.

This message is unique for a few reasons. It should be noted that epigraphic Old Mon exhibits irregularities with regards to spelling (Watson 2013), as can be seen in this inscription. A peculiar example is the concluding word, [kyāt'], written here with the final consonant [t]. This is an orthographic variant, as this word is usually written with a final [k]. However, this variant spelling can be explained by the fact that this word is pronounced with a final [t], so this instance is actually a closer phonetic representation than the usual spelling of [kyāk'].

Another notable feature is the two horizontal lines etched under the message, which might be considered as the final punctuation, quite possibly the double *daṇḍa* punctuation mark frequently appearing at the end of inscribed messages. Typically, this mark is written vertically, but here the final word of the second line leaves no remaining space for the punctuation mark, so it was perhaps moved down below and written, horizontally for stylistic appeal and to fill the space. The message can be summarized as such:

vau^{a}' puñ' trala^{a}' mra tā kyāt' ||

As can been seen, the first syllable in the second line is the final consonant of the last word from the first line. On the tablet, this first letter of the second line is not entirely legible and takes a slightly unusual shape. This might be attributable to stray marks on the tablet, or perhaps the scribe made an unintentional error and attempted to make a correction. In any case, the shape of [a] is clearly discernable, further supported by the fact that it carries the *virāma* symbol over the letter, indicating it as a final consonant, and the word [trala] is attested in other inscriptions with a final consonant [^{a}], presumably representing a glottal stop.

This inscribed message presents little difficulty in interpretation. The word [vau^{a}’] means “this”, [puñ’] means “merit”, [trala^{a}’] means “lord”, and [kyāt’] means “the Buddha”. There is no verb, which is a common feature of short, donative inscriptions in Old Mon. The only difficulty stems from the syllables [mra tā] in the second line. Kongkaew reads these together as [mratā], interpreted as a personal name (Prachya 2017 [2560 BE]: 29). This, however, is debatable, and it seems more likely that it actually represents two words, [mra] and [tā].

The word [ta] often appears before preceding the word [kyāk’] in Old Mon inscriptions. This normally takes the short vowel [ta] while in this inscription it bears a long vowel [tā], but this is less problematic when considering other instances of vowel length variation in epigraphic Old Mon. The word [ta] is interpreted in two ways by Harry Shorto. One way is as the preposition “to, towards” (Shorto 1971: 138); the other is as a nominal prefix recognizing the honorary status of male figures, understood as “father, grandfather” (Shorto 1971: 139). Shorto also defines the word [tā] as a question particle, but clearly in this inscription the word [tā] is not used as a question particle, and is thus better interpreted with one of the two meanings for [ta]. The words [ta] and [tā] also appear in Old Khmer inscriptions. Philip Jenner defines [ta] as a subordinating conjunction (Jenner 2009: 173) and [tā] as a verb meaning “to spread, increase” (Jenner 2009: 188), but Jenner notes that [ta / tā] are used interchangeably to denote “grandfather, ancestor; elderly man” or as a title for spirits (Jenner 2009: 585). While [ta kyāk’] in Old Mon has at times been understood as “to/toward the Buddha”, it seems more logical to interpret [ta / tā] in this context as an honorary title.

The remaining word is the syllable [mra] in the second line. While Kongkaew interprets this as the first syllable of the name [Mratā], reason has been given to interpret [tā] as a title for [kyāt’]. Nonetheless, it is likely that [Mra] can still be interpreted as a personal name. Following the word [trala^{a}’], it would thus be translated as “Lord Mra”. Other interpretations are likewise plausible. Shorto defines the word [mra] as a part of a knife (Shorto 1971: 302), which does not suit the context of this message. Shorto also gives the word [mar] as a verb meaning “to increase” (Shorto 1971: 287), and although the form is different from [mra], there are other instances of such syllable shifts in consonant clusters found in Old Mon inscriptions. However, it is uncommon to find a verb in this position of a phrase.

Shorto also gives the word [mrah] as a description of a Buddha image as seated, expressed as [Kyāk mrah] (Shorto 1971: 303), which is an interesting point in this context. In this case the word [mra] follows [trala^{a}’]; thus, it could possibly imply “the seated lord,” which corresponds with the image on the obverse showing a seated Buddha. Speculatively, it is possible to consider the word [mra] as a contraction of the Sanskrit and Pāli word [māra], the tempter of the Buddhist tradition who is also equated with death, seen elsewhere in Old Mon as [mār] (Shorto 1971: 292). This has been attested as [smiṅ mār], and because [smiṅ] is a cognate with [trala^{a}’], it would be plausible to consider [trala^{a}’ mār] as having a similar meaning. While the shift to a consonant cluster does not seem problematic, the contraction of a long vowel to a short vowel in a known Indic borrow word seems less likely, and other instances of such vowel contractions in Indic loans would need to be identified before this proposition could be seriously considered.

Consequently, this is the reading and translation which seems most plausible.

vau^{a}’	puñ’	trala^{a}’	mra	tā kyāt’ ||
This	merit	lord	Mra	the Buddha.

Although this phrase is lacking in verbs and prepositions, it could be interpreted as follows:

“This (is the) merit (made by) Lord Mra (for) the Buddha.”

Of course, all such interpretations are conjectural, as donative inscriptions in Old Mon tend to lack verbs and prepositions, and it is difficult to know with certainty how language users at the time of production of this tablet would have interpreted the meaning. Nevertheless, this inscribed tablet is a valuable discovery and is interesting for a number of reasons. Most significantly, this is the first known instance of any artifact inscribed in Old Mon discovered at U Thong, and indicates that, whether or not it was the local vernacular in ancient times, the Old Mon language was indeed present in some form at U Thong. Also, the variant spelling of [kyāt'] is an unusual occurrence which further indicates the level of spelling inconsistency in epigraphic Old Mon.

Acknowledgements

We thank Supamas Doungsakun, acting director of the U Thong National Museum, as well as the museum staff, and also Prachya Rungsaengthong, for the photographs and for bringing the finds from Phu Hang Nak to our attention.

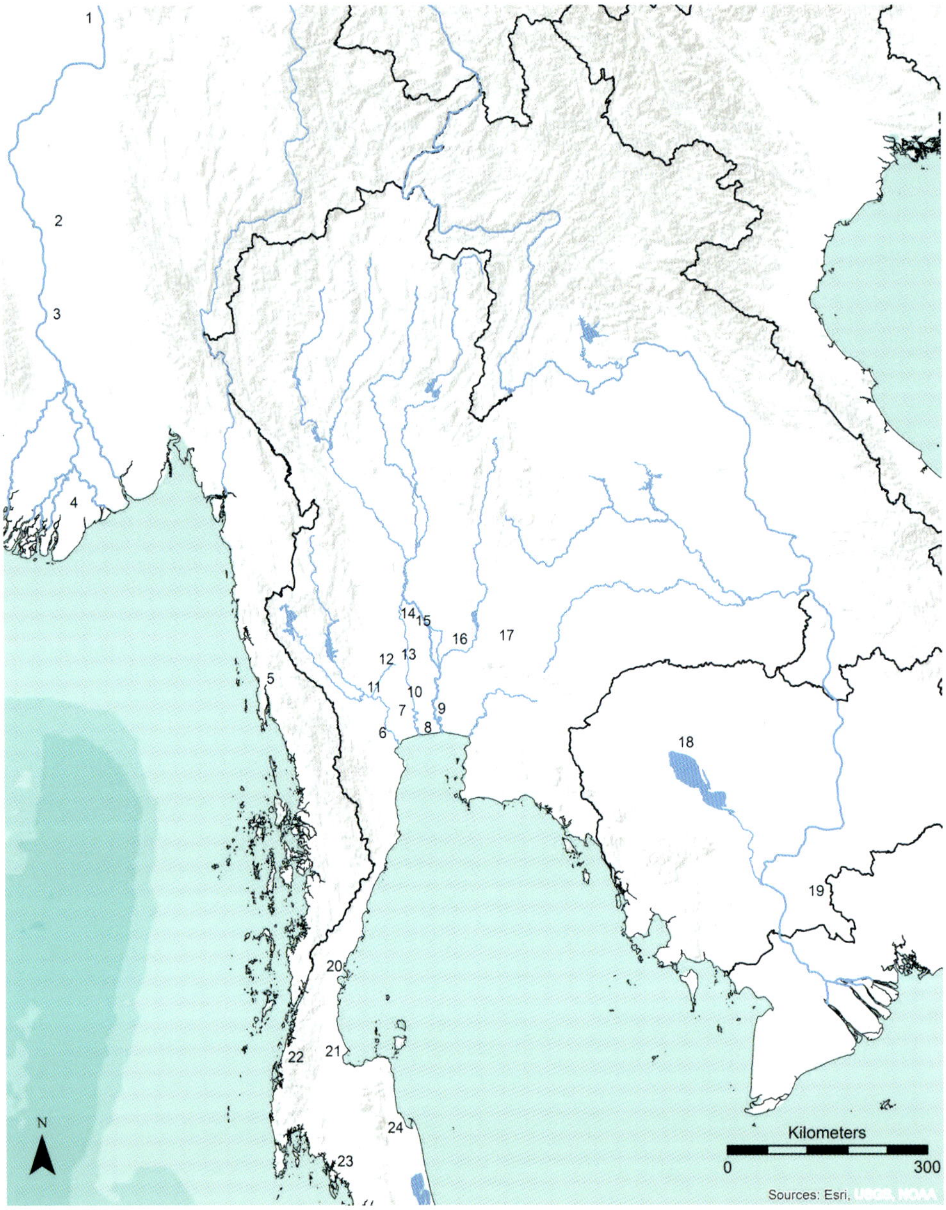

1. Halin
2. Beikthano
3. Sri Ksetra
4. Irrawaddy Delta
5. Dawei
6. Khu Bua
7. Nakhon Pathom
8. Phanom Surin shipwreck
9. Bangkok
10. Tha Chin River
11. Chorakhe Sam Phan River
12. U Thong
13. Suphan Buri
14. Dong Khon
15. Khu Mueang
16. Lop Buri–Pa Sak Basin
17. Wat Chanthuek
18. Preah Ko, Siem Reap
19. Prohear
20. Khao Sam Kaeo
21. Chaiya
22. Bang Kluai Nok, Phukhao Thong
23. Khuan Luk Pat, Wat Khlong Thom
24. Nakhon Si Thammarat

Fig.1 Map showing locations mentioned in the text (map by Hunter Watson).
All photographs belong to the author unless otherwise stated.

PRECIOUS METALS IN DVĀRAVATĪ CULTURE

Anna Bennett

Introduction

The extent to which religion and the spread of Hinduism and Buddhism over two thousand years ago accompanied trade suggests a mechanism other than that of missionary expeditions by which Buddhism arrived in Southeast Asia. Well before the advent of the Brahmanical and Buddhist civilisation of the Dvāravatī culture, characterised by moated settlements and elaborate resplendent white stucco and brick monuments, the communities in southern and west-central Thailand were part of a sophisticated and stratified society that was already trading directly or indirectly with India and China and had at least some contact with the Mediterranean world (Bellina and Glover 2004; Bellina et al. 2014; Borell et al. 2014; Bellina 2017; Borell 2017b, Borell 2017c, Borell 2018; Glover 1990, 1996a, 1996b, 2010a; Glover and Bellina 2011; Ray 1994, 2014; Xiong Zhaoming 2014, 2017). Ships sailed back and forth across the Gulf of Thailand and the South China Sea in a system of interconnected trade routes and, by the end of the first millennium BCE, the annals of the Western Han dynasty describe a sea voyage between the southern Chinese ports in the Gulf of Tonkin to a place called Huangzhi, which is thought to be Kāñcipuram in southern India. The text includes a description of a ten day land crossing, which is presumed to be that of the Kra Isthmus, the narrowest part of the Thai-Malay peninsula (Wang 1958: 19–20), and its use as a trans-penninsular crossing during the protohistoric and early historic periods would have connected the Gulf of Thailand and the Bay of Bengal. Caravans would have also travelled by land using the mountain passes and river systems to and from the Andaman Coast near Dawei, across lower Myanmar and the peninsula and up through Chaiya and Nakhon Si Thammarat to the areas which were to develop into the Dvāravatī polities of Nakhon Pathom and U Thong [Fig.1].

Dating of Dvāravatī

The Dvāravatī period may perhaps be viewed as a political unit of indigenous people who adopted and integrated elements of Indic culture into their own distinctive way of life. But the early centuries CE were not a process of Indian colonialisation. Rather, they witnessed a gradual and continuous cultural integration by which the political role of religion was sponsored by local rulers. The adoption of Buddhism by the people of Dvāravatī, first by the elite and then disseminating to the wider society was able to unify, both culturally and politically, the diverse communities which had coexisted in what is now central Thailand for hundreds of years. This created the ideal means of centralising power and local rulers thus enhanced their status and furthered their spheres of influence.

The term Dvāravatī has been used to describe a state or a kingdom, a period in history, and an art form. However, these terms which are not well defined may not have always coexisted chronologically and geographically. The sixth century CE, or even as late as the seventh century CE, has generally been accepted as the inception of the Dvāravatī period, albeit almost entirely based on artistic style (Woodward 1997; Baptiste and Zéphir 2009).

The excellent and comprehensive exhibition at the Musée Guimet made some headway to redress the dominant emphasis on Buddhist art (Phasook Indrawooth 2009), and recent archaeological evidence is increasing our understanding not only of the geographical and chronological complexities but also of the relationships between the known polities within the Dvāravatī sphere of influence (see Murphy 2016 for a summary).

New dating consistent with the idea of an uninterrupted occupation of some settlement sites in central Thailand, albeit with a much less dense population, supports the concept of an Early Dvāravatī or Proto-Dvāravatī period (Barram and Glover 2008; Glover 2010a, 2010b; Sawang Lertrit 2001: 231; Supamas 2005; Murphy 2016). Archaeological evidence together with the surviving ancient roads and irrigation canals which still surround the town of U Thong today, indicate that it was among the earliest urban centres in Southeast Asia. AMS carbon 14 analysis of brick and plaster by Andrew Barram (2003) from the 1967 excavation by Watson and Loof, together with new excavations by San Thaiyanonda (2011) and Saritphong Khunsong (2015) [Fig.2], have extended the occupation of the U Thong ancient settlement back to the fifth or perhaps fourth century CE.[1] This is a period well before that of a fully developed Dvāravatī culture, with its religion and religious buildings, the use of Old Mon language in inscriptions,[2] its moated settlement sites and stone sculptural tradition of the seventh century.

No.	*Sample*	*Grid*	*CM.DT.*	*Context*	*AMS(BP)*	*Dates*
1	*Charcoal*	G.1	113	Feature2	1521 ±22	429 CE ±22
2	*Shell*	G.1	130–140		1515 ±20	435 CE ±20
3	*Shell*	G.3	130–140		1480 ±21	470 CE ±21
4	*Charcoal*	G.1	190–200		1798 ±21	152 CE ±21
5	*Charcoal*	G.4	220–230	Infant Burial	1720 ±23	230 CE ±23
6	*Shell*	G.4	230–240		1709 ±20	241 CE ±20

Fig.2 Calibrated radiocarbon dates (Waikato University) from excavations at U Thong reproduced and adapted from Saritphong 2015 [2558 BE].

An engraved copper sheet found within the moated settlement of U Thong contains a Sanskrit inscription suggesting that the town may once have been a royal capital. "*I Śrī Harsavarman, grandson of the King, Śrī Isanavarman, who has expanded the sphere of his glory, obtained the lion throne by regular succession*" (U Thong Museum archive and Coedès 1963). Some scholars have suggested that the name Śrī Harṣavarman indicates Khmer lineage (Vickery 1998: 22; Guy, this volume) and there is debate therefore that this inscription may date to a period of Khmer occupation of the central plain, and should not be taken as evidence of a Dvāravatī kingdom (Phuthorn Bhumadhon, personnel communication).

The first confirmation of the name Dvāravatī is recorded in a Sanskrit inscription on two coin-like silver medallions[3] discovered in 1943 beneath the foundation of a ruined sanctuary[4] within the ancient settlement of Nakhon Pathom, today located along the road which leads to Bangkok. The medallions were found in an earthenware vessel together with silver conch coins and have a cow-and-calf on the obverse of one and a flowering vase on the obverse of the other. On the reverse an identical inscription *śrīdvāravatīśvarapuṇya* [Fig.3], translated by Cœdès in 1963 as "oeuvre méritoire du roi de Śrī Dvāravatī" (Boeles 1964: 100–102) and more recently as "merit of the glorious lord of Dvāravatī" (Skilling 2003: 94–95; see also Skilling this volume). A further group of nine coin-like medallions, three of which have the same inscription, were excavated in 1997 from beneath the foundation of a building at Khok Chang Din (Site 7), an extensive Brahmanical sanctuary comprising more than twenty buildings, lingas, and ritual ponds, to the southwest of U Thong (FAD 1966). The medallions which were found in an earthenware pedestal vessel together with cut silver ingots, presumably used for barter and trade, are on display in the U Thong National Museum[5] [Figs. 4a–e]. At least twenty-two other medallions with inscriptions have been recorded (Ronachai Krisadaolarn 2016: 31–32), including one from Ban Khu Mueang, Sing Buri Province, 150 km north of Nakhon Pathom, and one from Dong Khon, Sankhaburi, Chai Nat Province (Phuthorn Bhumadhon 1984 [2527 BE];1987 [2530 BE]; see also Bhumadhon this volume).

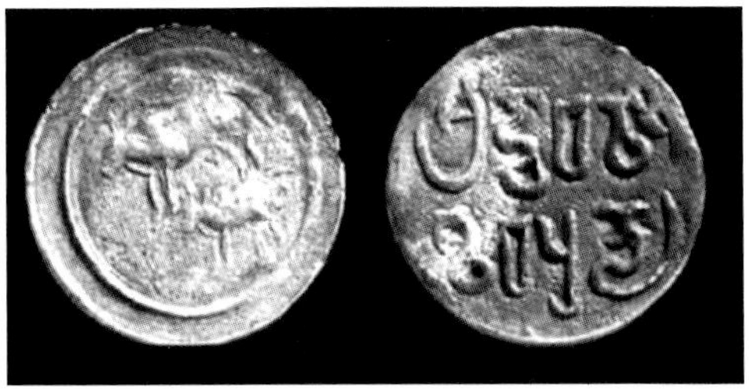

Figs.3 Coin-like silver medallion with the inscription śrīdvāravatīśvarapuṇya. Private collection. Photograph courtesy of Indrawooth.

Another Sanskrit inscription, which is the first inscription bearing the name Dvāravatī on stone to have been recovered, has been identified on a base for a Buddha statue from Wat Chanthuek in Pak Chong District, Nakhon Ratchasima Province. The inscription identifies a queen who is "*daughter of the Lord of Dvāravatī ... the queen*

1 Radiocarbon dates (uncalibrated) have also been published by Surapol Natapintu from excavations at U Thong, 2300 ± 310, 1790 ± 220 (reprinted in Sawang Lertrit 2001: 231).
2 Today ethnically Mon people are based in lower Myanmar and in communities scattered throughout Thailand.
3 There is debate about whether these objects are forms of standardised money (Wicks 1992: 159) or were medallions used ceremonially (Gutman 1978: 9–10).
4 Phra Pathom Chedi at Huay Chorokay, Tambon Noen Hin.
5 Ninth century Tang ceramics were also recovered.

set up the image ... this of the Tathāgata"[6] (Skilling 2003; see also Skilling this volume), thus indicating that the daughter of "the *Lord of Dvāravatī* " was sufficiently important to marry a king.

Religion

The symbiotic relationship of religion and trade in the late first millennium BCE and the early centuries CE would have been a powerful force behind economic development during the Dvāravatī period. Monasteries, which were primarily and strategically located close to trade routes, were large consumers of exotic goods, thus creating an expanding economic order which connected ancient production and trading centres across large parts of Asia. Traveling pilgrims would have established networks of intellectual exchange, making Buddhist teachings available within an interconnected sacred landscape through which craftsmen travelled, bringing new skills and perhaps raw materials and adapting readily to local tastes and conditions.

According to the Sri Lankan Buddhist tradition, monks were sent in small groups throughout South and Southeast Asia to propagate the Buddha's teaching during the reign of King Aśoka (268–233 BCE) (Kulke and Rothermund 2004: 66), who had converted to Buddhism. One group was sent to *Suvarṇabhūmi*, "Land of Gold", which has been interpreted as Southeast Asia, particularly Thailand and the Irrawaddy Delta in Lower Myanmar (Bunchar Pongpanich and Somchet Thinapong 2019).[7] Buddhist symbols such as the *triratna*[8] [Figs.5–7] and the *bhaddapitha*, or auspicious seat or throne [Fig.8], are represented in gold jewellery recovered from early Pyu sites in Myanmar and from sites such as Khao Sam Kaeo and Bang Kluai Nok in peninsular Thailand. By the fourth to fifth centuries CE, one of the most enduring symbols, that of the Wheel of the Law (*dharmacakra*) was mounted on a stone pillar, such as the one found near monument No.11 at U Thong [Fig.9] (Brown 1996, 2014). The three stone *dharmacakra* found there were in all probability manufactured at the Dvāravatī stone workshop sites such as the ones excavated to the south in Phetchaburi Province[9] (Phasook Indrawooth 2008), although earlier examples could possibly have been made of wood which no longer survives. However, this is disputed by Brown (2017) in his evaluation of the evidence behind the sudden appearance of a sophisticated and accomplished art style in central Thailand in the sixth century CE.

Although trade would have been one of the primary forces during the early Dvāravatī period, it was without doubt the fertility of the surrounding alluvial soils that allowed towns such as U Thong and Nakon Pathom, 80 km to the south of U Thong, which is the largest known Dvāravatī site and which covers an area of 5.7 square km, to grow into major urban centres. Ideal conditions for wet-rice cultivation, facilitated by the use of iron and animal traction using the water buffalo, would have resulted in a surplus of rice, a prerequisite to supporting the vast labour force and craft specialisation which would have been required to erect and embellish the monuments of the Dvāravatī culture.[10] These monuments would have served as pilgrimage centres but also as markers of prestige within the wider society, attracting followers from near and far. The magnificence of such monuments is described in an eighth century CE inscription on an Indian copper plate which has the following translation (Meltzer and Sander 2006).

"Whose *stūpas* even today light up the earth – mountain like *stūpas* resembling the colour of white frost, pearl necklaces, white water lilies, crystals and conch shells, raised high by parasols and possessing railings, with flames made up of waving flags, and worshipped by those who are worthy of being honoured by the three worlds–" (Meltzer and Sander 2006: 275).

"The place here which is the reason for our birth, which is adorned with *stūpas* resembling a multitute of white autumn clouds… . like lotus ponds, the surface of which has been purified by thousands of sunrays, ...may this great village of the noble ones (aryagrama) be constantly frequented by exalted beings just like heaven"
(Meltzer and Sander 2006: 277).

6 Although the elites would have followed Brahmanical practices, this inscription makes clear that these coexisted with Buddhist patronage.
7 Early forms of Buddhism were practiced in Sri Lanka and Andhra Pradesh since at least the third century BCE, producing, for example, the Great *Stūpa* at Amarāvatī, which show similar designs to those seen on the *dharmacakra*.
8 *Triratna* is a Sanskrit term meaning the Three Jewels, the Buddha, the Dharma and the Saṅgha (the community of all those who follow the teachings), and was used as an early Buddhist symbol.

9 Survey and excavation identified Dvāravatī workshop sites at Ban Nong Chik and Ban Tha Rua in Khao Yoi District and at Ban Lard in Ban Lard District, Petchaburi Province. Finds included a finished and unfinished Buddhist sculpture including *dharmacakra*, Buddha images and waste stone flakes.
10 The temper used in Dvāravatī bricks was husked rice, indicating a high level of rice agriculture. This rice has been used in the carbon dating of some of the structures.

The Dvāravatī period supported monastic Buddhism on a grand scale and at least thirty religious buildings have been recorded in the hills to the west of the city of U Thong alone, distributed along a seven kilometre route interspersed on the hilltops, at foothills, and on the slopes themselves. There were essentially two types of religious buildings, the *stūpa*, a reliquary or commemorative structure which may also have served for religio-political ceremonies, and the *vihāra*, an assembly hall or monastery, many of which were probably constructed of wood and would not have survived. The most renowned *stūpas* of U Thong are those at the top of Khao Rang Kapit, Khao Phra, and Khao Tham Thiam to the north, which remain sites of worship to the present day. The elites within the Dvāravatī communities are thought to have erected Brahmanical shrines, such as those of Khao Khok and Khok Chang Din, as a means of differentiating themselves from the wider population. These shrines were geographically distinct from the Buddhist sites, and in the case of U Thong were concentrated to the southwest of the settlement area (Bunchar Pongpanich and Phuthorn Bhumadhon 2015 [2558 BE]: 101; Supamas 2005). In 1966, a large number of Pyu rising-sun silver coins, which are thought to have been produced near the Pyu capital of Halin in Myanmar and which circulated from the fifth to ninth centuries CE (Moore 2007: 142–144), were recovered in an earthenware jar during excavations at Khok Chang Din [Fig.10a–c].[11] The standardised shape and weight of these coins imply a degree of centralised control although there is dispute as to whether they were used as a currency Wicks 1992: 159) or as bullion and royal gifts (Gutman 1978: 9–10) or, as in the case at Khok Chang Din, as consecration deposits. These coins are sometimes found cut into quarters [Figs.10d–e] and from information gathered from looters interviewed by this author, it is estimated that at least twenty burials within the Central Plain area have been found with a quarter of a coin placed in the mouth of the skeleton and that a few burials had a whole coin in the mouth area.

By the seventh to eighth centuries CE, the extent of cultural intermixing of Hinduism and Buddhism is clear. Inscriptions in Sanskrit and Pāli in scripts derived from Indic models have been found at U Thong and a carved figure of Viṣṇu and a liṅga from Khao Phra show that Bramanical practices co-existed with Buddhism (Phasook Indrawooth 2004; Guy 2014). The evidence points to a social structure in which Brahman priests performing Brahmanical rituals were sponsored by local rulers, their prerogative being the consecration of kingship which provided a basis for the relationship between ruler and ruled.

Trade

The Central Plain was ideally located to function as a crossroads for trade and commerce, to the west lay the Pyu urban centres of Beikthano, Sri Ksetra and Halin, with India and Sri Lanka beyond; to the north, the communities of the Chao Phraya-Pasak River Basins and China beyond; to the east the Khmer Empire and Champa; to the south the Thai-Malay peninsular region and the Gulf of Siam. Archaeological survey work suggests that the early moated settlements were in close proximity to the protohistoric sites from which they developed (Phuthorn Bhumadhon 2015). Settlements, populated by townspeople, traders, merchants and craftsmen, would have gradually grown and expanded into urban centres which would have been connected to each other and the surrounding smaller settlements via a complex system of waterways and land routes. Typically oval or irregular in shape, the larger settlements were located near waterways which fed their moats (Gallon 2014). Archaeological research (ibid.; Mudar 1999) has located over sixty small moated settlements on the Central Plain, and although many of these date to as late as the eleventh century CE, others may have been contemporary with the early settlement of U Thong, which, based on recent AMS carbon 14 dates, extended back to the fifth or perhaps fourth century CE [Fig.2]. Surrounded by an earthen rampart, a stone wall and a moat, and covering an area of approximately one square km (1.7 km x 0.8 km), with mountains to the north and the west, U Thong would have benefited not only from access to the close proximity of forest products and mineral wealth but also its strategic position, along the Chorakhe Sam Phan River, a tributary to the west of the Chao Phraya River which empties into the Gulf of Thailand, would have ensured its place as a truly cosmopolitan urban centre exemplified by, among other things, the portraits of West Asian merchants represented in the decoration, engraved on bricks and found on seal impressions [Figs.11a–e].

11 These coins have also been found at the Funan site of Oc Eo in southern Vietnam. They have the *srivatsa* (auspicious mark linked to ancient mother goddess who ensures fertility and good fortune) on the obverse and either a rising sun or the *bhaddapitha* (auspicious throne-stool) on the reverse. The other recurring motif is the conch (sankha), a water symbol linked to prosperity.

The recent discovery of a well-preserved eighth century Arab dhow in the delta of the Tha Chin River in Samut Sakhon Province [Figs. 12a–c] (Nareerat Preeyanuch 2014 [2557 BE]; (Guy 2017); Preeyanuch Jumprom 2019 [2562 BE]) further emphasises the connection with the wider world. Known as the Phanom Surin shipwreck,[12] with a keel of over seventeen metres in length, a stitched plank construction[13] which is still clearly visible, and its preserved cargo, it has provided evidence of trade with China in the form of Tang ceramics and with the Persian Gulf in the form of torpedo jars (Guy 2017). Although it is only the second Arab trading vessel to be found in Southeast Asia (Krahl and Guy 2011)[14] the scale of the sea trade and its importance by the early historic period is clearly illustrated by Indian coinage of the second century CE under the reign of King Vāsiṣṭhiputra Śrī Pulumāvi. A king of the Śātavāhana Dynasty, the coins are stamped with images of ships with masts, implying the use of sails and wind-driven ships. Three of these Śātavāhana copper-alloy coins showing a double-masted ship on one side and a humped bull on the reverse have been found at the ancient trading site of Khlong Thom on the southern peninsula in Krabi Province[15] [Fig.14]. Other small portable objects which indicate the importance of sea trade at this time include fourth to fifth century CE clay seal impressions with clear depictions of ocean-going trading vessels with stitched-plank construction, a single mast, lantern sails, and a lateral stern rudder board [Fig.14] (Baptiste and Zephir 2009: 54). These types of clay seals would have been used by Indian merchants, and while mostly found at Indian port sites such as Chandraketugarh (Ray 1994: Pl. 17), the find of a seal at Nakhon Pathom, the largest known early Dvāravatī site, suggests the presence of Indian merchants at this time. The Samkha Jātaka No.442 describes an inland port on the River Ganga near Varanasi which was used by merchants sailing to Suvarṇabhūmi, and Ray's research (1994: 22) into these texts has led her to conclude that the same boats were used on the rivers and for transoceanic expeditions. Clearly, these boats exploited the seasonal monsoon winds in the western Indian Ocean which blew from the southwest from April to September and from the northeast from November to February, thereby ensuring favourable voyages in both directions. Merchants leaving Southeast Asia would have sailed with the Northeast Monsoon and boats would also have departed from the west coast of India to supply consumers in the Roman Empire. The first to second century CE text *Periplus Maris Erythraei* (Voyage around the Erythraean Sea), written by an anonymous Greek-speaking Egyptian merchant, mentions two important Śātavāhana trade centres, Pratiṣṭāna and Tagara, which controlled much of the Indian sea coast and dominated trade with the Roman Empire.

There are numerous references to master mariners or sea-captains (*mahānāvika*) in India and a personal *mahānāvika* gold seal dated to the first or second century CE [Fig.8] was recently discovered at Bang Kluai Nok, a site located within hundreds of acres of seaside forest plantations near Phukhao Thong in Ranong Province, on the western coast of the peninsula (Bunchar Pongpanich 2009 [2552 BE]; Skilling 2015; Jacq-Hergoualc'h 2002: 214–15). Boats exploiting the monsoon winds in the western Indian Ocean would necessarily have made stopovers in riverine ports along the peninsula coast in order to not only replenish supplies and maintain their vessels, but in order to obtain and exchange both raw materials and locally manufactured items. The site of Bang Kluai Nok has produced a vast number of gold beads, cylinder agate beads, mosaic beads, amuletic stone beads, seals and intaglios, together with Eastern Han mirror fragments, clearly marking it as a site engaged in extensive trade (Bunchar Pongpanich 2009 [2552 BE]: 163–177; Bellina et al. 2014). The engraved inscription on the gold seal which reads *brahaspatiśarmasa nāvika* has been translated by Peter Skilling as "*of the mariner Brahaspati Navika*" and is only the second Brāhmī inscription referring to a mariner to have been found in Southeast Asia[16] (Skilling 2015: 63–77). The name Brahaspati surrounds the Buddhist *bhaddapitha*, or auspicious seat or throne, and the seal possibly belonged to a Brahmin who was wealthy enough to own such a seal and who had travelled to the area. An attachment soldered onto the reverse would have allowed the seal to be secured during its use and the extensive wear and overlapping scratches visible under the microscope (Bennett 2017: Figs.1.66–1.70) indicate that the seal had been in circulation and had been used for an extensive period before being lost at Bang Kluai Nok.

12 Named after the owners of the property on which the discovery was made.

13 A boat building technique confined to the west coast of India and the Middle East.

14 The other is the Belitung shipwreck, named after its find spot, a small island in the Java Sea. The cargo was a remarkable assemblage of lead ingots, bronze mirrors, spice-filled jars, intricately worked vessels of silver and gold, and more than 60,000 glazed bowls, ewers, and other ceramics.

15 One coin is in the Krabi Temple museum (Phasook Indrawooth 2004: 6.5) and two are in the collection of the SuthiRatana Foundation.

16 The first being the Kedah's Buddhagupta Mahānāvika inscription (Skilling 2011)

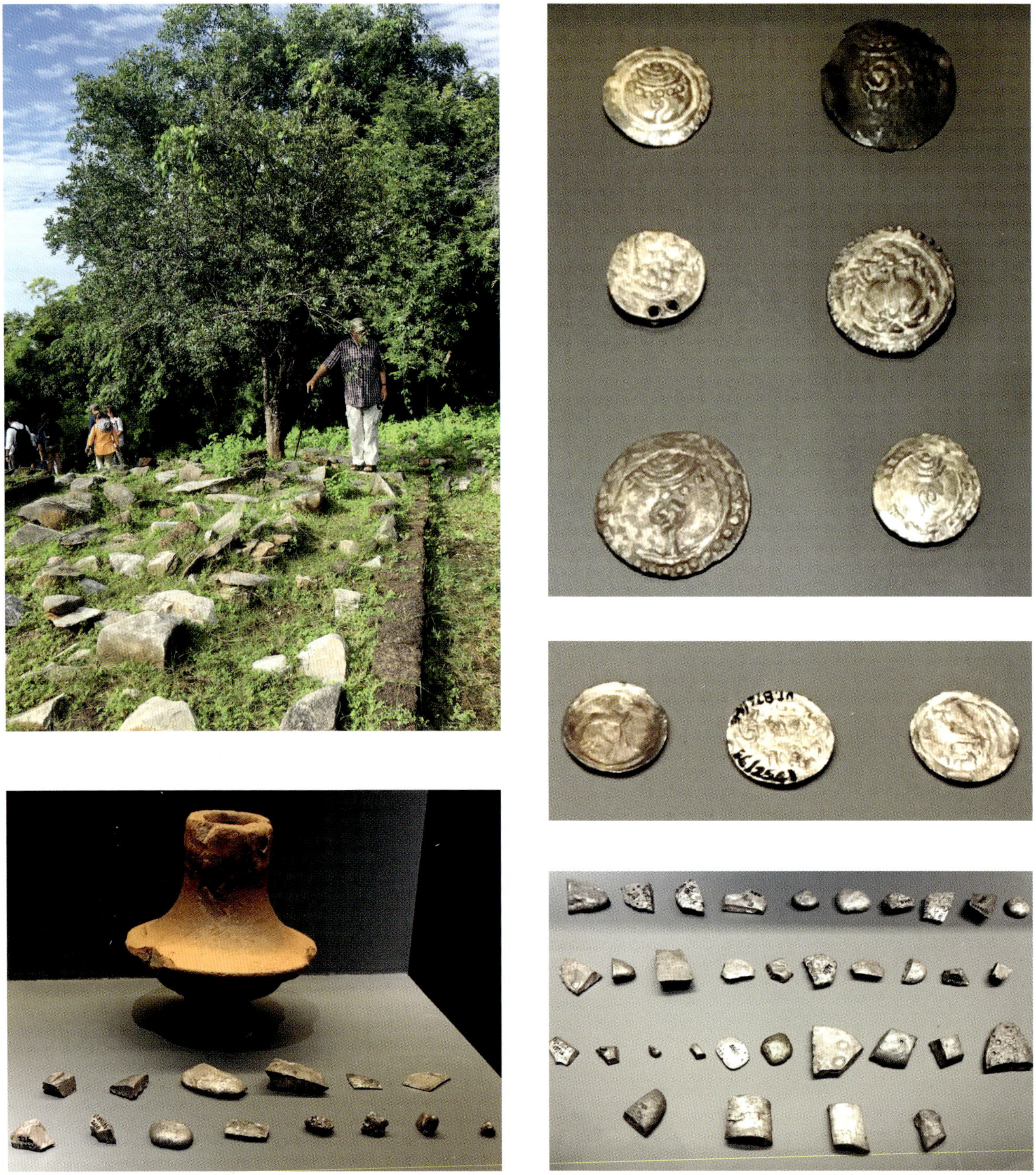

Figs. 4a–e Ian Glover in 2017 at the Brahmanical sanctuary of Khok Chang Din Site 7, pointing to the find spot of the nine silver coin-like medallions (top and middle right) found in an earthenware vessel (bottom left) together with cut silver ingots (bottom right). Three of the medallions (seen middle right) have the Sanskrit inscription *śrīdvāravatīśvarapuṇya* which has been translated as "merit of the glorious lord of Dvāravatī" and a cow-and calf on the other side. U Thong National Museum.

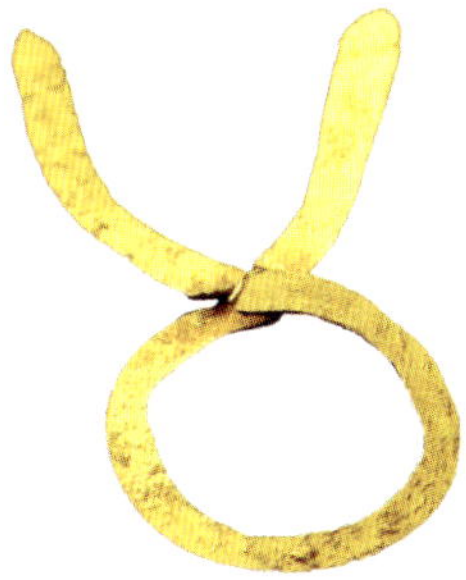

5

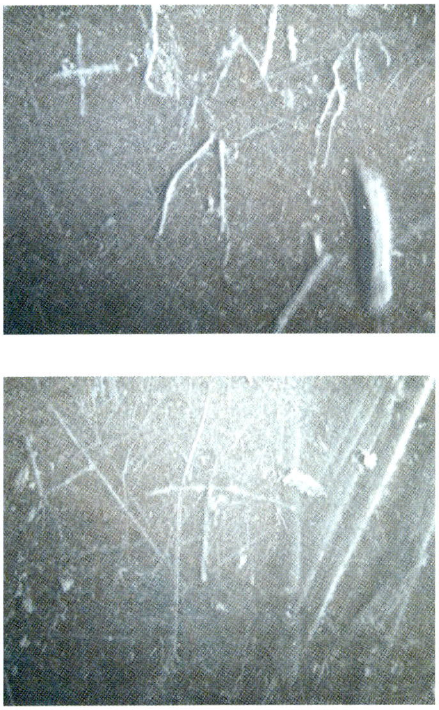

7

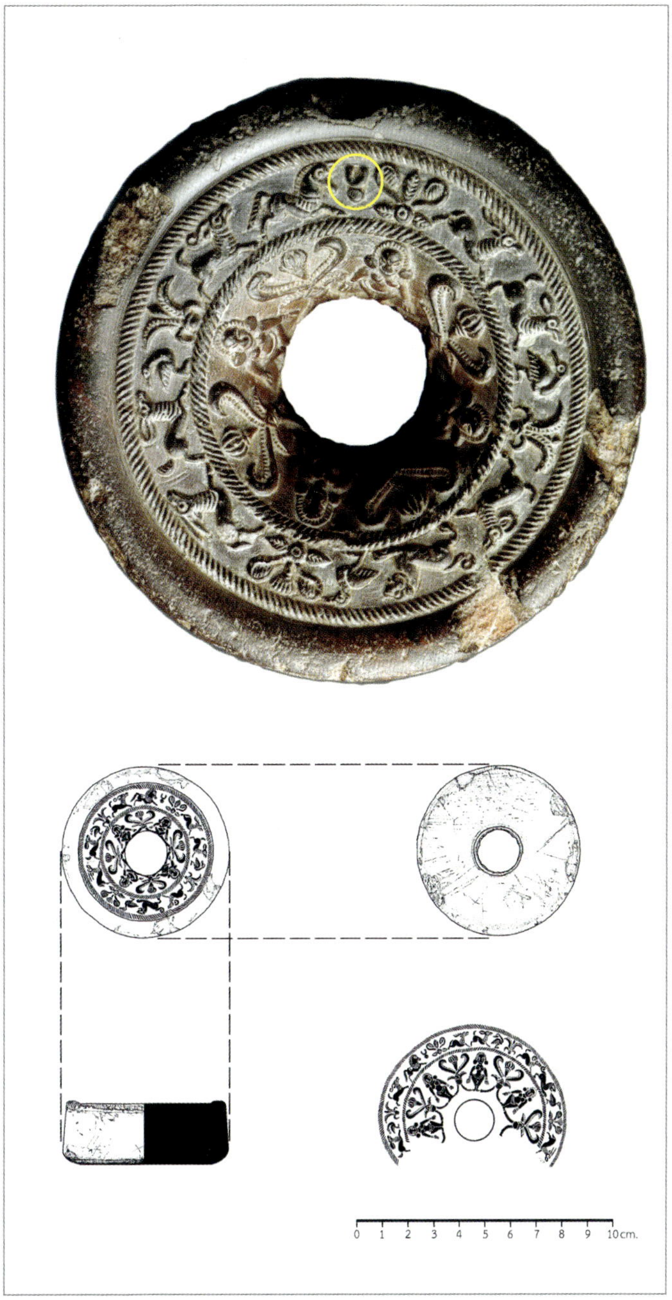

6

Fig.5 Gold *triratna* (a Sanskrit term meaning the Three Jewels, the Buddha, the Dharma and the Saṅgha) which was used as an early Buddhist symbol. Found at Khao Sam Kaeo on the east coast of the Thai-Malay peninsula, SuthiRatana Foundation, Bangkok, KSK355.

Fig.6 Mauryan–Śuṅga ringstone with several auspicious symbols including a *Trirata*, four standing nude female figures often interpreted as "fertility goddesses", alternating with Nāgapuṣpa flowers, the rhizome of the flowers emerging directly from the figure's legs. D. 5.8 cm. Found on the east coast of the Thai-Malay peninsula in the Ta Tapua River, adjacent to Khao Sam Kaeo archaeological site, and presumed to be used as a jewellery mould (Bennett 2017; 2019; forthcoming). SuthiRatana Foundation, Bangkok, KSK522 (Drawing by Khun Watinnee).

Fig.7 Photographs of the blank reverse face of the ringstone which bears a scratched inscription and parallel marks from use as a sharpening stone.

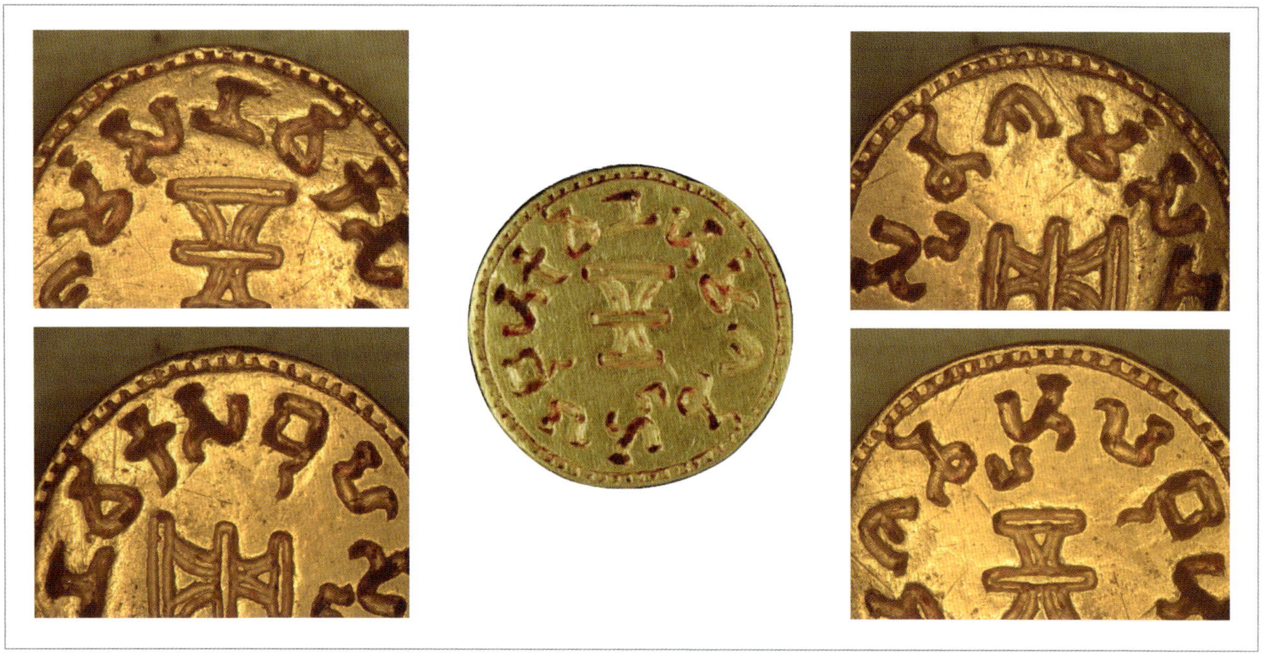

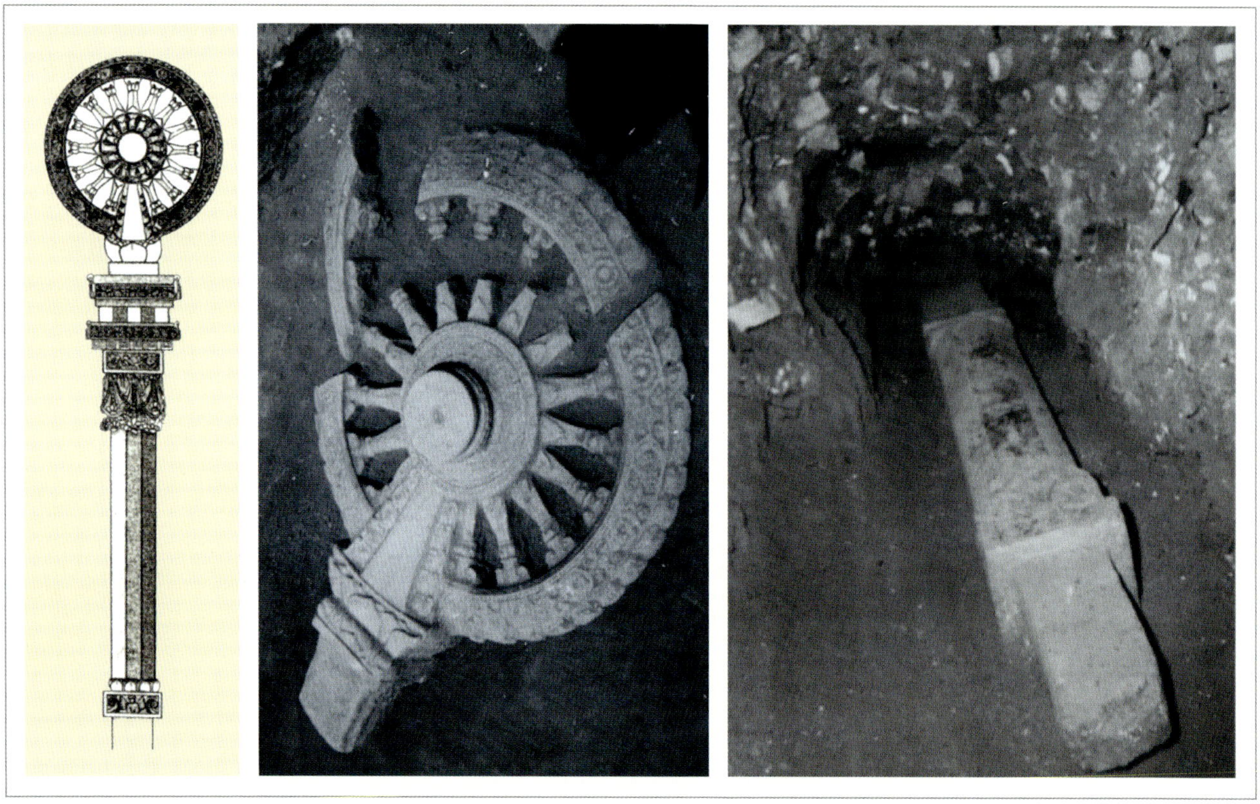

Fig.8 A first or second century CE gold seal bearing the Brāhmī inscription *brahaspatiśarmasa nāvika*, 'of the mariner Brahaspati'. The detailed photographs are reversed for ease of reading. Found at Bang Kluai Nok in Ranong Province on the western coast of the peninsula. SuthiRatana Foundation, Bangkok, BKN068.

Fig.9 Dharmacakra, the "wheel of the law" which is thought to represent the First Sermon by the Buddha, given at Sārnāth. This pillar, which was found near monument No.11 at U Thong, was probably manufactured at the Dvāravatī stone workshop sites such as the ones excavated in Phetchaburi Province. Courtesy of Phasook Indrawooth.

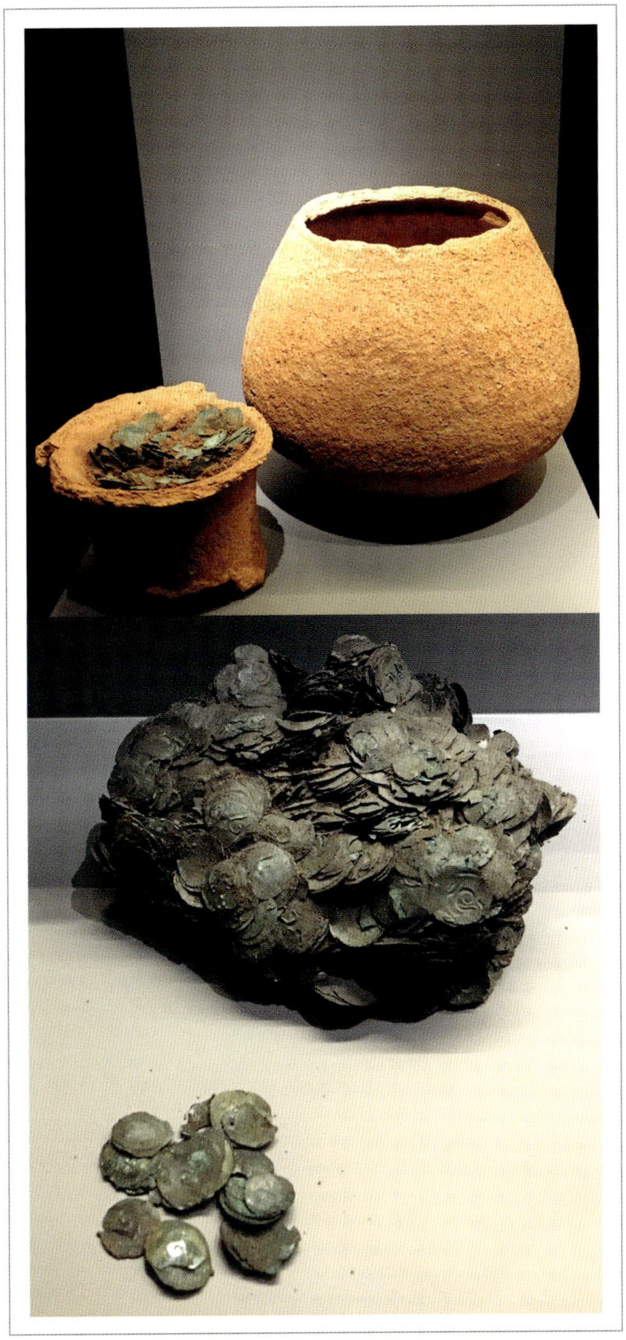

a–b

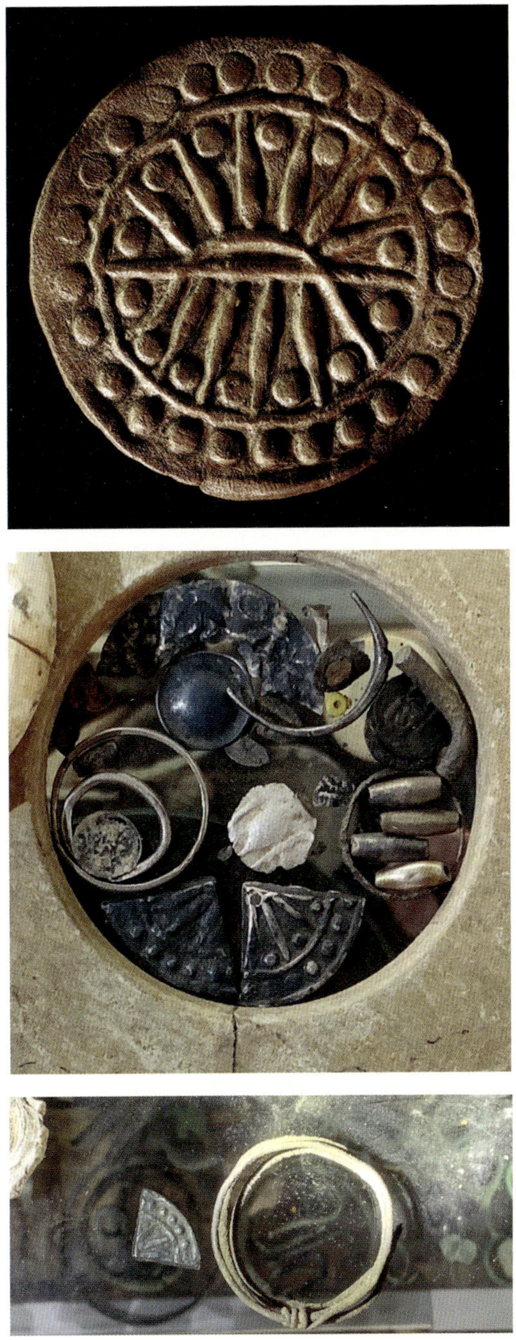

c–d

Fig.10a–b Large numbers of Pyu rising-sun silver coins, stamped with a conch motif, found in an earthenware jar during excavations in 1966 at the Brahmanical sanctuary of Khok Chang Din. *10c* Detail of a rising-sun coin, U Thong National Museum. *10d* Two quarters of rising sun coins found in the mouths of skeletons found by a looter at Khao Sam Pot, Tha Luang District, Lop Buri Province (shown left) and from Lam Sonthi District, Lop Buri Province (shown right). *10e* The quarter coin from Khao Sam Poi was found with a child's silver bracelet and carnelian and glass beads.

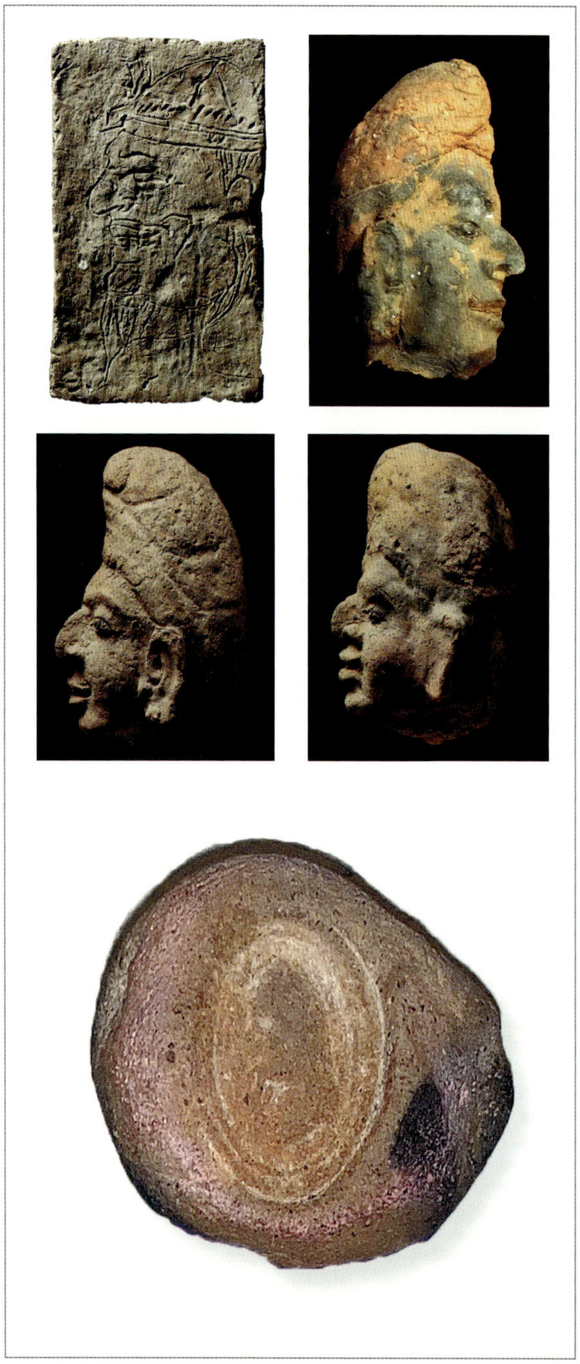

11a–e

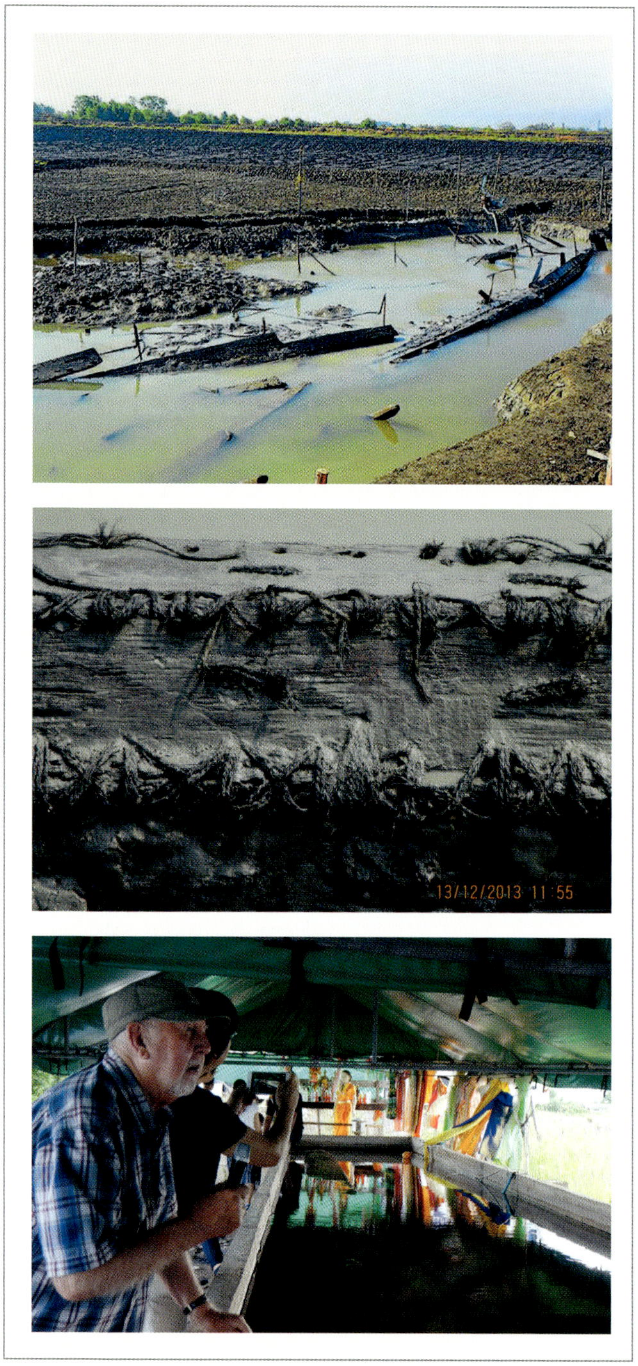

12a–c

Figs. 11a–e West Asian merchants are depicted in the brick and terracotta decoration of Dvāravatī monuments and clay seals. *11a* Inscribed brick depicting a West Asian merchant, found during the restoration of Chedi Chula Pathon, Nakom Pathom, ht. 27 cm, Phra Pathom Chedi National Museum, Nakhon Pathom, 609/2519. *11b* Baked clay portrait: Khu Bua, Ratchaburi Province, ht. 23 cm, Ratchaburi National Museum, *11c-d* ht. 23 and 20 cm, Phra Somdet Narai National Museum, Lop Buri Province, 1397/2504 and 1339/2504. Courtesy Musée Guimet, *11e* baked terracotta seal depicting a western face, diam. 4.5 cm, Sap Champa Museum, Lop Buri Province.

Figs. 12a–b Phanom Surin shipwreck, an eighth century Arab dhow trading ship found in the delta zone of the Tha Chin River in Samut Sakhon Province, carried cargo between China and the Persian Gulf. The stitched-plank construction has been perfectly preserved due to the waterlogged conditions (Courtesy of the Thai FAD). *12c* Ian Glover visiting the site of the shipwreck which has been partially lifted and is being kept submerged while awaiting conservation, 2017.

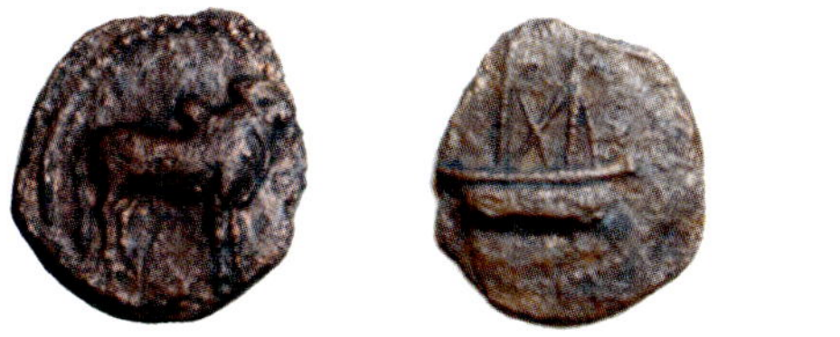

13

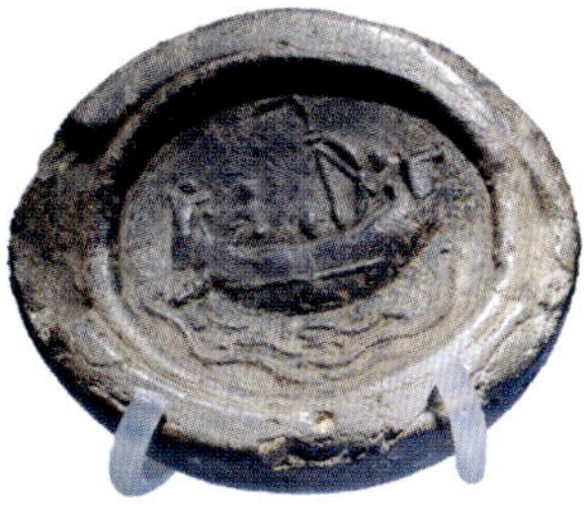

14

Fig 13 Śātavāhana copper-alloy coin, sixth century CE, with a double masted ship on one side and a humped bull on the other side found at Khlong Thom in Krabi Province on the peninsula. SuthiRatana Foundation, Bangkok, KLP399.
Fig 14 Baked terracotta impression of a fourth to fifth century CE Indian seal depicting an ocean-going vessel typical of the first millennium CE, found at Nakon Pathom, ht: 5 cm w: 4.5 cm, d. 3 cm. Bangkok National Museum, inv.no.2309.

Gold Ores

The Southeast Asian mainland, including lower Myanmar and the Thai-Malay peninsula region, was already known to Indian merchants of the first millennium BCE as Suvarṇabhūmi, 'Land of Gold', while *Suvarṇadvipa*, 'Islands of Gold', may refer to the Indonesian Archipelago including Sumatra. The question of whether Suvarṇabhūmi corresponds to a precise location is still a matter fuelled by national pride. It is a question which has fascinated scholars of both archaeology and early Buddhism for the last century with Myanmar, Thailand and Cambodia claiming to be the first nation in Southeast Asia to practice Buddhism. However, of the many references in ancient texts, none provide information as to a precise location for Suvarṇabhūmi, and it seems more appropriate to view the term as used in early Buddhist India to describe a mystical place to the east where early travellers and merchants sought wealth and prosperity. A place which is now generally regarded as denoting Southeast Asia, especially Thailand and the Irrawaddy Delta of Lower Myanmar (Srisakra Vallibhotoma 2018 [2561 BE]; Bunchar Pongpanich and Somchet Thinapong 2019). Historical sources inform us that the Chinese were impressed by the abundant quantities of gold on the Malay peninsula and Jin dynasty (265 CE–419 CE) Chinese emissaries refer to the Pre-Angkorian polity of Funan as having expanded its sphere of influence to encompass those parts of the Malay Peninsula with gold deposits. In his *Geography* (1.13–14),[17] Ptolemy (Stuckelberger and Grasshoff 2017) provides descriptions of the peninsula which he calls *Chryse Chersonesos*—golden peninsula. Sanskrit synonyms for gold such as *kanaka, hema* and *suvarṇa*, have been used to name rivers and mountains containing either alluvial or vein deposits of gold, and the word 'gold' is often associated with place names throughout the region. The *Rāmayāna* mentions Sugriva sending envoys to Hiranya Mountain[18] to the east, i.e. in the direction of Southeast Asia, which was known to be rich in precious metals, in search of Rāma's wife Sita. Another name for the region of modern Thailand is Laem Thong, which translates as "golden peninsula", and the word U Thong itself could be translated as gold workshop (Hunter Watson, personal communication).

Early Buddhist literature such as the *Supparaga Jātaka No. 463* describes merchants sailing from the pattanāma (port) of Bharuch, at the mouth of the River Narmada in Gujarat in western India. The *Supparaga Jātaka No.360* mentions merchants sailing from Bharuch to Suvarṇabhūmi and the *Jātaka Bk XXI No.539* describes a wealthy prince sailing to Suvarṇabhūmi (Ray 1994: 180). Although there is very little information about the capacity of these boats, *Jātaka Bk II No.196* mentions the transporting of 500 to 700 passengers, and Pliny (*Natural History VI.22)* (Bostock and Riley 1847–1848) mentions the carrying of 3,000 amphoras[19] in such ships. This search for Suvarṇabhūmi may be viewed as accompanying the expansion of Buddhism into Southeast Asia, and indeed there are supporting anecdotes for this within Theravada Buddhism. Buddhaswami's fifth century Sanskrit text *Bṛhatkathā - Lokasamgraha* relates the story of merchants who travelled to Suvarṇabhūmi by sea. Having crossed

17 Ptolemy of Alexandria completed his Geographical Guide in the mid-second century CE. His information is derived from accounts written in the late first to early second century CE by the cartographer Marinus of Tyre which are now lost.
18 *Hiranya* is Sanskrit for gold.
19 With regard to the tonnage of these ancient vessels, McCrindle (1927) says: "The amount of cargo carried by ancient ships was generally computed by the talent or the amphora, each of which weighed about a fortieth of a ton. The largest ships carried 10,000 talents or 250 tons. The talent and the amphora each represented a cubic foot of water, and as the Greek or Roman foot measured about .97 of an English foot, the talent and the amphora each weighed very nearly 57 lbs.

the "unfathomable" sea, they arrived at a coast and embarked on a long voyage on foot, travelling past the forested foothills of high mountains, which they crossed to finally reach a forest and a shallow river rich in gold sands (Dube 2003: 6). An eighth century Indian text known as the *Samaraiccakaha* describes a sea voyage to *Suvarṇadvipa* and the making of bricks from gold rich sands, which they inscribed with the name "Dhāraṇā" and then baked (Dube 2003: 6). The sintering of such gold rich sands by mixing the sand with water and shaping it into bricks may have afforded early gold explorers a relatively easy method of transporting the bulky raw material. Upon return it could then be carefully separated from its sand matrix in a more suitable environment.

Wherever it is found, alluvial and mined gold from primary vein deposits will invariably contain 5% to 40% silver and 0.1% to 1.5% copper by weight as the major impurities. There is evidence that early Asian explorers were aware of the differences in gold compositions, and an eleventh century Indian text refers to gold from Survarnadvipa as being of different types, being yellow gold colour and white shell colour, which presumably refers to the amounts of silver or copper contained in the alloy. An eleventh-century Sanskrit inscription of a Cham king by the name Rudravarman III found at Po Nagar Temple in Kauthara, near modern Nha Trang,Vietnam, mentions a donation by the king of seven *panas* of red coloured gold (*rakta kaladhautam*) and 23 *kattikas* and two *panas* of superior white gold (*sitatara kaladhautam*).[20]

Most metallic gold in today's world is retrieved by the deep mining of primary hard rock deposits, but in the prehistoric and early historic periods gold would undoubtedly have been extracted by panning alluvial sediments, a technique that requires little capital investment in equipment and no specialist technology. Villagers today can still be seen panning and dredging for gold on the on the Tenasserim River near Dawei, Myanmar using the same simple methods and the economic viability will be determined by the price of gold on the international market. When gold prices are at their highest, it becomes more economically advantageous to pan the gold bearing streams and the villagers sell their gold to middlemen who themselves sell it to merchants [Figs.15–17]. The author has also observed goldsmiths in Myanmar using locally panned gold to produce replica ancient beads (Bennett 2017).

While there is no modern commercial gold mining in the Lop Buri area, a nineteenth century map housed in the National Archives of Thailand and dated 1897 CE clearly shows the location of a gold mining area about 70 km north of Lop Buri city in Bo Thong Sub District, Nong Muang District, near Chan Sen archaeological site, Nakhon Sawan Province, which is now an agricultural field [Fig.18]. The gold mine was apparently still being worked after the Second World War but has now been abandoned (Bennett 2016).

Goldsmiths

Because a goldsmiths' tool set consists of only a few tools, the Indian goldsmiths would have been readily mobile and would have been drawn to early commercial centres close to riverine ports where there would have been not only a supply of the raw material they required but which would have been full of traders, merchants, and wealthy patrons. There is sadly no information concerning the identity and status of these craftsmen or their organisation and production system. How did the jeweller procure his gold? For whom was he making the items? What was the extent of political and/or religious control? Was there an unregulated private system? What was the goldsmiths' status within the society? Was there a guild structure as in India? Did the goldsmiths work in isolation or in workshops? Were the workshops in residential areas, religious compounds, or both? Were there masters and apprentices? What were the range of techniques employed and did they differ sufficiently to allow differentiation between workshops?

Because gold, silver and copper all melt together to form a complete solid solution series, an entire range of alloy compositions is technically possible. The alloy can be used as found, purified to remove the naturally occurring silver and copper, or debased by the addition of silver and copper for fraudulent purposes or in times of economic difficulty. In general, the composition of the gold jewellery and artefacts in societies that did not use a gold monetary system or in which the gold was not centrally controlled has been found to be much more random, varying from 45–99% gold, than in cultures where coins were widely circulated or where gold was used for fines or to settle disputes.[21] However, once gold

20 Majumdar (1986, 158–159) translated *rakta kaladhautam* as gold and *sitatara kaladhautam* as silver, but Daube (2003) has re-evaluated the texts and reached a more convincing explanation of *rakta kaladhautam* as red gold and *sitatara kaladhautam* as white gold.

21 By the time of the Khmer king Jayavarman V in the ninth century CE, punishments were according to the rank of the offender and royal princes were being fined twenty *pala* of gold (Majumdar 1953: 268–269).

was used as a measure of wealth, it would have become desirable to not only standardize the weights but at least to some extent to control the composition of gold by adding or removing other metals. Touchstones were certainly part of the goldsmiths' tool set as shown by the example recovered from the site of Khlong Thom, Krabi Province located along a tidal stream on the west coast of southern Thailand and now located about 20 kms from the Andaman Sea. This touchstone would have been the personal property of a Tamil goldsmith operating in the early century CE and has one of the earliest Tamil-Brāhmī script inscriptions found in Thailand, or indeed anywhere in Southeast Asia [Fig.19]. The two line inscription in Dāmili script and ancient Tamil language has been translated by K.V. Ramesh, an eminent South Indian epigraphist, as *Perumpatan̠ kal*, identifying it as being the stone belonging to the great "Goldsmith". *patan*, meaning "goldsmith" in ancient Tamil, occurs as *mahāsuvarṇakāra* in later Sanskrit inscriptions and was a professional designation (Ramesh 2012: 365). The dating of this inscription on paleographical grounds to the early centuries CE provides evidence of the early date at which Indian merchants and goldsmiths were travelling to the region in search of gold. The site of Khlong Thom which is also known as Khuan Luk Pat, which means "Bead Hill", has also produced a large number of locally produced gold coins which together with imitation gold pendants, tin-coin imitation pendants, their corresponding stone moulds and many waste gold fragments indicate that this was not only an internationally connected entrepôt but also an early production site operating by at least the third to sixth centuries CE (Bronson 1986: 213; Borell 2017a). The gold conch shell coins are of a standard weight (Borell 2017a:157) and the analysis of nine coins (Mitchiner and Pollard 1990) suggests that the goldsmihths were not purifying their raw material but were simply producing the coins from natural unrefined alluvial gold with between 56% and 77.8% gold and 22.1% and 43.7% silver with no added copper (0.1% to 0.49%).

Archaeological Evidence

That gold first appears in the archaeological record in about 400 BCE, at the same time as iron, semi-precious stone polishing, and glass working, suggests that the techniques of extracting and working gold were introduced to Southeast Asia via Indian and/or Chinese merchants seeking gold (Pryce et al. 2008; Bennett 2010, 2015; 2018). Until the end of the Iron Age, gold was sometimes placed in the inhumation burials that are found throughout Southeast Asia. Gold beads and ornaments have been reported from several protohistoric sites in the Lop Buri area [Figs. 20–21] including Bang Ka Pi, Ta Luang and Lop Buri Artillery Camp, where some 50 burials associated with a large number of both bronze and iron artefacts and gold beads were excavated (Bennett 1988). In Khok Samrong District, Lop Buri Province a looter found a spiral gold earring in the mouth of a burial, and at Dong Marum, Khok Samrung District, Lop Buri Province looters found gold beads and an unfinished agate bead which was shaped but not drilled.

Because gold can be hammered repeatedly to achieve very thin sheet and leaf without fracturing or cracking, it lends itself to the covering and/or coating of objects made of other materials. Beads produced by simply wrapping hammered gold foil over clay cores were excavated at the Iron Age cemetery site of Noen U-Loke in the Mun Valley in northeastern Thailand dating to the third to fourth centuries CE (Higham 2014: 239–256), and another burial at the site was of a man wearing silver ear coils covered in gold leaf. A gold-covered silver ear ornament, found at the site of Prohear (Reinecke 2015), about 65 km east of Phnom Penh, Cambodia and 40 km west of the Vietnamese border, dated to between the second century BCE and first century CE, indicates that gold was not confined to covering less expensive materials but was also used to cover other precious metals. The value attributed to gold in the protohistoric period may not have been that which we accord it today. This author interviewed a well-known looter who claims to have plundered over one hundred burials in the Central Plain area over the last two decades. He reported that graves had often been looted shortly after deposition, and that only large agate beads appeared to have been taken, leaving gold and other beads behind. He also reported that when he did recover burials which contained large agate beads, these had often been intentionally damaged prior to burial. This suggests that these large agate beads were more prestigious and sought after than the gold. The ancient inhabitants were aware of the dangers of looting and preferred to be buried with a small chip removed from their most precious beads in order to ensure they remained in the grave.

By the early centuries CE, these traditional practices had largely been replaced by Indianized burial practices and the gold recovered today is that which was deliberately concealed in hoards for safe keeping and never subsequently recovered, accidentally lost or misplaced, or deposited in the upper levels of the towers of religious sanctuaries. The head and the foot of a Buddha statue [Fig. 22] (Bennett 2017: Cat. Nos. 1 and 2) were recovered in 1963 by the Suphan Buri FAD during the restoration of Monument 2 at U Thong. Although both the head and the foot were found within the same monument, the head had been deposited on the terrace near the northwest corner of the building while the foot was found beneath the western entrance (FAD 2002 [2545 BE]).

Excavated finds are, however, extremely rare and the Dvāravatī gold objects [Figs. 23–26] which are on display in the U Thong and Bangkok national museums and those in private collections [Figs. 27–30] (Bennett 2017) have almost all without exception been discovered accidentally either during construction work accompanying the urbanisation of the rural landscape or by agricultural workers.

An exceptional jewellery assemblage was found ten years ago by looters in the ancient settlement area of U Thong in the direction of Khao Tham Thiam to the north west of the present day city and close to the Chinese cemetery. Eleven gold items were found in a small hole deep in the ground, in a position which suggested that they had been carefully placed there. Possibly wrapped in textile, which no longer survives, the jewellery was bundled together and there were no other associated objects.

A lone hinged split-ear ornament [Fig. 31] was recovered in 2010 during construction work in the U Thong National Museum compound, which is within the ancient settlement itself, and was presumably accidentally lost by its original owner. These hinged types of ear ornament are quite rare but an almost identical one was excavated at the ancient port site of Oc Eo in southern Vietnam, dated to the second to the fifth CE (Miksic 2003: Pl. 1.2; Richter 2000: Pl: 33). Other Javanese examples dated to the Classic Period are on display at Yale University Museum (Miksic 2011: Pl. 49) and in the Ghysels Collection, Brussels (van Custom 2001: 257). The more usual type of split-ear ornament is found over widespread areas in Southeast Asia and is shown on the Dvāravatī period terracotta friezes and in moulds for casting found at U Thong [Figs. 32–33].

There are a few surviving auspicious ornaments dating to the Dvāravatī period such as the *dharmacakra* [Fig.23], the gold *Kinnari*, a mythical creature half bird half woman [Fig.24], and the *Kirtimukha* [Fig.25], which have found their way to various national museums (Bennett 2017) but unfortunately, very little ancient gold survives. It was, and continues to be, melted down for reuse, thus avoiding possible conflict with the authorities (Bennett 2015). Estimates suggest that perhaps less than 5% of the gold artefacts that once circulated in Southeast Asia survives (Reinecke 2015) and the small amount of gold which does survive is mostly in the form of simple beads and a few elaborate items of jewellery which clearly do not represent the vast array of intricate jewellery which circulated during the Dvāravatī period. Only the stone and stucco sculptures, such as those from the important Buddhist site of Khu Bua, Ratchaburi Province , preserve evidence of the elaborate personal adornment which would have formed such a prominent part of Dvāravatī culture [Figs.36–38].

Conclusion

The quest for scarce and valuable raw materials such as gold would have acted as major stimuli for the Indian merchants who were not only sourcing gold ore but, from the archaeological evidence, were also involved in the significant production of finished objects to supply long distance markets. These commercial centres would therefore have facilitated not only the supply and exchange of raw materials and finished goods but also the exchange of ideas and cultural beliefs. The growth in trade of highly prized rare prestige goods and the spread of iconographic conventions which accompanied the expansion of the "newly" emerging power structures within the Dvāravatī sphere of influence, which was clearly much larger than any unified political unit, would no doubt have fuelled the instigation and development of new trade routes, both overland and overseas.

As part of a symbolic system used to indicate not only rank, status, and wealth within the community, jewellery would also have been used as a means of displaying political and cultural affiliations within a wider geo-political region and would have been especially susceptible to changes not only in terms of style but also in terms of materials used and techniques employed. The study of the few artefacts themselves and their representations in the sculpture can increase our understanding not only of the status of the jewellery but also of the functioning mechanisms and structure of the gold industry and the complexity of ancient trading connections which would have been strongly influenced by the political alliances which were in favour at a given moment. Certainly the

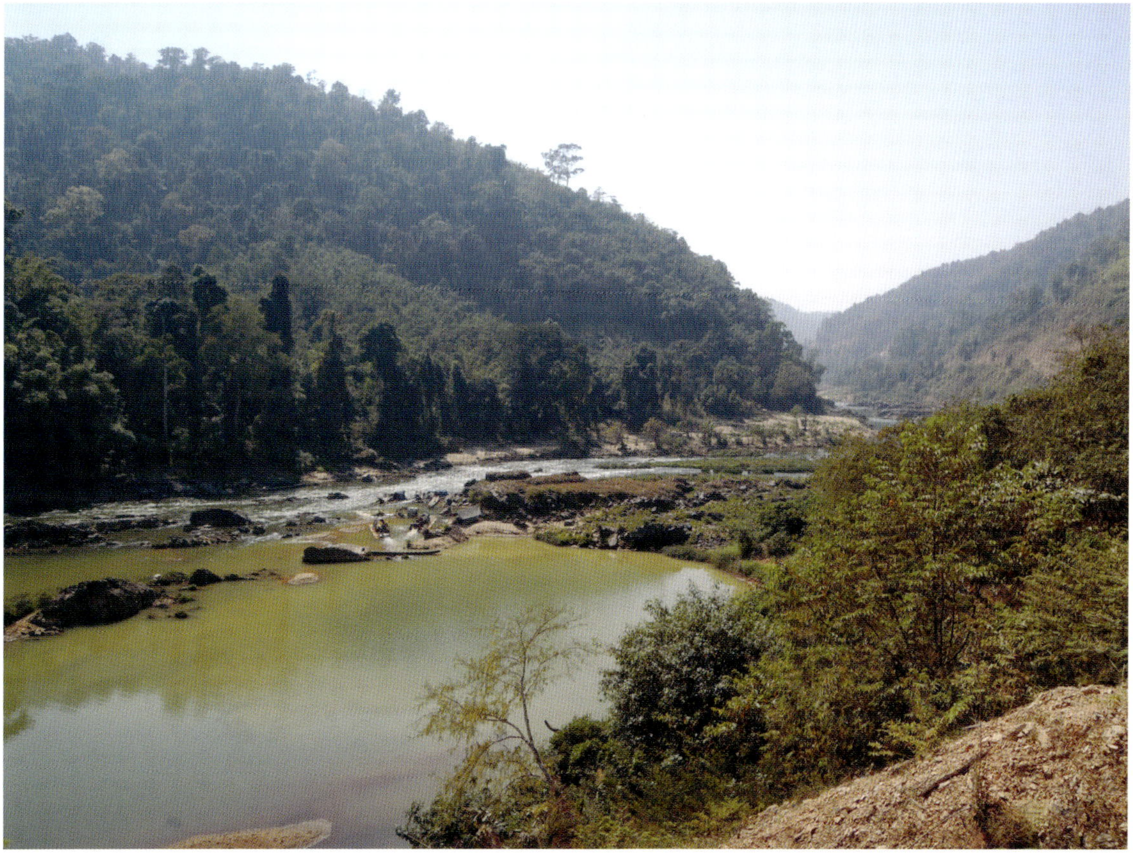

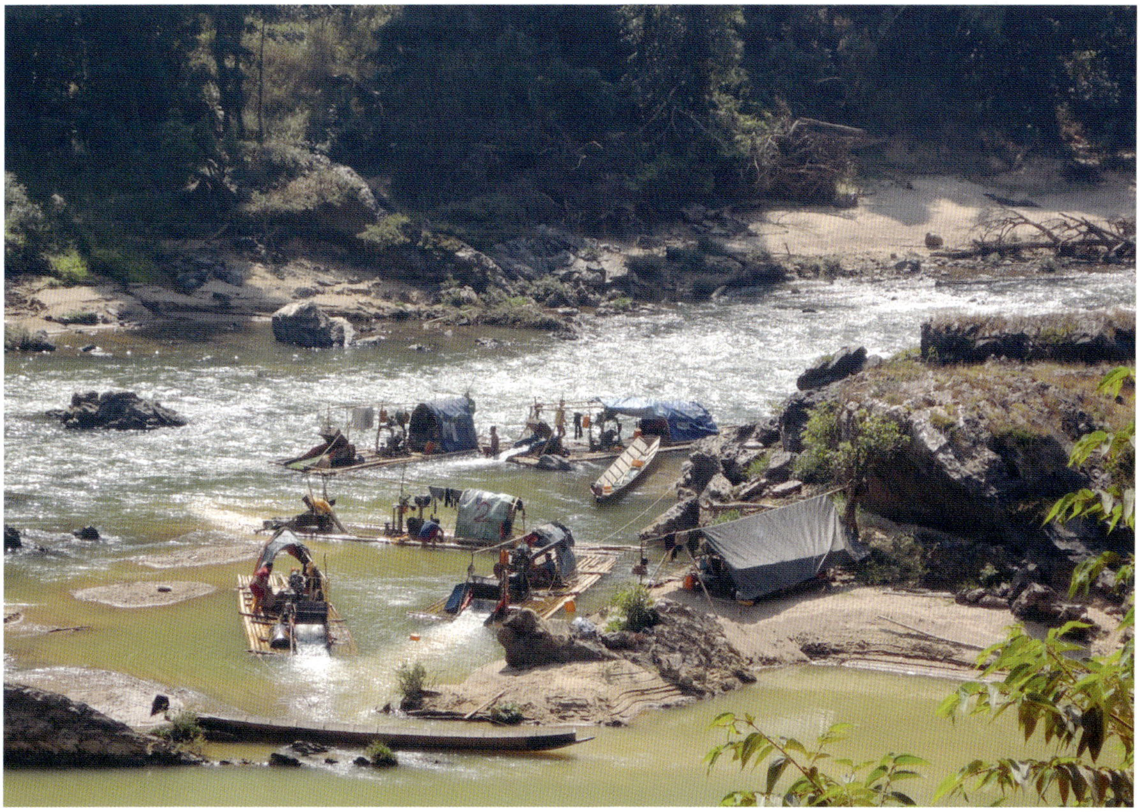

Figs. 15–16 Villagers today dredging for gold on the Tenasserim River near Dawei, Myanmar.

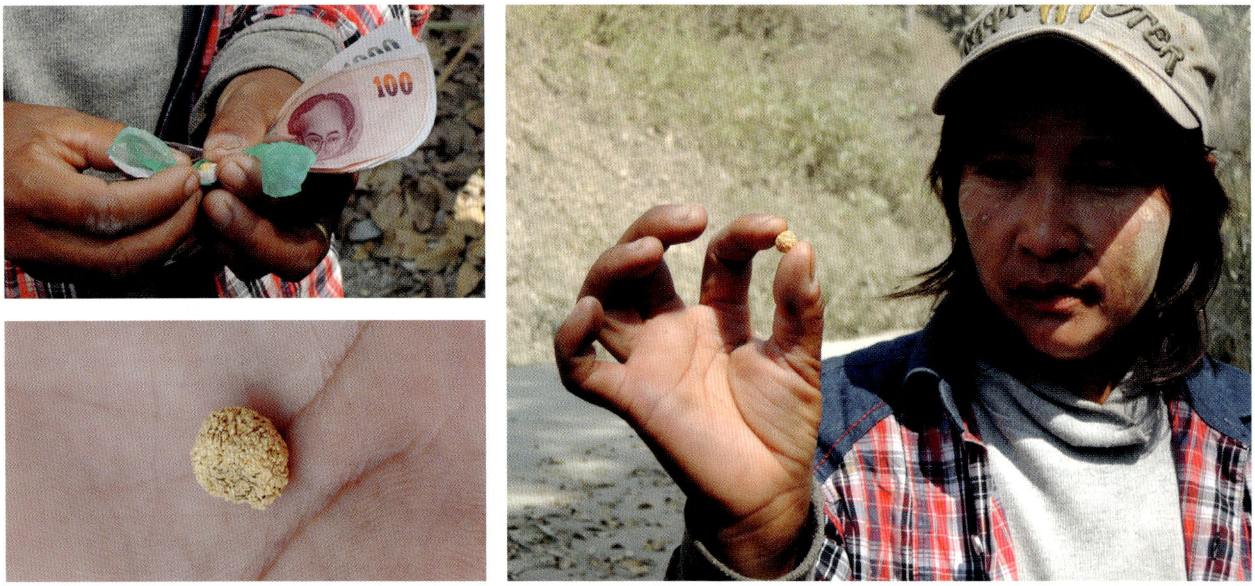

17

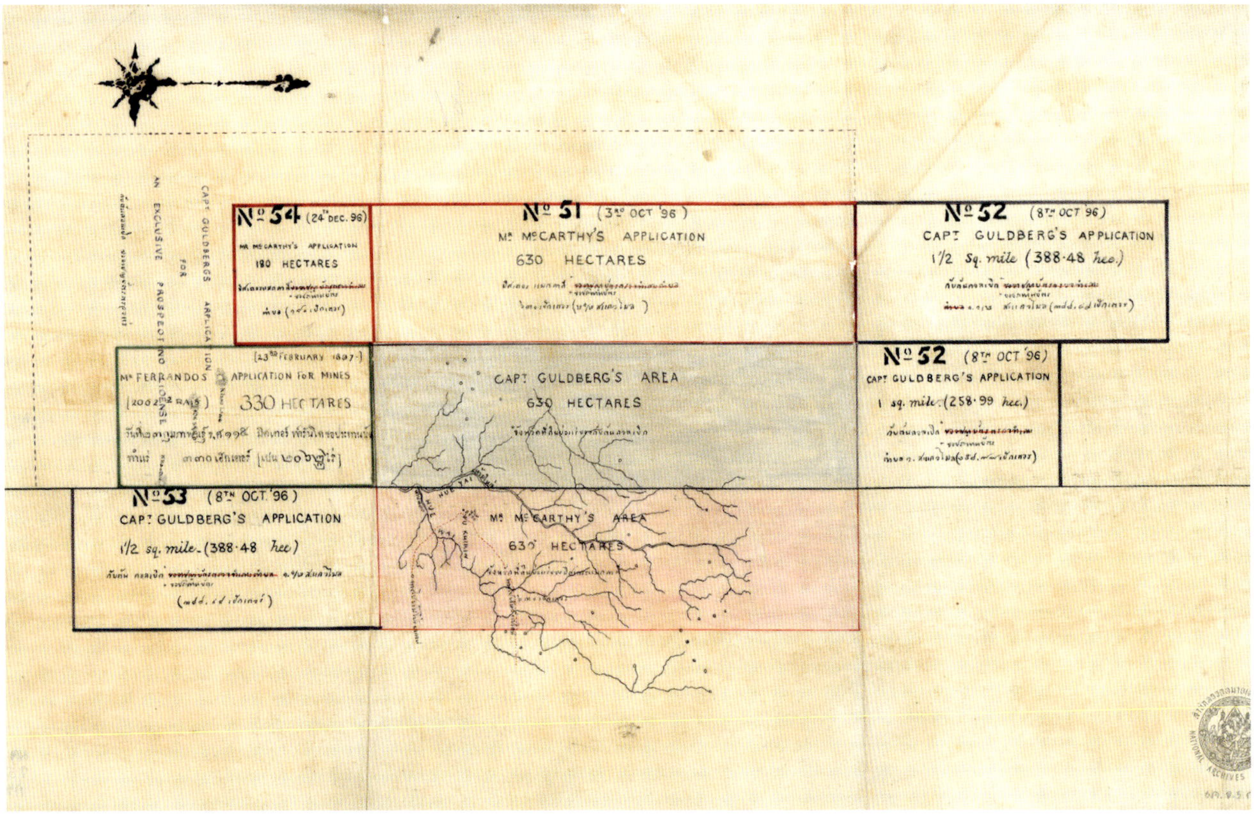

18

Fig 17 Villager on the Tenasserim River near Dawei selling gold to middlemen.
Fig 18 Map dated to 1897 CE, showing a gold mining area north of Lop Buri Province (National Archives of Thailand, Bangkok).

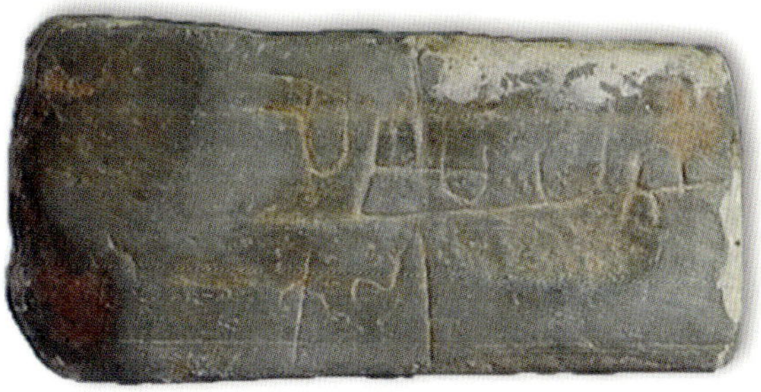

19

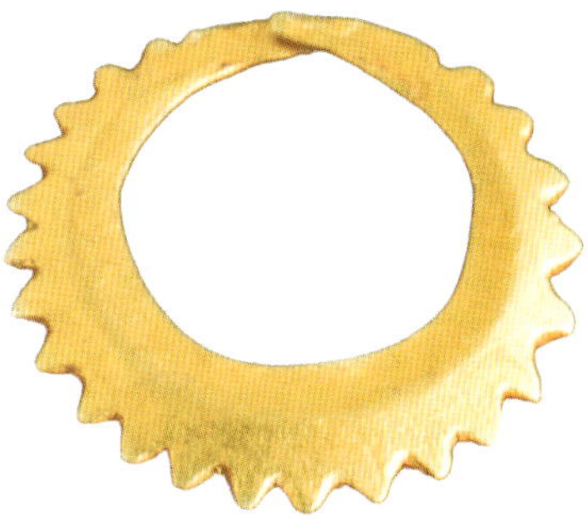

Weight: 0.53 g.
Ht: 11.41 mm
Width: 12.41 mm
Manufacture: hammered from a cast blank with the decorative edge cut with a chisel
Condition: complete
Find Location: close to Sap Champa archaeological site, Lop Buri Province
Present Location: private collection

20

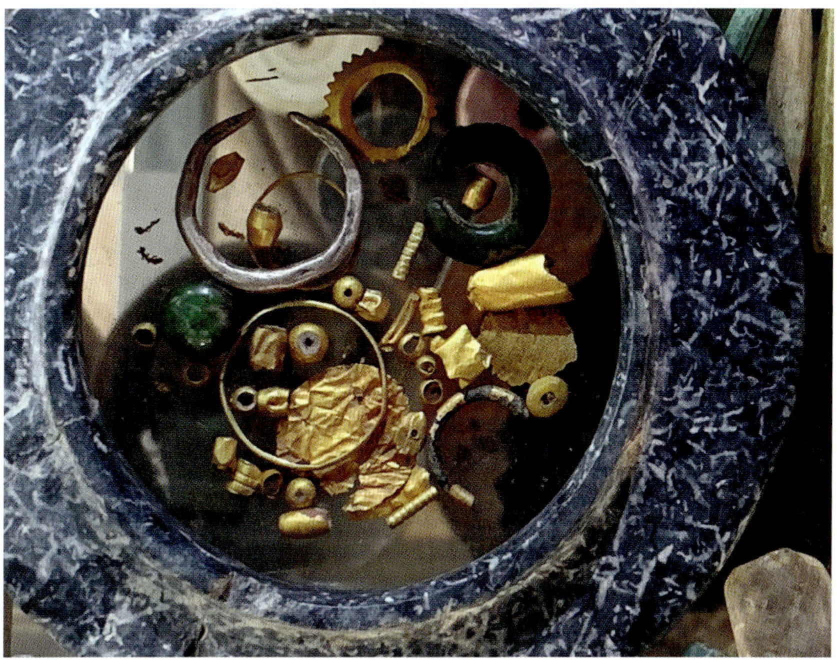

21

Fig. 19 A goldsmith's touchstone with a Brāhmī inscription identifying it as belonging to a Tamil goldsmith operating in the early centuries CE, Khlong Thom Phra Kru Athan Sankarakit Museum, Krabi Province.
Fig.20 The earring is hammered from a cast blank and the decorative edge cut with a chisel.
Fig. 21 Gold found by looters in the Lop Buri area.

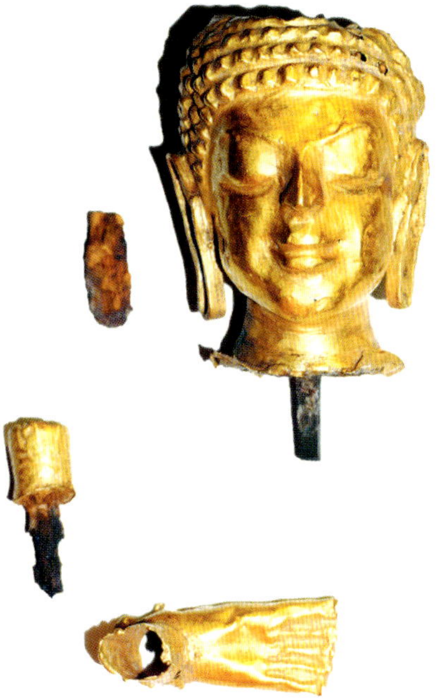

Weight: 57.95 g including iron armature and soil
Height of head without tang: 55.2 mm
Diameter of neck opening: 38.5 mm
Width: 35.3 mm
Width of left ear: 26.8 mm
Width of right ear: 26.5 mm
MT: 0.54, 0.55 and 0.62 mm
Manufacture: hammered gold sheet over a clay core and iron armature
Elemental composition:
Front of forehead: 94.62% gold, 4.57% silver, 0% copper, 0% tin, (0.79% iron from surface contamination)
Front of hair: 94.79% gold, 4.38% silver, 0% copper, 0.65% tin
cheek: 95.3% gold, 4.56% silver, 0% copper, 0% tin
Back of head: 91.84–95.09% gold, 4.56–5.19% silver, 0% copper, 0.2–0.54% tin
Find location: objects found in 1963 during the restoration of chedi No.2 UThong sanctuary by FAD Suphan Buri. Found on the terrace of the north west corner together with a stucco head, terracotta tablets, a terracotta *kinnari* and a fragment of a *dharmachakra*
Present location: U Thong National Museum
Inventory number: 10/76/2506 (1953 CE) (previous inventory number 8/2507)

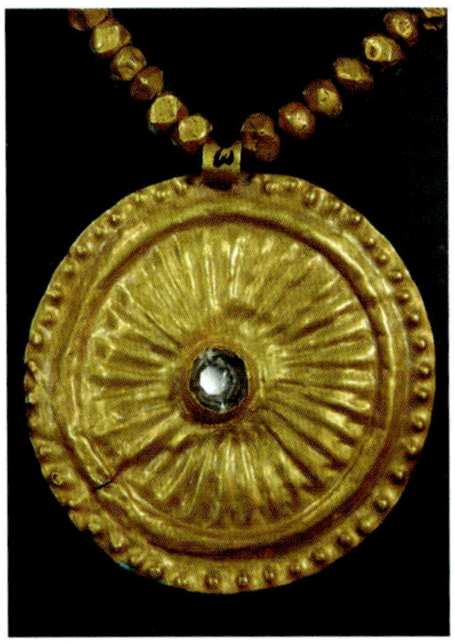

Diameter of pendant: 42.69 mm
Manufacture of pendant: Hammered into a stone mould. The stone inlay (not identified) in the centre of the pendant appears to be original and is mechanically held in place by crimping the surrounding gold. The suspension loop was made of a strip of gold sheet which was soldered to the top of the reverse of the pendant and simply folded over on itself
Elemental composition:
Front: 81.12% gold, 16.34% silver, 1.38% copper, 0.47% tin
Back: 81.86% gold, 16.54% silver, 1.09% copper, 0.50% tin
Condition: complete and in very good condition
Evidence of use: evidence of wear over the surface
Inventory number of pendant: 10/88/2503 (1960 CE)

Fig.22 Buddha head and foot recovered in 1963 by the Supan Buri FAD during the restoration of Monument 2 at U Thong.
Fig.23 Gold *dharmacakra* pendant, U Thong National Museum.

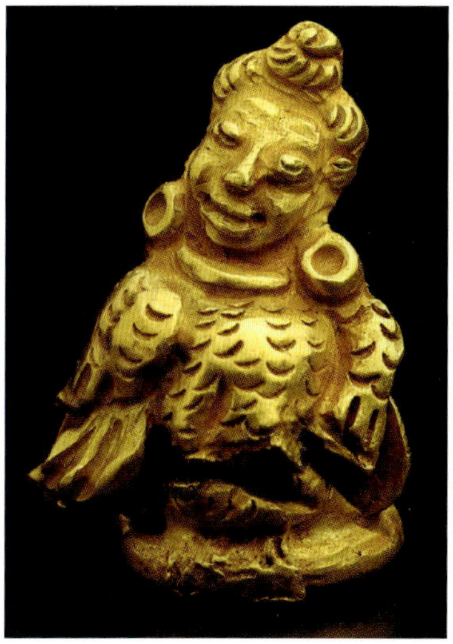

Weight: 2.87 g
Height: 18.89 mm
Width: 12.4 mm
Manufacture: The figure is made by repoussé with additional detail chased into the gold surface. A supporting backplate has been attached to the reverse of the figure and a wire loop has been soldered onto the base which would have allowed the object to be worn (width of wire: 1.9 mm)
Elemental composition: 87.1% gold, 16.15% silver, 0.96% copper, 0% tin
Find location: U Thong ancient settlement area
Present location: U Thong National Museum
Inventory number: 10/275/2509 (1956 CE)

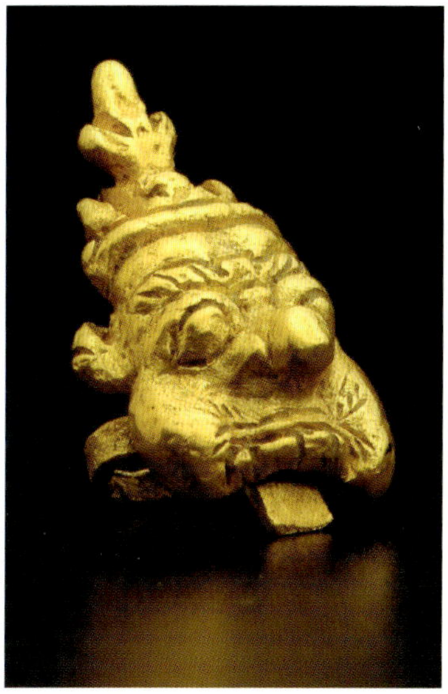

Weight: 4.57 g
Height: 18.8 mm
Width: 10.7 mm
Elemental composition: 72.25% gold, 19.07% silver, 0% copper, 0% tin, some soil contamination
Manufacture: cast gold, with some subsequent chasing. A slight feathering is visible around the mouth due to the use of a straight edged tool to chase around corners. The attachment ring on the reverse is soldered on.
Condition: complete
Evidence of use: no
Find location: unknown, register only says it was found in U Thong
Present location: U Thong National Museum
Inventory number: 10/274/2509

Fig.24 Gold *Kinnari*, a mythical creature half bird half woman, courtesy of U Thong National Museum.
Fig.25 Gold *Kirtimukha*. An attachment soldered onto the reverse allowed the object to be worn, courtesy of U Thong National Museum.

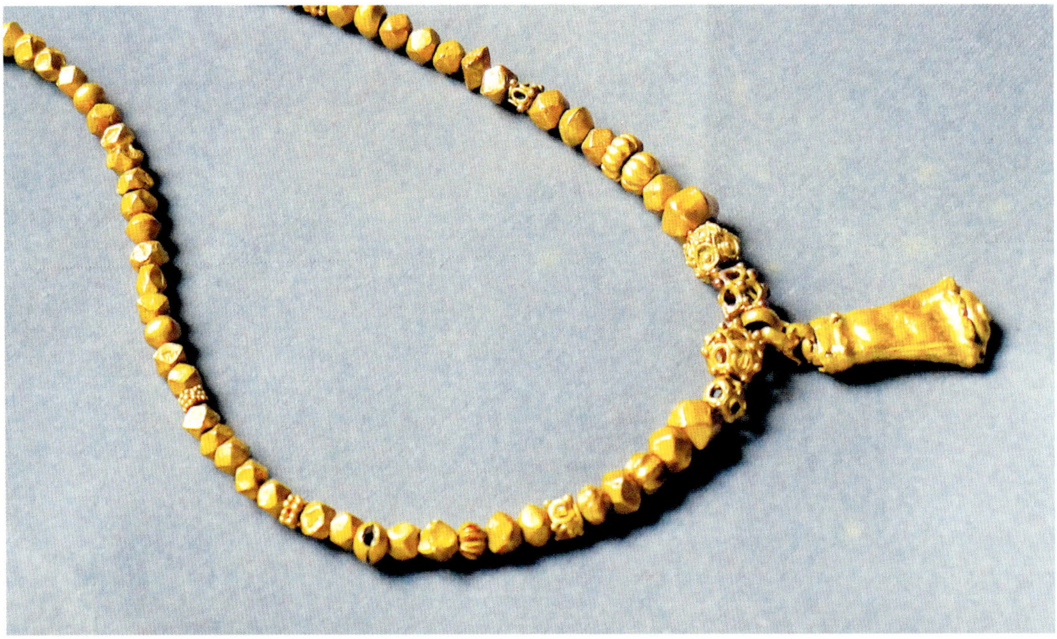

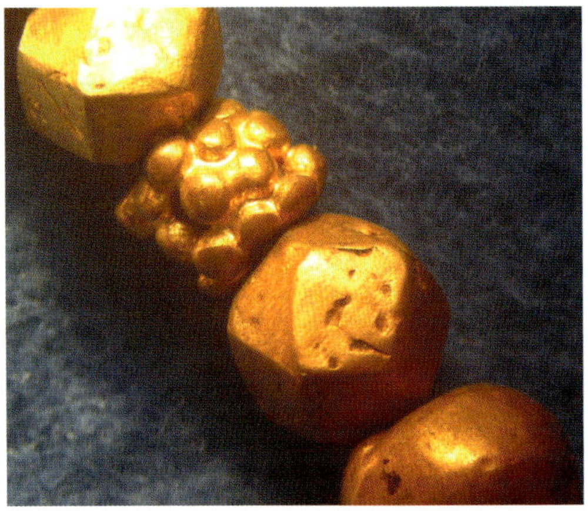

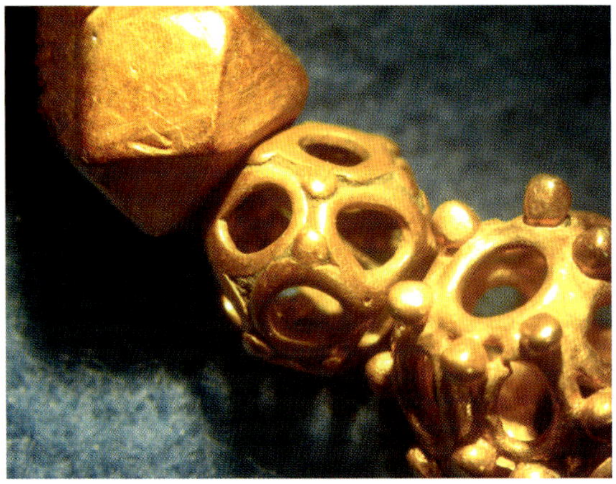

Weight of pendant and beads: 29.25 g (including modern clasp)
Length of necklace as displayed: 300 mm (including beads and pendant)
Length of necklace as displayed beads only: 275 mm
Height of pendant excluding clasp: 22.07 mm
Height of pendant including clasp: 25.8 mm
Manufacture of pendant: cast with a small amount of reworking
Elemental analysis of pendant:
Front: 94.26% gold, 4.77% silver, 0.29% copper
Reverse: 93.05% gold, 5.39% silver and 0.5% copper
Manufacture of beads: nine types of bead were identified. These include beads constructed from gold wire and individual granules, hammered gold sheet over clay cores of different shapes and cast beads
Condition: complete
Evidence of use: evidence of wear over the surface
Find location: acquired in 1975 reportedly with many other gold items which formed part of a colonel's collection. Present location: Bangkok National Museum
Inventory number: not available

Fig.26 Gold beads restrung as a necklace, Bangkok National Museum.

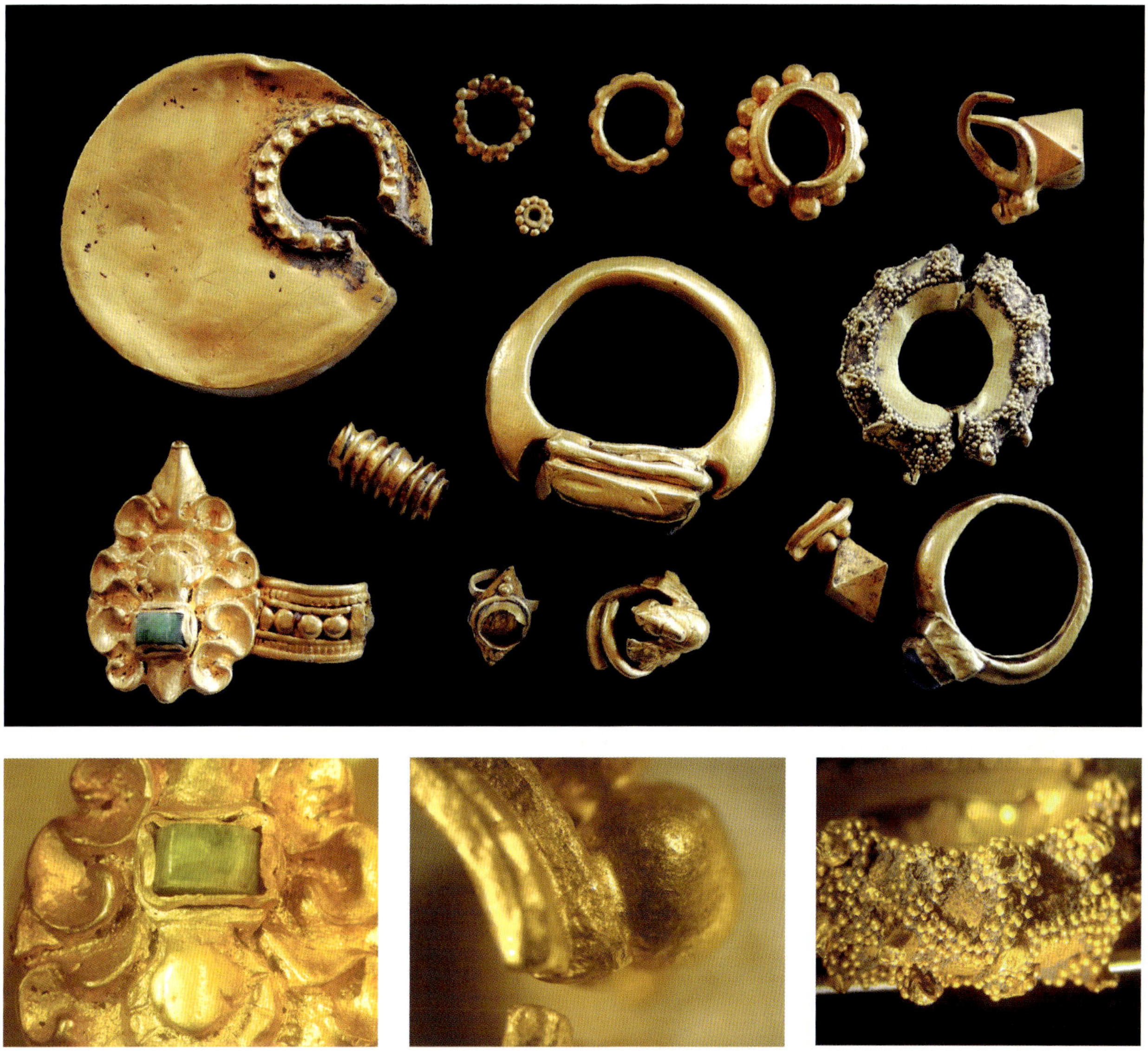

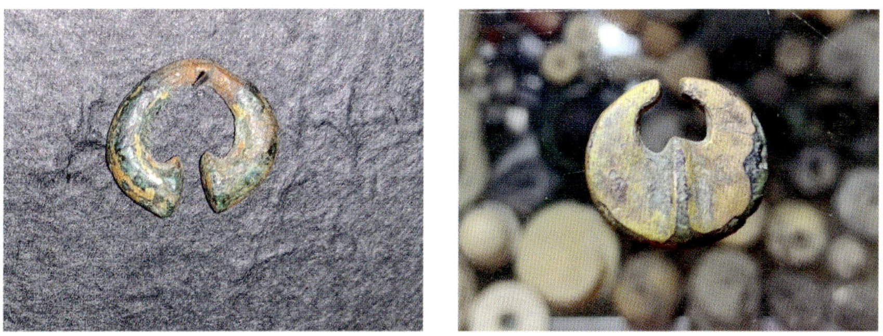

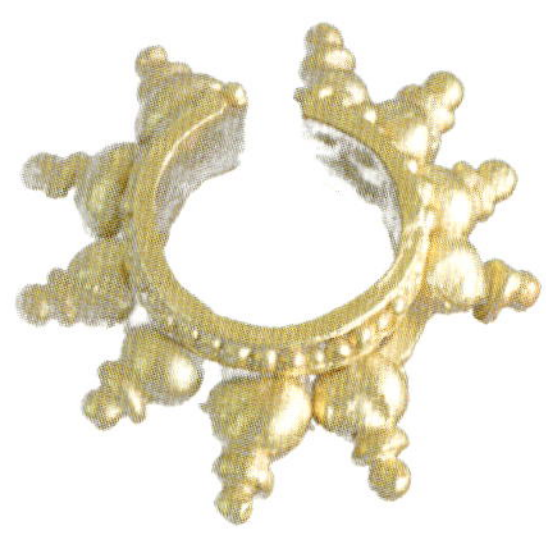

Figs.27a–d Gold jewellery found in U Thong ancient settlement, Private collection.
Figs.28a–b Gilt bronze earrings found by villagers near Sap Champa, Lop Buri Province, 30a diam 2 cm Sap Champa Museum, 29b Private collection.
Fig.30 Gold ornament found by looter, Wt: 6.98 grams Ht: 23.2 mm W: 23 mm. Inner width: 9.9 mm, made of wire, gold strip and granulation, Lop Buri Province, private collection.

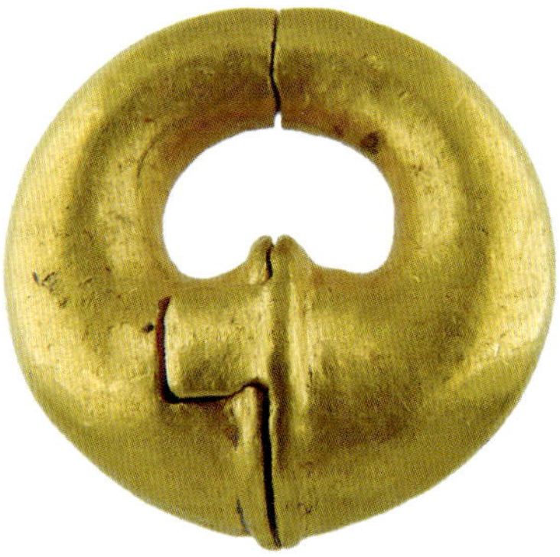

Weight: 26.11 g
Weight of half without tang: 12.27 g
Weight of half with tang: 13.86 g
Height: 19.7 mm
Diameter: 20.4 mm
Manufacture: cast in a two piece mould
Elemental composition: half without tang 98.76% gold, 1.15% silver, 0% copper, 0.0% tin, half with tang 98.31% gold, 1.22% silver, 0% copper, 0.0% tin
Find location: found accidentally in museum compound
Present location: U Thong National Museum
Inventory number: 10/001/2553

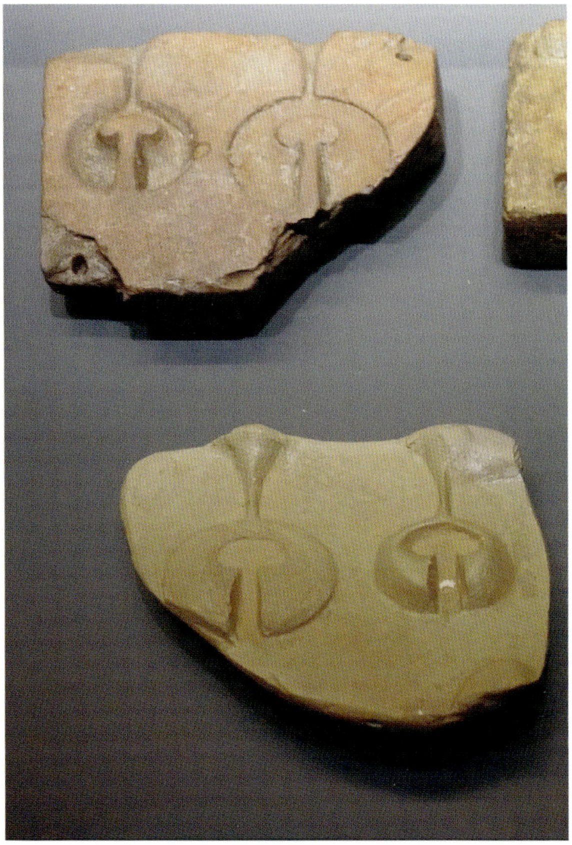

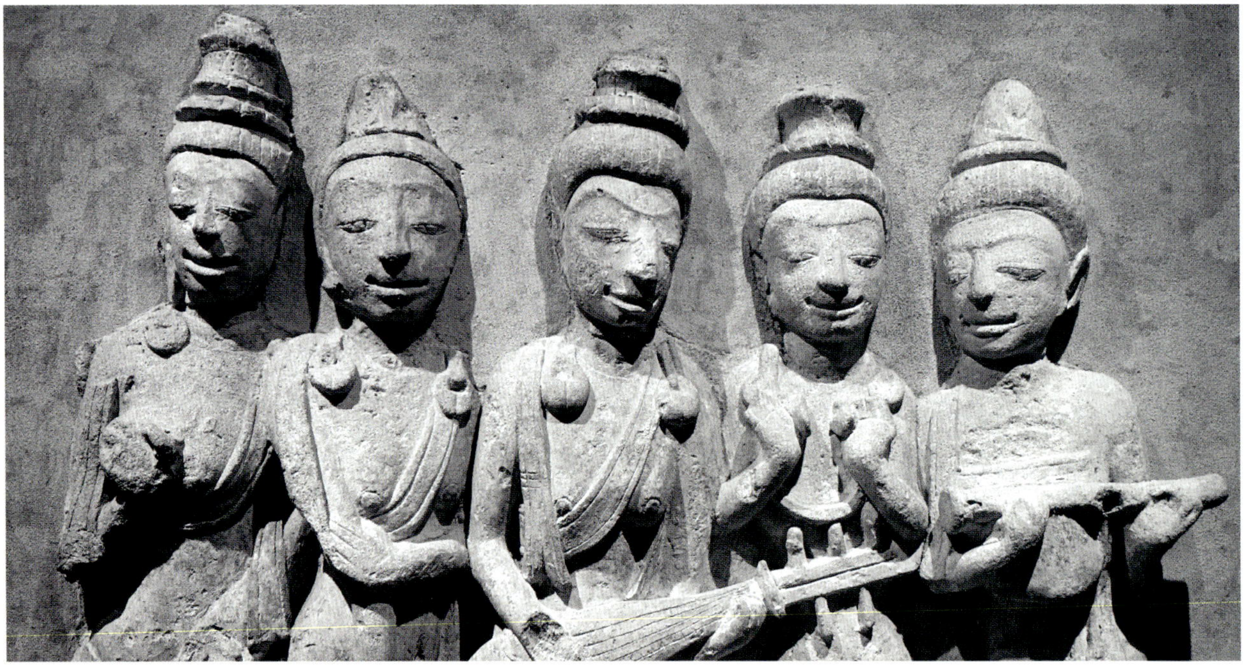

Fig.31 Dvāravatī period hinged split-ear ornament recovered in 2010 during construction work within the compound of the U Thong National Museum.
Fig.32 Sandstone mould and corresponding modern impression used for casting unhinged split-ear ornaments, UThong National Museum.
Fig.33 Terracotta relief from Khu Bua, Ratchaburi Province depicting musicians wearing split ears ornaments, Bangkok National Museum, 311/2511.

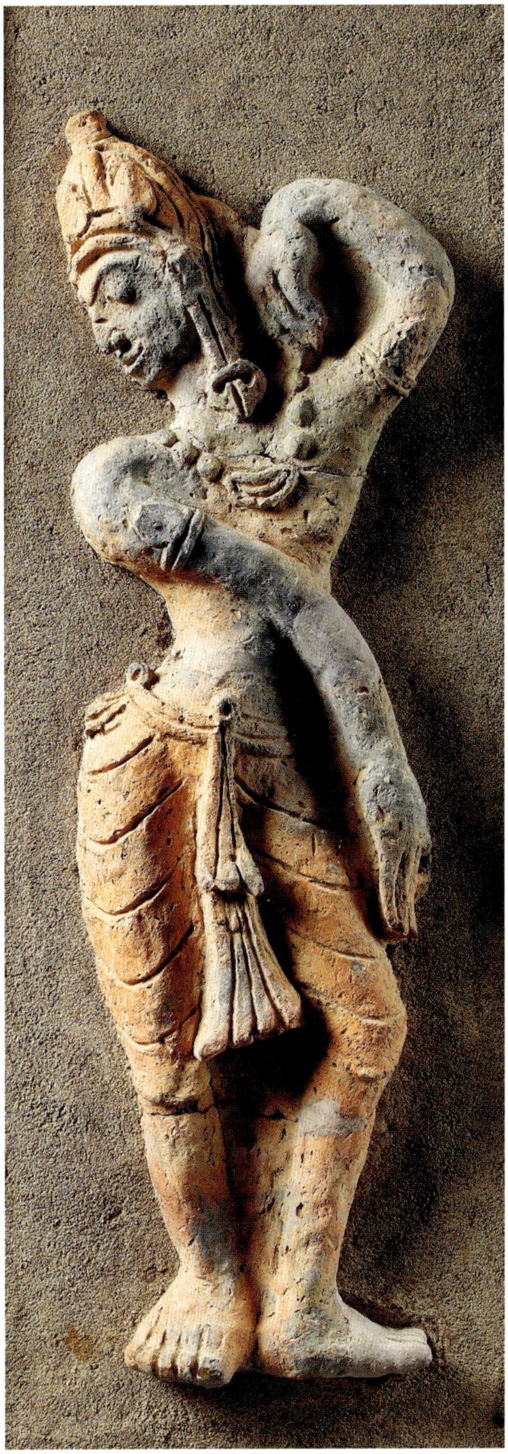

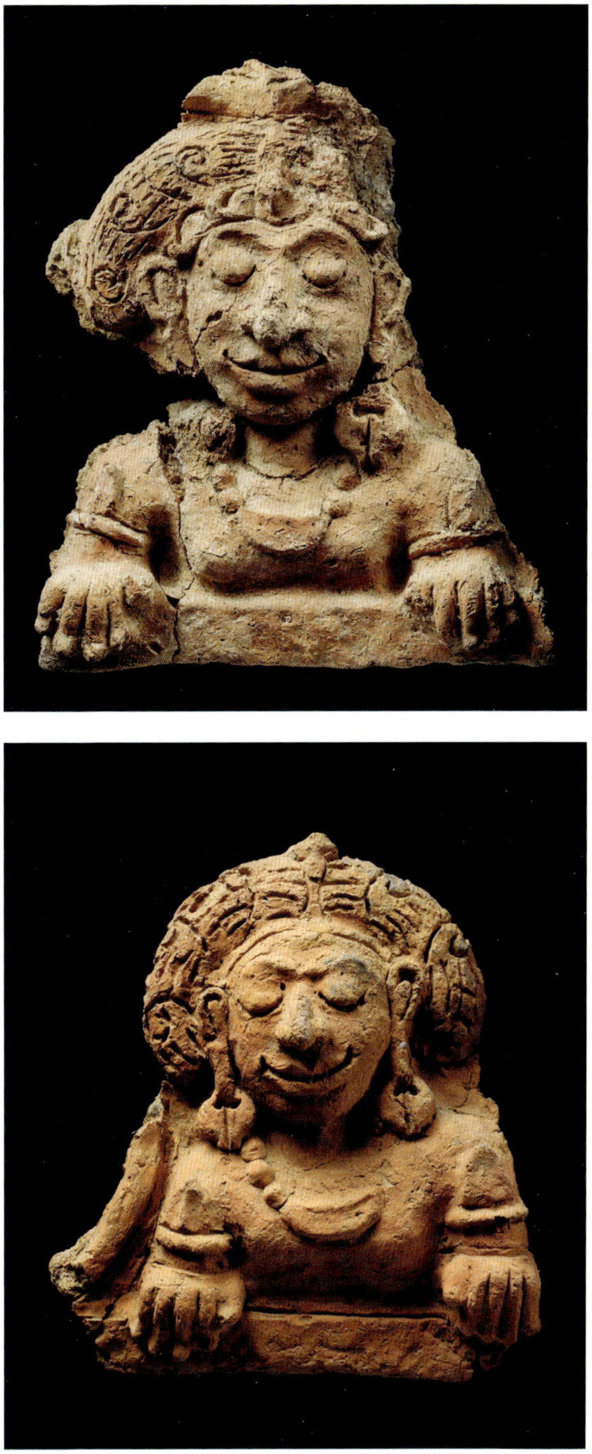

Figs.34 Terracotta relief depicting a male dancer showing the dress and elaborate jewellery including split-ear ornament, arm bands and necklace, U Thong National Museum 10/29/2543 (Baptiste and Zéphir 2009). Courtesy Guimet Museum.
Figs.35a–b Elaborate jewellery and split-ear ornament depicted on Dvāravatī period sculpture, Somdet Phra Narai National Museum, Lop Buri Province, 2003–2004/2518 2007/2518 and U Thong National Museum, 30/2543, 1/24, 2002/2518. Courtesy Musée Guimet.

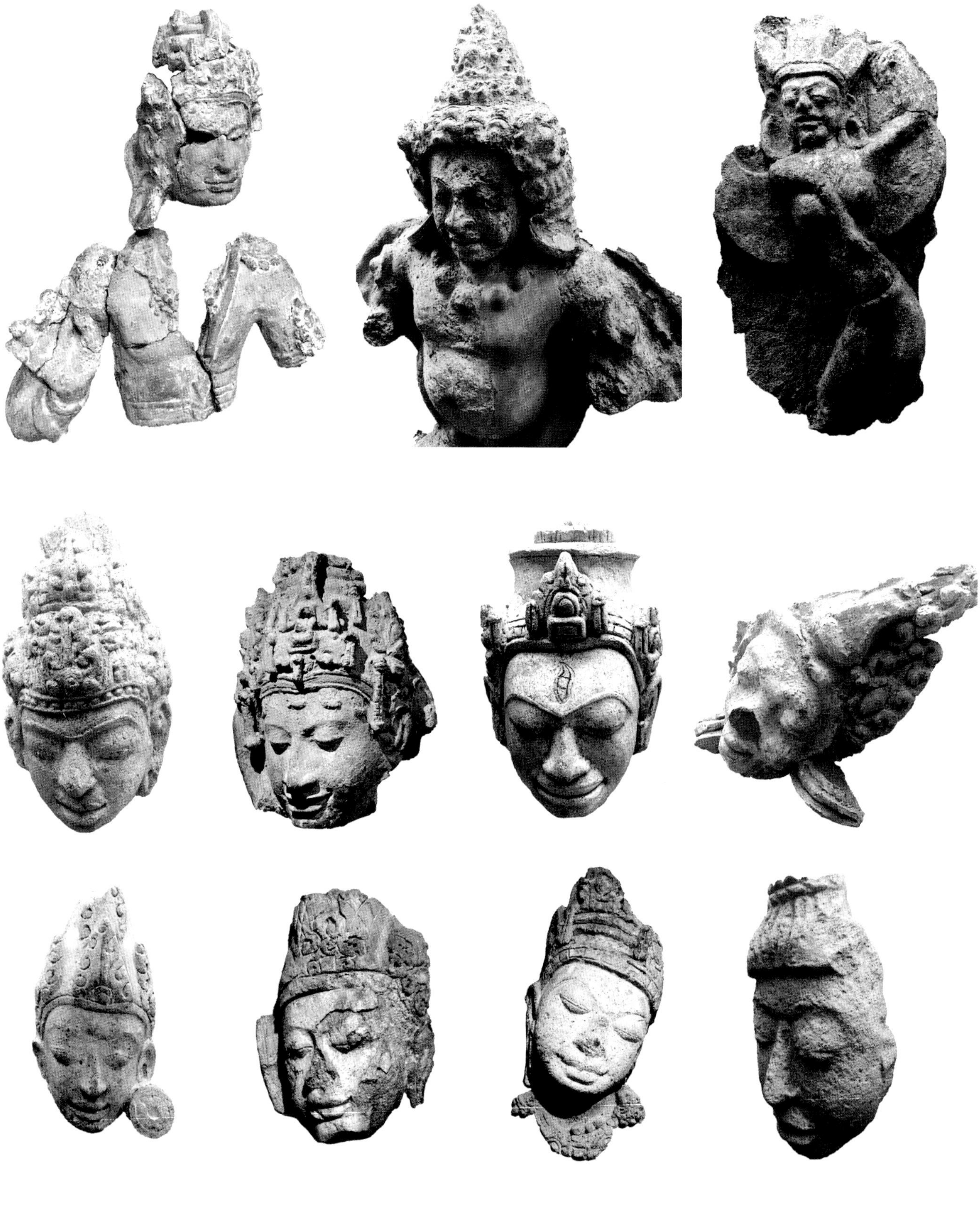

Fig.36 Terracotta sculpture depicting diadems with elaborate decoration. Many of these probably existed in gold or were perhaps made of leather and textile covered in gold foil. Phra Pathom Chedi National Museum, Nakhon Pathom and Bangkok National Museum.

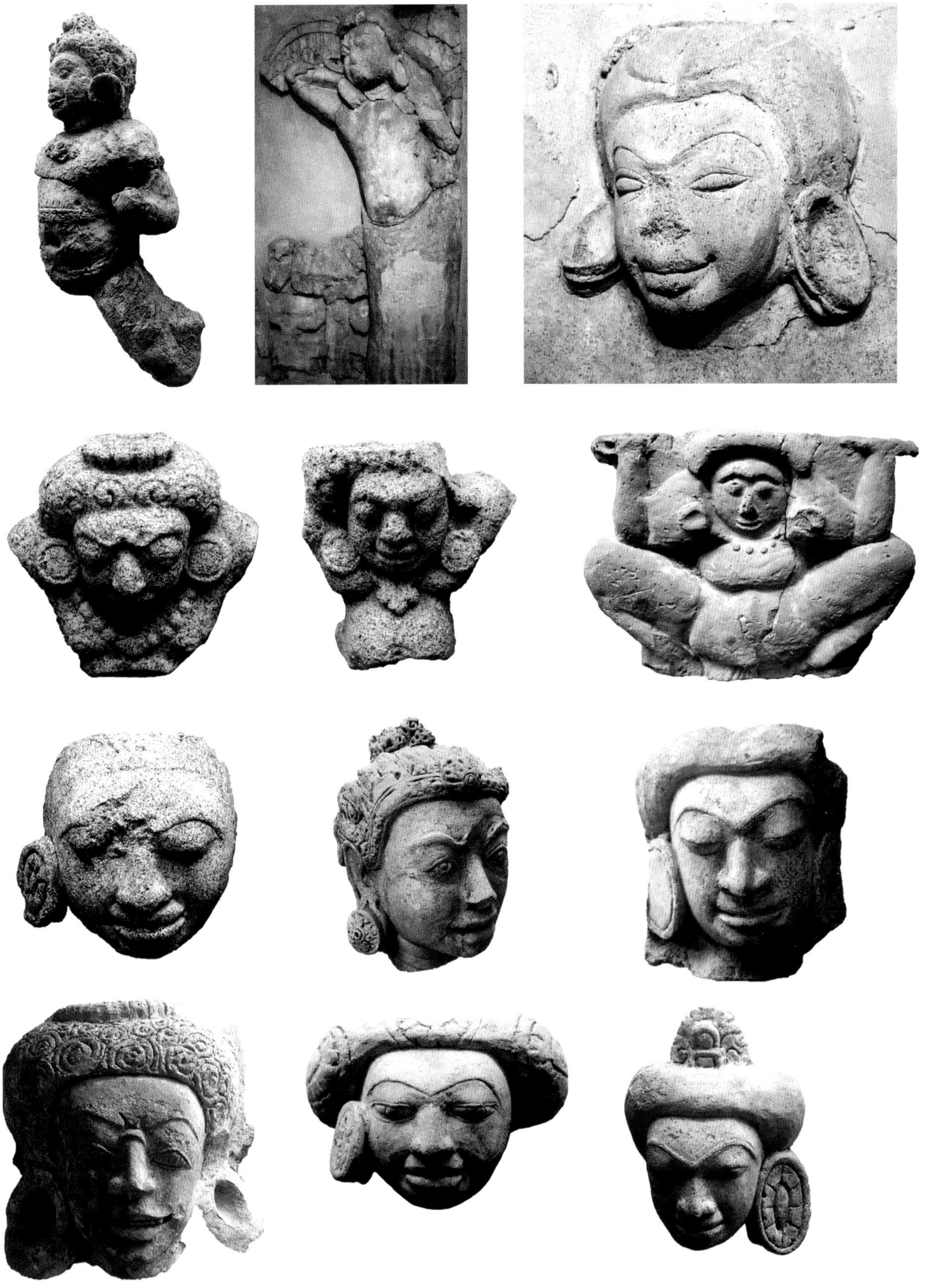

Fig.37 Stucco sculpture depicting figures wearing large discal ear ornaments. Many of these probably represent gold originals or those made of organic materials covered in gold foil. Khu Bua, Ratchaburi Province. Phra Pathom Chedi National Museum, Nakhon Pathom and Bangkok National Museum.

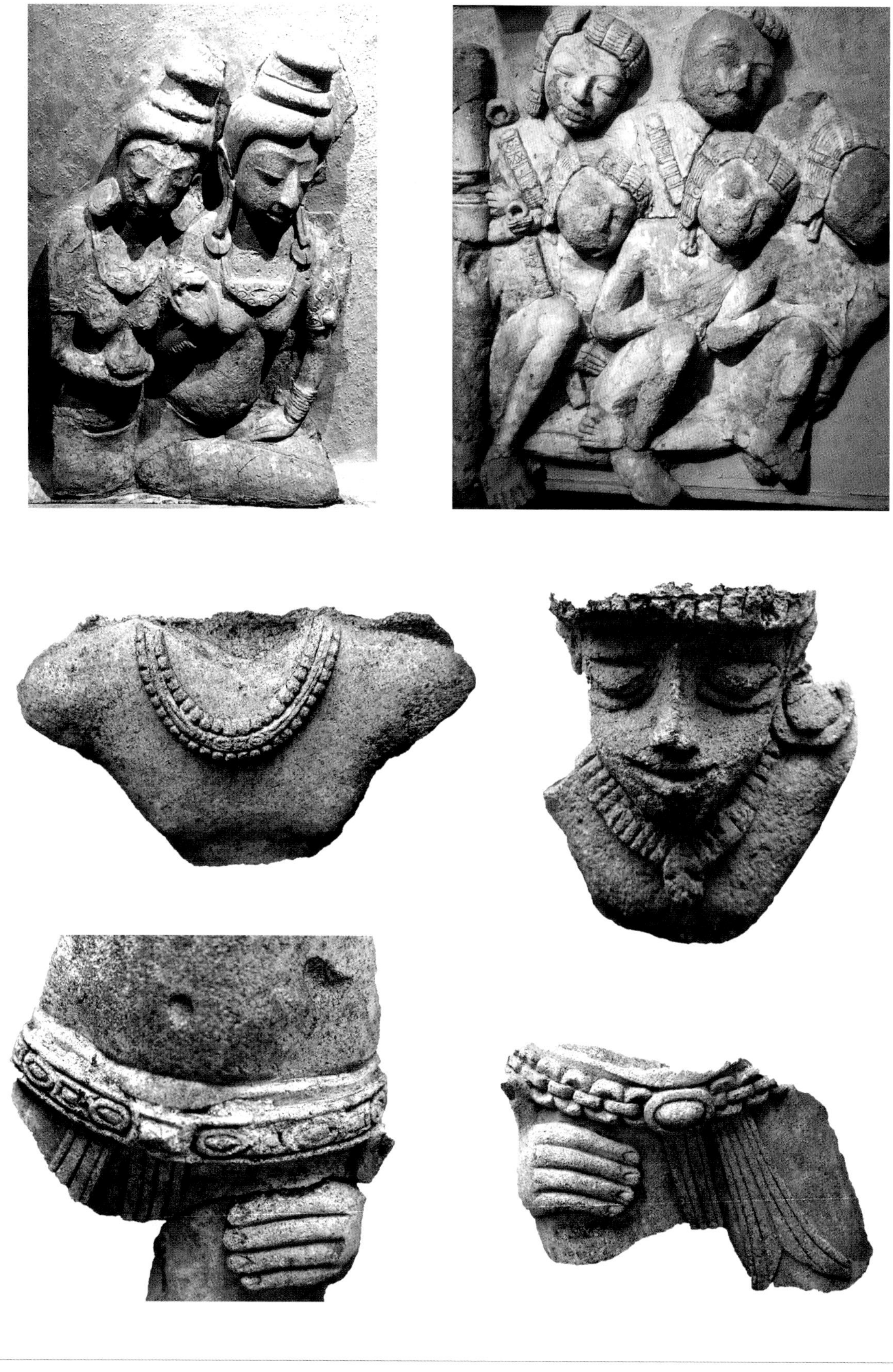

Fig.38 Stucco sculpture depicting figures wearing elaborate necklaces, belt ornaments, arm bands on the upper arm and holding items of adornment. Many of these probably represent gold originals. Khu Bua, Ratchaburi Province. Phra Pathom Chedi National Museum, Nakhon Pathom and Bangkok National Museum.

structure of a society and the status and organisation of the craftsmen within it would have influenced the techniques of production. If gold was centrally controlled, much like silver was in the Roman Empire, a direct consequence would be that the metal composition would have been of a consistent purity. One might also expect the technique of casting rather than hammering to be more prevalent, since the excess metal required in the process would have been of little consequence in a centrally controlled system and would simply have been melted down and reused.

The spread of Hinduism and Buddhism was necessarily accompanied by a transfer of culture and by following the means by which religion spread and co-opted local culture we can thread our way via commerce, travel, and trade to the societal and political roles that were established in what is now central Thailand in the early first millennium.

Acknowledgments

I most gratefully acknowledge the support of DASTA, a public organisation which was established in 2012 and the continued interest of its director, Taweebhong Wichaidit. I would like to thank Phnombootra Chandrajoti, Director of the Bangkok National Museum, Dendao Silapanon and Supamas Doungsakun, Director and acting director of the U Thong National Museum and their staff, Phuthorn Bhumadhon of Rearn Phra Lop and Lop Buri Conservation Committee, Bérénice Bellina and Praon Silapanth, the directors of Khao Sam Kaeo archaeological site, Bunchar Pongpanich and Pairot Singbun of the SuthiRatana Foundation for access to material. My thanks to Brigitte Borell, Daniella Simone and Corinna Wessels for interesting discussions. I am most grateful to Bunchar Pongpanich of the Buddhadasa Indapanno Archives (BIA), Bangkok for his continuous support. I cannot express enough thanks to Hunter Watson, my co-editor, for his formidable editorial skills and to Marine Penhouët and Pairot Singbun whose assistance with the layout of this volume has been invaluable.

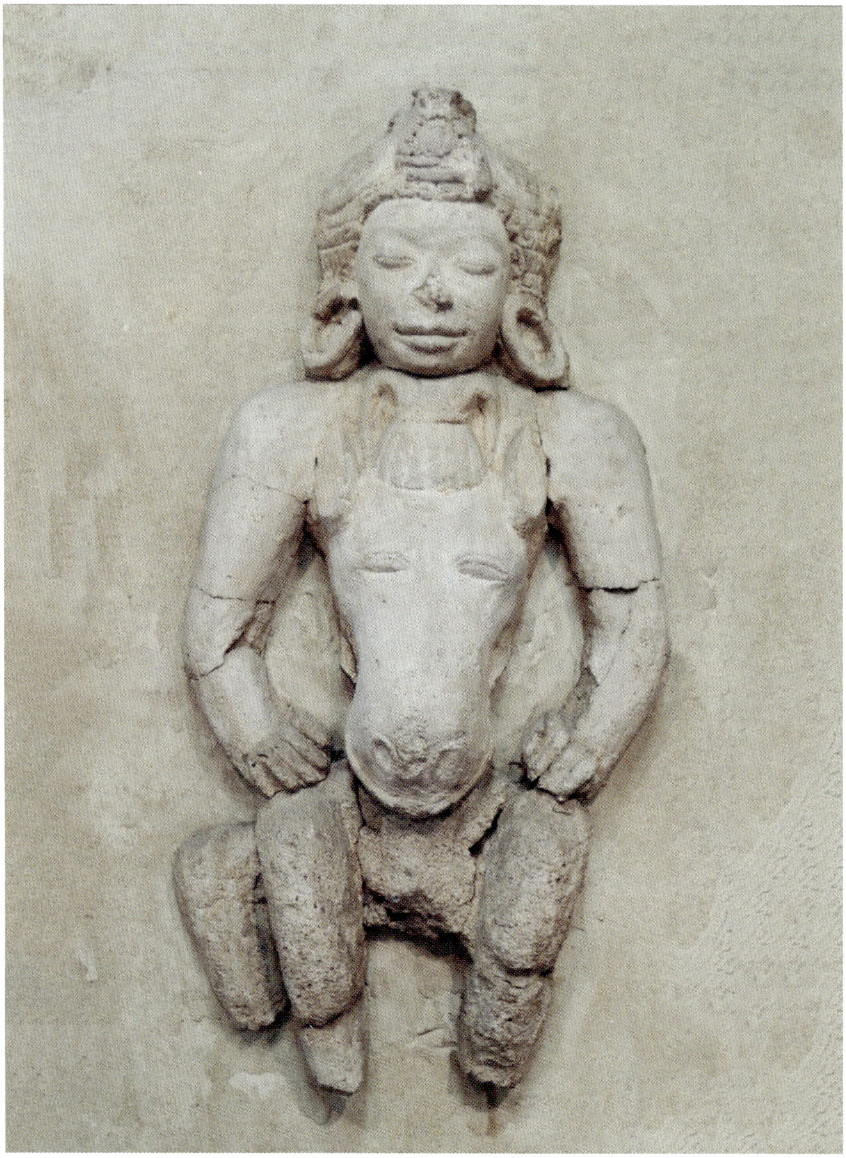

Fig.1 Stucco decorating the southwest corner of Chullapathon, courtesy Phra Pathom Chedi National Museum, Nakhon Pathom.

THE REQUEST FROM DVĀRAVATĪ FOR FINE HORSES

MEDIEVAL CHINESE TRIBUTE NOTES ON HORSE USAGE IN SOUTHEAST ASIA

Lin Ying and Huang Jiaxin

Introduction

In the classic monograph *Golden Khersonese*, Paul Wheatley (1961) took Chinese sources on the Malay Peninsula as the "single most valuable corpus of evidence available to the historical geographer of Malaya for the period prior to AD 1500." Nevertheless, his comment continued by pointing out the defects of these accounts, being that they were second-hand records. The dynastic histories (official histories) are recorded by bureaucrats "who were with rare exceptions uninterested in countries beyond the Chinese frontier." The authors of travels and topographies are not a "reliable guide," whereas encyclopedias, though they "achieved a high standard of factual accuracy," seldom provide sources of their information and indications of chronology. Last but not least, all these insufficiencies are added with another major problem: the transcriptions of foreign place names appear in records with varying spellings which attempted to represent the pronunciation of such names. As a result, a single state can often be found with different transcriptions in the dynastic histories, Buddhist travel notes, and encyclopedias.

When saluting the unsurpassed reading about early Chinese sources by this great Sinologist, the present authors would like to add a note about other facets of these texts. They were not originally intended for a historical geographer with modern academic training; instead, they were written for very different purposes. The tributes and envoys from foreign countries were recorded by Chinese government bureaucrats focusing on the rarity of their gifts as well as showing the glory and fame of certain foreign rulers. The travel notes, for instance, like Yi Jing's *Datang xiyu qiufa gaoseng zhuan*, was a memoir with deep sympathy to record his contemporary Buddhist monks who brought the same firm determination as him and their adventures sailing to India to obtain the Dharma. In other words, these records are not only historical sources for identifying names in foreign geography but are also a path to guide us into the cultural milieu several centuries ago.

Wheatley divides Chinese documents on the Malay Peninsula into three categories: dynastic histories, encyclopedias, and travels and topographies. These documents can be further analyzed according to the writing format. For instance, the writing format of the chapter on foreign countries in dynastic histories was invented by Ban Gu, author of *Han Shu* (written in the first century CE). He arranged each country according to the routes from China to the west, starting from the states closest to the border of China and gradually expanded westward to the most remote countries. He also noted the distance from each country to the station of the general's house in the frontier, as well as the capital of China.

This writing format was generally followed by the historians of successive dynasties when compiling their own dynastic histories. As a result, the chapter on foreign countries in dynastic histories preserved a quite regular format. The information is organized under the item of country, with a report about each country including their politics, local customs, and diplomatic relations with China (usually war and tributes). The ordering of countries in these writings is arranged according to the route. The sea routes before the tenth century, however, were vague and changing. It was not easy to organize maritime countries according to the sequence established by land routes. Therefore, in the reports on countries in the South Seas, the countries closest to China and usually in more frequent contact with China became the coordinates for locating other countries. Remote countries, who only occasionally had contact with China, were positioned as "in the sea" or sometimes labeled by the distance sailing from Chinese ports. Usually, details of these countries "in the sea" did not include the geographic distances from Chinese borderlands or the capitals of these foreign kingdoms.

When analyzing the documents, the accounts in dynastic histories are most important because they provide reliable chronology. These reports can be supplemented with more information from encyclopedias, travel notes and topography, and other genres of literature, such as fiction and poetry. Actually, this approach is not the new finding of the current authors but is the basic training for students of Chinese history when reading traditional documents. Versatile Sinologists like Wheatley knew these techniques well. However, his study in the 1960s was comprehensive and centered on historical geography, i.e. the identification of place names. The current authors, conversely, hope to return to the original point to see if a case study, based on these often-cited sources, could contribute some fresh ideas when new questions are posed.

Thus, the paper starts from an unusual note, a request from Dvāravatī to the Tang court for horses, as preserved in the dynastic histories *Jiu Tang Shu* (written in 945 CE) and *Xin Tang Shu* (written in 1060 CE) (Wheatley 1961: 104–113). The brief record will be examined with more information provided by the tribute inventory preserved in *Cefu Yuangui*, an encyclopedia written in 1005 CE (see Appendix I). After that, the authors will try to expand the scope of the search, examining the chronological characters of tribute records on the South Seas in the dynastic histories in the first millennium CE and briefly describe the accounts of horses in this repertoire. Finally, we return to Dvāravatī, sketching out the image of Dvāravatī in the Tang worldview.

The request from Dvāravatī for horses: Why it looked unusual in the context of a tribute note

The request of Dvāravatī for fine horses from the Tang court was recorded in *Jiu Tang Shu*, chapter 147, "In 649 (the twenty third year of the Zhenguan reign), the king of Duo-he-luo sent an envoy again, with tribute of ivory and huozhu (fire bead),[1] and requested fine horses."

We can find another account in the encyclopedia *Tongdian*, written by Du You in 801 CE: "People in this state ride elephants and horses. The number of horses is very limited, less than one thousand. The horses do not wear harnesses. Riders only fasten a bridle through the mouth of a horse for control." According to *Jiu Tang Shu*, Tuoheng, a vassal of Dvāravatī, also asked for horses and a bronze bell in 647 CE (the twenty first year of Zhenguan reign, in *Jiu Tang Shu*, chapter 147).

According to the tribute inventory preserved in the *Cefu Yuangui* (see Appendix), Dvāravatī made tribute five times during the Zhenguan reign of Emperor Taizong (twelfth year, 638; fourteenth year, 640; seventeenth year together with Tuoheng, 643; twenty first year Tuoheng, 647; twenty third year, 649). Afterwards, they no longer appeared in the tribute inventory during the Tang Dynasty.

A noteworthy event in 647 was that Guligan, a state in the Western Regions, sent one hundred "fine horses" to the Chinese court. These horses were so praiseworthy, being recorded as "youjun," excellent horses, that Emperor Taizong, a noted horse connoisseur, personally selected and named the ten best horses. It is plausible that envoys from Tuoheng, a vassal state of Dvāravatī, saw these steeds and thus made a request.

For the Tang court, giving fine horses to a very distant state like Dvāravatī and its vassal would have been unusual. The politically-oriented tribute system was more hierarchical and symbolic, focusing on establishing the world order viewing China as the central kingdom rather than being a practical trading network. The tribute list in *Cefu Yuangui*, for instance, may give us an idea for this diplomacy expressed by gift-exchange under the pretense of a trading system. We can find that tributes from the South Seas are always "tame elephant," "white parrots," or "five-colored parrots" and "women or children slaves from Seng-zhi" (possibly a state in Africa). Usually, the gift in return from the Tang court was silk, as recorded in the tribute list, "in the twelfth year of Kaiyuan reign, Moluo, the envoy from Srivijaya, was granted the official title of Zhechong, one hundred rolls of silk as a return gift, and allowed to return to his own state." Occasionally, horses were taken as gift to some kingdoms that showed great loyalty to the court. In the tribute inventory of *Cefu Yuangui*, the only record was in the first year of Kaiyuan reign of Emperor Xuanzong (713 CE). The emperor, after taking the throne in a bloody coup, eagerly wanted any sign of support from either inside or outside. When the king of Linyi sent five elephants, the emperor sent horses as a gift, with the following edict:

"Your kingdom is afar, in the South Seas. Your envoys take a long way to send tribute to me. The gift from you shows fully your sincerity to me. Now I send you two horses as an expression of my heart."

1 According to *Jiu Tang Shu*, fire bead was sent by Linyi to China. See Appendix I, tribute in 631.

If the request for fine horses from Dvāravatī looked unusual, why did the Tang court allow it, and even on two occasions. Why would the envoys from Dvāravatī not care about the limitations set up by the tribute system and have the audacity to request fine horses from the emperor? If we examine the contemporary accounts on this country, we could find more clues for these questions.

Image of Dvāravatī in the Tang tribute inventory and official histories

In the complete tribute inventory during the Tang period, preserved in the *Cefu Yuangui*, tribute notes are arranged chronologically, with the name of states, the names of kings and envoys (occasionally), the content of tributes (selectively), and brief comments about the tributes and related kingdoms. In comparison to the more standard records organized under the items of each country in the dynastic histories (*Jiu Tang Shu* and *Xin Tang Shu*), the documents in *Cefu Yuangui* provide more vivid depictions and were closer to the original face of Tang diplomatic archives.

In Appendix I, a list of all tributes from states in the South Seas is given, taken from the *Cefu Yuangui*. Chronologically, the envoys from the South Seas frequently visited China from the beginning of the Tang period in 618 CE to the mid-eighth century. After the reign of Emperor Xuanzong (712–756 CE), tribute from this region declined abruptly.

Among the states sending tribute to China, Linyi was no doubt the most prominent during the three hundred years of the Tang Dynasty. The other countries that kept frequent tribute-visits were Zhenla, Shilifoshi (sometimes Foshi, Srivijaya) and Heling or Keling (Wade 2014). It is noteworthy that states keeping frequent tribute liaison with China had quite uniformed names, for instance, the names of Linyi and Zhenla were not changed in the inventory through the time span of the Tang, showing that the Chinese were very familiar with them.

When connecting this tribute list with the records in two official histories, the *Jiu Tang Shu* and *Xin Tang Shu*, we find that Tang geography based on tribute notes and diplomatic affairs about the South Seas could be divided into two spheres. The center of the first sphere was doubtlessly Linyi, and shortly afterward Zhenla was added. Linyi, in particular, became a coordinate point for locating other countries in the first sphere. The second sphere covered Srivijaya, Heling, Dvāravatī and other countries mainly positioned around the Malay Peninsula. Though these countries are frequently mentioned in the travel notes of Buddhist monks, the coordinates for locating them is actually Guangzhou, the biggest port in southern China in the Tang period. Clearly, the geography in official histories is politically oriented. Countries in the second sphere, not like Linyi which was officially admitted as a vassal by the Tang court, were not within the political sphere of the Tang government.

It is in such a context (tribute system and political milieu) that Dvāravatī came to the stage. In 638 CE (the sixth month, the twelfth year in the Zhenguan reign, Emperor Taizong), Dvāravatī (Du-he-luo) made the first visit, not accompanied by Linyi. There was a one-sentence comment beside its first appearance, "from the wilderness of southern distant land, belonging to the category of Kunlun people[2]." Two years later (640 CE), the envoy of Dvāravatī came again with Tuoheng (a vassal of Dvāravatī according to *Jiu Tang Shu*).

Dvāravatī, on the other hand, was frequently mentioned in the account of countries in the second sphere. The locations of these countries were explained with reference to Dvāravatī. It illustrates the important role of this polity in the region beyond the Linyi sphere. Possibly, horses reflected the power and influence of Dvāravatī as an important polity in the Malay peninsular region and adjacent areas, and this might be why envoys from Dvāravatī made a request for fine horses from the Tang court.

Chronological characters of Chinese official histories on medieval Southeast Asia and horse usage

We can discern some chronological features in Chinese official histories concerning Southeast Asia in medieval times. From the third to sixth centuries, most reports were actually from Funan, where Chinese envoys Zhu Ying and Kang Tai visited personally in the 220s CE. The envoys recorded geographical knowledge and

2 Kunlun was general reference to people in the South Seas, "South to Linyi, people are all black and curl-haired, being called Kunlun generally", in *Jiu Tang Shu*, chapter 147.

even rumors obtained from Funan, arousing curiosity in this region among the class of Chinese intellectuals. Down to the fifth century, we find some new visitors arrived in China from modern-day central Thailand and the Malay Peninsula, including Dandan, Panpan, Langyaxiu, and others (Wade 2014). Starting from this era, more states sent envoys and merchants to China. These visits reached a zenith in the mid-eighth century as we find from the above-discussed tribute inventory. The tribute institution and political grading was expressed by the description and report focusing on the rarity and unique traits of tributes, rituals, palaces, and administrations of foreign kings, as well as exotic customs of foreign populations. It finally constructed a political world map, covering China as the centre and other countries keeping graded political and diplomatic distance from this central kingdom. By the end of the tenth century, a new trend can be clearly seen that commercial activities aimed at obtaining economic benefits were the major pursuit, and trade networks connecting southern China and Southeast Asia were established based on regular sailing routes, under firm control of Chinese dynasties. After the tenth century, visits recorded in the official histories from this region were mostly commercial activities, though they continued to be written in the framework of tribute notes.

The reports of horses in the official histories reflected this chronological change, as well. In the first phase (third to sixth centuries), we can find that Kuṣāṇa horses arrived in Funan, together with the building of new diplomatic ties between northern India and Funan, as recorded by Chinese envoys to Funan, and were gradually transmitted into fiction and poetry in China, becoming a part of legendary geography of Southeast Asia at that times.

The horses recorded in official history after the tenth century, however, presented another face, rightly matching the commercial nature of the new age. In *Song Shi* (chapter 489, biography 240, written in 1343), we read the following notes: "Zhancheng (Champa): People in this state take the elephant chariot and randou (a kind of cart?). They also go to Jiaozhou (northern Vietnam) to buy horses.

In 1171 CE, some people from Fujian (modern-day Fujian Province, China) sailed to Jiyangjun (modern-day Sanya, Hainan Province, China) and encountered a big storm. They finally arrived at Zhancheng. The country was at war with Zhenla. Both armies took elephants and the victory could not be decided. The people from Fujian taught the king of Zhancheng about cavalry and archery. The king was delighted. He prepared a ship and sent the Fujian people to Jiyangjun, bringing back dozens of horses. After that, the king of Zhancheng won a big victory. In the next year, they came again to purchase additional horses. The people in Hainan Province refused their request. The sailors from Zhancheng were offended. They looted the local people and returned to their state. In 1175, the court issued a strict prohibition edict not allowing horses to be sold to foreign countries."

In the second phase (seventh to tenth centuries), accounts on Southeast Asia had many vivid descriptions on the royal palaces, dress, and ceremonies. The *Sui Shu*, for instance, recorded the splendid court and diplomatic ceremonies for welcoming Chinese envoys in the Chitu kingdom (red-earth kingdom):

"The king lives in the Sengzhi city (Sangra? Lion) which has three gates, with a distance of several hundred steps, respectively. The gate pictured flying celestial beings, Bodhisattvas, with hanging golden flowers and golden bells. Dozens of women performed music and took golden flowers before the gates. Four other women, decorated like the Vajra Guardians next to the Buddhist Pagoda, stood aside the gates. The attendants outside the gates held weapons, while the others inside held white fly-whisks. Along the route (to the palace) hung white nets adorned with flowers. The palaces were all multi-floor pavilions with windows opening to the north. The king sat on a three-tiered throne. He dressed on the Zhaoxia clothes, wearing a crown decorated with golden flowers, precious stones, and a tassel. Four female attendants stood around the king, and over one hundred guards stood to the right and left of his throne. Behind the king's throne was a wooden shrine inlaid with gold, silver, and fragrant wood. Behind the shrine hung a golden decoration with the pattern of sunlight. On both sides of the throne were erected two mirrors. Two gold jars were placed before the mirrors, and two golden incense burners in front of the jars. In the front of the incense burners was placed a gold groveling bull. Before the bull was erected a golden umbrella and fan decorated with precious stones on the left and right. Several hundred Brahman sat in rows, on the east and west sides, facing each other."

The expressions of kingship in this region combining indigenous culture with elements from India impressed the Chinese. Similar descriptions like this are found in accounts of other states, including Dvāravatī. Were the fine horses from China taken into the royal ritual and paraded there? An enthralling question awaits more evidence from inscriptions and archaeological discoveries in Southeast Asia.

Conclusion

The fragmented reports in Tang dynastic histories and other documents gave us a glimpse of Dvāravatī, a large, distant country in the South Seas. Dachengdeng, the Sanskrit teacher and guide of Yi Jing in his travels in India, sailed to this country with his parents in childhood and later became a monk there.

In the *Tongdian*, the country was described as "having six markets. Traders there used silver coins, small, like the elm pods, and the king's name is Touheluo (Dvāravatī?) and the given name is Puyeqiyao. He ruled several cities indirectly. Inside his city there was only the king's palace and administrative offices. Outside of the city inhabited ten thousand households...... people in this country do not need to pay taxes. They live on agriculture and trading. They ride elephants and horses."

Possibly, Chinese sources, as the "single most valuable corpus of evidence," could contribute more to understanding this Dvāravatī kingdom if considered with new archaeological findings, site excavations and readings of inscriptions (Revire and Murphy 2014).

Appendix

Tribute inventory in the Tang period (618–907 CE) according to Cefu Yuangui, chapter 970 and chapter 971

Emperor Gaozu, r. 618–626

623, 2nd month	Linyi
626	Zhenla
625, 4th month	Linyi
625, 9th month	Zhenla and Canzhu

Emperor Taizong, r. 627–649

628, 10th month	Linyi, Zhenla, Canban, Shunai
631	Linyi, Poli The tribute is huozhu (fire bead). Comment: It looks like crystal. In the midday sunlight, the bead mirrors the sun. When taking moxa floss to cover it, fire can be seen. It is reported to be obtained from Poli. The Poli emissary followed the emissary of Linyi to make tribute.
631	Linyi The tribute is a five-colored parrot and a white parrot. Comment: The bird is sympathetic and wise, good at replying to questions. From this year onwards, the tribute from Linyi does not stopped.
635, 4th month	Zhenla
638, 1st month	Senggao, Wuling, Jiazuo, Jiumi, four countries made tribute together. Comment: All the four states are small. It is the first time for them to contact with China. Their clothing and language are similar to Linyi. They belong to the category of Kunlun, living in the wilderness of the south.
638, 6th month	Duheluo (Dvāravatī) Comment: The state belongs to the category of Kunlun, living in the wilderness of the south.
640	Heling and Duheluo (Dvāravatī)
641, 2nd month	Panpan
642, 1st month	Poluo, Taling and Canban
642, 5th month	Linyi
643, 1st month	Duheluo (Dvāravatī)
643	Tuoheng (according to Xin Tang shu, it is a vassal of Dvāravatī)
647	Tuoheng (vassal of Dvāravatī?) The tribute is a white parrot. Comment: It has shiny white feathers. On its head there are bunches of red hair. The red hair hangs down to its wings. Also, one five-color parrot, and fragrant ointment from Polu (Poli?).
647	Zhuipodeng (Dvāravatī?)
649	Duoheluo (Dvāravatī) The tribute is fire bead and ivory.

Emperor Gaozong, r. 650–668

651, 10th month	Zhenla The tribute is a tame elephant.
651, 10th month	Tuoheng (vassel of Dvāravatī?)
653, 4th month	Linyin The tribute is a tame elephant.
654	Linyi The tribute is a tame elephant.
657, 2nd month	Linyi
657, 6th month	Zhanbo (Champa?) a tame elephant, a rhinoceros
661, 5th month	Poan
662, 2nd month	Linyi
662, 6th month	Zhanbo (Champa?), a tame elephant, a rhinoceros
663, 8th month	Three states from South India Comment: The envoys sailed in the big sea for several months and finally arrived at Jiaozhou and made tribute.
664, 8th month	Three small states to the south of Linyi came to make tribute.

665, 5th month	Yufo, Mola, Sanpu, Geluoshefen, Xiuluofen, Ganbi sent tributes together. Comment: Geluoshefen is in the southern part of the South Seas. To the east it is connected with Duoheluo (Dvāravatī). The king's name is Pujiayuemo. The state has an army of 20,000 warriors. The envoy started his journey in 656 and arrived in China in 665. Xiuluofen is in the northern part of the South Seas. The city is constructed of wood. To the east it is connected with Zhenla, to the south is the sea. The king's name is Shidamotipo. The state has an army of 20,000 warriors.
666	Dandan, Heling
669, 8th month	Linyi, Moluopo
670	Linyi, Shizi (lion state), Heluo, Dandan
671	Shilijiumo, the king of Jiumi, and Shilitipobamo, the king of Funan made tribute.
672, 3rd month	States in south India
682, 5th month	Zhenla
682, 12th month	States from south India
686, 3rd month	Linyi Tribute is a tame elephant.
691, 11th month	Linyi Tribute is a tame elephant.
695, 1st month	Linyi Tribute is a war elephant.
695, 4th month	Linyi
698, 1st month	Zhenla
699, 6th month	Linyi
701, 12th month	Foshi (Srivijaya)
703, 12th month	Linyi
704, 1st month	Linyi
704, 8th month	Linyi
Emperor Zhongzong, r. 705–710	
705, 7th month	Linyi
707, 5th month	Zhenla
707, 8th month	Linyi Tribute is a tame elephant.
709, 3rd month	Kunlun
709, 11th month	Linyi Tribute is a white elephant.
710, 1st month	Nantianzhu (South India?), Zhenla
Emperor Ruizong, r. 711–712	
711, 9th month	Nantianzhu
712, 11th month	Linyi, Shizi (Lion state?)
712	Linyi
Emperor Xuanzong, r. 712–756	
713, 6th month	Nantianzhu (South India?)
713	Jianduodamo, the king of Linyi Tribute is five elephants. Comment: Your kingdom is afar, in the South Seas. Your envoys take a long way to send the tribute to me. The gift from you shows fully your sincerity to me. Now I send you two horses as an expression of my heart.
714, 6th month	Linyi
716, 3rd month	Foshi (Srivijaya)
716, 5th month	Zhenla, Wendan
718, 7th month	Sufosheli, king of Folu
719, 5th month	Nantianzhu Tribute is a leopard, a five-colored parrot, and a wenri bird (asking-sun bird in Chinesse)
719, 11th month	
719, 2nd month	Nantianzhu
724, 2nd month	Sumoluo, the big chief of Folu
724, 11th month	Shilifoshi (Srivijaya) send envoy Jumoluo. Tribute is two dwarves, two Sengzhi female slaves, one band of musicians, and a five-colored parrot.
727, 11th month	Foshi (Srivijaya) A five-colored parrot.
731, 10th month	Linyi Four elephants.
734, 6th month	Linyi Aloes

735	Linyi A white elephant.
741, 8th month	the prince of Foshi (Srivijaya)
	746, 1st month Shizi (lion state?) send envoy Shiluomijia, Brahman monk Guanding sanzang (abhisaca? Tripitaka?) A-ri-jia-bo-zhe-luo to visit the court. Tribute: strings of ornaments inlaid with gold and precious stone, one Mahāprajñāpāramitā Sutra, written in Sanskrit on palm-leaf, forty pieces of fine white cotton cloth.
748, 6th month	Linyi Tribute is ivory, cotton cloth with floral pattern.
749, 9th month	Lutuo, the Chief of City in Linyi. Tribute: One hundred strings of pearls, thirty jin of black aloes, twenty rolls of fresh white cotton cloth.
750, 3rd month	Shizi (lion state) Tribute: ivory and pearl
750, 3rd month	Linyi Tribute: ivory, pearl, and white cotton with floral pattern?
750, 6th month	Zhenla Rinoceros
753, 9th month	Prince of Wendan and his subordinates, twenty-six people.

Emperor Daizong, r. 762–779

763	Heling

Emperor Dezong, r. 780–805

793, 10th month	The king of Huan state sent a rhinoceros.

Emperor Xianzong, r. 806–820

813	Zhenla sent the envoy Li Mona, possibly an Arab (Wade 2014)
814, 9th month	Heling Tribute: Sengzhi child slaves, five-colored parrot, Pinjia bird, and many exotic treasures.
818	Heling Tribute: Two Sengzhi female slaves, a parrot, a tortoise shell, a rhinoceros horn.

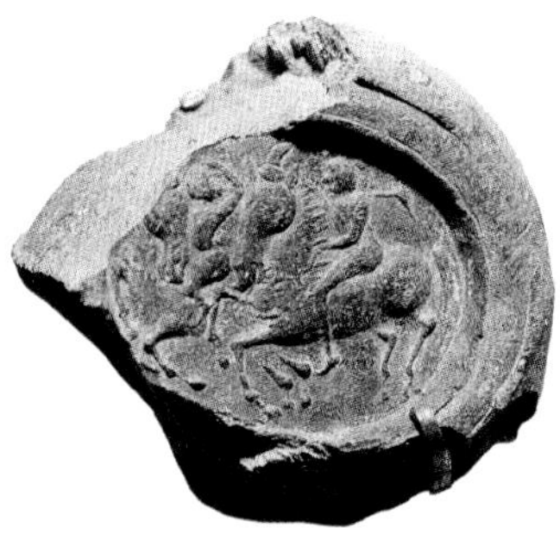

Fig.2 Terracotta seal depicting horse and rider, courtesy Somdet Phra Narai National Museum, Lop Buri.

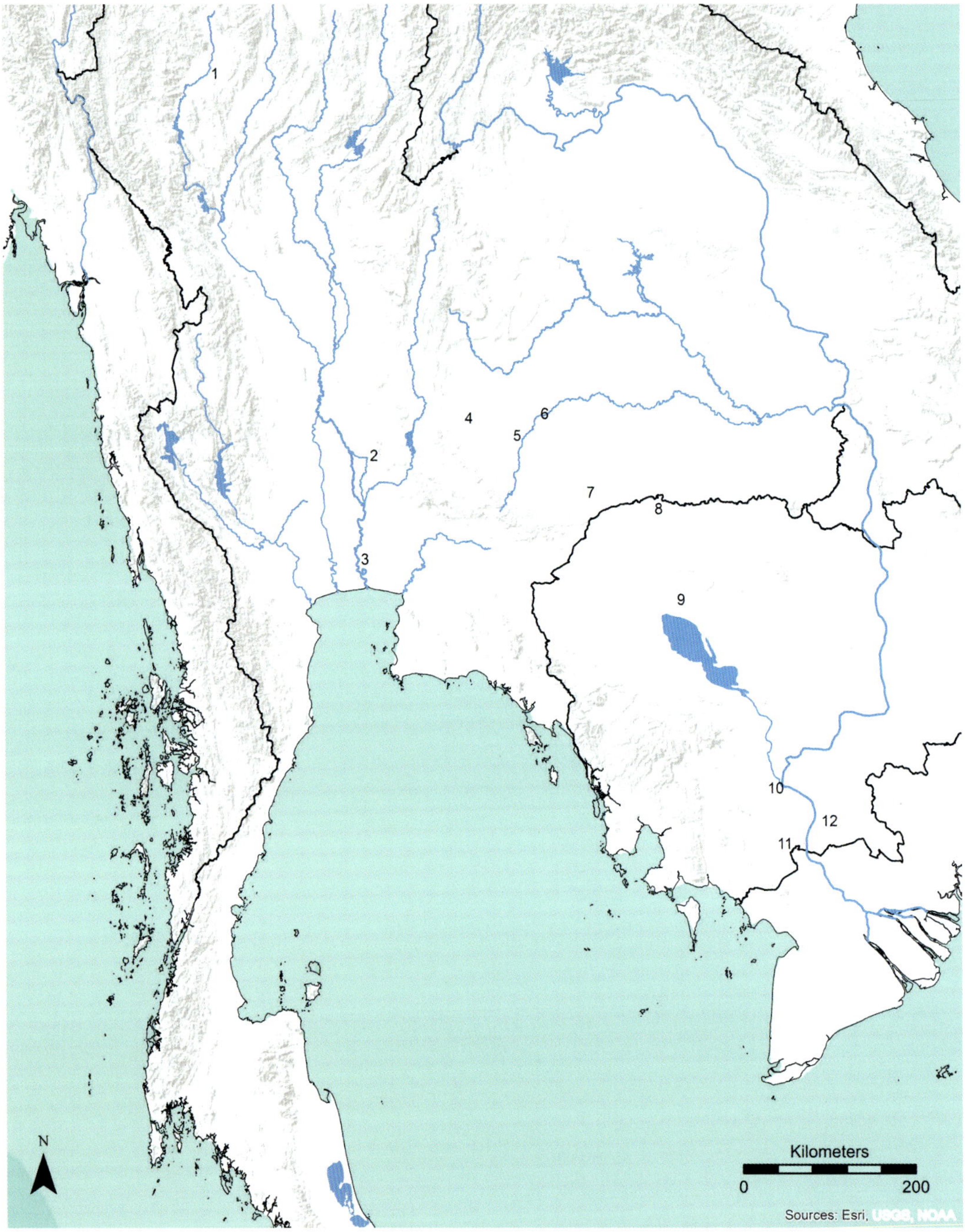

1. Hariphunchai (Lamphun)
2. Lop Buri
3. Bangkok
4. Wat Cong Ko, Nakhon Ratchasima
5. Phanom Wan
6. Phimai
7. Phanom Rung
8. O Smach
9. Angkor
10. Phnom Penh
11. Angkor Borei
12. Ba Phnom

Fig.1 Map showing locations mentioned in the text (map by Hunter Watson).
All photographs belong to the author unless otherwise stated.

THE FALL OF DVĀRAVATĪ AS MENTIONED IN THE KHMER INSCRIPTION K.1198

U-tain Wongsathit, Kangvol Katshima, and Chatupohn Khotkanok

Introduction

The mention of Dvāravatī in Khmer inscriptions is very rare. The appearance of inscriptions by Khmer kings at sites associated with Dvāravatī gives a clue to the fall of Dvāravatī. The focus of this article, however, is inscription K.1198/Ka.18 (Figs. 1& 2), for which the Sanskrit portion has never been published. This inscription records the biography of Lakṣmipativarman, an army general of King Sūryavarman I, and the installation of Śaiva divinities and donations. The mention of the appointment of Lakṣmipativarman as the governor of Rāmanya (Mons) in line 20 is very fascinating. The reference to Lavapura in line 27 gives new considerations for the fall of Dvāravatī.

Cœdès cites only two occurrences of the place name "Dvāravatī", being inscriptions K.165 and K.89. Inscription K.165 from the site Thar Kdei, Kompong Thom Province, with the year 874 Śaka, corresponding with 952 CE, records "sruk dvāravatī" as a place name. Inscription K.89, from the site Preah Nan, Kampong Cham Province, with the year 92 Śaka or 1002 CE, mentions "teṅ tvan dvāravatī" as a personal name.

The appearance of inscriptions by Khmer kings at sites associated with Dvāravatī may give a clue to the fall of Dvāravatī. Cœdès (1968:137) stated that "Evidence of the Khmer occupation in the lower Menam in the eleventh century is given by a group of inscriptions from Lopburi, at least one of which emanates from Sūryavarman I." Cœdès made reference to K.410 from Lop Buri as solid evidence for the expansion of Khmer civilisation into central Thailand, concluding that "In the eleventh Khmers had established themselves at Lavo, and in the twelfth they had extended their domination to the borders of the kingdom of Hariphunchai, coming into conflict with King Ādityarāja." (Cœdès 1968: 194)

The current study made use of numerous scholarly sources which are not specifically cited in this article, as follows. The study of inscriptions in Cambodia was facilitated by reference to works by George Cœdès (1937-1966), Saveros Pou (1989; 2001), and Von Sotheara et al (2002). Information about the history and culture of ancient Cambodia can be gleaned from various sources, the most notable of which in this case were the works of Lawrence Briggs (1951), Kamaleswar Bhattacharya (1961), Adhir Chakravarti (1978; 1980), Michael Vickery (1998; 2002), and Chhany Sak-Humphry (2005). The translation and understanding of vocabulary appearing in the inscription was aided by multiple dictionaries and other texts, namely works by Sir Monier Monier-Williams (1899), Franklin Huffman (1978), Long Seam (1997; 2000), and U-tain Wongsathit (2012).

The war between Jayavīravarman (r. 1002-1008 CE) and Sūryavarman I (r. 1002-1049 CE)

The starting point of the expansion of Khmer civilisation into central Thailand seems to have been the civil war in the Angkorian empire between Jayavīravarman and Sūryavarman I. The war started after the death of Udayādityavarman I, in 1001 CE. There was a period of acute violence and a fierce struggle for the imperial throne. The principal challengers were two rival princes, Jayavīravarman and Sūryavarman I. Notably, both claimed to have been consecrated in the same year, 1002 CE. Inscriptions K.158 and K.989 both state that Jayavīravarman succeeded the throne in 924 Śaka, or 1002 CE. The locations of the inscriptions show that Jayavīravarman ruled at Angkor and the western regions, while Sūryavarman I ruled in the eastern regions of the Angkorian empire. An inscription, K.834, found at Tuol Don Srei, mentions that the war lasted for nine years, and finally Sūryavarman I was victorious. From a recently found inscription, the Wat Cong Ko Inscription, dated 1008 CE, it is known that after losing his power at Angkor, Jayavīravarman shifted to the eastern part of modern-day Thailand and probably died there (U-tain Wongsathit 2015). It seems that Jayavīravarman, who became king of Angkor, was the ruler on the Khorat Plateau, perhaps from the Mahīdharapura Dynasty. Inscription K.275 states that Sūryavarman I was born in the family of

Indravarman I and ascended the throne in 924 Śaka, or 1002 CE, in the eastern region. Inscriptions K.380 and K.660 give the information that Sūryavarman's queen, Vīralakṣmī, was born of the royal line of Haraṣavarman I and Īśānavarman II. In any case, Sūryavarman I had no legitimate claim to the throne from the immediate predecessors by bloodline. Inscriptions K.136 and K.161 show that Sūryavarman I obtained the kingdom by defeating his rivals in battles. The theory that Sūryavarman I originated from a ruling family in what is now Thailand, or the Malay Peninsula, is an ingenious speculation, but lacks convincing proof (Vickery 2000: 99-100). Although Sūryavarman I adopted the Buddhist faith, he did not give up the royal tutelary deity, as he constructed both Śaiva and Vaiṣṇava temples. His religious generosity was also shown in inscription K.161, which starts with an invocation to the Buddha followed by an invocation to Śiva.

The civil war between Jayavīravarman and Sūryavarman I continued for nine years, until 1010 CE. After winning the war and gaining control of the Angkor region, Sūryavarman I ordered the provincial officials to swear an oath of loyalty and serve his family; these oaths were recorded in six inscriptions: K.292, K.466-468 and K.541-542, all of which date to 1011 CE. Some portions of the inscriptions are very interesting. The officials swore that they would not honour any other king, would never be hostile (to their king) and would not be the accomplices of any enemy.

King Sūryavarman I built the royal palace at Angkor and probably a new reservoir, the West Baray, measuring eight kilometres in length and two kilometres in width. This reservoir is still in use until the present. He was credited with the completion of the Preah Vihear Temple, which is located on an escarpment of the Dangrek Mountain Range, as well as many other temples outside the Angkor region. Sūryavarman I had Vīralakṣmī as his principal queen. He also had another queen, Nṛpatīndralakṣmī, who gave birth to Prince Vīravardhana (mentioned in inscription K.989). Sūryavarman I died in 1049 CE and was given the posthumous name Paramanirvānapada, or simplified as Nirvānapada.

Inscription K.410 of Sūryavarman I

In 1025 CE, Sūryavarman I issued inscription K.410, which is today in Lop Buri, Thailand, located 138 km from Bangkok. This inscription contains regulations about monasteries in which it was lain down that the ascetics and Buddhist monks should earn merit on behalf of the king. His power seems to have extended into what is now central Thailand, as this is where the inscription was discovered. The question why King Sūryavarman I of Angkor installed an inscription, K.410, in Lop Buri in 1025 CE is controversial among scholars. The answer might be found in the Sanskrit portion of inscription K.1198 / Ka.18 of Lakṣmipativarman, an army general of Sūryavarman I.

Khmer Inscription K.1198 / Ka.18

The content of inscription K.1198 / Ka.18 gives important information about the history, society, customs and daily lives of ancient Khmer people during the time of King Sūryavarman I. Two eminent scholars have studied the Khmer portion of this inscription. Saveros Pou (2001: 240-260) published the reading and a French translation of the Khmer text on both sides of the inscription. Long Seam translated the Khmer portion into modern Khmer with valuable footnotes in a handout at a seminar at Silpakorn University, Bangkok. The focus of the present article is inscription K.1198 / Ka.18, for which the Sanskrit portion has never been published. The reading and translation is limited to only a few lines and verses relating to the fall of Dvāravatī.

The Rebellion against King Sūryavarman I in Nakhon Ratchasima Province, Thailand

Inscription K.1249, from Wat Cong Ko, Nakhon Ratchasima Province, Thailand, dated 1008 CE, relates how after losing his power at Angkor, Jayavīravarman escaped to what is now the eastern part of Thailand. The event was followed by a rebellion against King Sūryavarman I in what is now Nakhon Ratchasima Province, as mentioned in the Khmer portion of inscription K.1198. The text narrates as follows:

> "In 1011 CE, the Vau family together with the Tampāṅ family rebeled against King Sūryavarman I.

Fig. 1 Photograph by Ian Glover, courtesy National Museum of Cambodia.

Discovery:	In 1994, Cambodian police arrested men in a truck illegally carrying the inscription at O'Smech, a small Cambodian town on the Thai border in Samraong District of Oddar Meanchey Province, Cambodia.
Exhibition:	The inscription is currently in the permanent exhibition of the National Museum of Cambodia in Phnom Penh.
Register No.:	K.1198/Ka.18
Material:	Sandstone
Form:	Stele
Size:	85 cm. width; 151 cm. height; 13 cm. thick
Face/Lines:	2 faces; contains 116 lines, face I has 57 lines, face II has 59 lines
Script:	Ancient Khmer Script of the eleventh century CE
Languages:	Old Khmer and Sanskrit
Date:	Śaka 936 / 1014 CE
Content:	The inscription records the biography of Lakṣmipativarman, an army general of King Sūryavarman I, and the installation of Śaiva divinities and donations.

The king took all properties including Sukhāvasa of Tāñ Tri from the Vau family and gave it to Lakṣmipativarman. The king ordered Lakṣmipativarman to replace the Buddha with a Śivaliṅga. Vraḥ Kamrateṅ Añ Vidyāśrama presided over the ceremony and formed the place of worship."

K.1198, lines 23-27

This rebel, according to the inscription, was from a family around the place named Sukhāvāsa. It is clear that Sukhāvāsa, meaning "the happy residence," was a lake (Khmer /Piṅ/), as mentioned in inscription K.393, dated 1055 CE, from Phanom Wan, Thailand. Thus, Sukhālaya was located in the adjoining area of Phanom Wan. This is evidence that the rebel was from the region of Nakhon Ratchasima Province in modern-day Thailand. It may be expected that both families were supporters of Jayavīravarman. They fought for Jayavīravarman against King Sūryavarman I. This corresponds with the content of inscription K.1249, which records the donation of Jayavīravarman to the god Vimāya, today known as Phimai. This explains why Jayavīravarman escaped to the eastern part of Thailand. The inscriptions explicitly show that he had enough power to make a huge donation to a deity there in 1008 CE, and in 1011 CE he gained the support from two influential families to fight against Sūryavarman I. The inscriptions also state that they were Buddhists. This incident ended with a defeat by Suryavarman's army.

It seems the king was very angry. He confiscated all property of the Vau family, including Sukhāvasa, the place around Nom Van Temple, and gave it to Lakṣmipativarman. The king ordered the Buddha statue to be replaced with a Śivaliṅga. This might show why Sūryavarman I came to support Śaivism.

The invasion of Sūryavarman I as mentioned in the Sanskrit Text

The inscription begins with a tribute to Śiva, Umā, Viṣṇu and Lakṣmī. Then, there is a long eulogy of King Sūryavarman I. After that, the text relates the story of Lakṣmipativarman, the army general who became the governor of Mons at Lavapura.

Who is Lakṣmipativarman ?

In line 20 of Face II of the inscription, verses 22-23 reads as follows:

(20)	*śrīsūryyavarmmadevasya*	*tasya vyādhapurānvyaḥ*
	śrīlakṣmipativarmmā ya	*s senāṇir atraṇir yudhāṃ*
	ādau yas tena bhūbhartrā	*paścimāśāvakāśināṃ*
	rāmanyānām adhīśatve	*niyutto yuddhā dahada//*

These two verses can be translated as follows:

Verse 22.
This King Śrī Sūryavarman had a general, Śrī Lakṣmīpativarman, of the lineage of Vyādhapura, (marching) at the head of the warriors.
Verse 23.
He was initially charged by this king of the government Rāmanya, who occupy the western region and burnt the enemies with warfare.

Lakṣmīpativarman was a descendant of Vyādhapura. It is interesting to note that Vyādhapura, "the City of Hunters." Cœdès (1968: 36) argued that it had been an important city in the Pre-Angkorian Period and was the capital of Funan. According to Chinese sources, the city was defeated and merged with Chenla by King Īśānavarman I. According to the inscriptions of Yaśovarman I and of Rājendravarman II, Vyādhapura was ruled by Rājendravarman I and then was united with Śambhupura in the last phase of the Chenla Period. The location was previously identified with Bā Phnom in Southern Cambodia, but from but following archaeological excavations, Michael Vickery (2000:70-73) suggested that Angkor Borei was the ancient Vyādhapura. The origin of the city's name, Vyādhapura, is obscure. The name is mentioned in inscription K.61, dated 912 CE, as Adrivyādhapura. Lakṣmīpativarman, a descendant of Vyādhapura, became the general of King Sūryavarman I. This indicates that Sūryavarman I ruled in the eastern and southern regions while Jayavīravarman was ruling at Angkor.

Lakṣmīpativarman was appointed by King Sūryavarman I as the governor of Rāmanya in the western part of the empire. It is clear that Rāmanya is an alternative form of Rāmañña, a reference to the Mons. The closest Rāmanya or Mons (?) to the west of Angkor is Dvāravatī. And it seems that the Mons (?) in Myanmar were quite far from Angkor. So, it may be presumed that after the war with Dvāravatī, Lakṣmīpativarman became the governor of the Mons. This corresponds with the reference of Lavapura in line 27.

Line 27, which contains verses 36-37, can be transliterated as follows:

pṛthuparvvataśarvvasya akṛtvā śramamuktam imaṃ
pūjāvalividhibhaktyā kalpayat prativatsaram //
kāleyadoṣair lavapur ānyaṃ
pradaṣṭarupā hatasarvvaśobhā
vyāghrādibhír vyālamṛgaiḥ prakarṇnā
śmaśānabhūmer api bhīmarupā //

These two verses read as follows:

Verse 36
He built for the god Śiva of the Pṛthuparvata, an excellent hermitage, and set up an annual ceremony consisting of adorations and offering oblations.
Verse 37
By the defects of the Kali Age, Lavapur is like a jungle having lost its beautiful form, all its ruined beauty, traveled by beasts of prey such as tigers, etc., apparently more terrifying than that of a place of cremation.

From the text, it seems that Lakṣmīpativarman first led the army to Phnom Rung, in modern-day Buri Ram Province of Thailand, denoted by the name Pṛthuparvata. Then he attacked Lavapura, or modern-day Lop Buri. Thus, the marching route of Lakṣmīpativarman was from Angkor to Phnom Rung (in modern-day Buri Ram Province), then to Nom Van Temple (in modern-day Nakhon Ratchasima Province), as the Khmer text denotes. After defeating the rebel in the area around Nom Van Temple, he marched to Lavapura (modern-day Lop Buri Province) to conquer the Mons of Dvāravatī. It is the tradition of Sanskrit *Kāvya* that the text will blame the faults of the Kali Age, there is no mention of the army led by Lakṣmīpativarman, which burnt Lavapura to ashes.

Line 28, which contains verse 38, reads as follows:

sarvve śūnyatamāśviraṃ kaliyugena 'ṣṭādhruvaṃ
vāruṇāḥ saṃruphadrumarāgarye pivimayārājñā niyuktena ye
śrīlakṣmīpativarmmaṇā kila punaḥ kartu yathā pūrvvakaṃ
te kṛtvādiyuge yathātihitan nitassamṛṣṭapunaḥ //

Fig. 2 Sūryavarman I inscription, K.1198/Ka.18, in Khmer and Sanskrit, at the National Museum of Cambodia. Photograph by Ian Glover.

Verse 38.

In the Kali Age, all the western districts had been perfectly abandoned for a long time, ruined surely and invaded by masses of trees; the king charged Lakṣmīpativarman to restore them to their former state, kila; repopulating them as they were at the first age, he led them again to prosperity.

This stanza describes how after conquering Lavapura, Lakṣmīpativarman became the governor of the Mons and had a mission to renovate the ruined city to its former glory.

Conclusion

Inscription K.1198 / Ka.18 may provide new insight into the fall of Dvāravatī. The inscription provides evidence that the army of King Sūryavarman I led by General Lakṣmīpativarman first marched to Phnom Rung, then to the area which is today Nakhon Ratchasima Province to squash the rebellion against the king. After conquering the rebel, Lakṣmīpativarman led the army to defeat the Mons of Dvāravatī at Lavapura, or modern-day Lop Buri. After that, Lakṣmīpativarman was appointed as the governor there. He had the mission to renovate the city destroyed by war to be as it was before. This is the first mention of the fall of Dvāravatī caused by the Khmer army.

Appendix

A concise translation of the Khmer text

The inscription records how in the year 1014 CE, King Sūryavarman I gave an audience at the grand palace.[1] The king ordered the installation of this inscription at Madhyadeśa and gave respect to a golden liṅga. Then the inscription relates a previous story that, in the year 1009 CE, Mratāñ Khloñ Nṛpendropakalpa[2] purchased a plot of land at Madhyadeśa and offered it to Lakṣmipativarman. In 1011 CE, Vraḥ Kaṃ Steṅ Añ Śrī Lakṣmipativarman purchased land with a mountain and established a Śivaliṅga on that mountain. In 1014 CE, Lakṣmipativarman performed the ceremonies of Brahmayajña and Matṛyajña and paid respect to the golden liṅga. Then, together with a gathering of royal officials, he installed this inscription. In the assembly, Vraḥ Kaṃ Steṅ Añ Kanlaḥ Vnaṃ gave the promise to offer plots of land to the Śivaliṅga at Madhyadeśa and the Śivaliṅga on the mountain. In 1011 CE, the Vau family together with the Tampāṅ family rebeled against King Sūryavarman I. The king took all property from the Vau family, including Sukhāvasa of Tāñ Tri, and gave it to Lakṣmipativarman. The king ordered Lakṣmipativarman to replace the Buddha image with a Śivaliṅga. Vraḥ Kamrateṅ Añ Vidyāśrama presided over the ceremony and formed the place of worship. In 1012 CE, Vāp Le, an official of god, from Daśagrāma, borrowed gold from Lakṣmipativarman. He could not return the gold with interest, so he gave a plot of land in Trāc village to repay the debt. In 1012 CE, Lakṣmipativarman purchased an inherited plot of land at Mat Caṅvā from Vāp Jū Pralāy for the value of four silver bowls, four rings, one cup, one jar and ten pieces of cloth. The plot of land was demarcated. In 1013 CE, Kaṃ Steṅ Mlvay had an argument with Lakṣmipativarman about the right to govern the plot of land at Vraḥ Vnūk. So, Kaṃ Steṅ Mlvay sent his servants to harvest the rice planted in that location. Lakṣmipativarman beseeched the king regarding his claim to that plot of land. The king was very angry at Kaṃ Steṅ Mlvay and granted rights to Lakṣmipativarman. The death penalty was sentenced to Vāp Jū, the servant leader of Kaṃ Steṅ Mlvay. Vāp Jū appealed the penalty by giving all his property to Lakṣmipativarman. The king donated the land to Dvihasta Śivaliṅga at Madhyadeśa. The king ordered the elders and leaders of the village to properly demarcate the land. Lakṣmipativarman was very delighted and made many donations to the god. In 1013 CE, Vāp Vai, the royal official who resided in Tampuṅ village, offered land to Lakṣmipativarman. The plot of land was to the east of Kamrateṅ Jagat Śivapāda. In 1013 CE, on the 1st day of the waxing moon of the eighth lunar month, King Sūryavarman I gave an audience at the grand palace. The king gave an order to Vidyādhipaṇḍita and Mratāñ Khloñ Nṛpendropakalpa from Aninditapura with all his offspring, who were the officials of the worship chamber, to unite their properties with Lakṣmipativarman for the purpose of taxation.

In 1014 CE, Loñ Sikhvindu and senior relatives along with the village headsman offered the land of Kaṃ Tvat Tol to Lakṣmipativarman.

1 Caturdvāra, Silātatāka of Śrī Jayendragiri.

2 All -kalpa ending names are only mentioned in inscriptions from the reigns of King Harṣavarman II to Suryavarman I.

Then, Lakṣmipativarman contributed many donations to the Śivaliṅga at Kaṃ Tvat Tol. It was decreed that virtuous men who came to this place may obtain the merit of Lakṣmipativarman, while those who desecrated this hermitage must to go to hell as long as the sun and the moon shine. In 1014 CE, Mratāñ Khloñ Śrī Vīrendravallabha gave a plot of land and many slaves to the Śivaliṅga of Madhyadeśa. This is the message of Mratāñ Śrī Vīrendravallabha, son of Lakṣmipativarman. Then there is a list of donations of Kaṃ Steṅ Añ to the god of Madhyadeśa.

Acknowledgements

I am very thankful to Bunchar Pongpanich and Phuthorn Bhumadhon for inviting me and encouraging me to write about this topic. I would also like to show my gratitude to Sombat Mangmeesukhsiri for translating the Sanskrit text. I am indebted to Hunter Watson for helping to edit the language of this article.

EXHIBITION OF PRE-DVĀRAVATĪ ARTEFACTS AND POST WORKSHOP VISITS

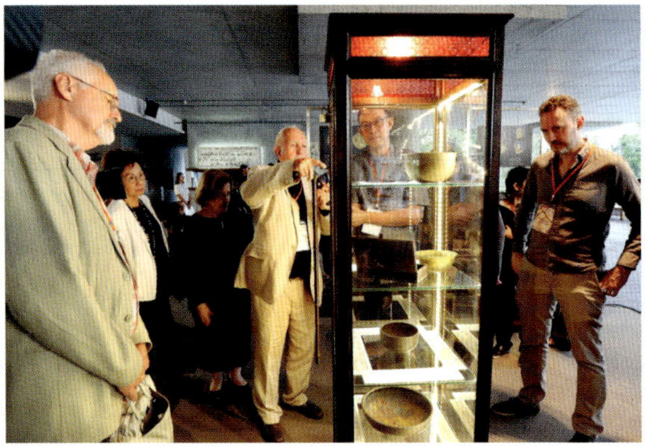

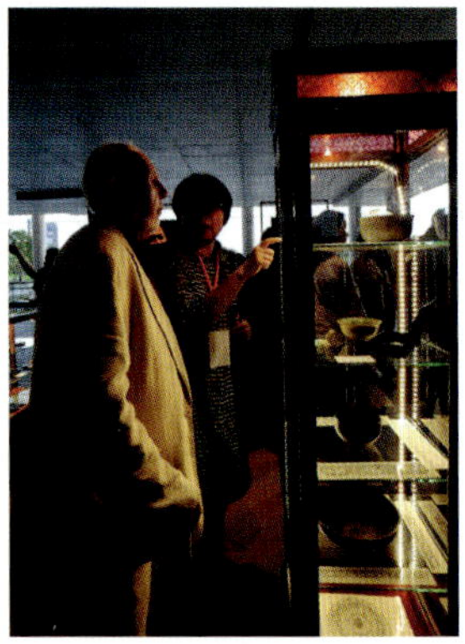

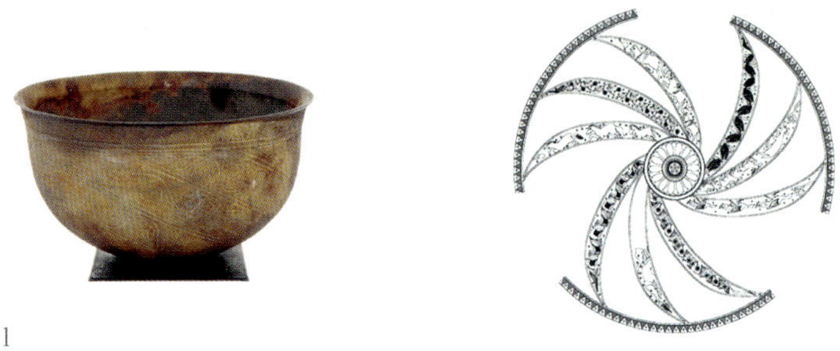

Bowl 1

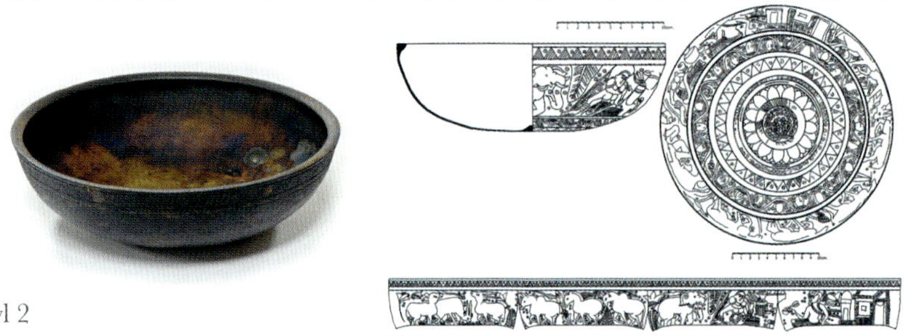

Bowl 2

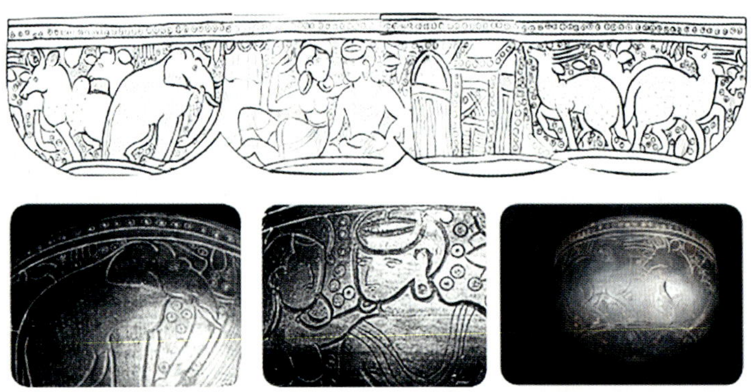

Bowl 3

Figs. 1a-b Ian Glover lecturing on the bronzes found at Khao Sam Kaeo in Chumphon Province, on the southeast coast of the peninsula, which were displayed in the special exhibition "Recently discovered Pre-Dvāravatī artefacts". SuthiRatana Foundation, Bangkok.
Fig 2 Bowl 1 (KSK 525) (Glover and Shahnaj Husne Jahan 2014).
Fig 3 Bowl 2 (KSK554) drawing by Nguan Tretappratina.
Fig 4 Bowl 3 (KSK528) drawing by Nguan Tretappratina.

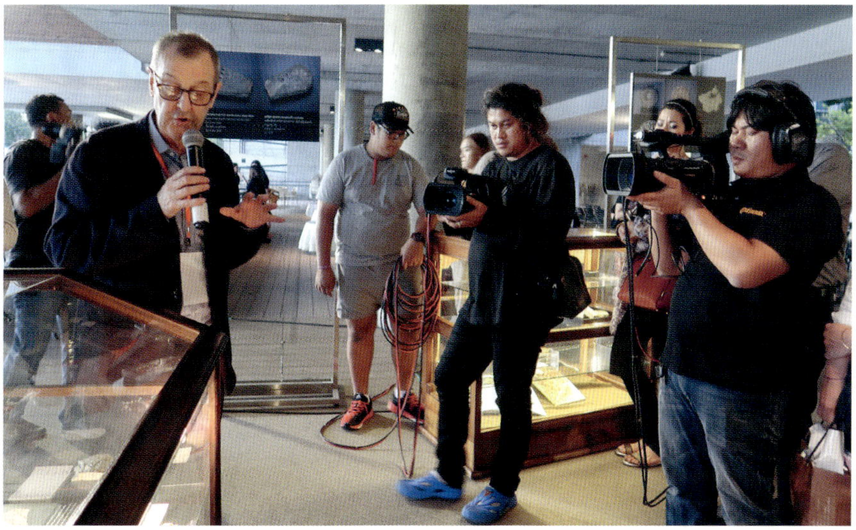

5

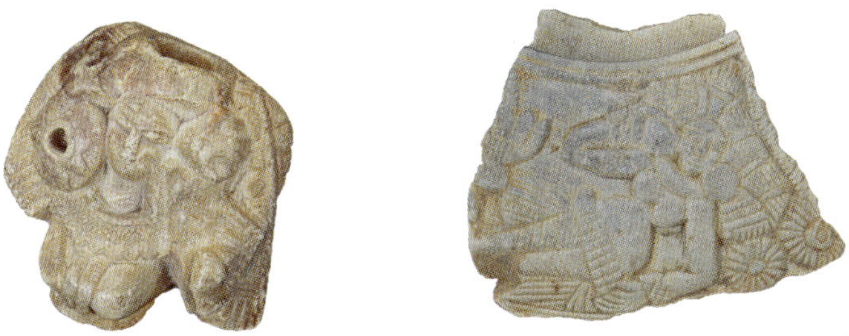

6a-b

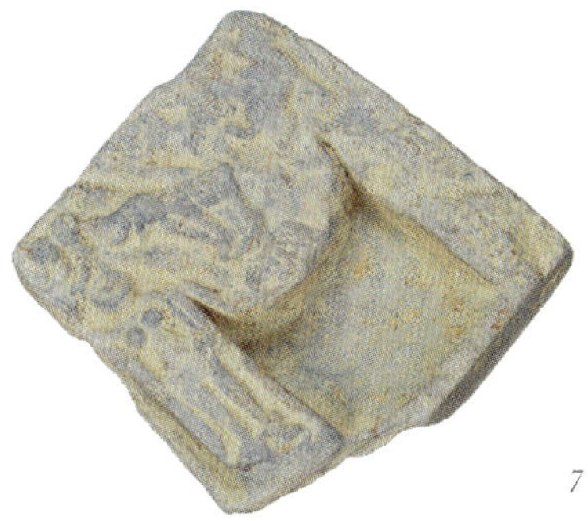

7

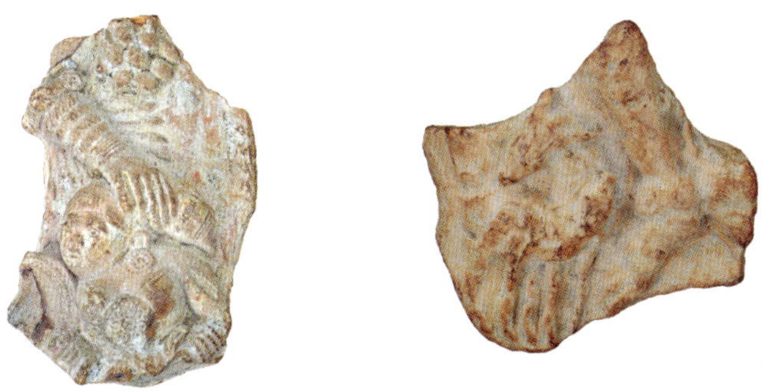

8a-b

Fig.5 John Guy lecturing on the stone artefacts from SuthiRatana Foundation, Bangkok, which were displayed in the special exhibition "Recently discovered Pre-Dvāravatī artefacts".
Fig.6a-b Fragments of decorated stone depicting adorned ladies similar to the so-called Indian Śuṅga style. Found on the west coast of the Myanmar-Thai-Malay peninsula in the Kawthaung area of lower Myanmar.
Fig.7 Decorated stone with the low relief of an elephant standing on a lotus flower pouring water over a female figure. Found at Klong Hnoo, a site on the west coast of the Myanmar-Thai-Malay peninsula in the Kawthaung area of lower Myanmar.
Fig.8a-b Decorated terracottas with female figure (left) and an antelope (right). Found on the west coast of the Myanmar-Thai-Malay peninsula in the Kawthaung area of lower Myanmar.

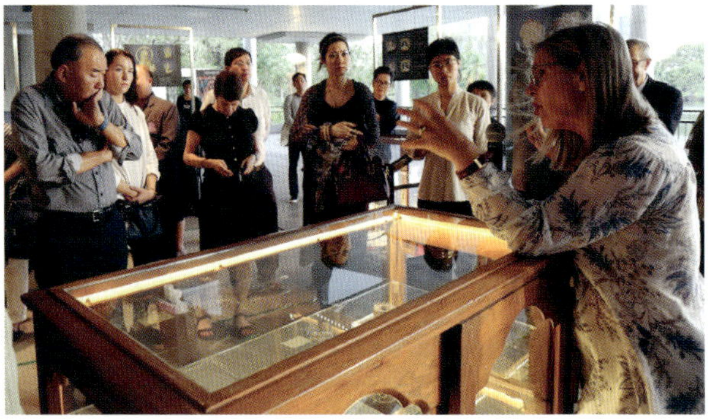

9

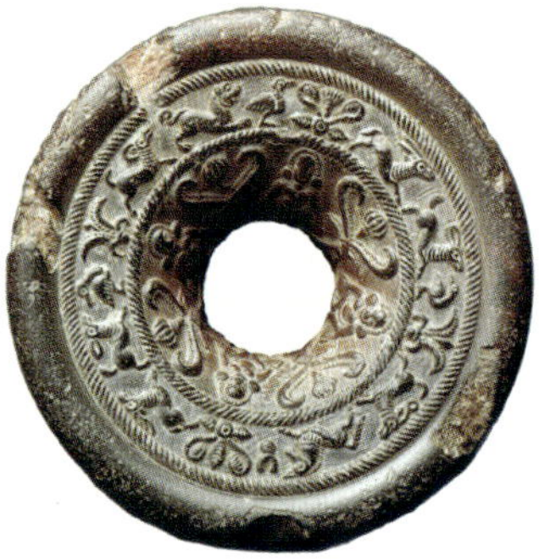

10

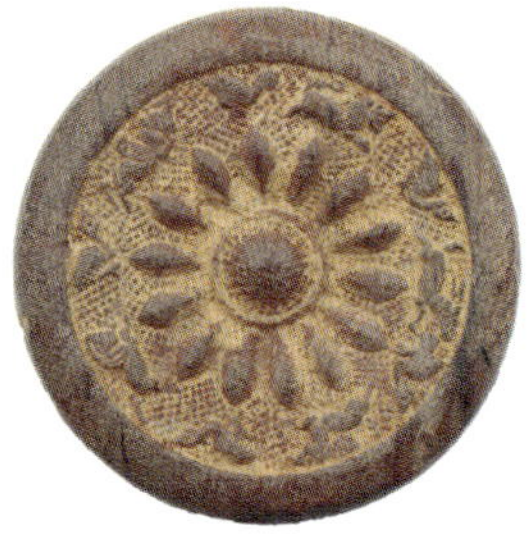

11

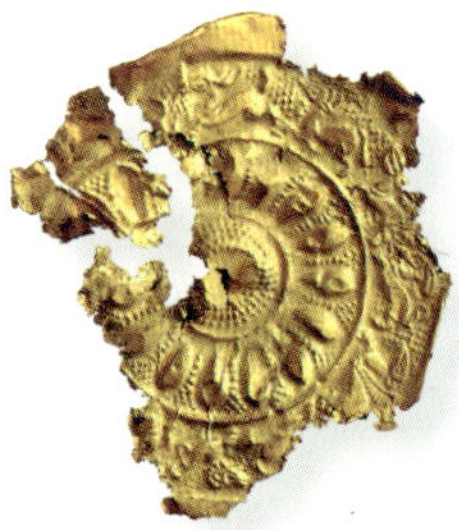

12

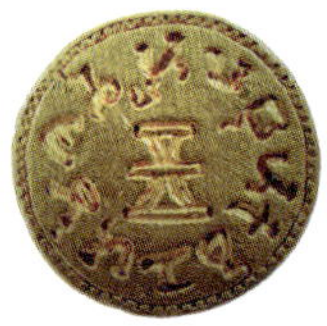

13

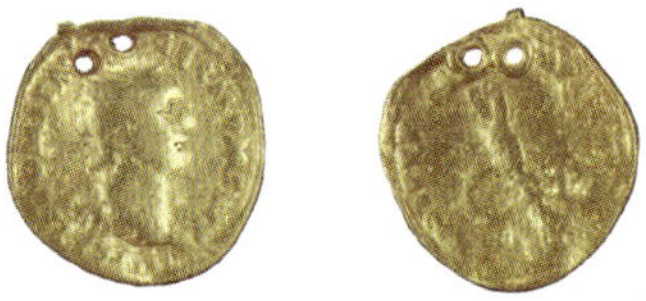

14a-b

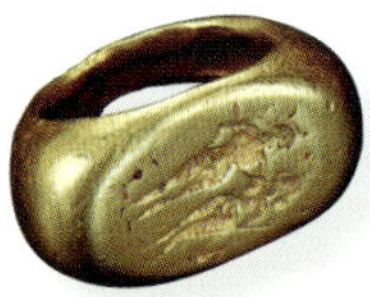

15

Fig.9 Anna Bennett lecturing on the Khao Sam Kaeo Ringstone (KSK522) and the Khamaukgyi Discstone (KMY/MYM526) which were displayed in the special exhibition "Recently discovered Pre-Dvāravatī artefacts". SuthiRatana Foundation, Bangkok.
Fig.10 Khao Sam Kaeo Ringstone with intricately carved upper face showing two bands of cable-moulding between which a ring of eleven animals and birds: lion, crane, ibex, antelope, goose, markhor goat, horse, deer, antelope, goose, and ram run towards the right separated by four floral designs. KSK522.
Fig.11 Khamaukgyi Discstone with a central lotus flower around which is a ring of ten animals and birds: winged lion, goose, lion, flying bird, ibex, flying bird, deer, bird, horse and flying bird run towards the right. KMY/MYM526.
Fig.12 Gold foil with repoussé decoration of a central lotus flower with bird and animal frieze, (Wt.: 0.57g, D: 4.5 cms) (composition: 84.5% gold, 12.1% silver, 2.6% copper) SuthiRatana Foundation, Bangkok KSK512 (Bennett 2017: 62–63; 2019: 103-104).
Fig.13 A first or second century CE gold seal bearing the Brāhmī inscription *brahaspatiśarmasa nāvika*, 'of the mariner Brahaspati'. Found at Bang Kluai Nok in Ranong Province on the western coast of the peninsula. SuthiRatana Foundation, Bangkok, BKN068.
*Fig.*14 Aureus of Domitian of 86 CE Pendant, found near a huge wooden plank on Bang Kluai Nok Beach and probably part of an ancient shipwreck, D. 2.0 cm Wt. 7.07 g. Bang Kluay Nok, Ranong Province, Southern Thailand. SuthiRatana Foundation, Bangkok.
*Fig.*15 Gold Ring with crowned couple holding a vessel, found at Klong Hnoo, a site on the west coast of the Myanmar-Thai-Malay peninsula in the Kawthaung area of lower Myanmar.

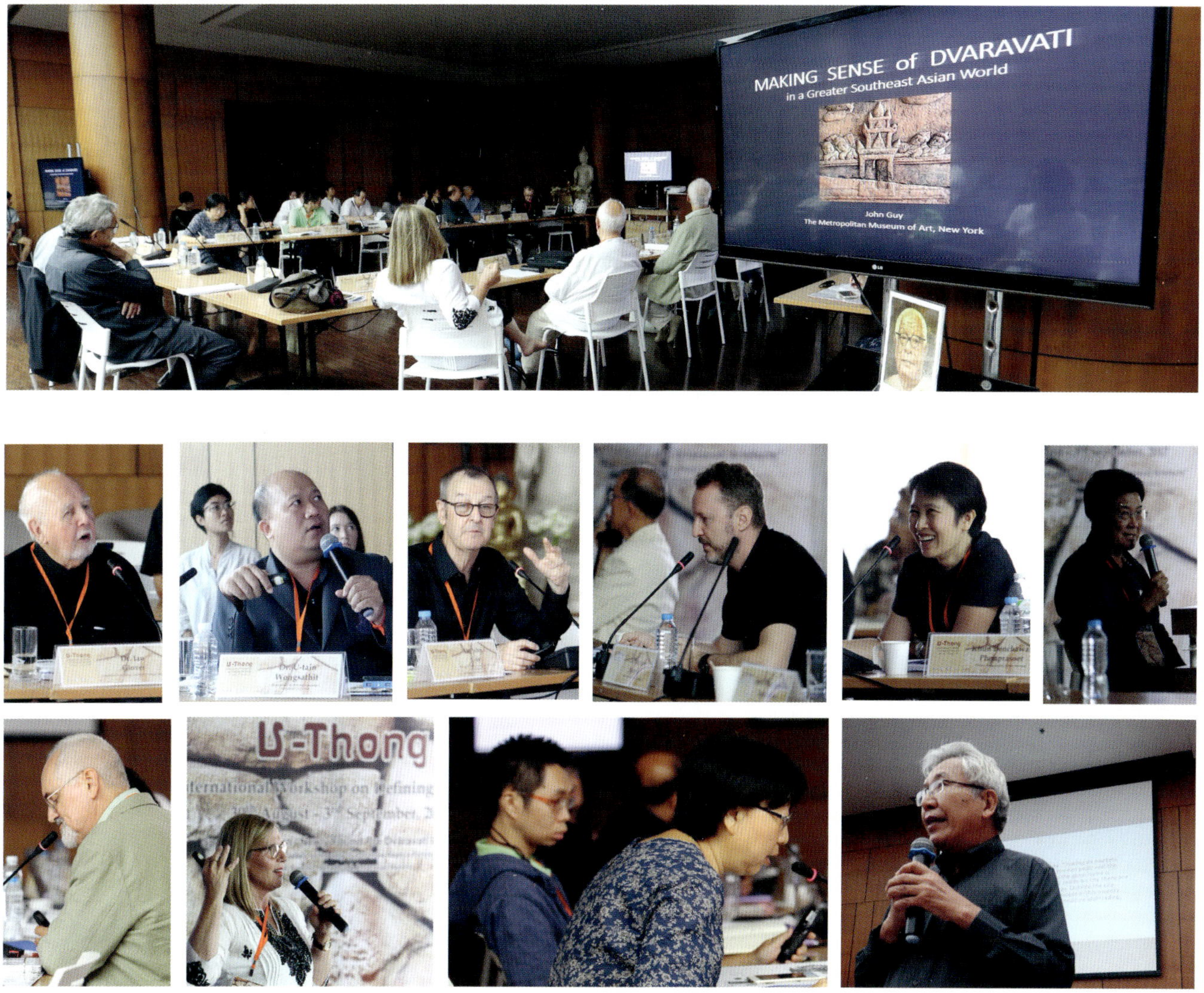

Fig.16 Eleven talks relating to Dvāravatī were presented. These included *The Pre-Dvāravatī Gap* by Ian C. Glover; *The Fall of Dvāravatī as mentioned in Khmer Inscription* K.1198/Ka.18 by U-tain Wongsathit; *Making Sense of Dvāravatī in a Greater Southeast Asian World* by John Guy; *The Extent of Dvāravatī: How much can sema stones tell us?* by Stephen Murphy, Asian Civilisation Museum, Singapore; *The Traces of Dvāravatiī in Hariphunchai Kingdom* by Benchawan Phonprasoet, curator of Hariphunchai National Museum; *Religion of Dvāravatī: The Art Historical Evidence* by Piriya Krairiksh, Piriya Krairiksh Foundation, *Phong Tuek Comlexities* by Wesley Clarke; *Science, Technology & Economy of Dvāravatī: The role of the precious metals trade* by Anna Bennett; and *Request for fine horses: Medieval Chinese tribute notes on horse usage in Dvāravatī and Southeast Asia* by Lin Ying and Huang Jiaxin, Sun Yat-sen; an address on *New knowledge on Dvāravatī, the Earliest Proto Historic period of Thailand* by Phuthorn Bhumadhon, as well as a paper by Hunter Watson which was read by U-tain Wongsathit on his behalf.

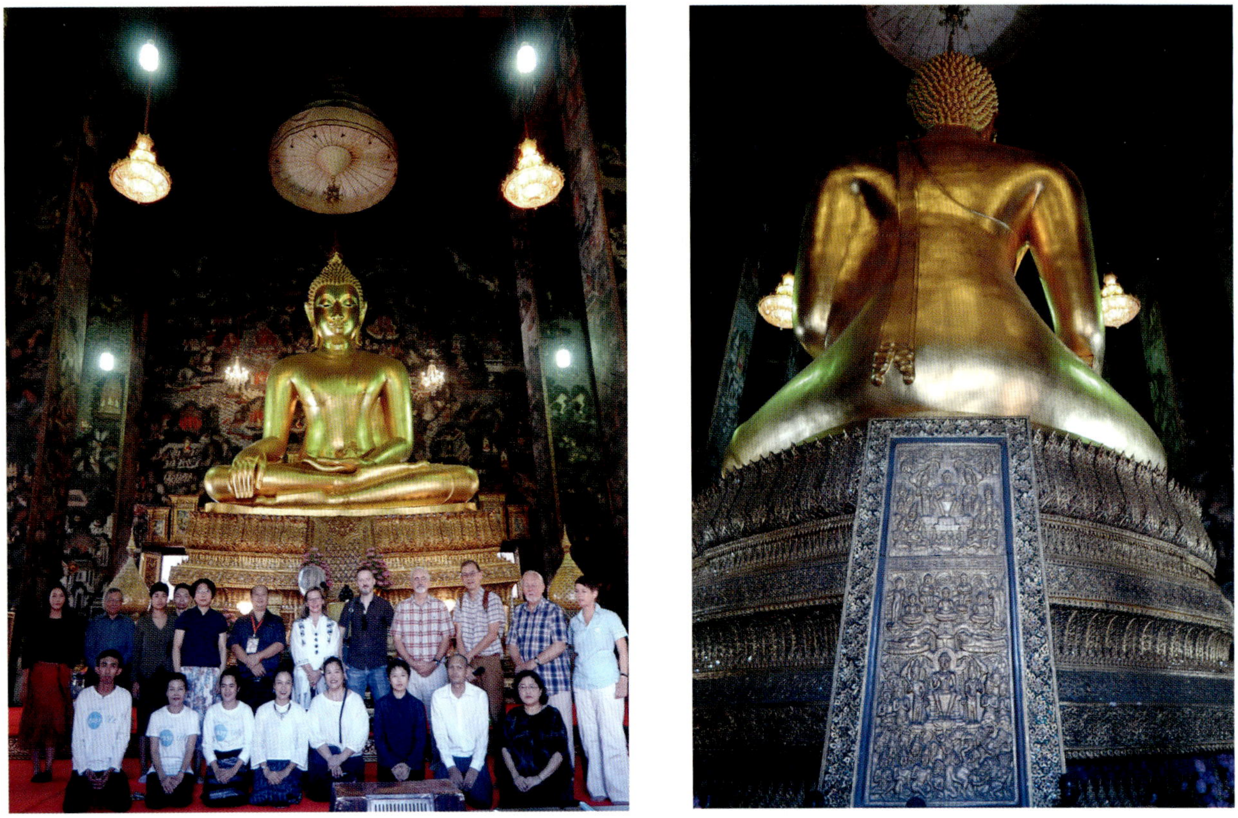

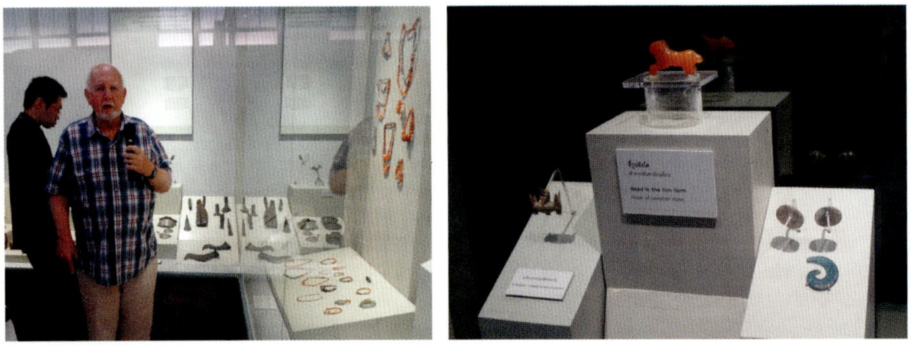

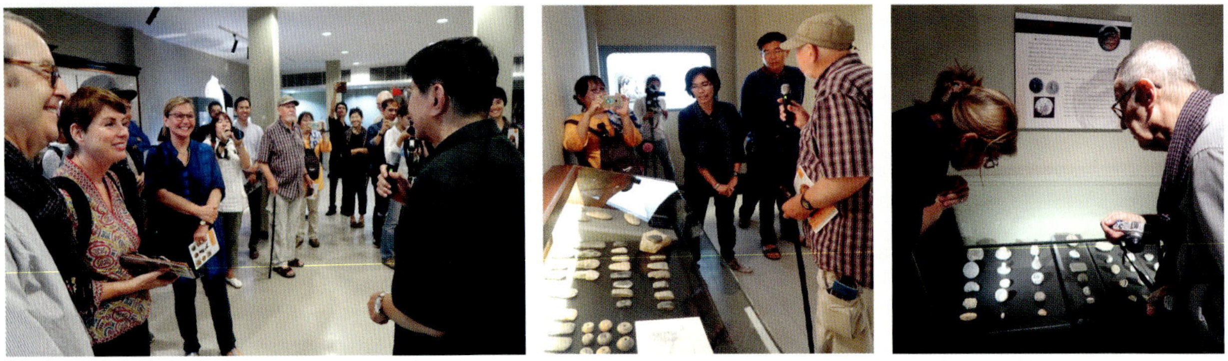

Fig.17a-b The great Dvāravatī stone relief slab on The Great Miracle of Lord Buddha from Nakhon Pathom preserved behind the Great Śākyamuni Buddha statue at Wat Suthat Thepwararam.
Fig.18a-b Walk with Ian Glover in the Pre-Dvāravatī gallery in the Bangkok National Museum.
Fig.19a-c Dvāravatī galleries, Bangkok National Museum and U Thong National Museum.

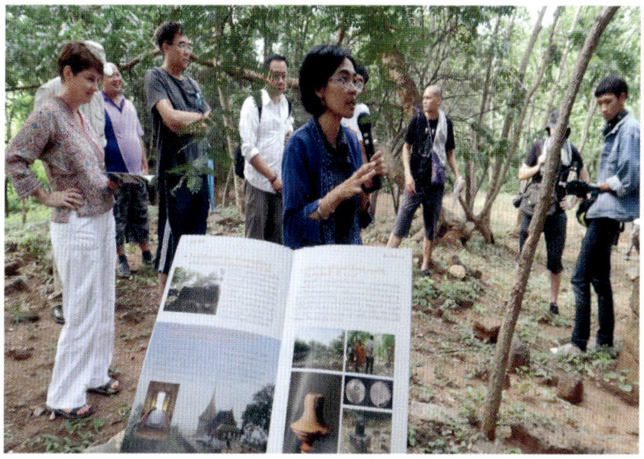

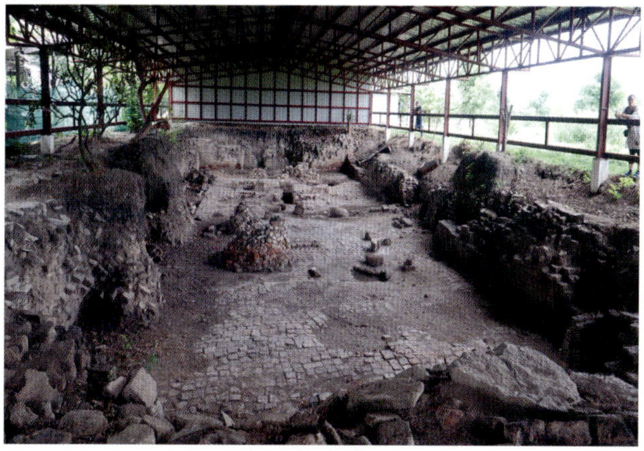

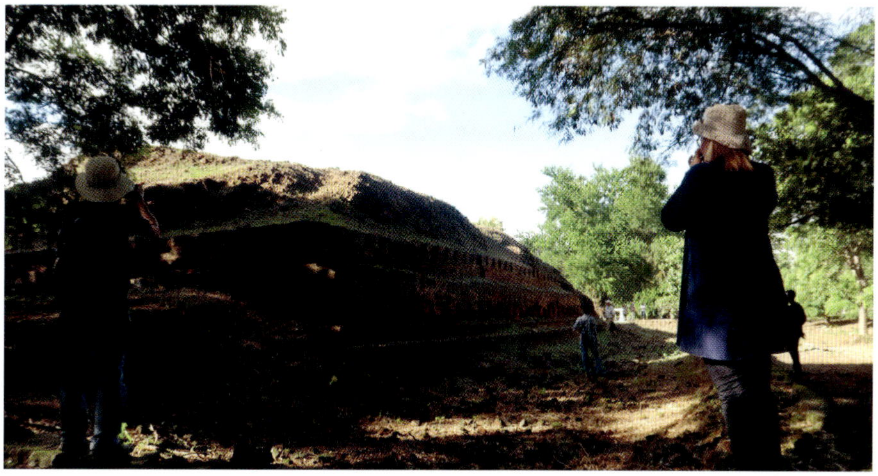

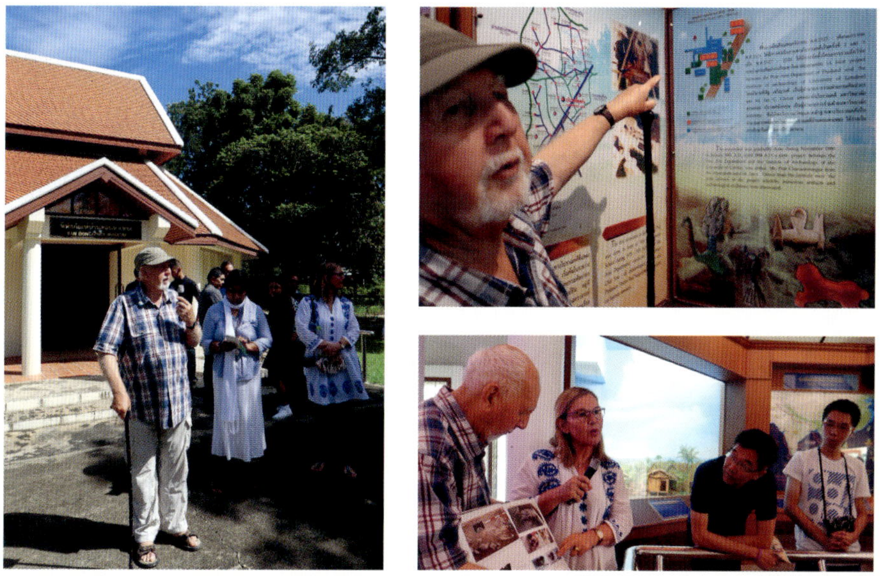

Fig.20 Kok Chang Din archaeological site with Supamas Duangsakul from U Thong National Museum and the FAD Suphan Buri Office.
Fig.21 A recently excavated site at U Thong.
Fig.22 Monument no.1, U Thong.
Fig.23a-c Ian Glover at Ban Don Ta Phet Museum and archaeological site, Kanchanaburi Province.

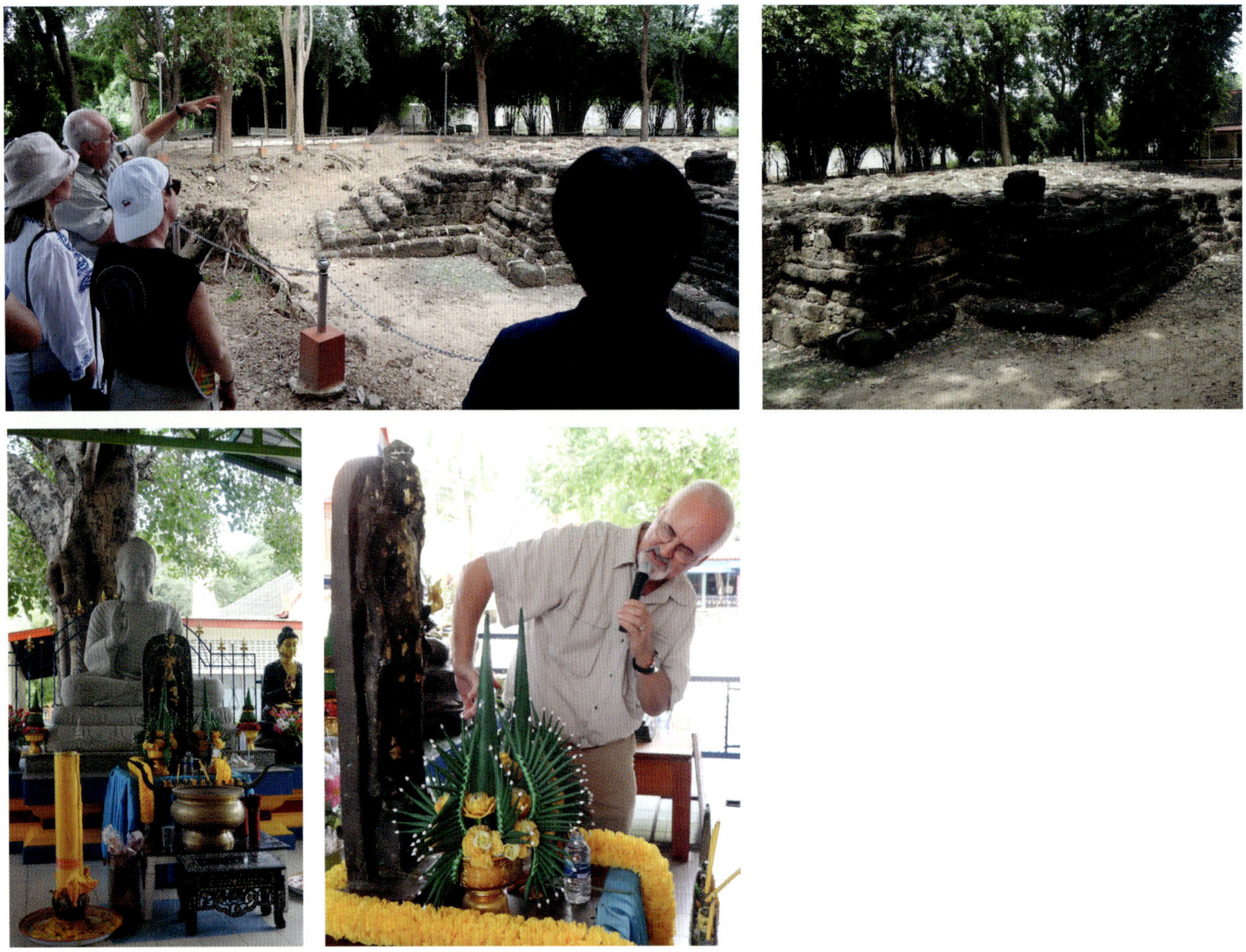

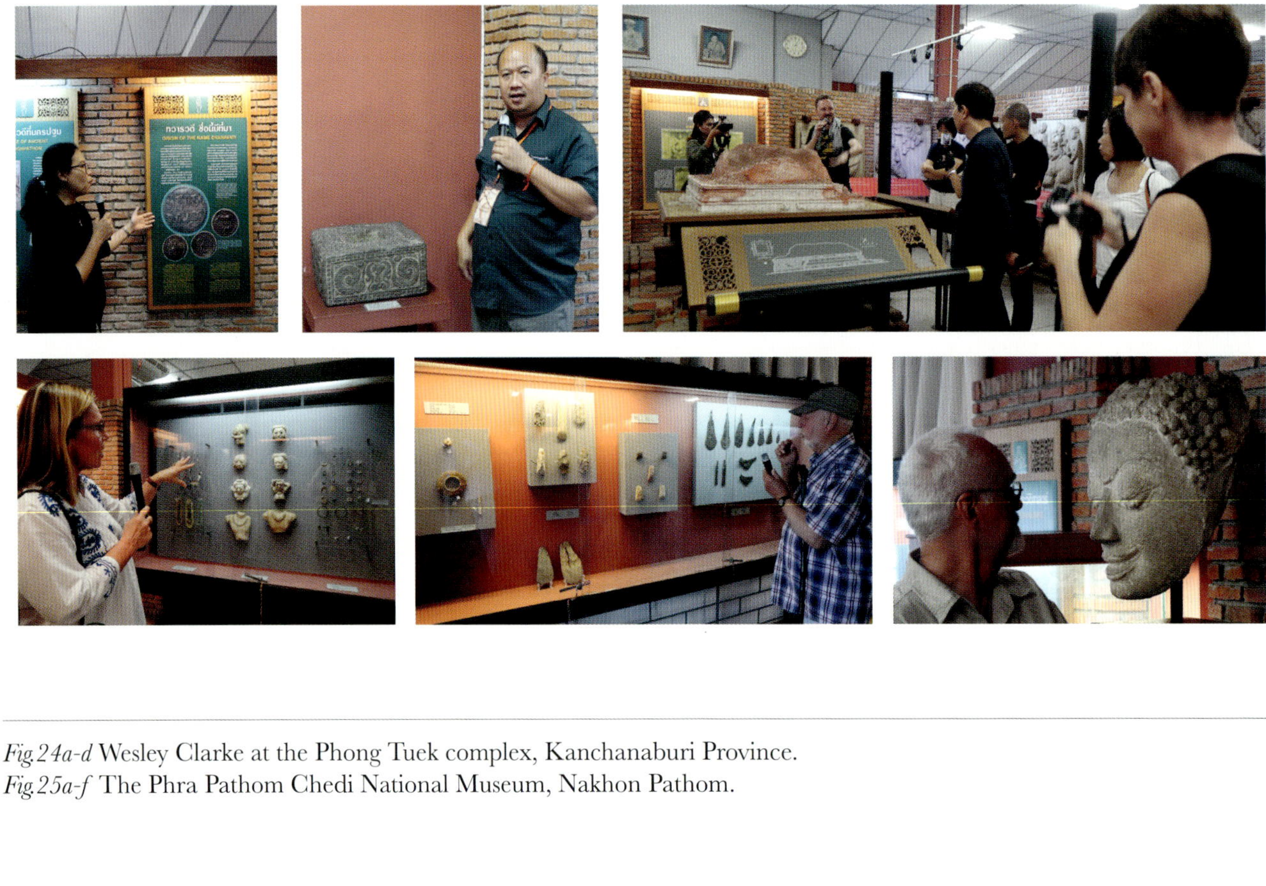

Fig.24a-d Wesley Clarke at the Phong Tuek complex, Kanchanaburi Province.
Fig.25a-f The Phra Pathom Chedi National Museum, Nakhon Pathom.

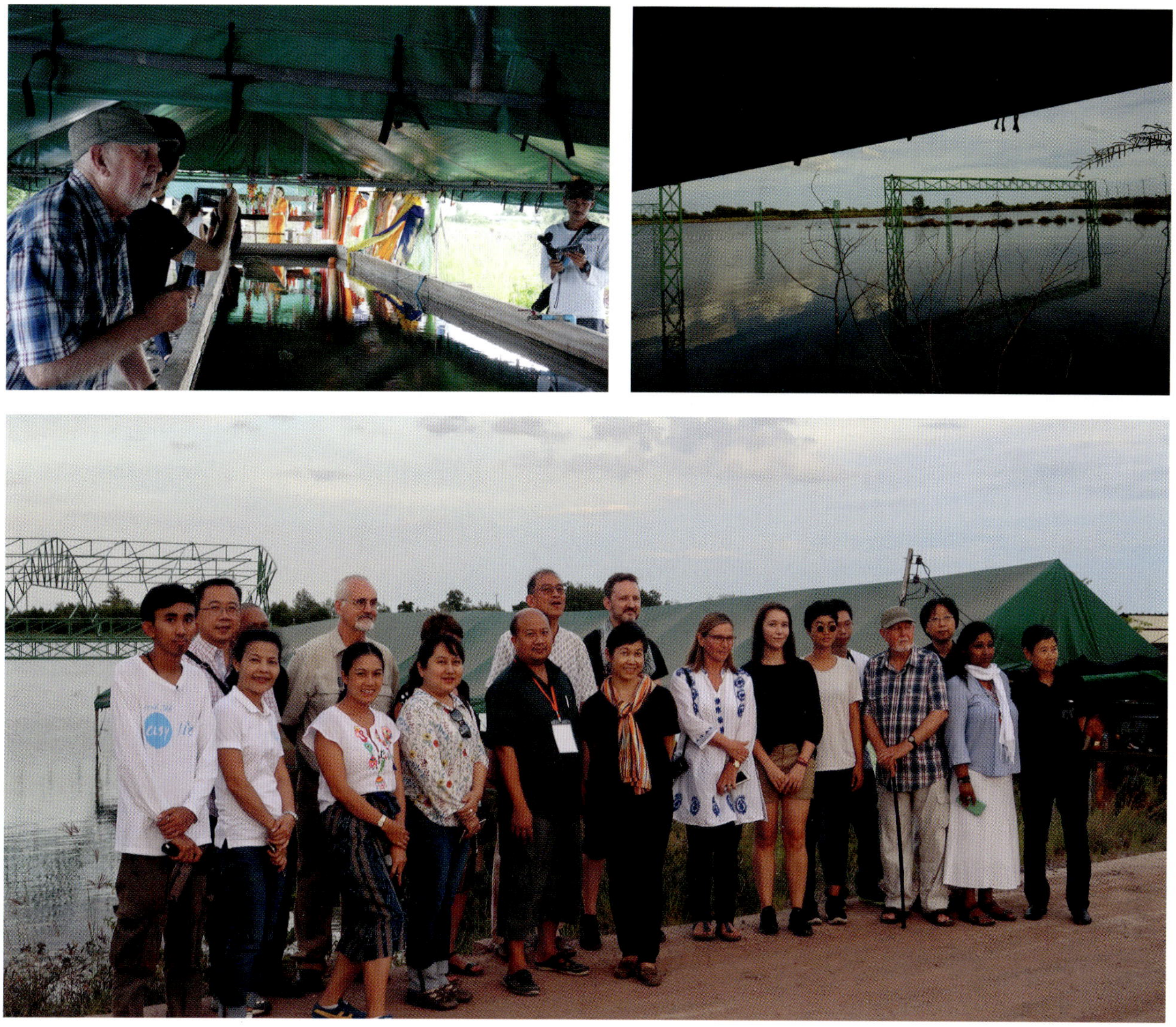

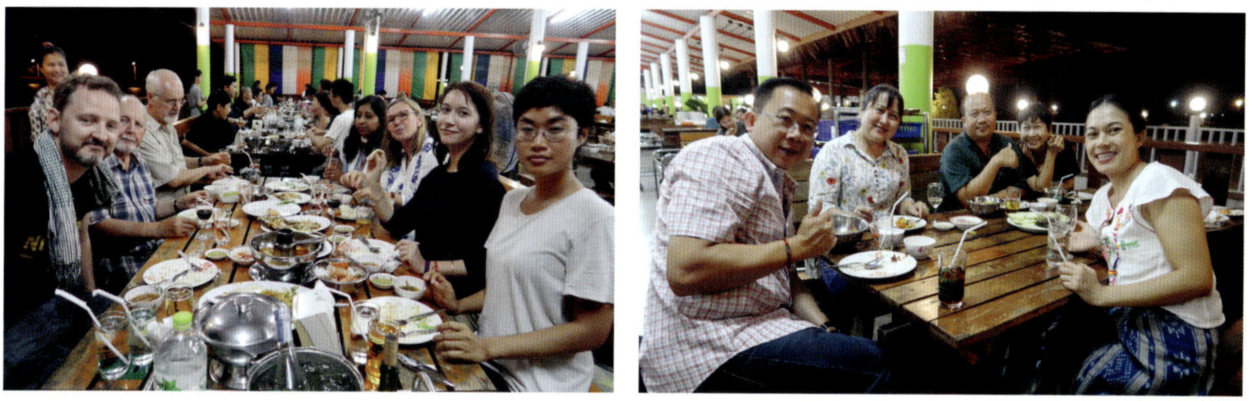

Fig.26a-c The Phnom Surin shipwreck near the mouth of the Tha Chin River.
Fig.27a-b The farewell dinner.

BIBLIOGRAPHY

Ian C. Glover
THE PRE-DVĀRAVATĪ GAP

Barram, Andrew, and Ian Glover 2008. "Re-thinking Dvavaratī." In *Archaeology in Southeast Asia—from Homo erectus to the Living Traditions, Selected papers from the 11th International Conference of the European Association of Southeast Asian Archaeologists, Bougan, 25–29th September 2006,* Eds. J.P. Pautreau, P.S. Méry, V. Zeitoun & E. Rambault, Chiang Mai: Silkworm Press: 175–182.

Basa, Kishor Kumar 1991. *The Westerly Trade of Southeast Asia From C.400 BC to C. AD 500: With Special Reference to Glass Beads.* Ph. D. Institute of Archaeology, UCL

Bellina, Bérénice 2003. "Beads, social change and interaction between India and Southeast Asia." *Antiquity* 77: 285–297.

Bennett, Anna T.N. 1982. *Metallurgical Analysis of Iron Artifacts from Ban Don Ta Phet, Thailand.* MA Thesis. Institute of Archaeology, UCL.

Bennett, Anna T.N. 2013a. "Protohistorical iron tools and weapons from a burial site in West Central Thailand." In *The World of Iron*, pp.371–382. Edited by J. Humprhis and T. Rehren. London: Archetype.

Bennett, Anna 2013b. "The Importance of Iron—its Development and Complexity in the Southeast Asian Iron Age." In *Selected Papers from the 12th International Conference of the European Association of Southeast-Asian Archaeologists, Leiden, September 2008*, pp.107–121. IAS Publication series, Amsterdam UniversityPress.

Bennett, Anna 2015. "Metallography, Experimental Smithing and Ethnographic Interpretation of Late Prehistoric Iron Billhooks from Mainland Southeast Asia." In *Metals and Civilizations Proceedings of the Seventh International Conference on the Beginnings of the Use of Metals and Alloys (BUMA VII)*, pp. 68–77. Edited by S. Sriniyasan, S. Ranganathan, A. Guimlia-Mair. Bangalore: National Institute of Advanced Studies.

Bennett, Anna 2017. *The Ancient History of U-Thong, City of Gold.* River Books, Bangkok.

Bennett, Anna, and Ian C. Glover 1992. "Decorated high-tin bronzes from Thailand's prehistory." In *Southeast Asian Archaeology, 1990: Proceedings of the Third Conference of the European Association of Southeast Asian Archaeologists,* pp.187–208. Edited by I. Glover. Hull UK: Centre for Southeast Asian Studies, University of Hull.

Brown, Robert 1996. "The Dvāravatī Wheels of Law and the Indianization of South East Asia." *Studies in Asian Art and Archaeology* 18. Leiden: Brill.

Chin You–Di 1976. *Ban Don Ta Phet 1975–76: Excavation Report.* Bangkok: FAD. Translated by Oraphan Chaivorart.

Clarke, Wes 2009. *The Skeletons of P'ong Tuk: A Preliminary Consideration of Human Remains in Dvāravatī Ritual Contexts.* Presented at 19th Indo-Pacific Prehistory Association Congress, Hanoi December 5th, 2009

Glover, Ian C. 1983. "The cemetery of Ban Don Ta Phet, results from the 1980-81 excavation season." In *South Asian Archaeology 1981*, pp.319–330. Edited by B. Allchin. Thailand: Cambridge University Press.

Glover, Ian C. 1990. "Ban Don Ta Phet: The 1984–85 excavation." In *Southeast Asian archaeology 1986*, pp.139–184. Edited by I. C. Glover and E. Glover. Oxford: BAR International Series 561.

Glover, Ian C. 2010. "The Dvāravatī Gap – Linking Prehistory and History in Early Thailand." *Bulletin of the Indo-Pacific Association* 30: 79–86.

Glover, Ian C. 2017. "Chin You–Di – A brief tribute." *SPAFA Journal* 1.

Glover, Ian C. and Anna Bennett 2012. "The High-Tin Bronzes of Thailand." In *Scientific Research on Ancient Asian Metallurgy*, pp.101–113. Edited by P. Jett., B. McCarthy and J. Douglas. Washington D.C.: The Smithsonian Institution.

Lankton, James and Laure Dussubieux 2006. "Early glass in Asian maritime trade: A review and an interpretation of compositional analysis." *Journal of Glass Studies* 48: 121–144.

Rajpitek, W. and N.J. Seeley 1979. "The bronze bowls from Ban Don Ta Phet: An enigma of prehistoric metallurgy." *World Archaeology* 11 (1): 26–31.

Rajpitek 1979. "The Technology of Copper Alloy Artefacts from Ban Don Ta Phet, Thailand." BSc. Report. London: Institute of Archaeology.

Saritpong Khunsong, Phasook Indrawooth, and Surapol Natapintu 2011. "Excavation of a pre-Dvāravatī site at Hor-Ek in ancient Nakhon Pathom." *Journal of the Siam Society* 99: 150–171.

Wasan Dhepsuriyanon 2001. *The Archeological site of Ban Don Ta Phet.* Bangkok: FAD. [In Thai]

Woods, M. 2002. *A Spatial and Statistical Analysis of Ban Don Ta Phet.* MA Thesis, SOAS London.

Wesley Clarke
DVĀRAVATĪ FROM THE BOTTOM UP

Acri, Andrea 2017. "'Local' vs. 'cosmopolitan' in the study of premodern Southeast Asia." *Suvannabhumi* 9 (1): 7–52.

Adams, Ron L. and Stacie M. King 2011. "Residential burial in global perspective." *Archaeological Papers of the American Anthropological Association* 20 (1): 1-16.

Banning, E. B. 2002. *Archaeological Survey.* New York: Kluwer Academic.

Bayly, Susan 2000. "French anthropology and the Durkheimians in colonial Indochina." *Modern Asian Studies* 34 (3): 581–622.

Bayly, Susan 2002. "Racial readings of empire: Britain, France, and colonial modernity in the Mediterranean and Asia." In *Modernity and Culture: From the Mediterranean to the Indian Ocean,* pp.285–313. Edited by L. T. Fawaz and S. Bayly. New York: Columbia University Press.

Bayly, Susan 2004. "Imagining 'Greater India': French and Indian visions of colonialism in the Indic mode." *Modern Asian Studies* 38 (3): 703–744.

Bentley, R. Alexander and Herbert Maschner 2003. "Preface: Considering complexity theory in archaeology." In *Complex Systems and Archaeology: Empirical and Theoretical Applications,* pp.1–8. Edited by R.A. Bentley and H. Maschner. Salt Lake City: University of Utah Press.

Bintliff, John L. 2006. "Time, structure, and agency: the Annales, emergent complexity, and archaeology." In *A Companion to Archaeology*, pp.174–194. Edited by J. L. Bintliff. Hoboken, New Jersey: Blackwell Publishing.

Bray, Warwick and Ian C. Glover 1987. "Scientific investigation or cultural imperialism: British archaeology in the Third World." *Bulletin of the Institute of Archaeology* 24: 109–125.

Briggs, Lawrence P. 1945. "Dvāravatī, the Most Ancient Kingdom of Siam." *Journal of the American Oriental Society* 65 (2): 98–107.

Brown, Robert L. 1996. *The Dvāravatī Wheels of the Law and the Indianization of South East Asia.* Leiden, New York, Köln: E.J. Brill.

Brown, Robert 2017. "The Trouble with Convergence." In *India and Southeast Asia Cultural Discourses,* pp.37–50. Edited by A. Dallapiccola. Mumbai: K.R. Cama Oriental Institute.

Burger, Oskar, and Lawrence C. Todd 2006. "Grain, extent, and intensity: The components of scale in archaeological survey." In *Confronting Scale in Archaeology: Issues of Theory and Practice,* pp.235–255. Edited by G. Lock and B. L. Molyneaux. Boston: Springer.

Canuto, Marcello and William L. Fash, Jr. 2004. "The blind spot: Where the elite and non-elite meet." In Continuities and Changes in Maya Archaeology: Perspectives at the Millennium, pp.47–70. Edited by C.W. Golden and C. Borgstede. New York and London: Routledge.

Charnvit Kasetsiri 1979. "Thai historiography from ancient times to the modern period." In *Perceptions of the Past in Southeast Asia,* pp.156–170. Edited by A. Reid and D. Marr. Singapore: Asian Studies Association of Australia/Heinemann Education Books.

Cherry, Haydon L 2004. "Social communication and colonial archaeology in Viet Nam." *New Zealand Journal of Asian Studies* 6 (2): 111–126.

Clarke, David L. 1973. "Archaeology: The loss of innocence." *Antiquity* 47: 6–18.

Clarke, Wesley 2011. *Return to P'ong Tuk: Preliminary Reconnaissance of a Seminal Dvāravatī Site in West- Central Thailand.* MA thesis, Center for International Studies, Southeast Asia Studies Program, Ohio University, Athens, Ohio.

Clarke, Wesley 2014. "The skeletons of Phong Tuek: Human remains in Dvāravatī ritual contexts." In *Before Siam: Essays in Art and Archaeology,* pp.205–223. Edited by N. Revire and S. Murphy. Bangkok: River Books & The Siam Society.

Clarke, Wesley 2015. "New observations at P'ong Tuk and ongoing issues with the conceptualization of Dvāravatī." In *Advancing Southeast Asian Archaeology 2013 - Selected Papers from the First SEAMEO-SPAFA International Conference on Southeast Asian Archaeology*, pp.289–305. Edited by N. H. Tan. Bangkok: SEAMEO SPAFA.

Cœdès, Georges 1925a. "Documents sur l'histoire politique et religieuse du Laos occidental." *Bulletin de l'École française d'Extrême-Orient* 25: 1–201.

Cœdès, George 1925b. "Tablettes votives bouddhiques de Siam." *Publications de École française d'Extrême-Orient, Études asiatiques* 20: 145–167.

Cœdès, George 1926. "Une Exposition de Sculptures Khmères et Siamoises au Musée Cernuschi." *Artibus Asiae* 1 (3): 190–202.

Cœdès, Georges 1928a. *Les collections archéologiques du Musée National de Bangkok.* Paris & Bruxelles: G. Van Oest.

Cœdès, George 1928b. "The Excavations of P'ongtük and their importance for the ancient history of Siam." *Journal of the Siam Society* 21 (3): 195–209. (Reprinted in *The Siam Society Fiftieth Anniversary* 1, pp.205–238. Bangkok: Siam Society, 1954).

Cœdès, Georges 1929. *Recueil des inscriptions du Siam, Deuxième partie: Inscriptions de Dvāravatī, de Çrīvijaya et du Lăvo.* Bangkok: Bangkok Times Press.

Cœdès, George 1964. "Some problems in the ancient history of the Hinduized states of South- East Asia." *Journal of Southeast Asian History* 5 (2): 1–14.

Cœdès, George 1968. *The Indianized State of Southeast Asia.* Translated by S.B. Cowing. Honolulu: The University Press of Hawai'i.

Crumley, Carole 2007. "Notes on a new paradigm." In *Socializing Complexity: Structure, Interaction and Power in Archaeological Discourse*, pp.30–36. Edited by S. Kohring and S. Wynne-Jones. Oxford: Oxbow Books.

Damrong Rajanubhab 1919. "Siamese history prior to the founding of Ayuddyā." *Journal of the Siam Society* 13 (2): 1–65.

Damrong Rajanubhab 1928. "[คำนำ] ยอร์ช เซเดส์ส, *โบราณวัตถุในพิพิธภัณฑสถานสำหรับพระนคร*" ([Introduction to] Cœdès, George: Les collections archéologiques du Musée national de Bangkok). *Ars Asiatica.* Bruxelles; Paris: G. Van Oest.

Damrong Rajanubhab 1973 [1926]. *Monuments of the Buddha in Siam*, 2nd edition. Translated by S. Sivaraksa and A.B. Griswold. Bangkok: The Siam Society.

de Laguna, F. 1957. "Some problems of objectivity in ethnology." *Man* 228: 179–182.

Desjeux, Dominique 1996. "Scales of observation: A micro-sociological epistemology of social science practice." *Visual Studies* 11 (2): 45–55.

Dunnell, R.C. and William S. Dancey 1983. "The siteless survey: A regional scale data collection strategy." In *Advances in Archaeological Method and Theory* 5, pp.267–286. Edited by M.B. Schiffer. New York: Academic Press.

Dupont, Pierre 1959. *L'archéologie Mône de Dvāravatī*, 2 Vol. Publications de l'École Française d'Extrême-Orient 41. Paris: École française d'Extrême-Orient.

Embree, Lester 1989. "The structure of American theoretical archaeology: A preliminary report." In *Critical Traditions in Contemporary Archaeology*, pp.28–37. Edited by V. Pinsky and A. Wylie. Cambridge: Cambridge University Press.

Evans, Caitlin, Nigel Chang and Naho Shimizu 2016. "Sites, survey, and ceramics: Settlement patterns of the first to ninth centuries CE in the Upper Mun River Valley, northeast Thailand." *Journal of Southeast Asian Studies* 47 (3): 438–467.

Fournereau, Lucien 1895. *Le Siam ancien, archéologie, épigraphie, géographie.* Paris: Ernest Leroux.

Wesley Clarke
DVĀRAVATĪ FROM THE BOTTOM UP

Fornereau, Lucien 1908. *Le Siam Ancient, Archéologie - Epigraphie - Géographie*. Paris: Tome trente-unième (deuxième partie) des Annales du Musée Guimet. Edited by Ernest Leroux.

Gallon, Matthew D. 2013. *Ideology, Identity and the Construction of Urban Communities: The Archaeology of Kamphaeng Saen, Central Thailand (c. Fifth to Ninth Century CE)*. Ph.D. Diss., University of Michigan, Ann Arbor.

Gallon, Mathew 2014. "Monuments and Identity at the Dvāravatī Town of Kamphaeng Saen." In *Before Siam: Essays in Art and Archaeology*, pp.331–351. Edited by N. Revire and S. Murphy. Bangkok: River Books & The Siam Society.

Glover, Ian 1993. "Other peoples' pasts – Western archaeologists and Thai prehistory." *The Journal of the Siam Society* 81 (1): 45–53.

Glover, Ian 2010. "Thinking about Dvāravatī." In *Abhinandanamālā: Nandana Chutiwongs Felicitation Volume*, pp.47–65. Edited by L. Prematilleke et al. Bangkok: SPAFA Regional Centre of Archeology and Fine Arts, in collaboration with the Abhinandanamālā Committee, Colombo.

Guillon, Emmanuel 1999. *The Mons: A Civilization of Southeast Asia*. Bangkok: The Siam Society.

Gupta, Sunil 2003. "From archaeology to art in the material record of Southeast Asia." In *Fishbones and Glittering Emblems: Southeast Asian Archaeology 2002*, pp.391–404. Edited by A. Karlström and A. Källén. Stockholm: Museum of Far Eastern Antiquities.

Hennequin, Laurent 2010. "The French Contribution to the Rediscovery of Dvāravatī Archaeology." *Journal of the Siam Society* 98: 1–48.

Hodder, Ian 2012. "Introduction: Contemporary theoretical debate in Archaeology." In *Archaeological Theory Today*, 2nd edition, pp.1–14. Edited by I. Hodder. Malden, Massachusetts: Polity Press.

Hodder, Ian and Clive Orton 1976. *Spatial Analysis in Archaeology*. Cambridge: Cambridge University Press.

Holland, John 2014. *Complexity: A Very Short Introduction*. Oxford: Oxford University Press.

Indorf, Pinna, Swati Gudur and Wesley Clarke 2014. "Describing architectural change and continuity in early historic central Thailand: a Dvāravatī example." Paper presented at the 20th Congress of the Indo-Pacific Prehistory Association, January 16, 2014, Siem Reap, Cambodia.

Kohler, T. 2012. "Complex systems and archaeology." In *Archaeological Theory Today*, 2nd edition, pp.93–123. Edited by I. Hodder. Malden, Massachusetts: Polity Press.

Kulke, Hermann 1990. "Indian colonies, Indianization or cultural convergence? Reflections on the changing image of India's role in South-East Asia." *Semaian* 3: 8–32.

Lavy, Paul, and Wesley Clarke 2015. "Integrating the Phong Tuek Viṣṇu: The archaeology and art history of a forgotten image." *Journal of the Siam Society* 103: 19–62.

Lock, Gary and Brian L. Molyneaux 2006. "Introduction: Confronting scale." In *Confronting Scale in Archaeology: Issues of Theory and Practice*, pp.1–11. Edited by G. Lock and B.L. Molyneaux. Boston, Springer.

Lukas, Helmut 2003. "Theories of Indianization, exemplified by selected case studies from Indonesia." In Proceedings of Papers: *Sanskrit in Southeast Asia: The Harmonizing Factor of Cultures, International Sanskrit Conference, Silpakorn University*, pp.82–107. Bangkok: Mahachulalongkornrajavidyalaya Press.

Lyons, Elizabeth 1979. "Dvaravati, a consideration of its formative period." In *Early South East Asia, essays in archaeology, history, and historical geography*, pp.352-359. Edited by R.B. Smith and W. Watson. New York and Kuala Lumpur: Oxford University Press.

Mabbett, Ian W. 1977. "The 'Indianization' of Southeast Asia: Reflections on the historical sources." *Journal of Southeast Asian Studies* 8: 143–161.

MacDonald, William K. 1980. "The Bang Site, Thailand: An alternative analysis." *Asian Perspectives* 21 (1): 30–51.

McNeill, Judith R. 1997. "Muang Phet: Quaritch Wales' moated site excavations re-appraised." *Bulletin of the Indo-Pacific Prehistory Association* 16: 167–176.

Miksic, John N. 1995. "Evolving archaeological perspectives on Southeast Asia." *Journal of Southeast Asian Studies* 26 (1): 46–62.

Miksic, John N. and Geok Yian Goh 2017. *Ancient Southeast Asia.* Milton Park and New York: Routledge.

Molyneaux, Brian L. 2005. "Archaeological survey." In *Handbook of Archaeological Methods* 1, pp.106-132. Edited by H.D.G. Maschner and C. Chippindale. Lantham, Maryland and Oxford: AltaMira Press.

Mudar, Karen M. 1999. "How many Dvaravati kingdoms? Locational analysis of first millennium A.D. moated settlements in Central Thailand." *Journal of Anthropological Archaeology* 18: 1–28.

Nandana Chutiwongs 2009. "Le bouddhisme à Dvāravatī et à Hariphunchai." In ***Dvāravatī: aux sources du bouddhisme en Thaïlande,*** pp.59–73. Edited by P. Baptiste and T. Zéphir. Paris: Réunion des Musées nationaux.

Phasook Indrawooth 1983. *The Excavation at the Ancient Town of Nakhon Phatom, Tambon Phra Praton,Amphoe Muang, Changwat Nakhon Pathom.* Nakhon Pathom: Silpakorn University Press.

Phasook Indrawooth 1999 [2542 BE]. ทวารวดี : การศึกษาเชิงวิเคราะห์จากหลักฐานทางโบราณคดี (*Dvaravati: A critical study based on archaeological evidence*). Bangkok: Faculty of Archaeology, Silpakorn University. [In Thai]

Phasook Indrawooth, S. Krabuansang, and P. Narkwake 1991. "Muang Fa Daed Song Yang: New archaeological discoveries." In *Récentes Recherches en Archéologie en Thaïlande: Deuxieme Symposium Franco-Thai*, pp.98–111. Bangkok: Silapkorn University.

Phattharaphong Kaongoen 2002 [2545 BE]. โบราณคดีคอกช้างดิน(*The Archaeologyof Khok Chang Din*). Suphan Buri: FAD. [In Thai]

Peleggi, Maurizio 2004. "Royal antiquarianism, European orientalism and the production of archaeological knowledge in modern Siam." In Project MUSE: *Asia in Europe, Europe in Asia.* Edited by S. Ravi, M. Rutten, B. Goh. Institute of Southeast Asian Studies. Web <http://muse.jhu.edu/>.

Pelliot, Paul 1904. "Deux itinéraires de Chine en Inde à la fin du VIIIe siècle." *Bulletin de l'École française d'Extrême-Orient* 4: 131–413.

Peregrine, Peter N. 2017. *Archaeological Research: A Brief Introduction.* New York: Routledge.

Piriya Krairiksh 2012. *The Roots of Thai Art.* Translated by N. Chakrabongse. Bangkok: River Books.

Ray, Himanshu Prabha 1997. "The emergence of urban centres in Bengal: Implications for the late prehistory of Southeast Asia." *Indo-Pacific Prehistory Association Bulletin* 16 (3): 43-48.

Revire, Nicolas 2011. "Review article, Pierre Dupont's L'archéologie mône de Dvāravatī and its English translation by Joyanto K. Sen, in relation with continuing research." *Journal of the Siam Society* 99: 196–225.

Revire, Nicolas 2015. "What's in a name? The status of Dvāravatī today." Paper presented at the 15th International Conference of the European Association of Southeast Asian Archaeologists, Paris, July 6–10.

Revire, Nicolas 2016. "Dvāravatī and Zhenla in the seventh to eighth centuries: A transregional ritual complex." *Journal of Southeast Asian Studies* 47 (3): 393–417.

Rispoli, Fiorella, Roberto Ciarla, Vincent C. Pigott 2013. "Establishing the prehistoric cultural sequence for the Lopburi region, central Thailand." *Journal of World Prehistory* 26: 101–171.

Saritpong Khunsong, Phasook Indrawooth, and Surapol Natapintu 2011. "Excavation of a pre-Dvāravatī site at Hor-Ek in ancient Nakhon Pathom." *Journal of the Siam Society* 99: 150–171.

Wesley Clarke
DVĀRAVATĪ FROM THE BOTTOM UP

Souvatzi, Stella 2007. "Social complexity is not the same as hierarchy." In *Socialising Complexity: Structure, Interaction and Power in Archeological Discourse,* pp.37–59. Edited by S. Kohring and S. Wynne-Jones. Oxford: Oxbow Books.

Srisakra Vallibhotoma 1986. "Political and cultural continuities at Dvāravatī sites." In *Southeast Asia in the 9th-14th Centuries,* pp.229–238. Edited by D.G. Marr and A.C. Milner. Singapore: Australian National University and the Institure of Southeast Asian Studies.

Stark, Miriam T. 1993. "Re-fitting the 'cracked and broken façade': The case for empiricism in post-processual ethnoarchaeology." In *Archaeological Theory: Who Sets the Agenda?*, pp.93–104. Edited by N. Yoffee and A. Sherratt. Cambridge: Cambridge University Press.

Stark, Miriam T. 2006. "Early mainland Southeast Asian landscapes in the first millennium A.D." *Annual Review of Anthropology* 35: 21.1–21.26.

Stark, Miriam 2015. "Looking forward by studying the past in East and Southeast Asian archaeology: The next 50 years." *Journal of Indo-Pacific Archaeology* 35: 67–75.

Stark, Miriam T. 2016. "Inscribing legitimacy and building power in the Mekong Delta." In *Social Theory in Archaeology and Ancient History; the Present and Future of Counternarratives,* pp.75–105. Edited by G. Emberling. New York: Cambridge University Press.

Stark, Miriam T. 2017. "Book review of *Before Siam: Essays in Art and Archaeology*, N. Revire and S.A. Murphy, editors, Bangkok: River Books, 2014." *Asian Perspectives* 56 (2): 260–261.

Stark, Miriam T., David C. W. Sanderson, and Robert G. Bingham 2006. "Monumentality in the Mekong Delta: Luminescence dating and implications." *Bulletin of the Indo-Pacific Prehistory Association* 26: 110–20.

Thanik Lertcharnrit 2005. "Late prehistoric and early historic archaeology in Thailand: Recent evidence from the central Highland." *Silpakorn University International Journal* 5 (1–2): 55–72.

Thanik Lertcharnrit 2006. "The moated site of Promtin Tai and the transition from late prehistory to early history in central Thailand." In *Uncovering Southeast Asia's Past: Seclected Papers from the 10th International Conference of the European Associtaion of Southeast Asian Archaeologists,* pp.258–265. Edited by E. Bacus, I. Glover, and V. Pigott. Singapore: National University of Singapore Press.

Thanik Lertcharnrit 2009 [2552BE]. "เครื่องประดับโบราณที่บ้านพรหมทินใต้" (Prehistoric ornaments from an Iron Age site in central Thailand). *Sarakadee* 298: 26–30. [In Thai]

Thanik Lertcharnrit 2010. "An early ivory bracelet from central Thailand." *Expedition* 52 (2): 8.

Thanik Lertcharnrit 2011. "Zoomorphic spouts from central Thailand." *Bulletin of the Indo-Pacific Prehistory Association* 31: 25–29.

Thanik Lertcharnrit 2014. "Phromthin Tai: An archaeological perspective on its societal transition." In *Before Siam: Essays in Art and Archaeology*, pp.119–131. Edited by N. Revire and S.A. Murphy, Bangkok: River Books and The Siam Society.

Thanik Lertcharnrit and Alison Carter 2010 [2553 BE]. "ผลวิจัยล่าสุดเรื่องลูกปัดหินและลูกแก้วยุคเหล็กจากแหล่งโบราณคดีพรหมทินใต้ลพบุรี" (Recent research on Iron Age glass and stone beads from PromtinTai, central Thailand). *Muang Boran Journal* 36 (4): 53–68. [In Thai]

Wales, H.G. Quaritch 1936. "Further excavations at P'ong Tuk (Siam)." *Indian Arts and Letters, New Series* 10 (1): 42–48.

Wales, H.G. Quaritch 1937a. "Early Indian art from the Siamese jungle." *Illustrated London News* 30: 174–176.

Wales, H.G. Quaritch 1937b. Towards Angkor: In the *Footsteps of the Indian Invaders.* London: Harrap & Co.

Wales, H.G. Quaritch 1937c. "Some ancient human skeletons excavated in Siam." *Man* 37: 89– 90.

Wales, H.G. Quaritch 1951. *The Making of Greater India: A Study in South-East Asian Culture Change.* London: Bernard Quaritch.

Wales, H. G. Quaritch 1964. "Some ancient human skeletons excavated in Siam: A correction." *Man* 64: 121.

Wales, H. G. Quaritch 1966. "Dvāravatī in South-East Asian cultural history." *Journal of the Royal Asiatic Society, New Series* 98 (1): 40–52.

Wales, Quaritch 1969. *Dvāravatī: The earliest kingdom of Siam (6th to 11th century A.D.).* London: Bernard Quaritch.

Wheatley, Paul 1983. *Nāgara and Commandery: Origins of the Southeast Asian Urban Traditions.* Chicago: Department of Geography, The University of Chicago.

White, Joyce C. 2017. "Changing paradigms in Southeast Asian archaeology." *Journal of Indo- Pacific Archaeology* 41: 66–77.

Wiens, J. A. 1989. "Spatial scaling in ecology." *Functional Ecology* 3: 385–397.

Wolters, Oliver W. 1982. *History, Culture, and Region in Southeast Asian Perspectives.* Singapore: Institute of Southeast Asian Studies.

Woodward, Hiram 2005. *The Art and Architecture of Thailand.* Leiden and Boston: Brill.

Wynne-Jones, Stephanie and Sheila Kohring 2007. "Socializing complexity." In *Socializing Complexity: Structure, Interaction and Power in Archaeological Discourse.* Edited by S. Kohring and S. Wynne-Jones, pp.1–12. Oxford: Oxbow Books.

Phuthorn Bhumadhon
NEW KNOWLEDGE ON DVĀRAVATĪ

Bunchar Pongpanich 2019 (forthcoming). "Suvannabhumi: The Preliminary Conclusion." In *Suvarnabhumi The Golden Land, pp.*251–254. Edited by B. Pongpanich and S. Thinapong. Bangkok: GISTDA Geo-Informatics and Space Technology Development Agency.

Lankton, James and Bernard Gratuze 2019 (forthcoming). "Suvarnabhumi in the 1st Century CE: The glass Evidence." In *Suvarnabhumi The Golden Land, pp.*68–77. Edited by B. Pongpanich and S. Thinapong. Bangkok: GISTDA Geo-Informatics and Space Technology Development Agency.

Phattharaphong Kaongoen 2002 [2545 BE]. *โบราณคดีคอกช้างดิน* (*The Archaeologyof Khok Chang Din*). Suphan Buri: FAD, Office 2. [In Thai]

Piriya Krairiksh 1977. *Art styles in Thailand: a selection from national provincial museums, and an essay in conceptualization.* Bangkok: Ministry of Education, Dept. of Fine Art.

John Guy
MAKING SENSE OF DVĀRAVATĪ

Abraham, Meera 1988. *Two Medieval Merchant Guilds of South India*. New Delhi: Manohar Publications.

Baptiste, Pierre, and Thierry Zéphir (eds.) 2009. *Dvāravatī: Aux sources du bouddhisme en Thaïlande.* Paris: Réunion des Musées Nationaux and Musée des arts asiatiques Guimet.

Bellina, Bérénice (ed.) 2017. *Khao Sam Kaeo: An Early Port-City between the Indian Ocean and the South China Sea.* Paris: École Française d'Extrême-Orient.

Bennett, Anna 2017. *The Ancient History of U Thong City of Gold: A scientific study of the Gold from U Thong*. Bangkok: River Books.

Bennett, Anna 2019. Suvarṇabhūmi 'Land of Gold'. In *Suvarnabhumi, The Golden Land*, pp.79–115. Edited by Bunchar Pongpanich and Somchet Thinapong. Bangkok: GISTDA Geo-Informatics and Space Technology Development Agency.

Bhattacharya, Kamaleswar 1961. *Les Religions brahmaniques dans l'ancien Cambodged'apres l'epigraphie et l'iconographie.* Publications de l'École Française d'Extrême-Orient 49. Paris: École Française d'Extrême-Orient.

Boeles, Jan Jetso 1964. "The king of Śri Dvāravatī and his regalia." *Journal of the Siam Society* 52 (1): 99–114.

Borell, Brigitte 2008. "Some Western Imports Assigned to the Oc-Eo Period Reconsidered." In *From Homo Erectus to the Living Traditions: Choice of Papers from the 11th International Conference of the European Association of Southeast Asian Archaeologists, Bougon, 25th–29th September 2006,* pp.165–174. Edited by J.P. Pautreau et al. Chiang Mai: Siam Ratana.

Borrell, Brigitte 2008. "Some Western imports assigned to the Oc-Eo period reconsidered." In *From Homo Erectus to the Living Traditions: Choice of Papers from the 11th International Conference of the European Association of Southeast Asian Archaeologists*, Bougan, 25th-29th September 2006, pp.165-174. Edited by J-P. Pautreau et al. Chiang Mai.

Brown, Robert L. 1996. *The Dvāravatī Wheels of the law and the Indianization of South East Asia.* Leiden, New York, Köln: EJ. Brill.

Coedès, George 1963. "Découverte numismatique au Siam intéressant le royaume de Dvāravatī." *Comptes rendus de L'Académie des Inscriptions et Belles-Lettres* 107 (3): 285–291.

Dupont, Pierre 1959. *L'archéologie Mône de Dvāravatī*, 2 Volumes. Publications de l'École Française d'Extrême-Orient 41. Paris: École française d'Extrême-Orient.

Ghosh, Sucandra and Lipi Ghosh 2011. "Seals, Amulets and Coinages of Dvāravatī Cultural Sites: Understanding Their Social Environment and Religious Network." *Bulletin of the Indo-Pacific Prehistory Association* 31: 25–29.

Glover, Ian 2010. "The Dvāravatī Gap - Linking prehistory and history in early Thailand." *Bulletin of the Indo-Pacific Prehistory Association* 30: 79–86.

Glover, Ian 2002. "West Asian Sassanian-Islamic Ceramics in the Indian Ocean, South, Southeast and East Asia." *Man and Environment* 27 (1): 165–177.

Griffiths, Arlo 2014. "Early Indic Inscriptions of Southeast Asia." In *Lost Kingdoms: Hindi-Buddhist sculpture of early Southeast Asia*, pp.53–57. Edited by J. Guy. New York: The Metropolitan Museum of Art.

Griffiths, Arlo and William Southworth 2011. "Études du corpus des inscriptions du Campā II. La stèle d'installation de Śrī Ādideveśvara: une nouvelle inscription trouvée dans le temple de Hoà Lai et son importance pour l'histoire du Pāṇḍuranga." *Journal Asiatique* 299 (1): 271–317.

Gupta, Swaraj Prakash 1980. *The Roots of Indian Art.* Delhi: B.R. Publishing.

Guy, John 1989. *Ceramic Traditions of South-East Asia,* Singapore, Kuala Lumpur: Oxford University Press.

Guy, John 1999. "The Art of the Pyu and Mon." In *The Art of Burma: New Studies.* Edited by D. Stadtner. *Marg* 50 (4): 12–28.

Guy, John 2000. "The Kosa Masks of Champa: New Evidence." In *Southeast Asian Archaeology 1998: Proceedings of the 7th International Conference of the European Association of Southeast Asian Archaeologists, Berlin, 31 August–4 September 1998,* pp.51–60. Edited by W. Lobo and S. Reimann. Hull: Centre for South-East Asian Studies.

John Guy
MAKING SENSE OF DVĀRAVATĪ

Guy, John 2003. "Early Asian Ceramic Trade and the Belitung ('Tang') Cargo." *Transactions of the Oriental Ceramic Society* 66: 13–27.

Guy, John 2006. "Early Ninth-Century Chinese Export Ceramics and the Persian Gulf Connection: The Belitung Shipwreck Evidence." *Chine-Méditerranée: Routes et Echanges de la Céramique Jusqu'au XVI e Siècle. TAOCI,* Paris, Vol. 4: 9–20.

Guy, John 2011. "Rare and Strange Goods: International Trade in Ninth-Century Asia." In *Shipwrecked. Tang Treasures and Monsoon Winds*, pp.18–25. Edited by R.Krahl et al. Washington D.C.: Freer-Sackler.

Guy, John (ed.) 2014. *Lost Kingdoms: Hindu-Buddhist Sculpture of Early Southeast Asia.* New York: The Metropolitan Museum of Art, Yale University Press; Bangkok: River Books.

Guy, John 2017a. "The Phanom Surin Shipwreck, a Pahlavi Inscription, and their Significance for the History of Early Lower Central Thailand." *Journal of the Siam Society* 105: 179–196.

Guy, John 2017b. "Hollow and useless luxuries: The Tang Shipwreck and the emerging role of Arab traders in late first millennium Indian Ocean - Nanhai World." In *The Tang Shipwreck. Art and exchange in the 9th century,* pp.160–176. Edited by A. Chong and S.A. Murphy. Singapore: Asian Civilisations Museum.

Guy, John 2018. "Saliva ritual: liṅgakośa and mukhakośa in Champa." In *Vibrancy in Stone: Masterpieces of the collection of the Đà Nẵng Museum of Cham Sculpture,* pp.89–96. Edited by Trần Kỳ Phương, Võ Văn Thắng, and P. Sharrock. Bangkok: River Books.

Guy, John 2019. "Shipwrecks in Late First Millennium Southeast Asia: Southern China's Maritime Trade and Emerging Role of Arab Merchants in Indian Ocean Exchange." In *Early Global Interconnectivity across the Indian Ocean World,* pp.121-163. Edited by A. Schottenhammer. Cham, Switzerland: Palgrave.

Higham, Charles 2002. *Early Cultures of Mainland Southeast Asia.* Bangkok: River Books.

Jett, Paul 2010. "A Technical Study of the Kampong Cham Figure Group." In *Gods of Angkor. Bronzes from the National Museum of Cambodia*, pp.78–87. Edited by L. Cort and P. Jett. Washington D.C.: Smithsonian Institution.

Karashima, N. (ed.) 2002. Ancient and Medieval Commercial Activities in the Indian Ocean: Testimony of Inscriptions and Ceramic-sherds. Tokyo: Taisho University.

Krahl, Regina and John Guy (eds.) 2010. *Shipwrecked: Tang Treasures and Monsoon Winds*. Washington D.C.: Sackler Gallery.

Lamb, Alastair 1964. "Takuapa: The Probable Site of a Pre-Malaccan Entrepot in the Malay Peninsula." In *Malayan and Indonesian Studies*, pp.76–86. Edited by J. Bastin and R. Roolvink. Oxford: Oxford University Press.

Li Rongxi (trans.) 1996. *Xuanzang: The Great Tang Dynasty Record of the Western Regions.* Berkeley: Numata Center for Buddhist Translation and Research.

Li Rongxi (trans.) 2000. *Buddhist Monastic Traditions of Southern Asia: A Record of the Inner Law Sent Home from the South Seas*. Berkeley: Numata Center for Buddhist Translation and Research.

Lorrillard, Michel 2010-2011. "Par-delà Vat Phu: Données nouvelles sur l'expansion desespaces khmer et môn anciens au Laos." *Bulletin de l'École française d'Extrême-Orient* 97–98: 205–270.

Mahlo, Dietrich 2012. *The Early Coins of Myanmar (Burma): Messengers from the Past, First Millennium AD.* Bangkok: White Lotus Press.

Malleret, Louis 1959–1963. *L'archeologie du delta du Mekong: L'exploration archéologique et les fouilles d'Oc-éo,* Vols.1–4. Paris: École Française d'Extrême-Orient.

Nareerat Preecharpeechagupt 2014 [2557 BE]. "เรือโบราณพนมสุรินทร์" (The Phanom Surin Shipwreck). *Silpakorn Journal* 57 (3): 22–35. [In Thai]

Pan Hla, Nai 1991. "The Major Role of the Mons in Southeast Asia." *Journal of the Siam Society*, 79 (1): 13–21.

Piriya Krairiksh 2012. *The Roots of Thai Art*. Translated by N. Chakrabongse. Bangkok: River Books.

Revire, Nicolas 2014. "Five Monumental Bhadrasana Buddhas from Nakhon Pathom." *Orientations* 45 (3): 64–70.

Sanskrit Studies Centre 2003. *Sanskrit in Southeast Asia: The Harmonizing Factor of Cultures. International Sanskrit Conference, May 21–23, 2001.* Bangkok: Sanskrit Studies Centre, Silpakorn University.

Sastri, K.A. Nilakanta 1949. "Takua Pa and Its Tamil Inscription." *Journal of the Malaysian Branch of the Royal Asiatic Society* 22 (1): 25–30.

Schopen, Gregory 1997. "On monks, Nuns and 'Vulgar' Practices: The Introduction of the Image Cult into Indian Buddhism." In *Bones, Stones an Buddhist Monks. Collected Papers on the Archaeology, Epigraphy, and Texts of Monastic Buddhism in India*, pp.238–257. Edited by G. Schopen. Honolulu: University of Hawai'i Press.

Scott, James 2009. *The Art of Not Being Governed: An Anarchist History of Upland Southeast Asia*. New Haven: Yale University Press.

Shanmugan, P. 1996. "An Early Tamil Brāhmī Inscription from Thailand." *Journal of the Epigraphic Society of India* 22: 100–103.

Skilling, Peter 1992. "Two Ports of Suvarnabhuumi: A Brief Note." *Journal of the Siam Society* 80 (1): 131.

Skilling, Peter 2003. "Dvāravatī: Recent revelations and research." In *Dedications to Her Royal Highness Princess Galyani Vadhana Krom Luang Naradhiwas Rajanarindra on her 80th birthday*, pp.87–112. Edited by C. Baker. Bangkok: The Siam Society.

Skilling, Peter 2009. "Des images moulées au service de l'idéologie du mérite." In *Dvāravatī aux sources du bouddhisme en Thailande*, pp.107–113. Edited by P. Baptiste and T. Zephir. Paris: Musée Guimet.

Skilling, Peter 2015. "The Circulation of Artefacts Engraved with '*Apramāda*' and Other Mottos in Southeast Asia and India: A Preliminary Report." In *Annual Report of The International Research Institute for Advanced Buddhology at Soka University for the Academic Year 2014* Vol.18, pp.63–77. Tokyo: Soka University.

Srivastava, A.L. 2008. "Taurine Symbol on Stone Discs from Murtaziganj and Other Places." In *Recent Researches in Indian Art and Iconography. Dr. C.P. Sinha Felicitation Volume*, pp.51–61. Edited by Bhagwant Sahai et al. New Delhi.

Stargardt, Janice 1990. *The Ancient Pyu of Burma, Vol. 1: Early Pyu Cities in a Man-Made Landscape*. Cambridge: Cambridge University Press.

Vickery, Michael 1998. *Society, Economics, and Politics in Pre-Angkor Cambodia: The 7th–8th Centuries*. Tokyo: The Centre for East Asian Cultural Studies for UNESCO, The Tokyo Bunko.

Wade, Geoff 2014. "Beyond the Southern Borders: Southeast Asia in Chinese Texts to the Ninth Century." In *Lost Kingdoms: Hindu-Buddhist Sculpture of Early Southeast Asia*, pp.25–32. Edited by J. Guy. New York: The Metropolitan Museum of Art, Yale University Press; Bangkok: River Books.

Watson, Hunter I. 2018. "A group of clay artefacts from Tap Chumphon inscribed in Pali and Old Mon." In *Advancing Southeast Asian Archaeology 2016: Selected Papers from the Second SEAMEO SPAFA International Conference on Southeast Asian Archaeology*, pp.118–129, 329–335 Edited by N.H. Tan. Bangkok: SEAMEO SPAFA.

Watson, Hunter and Peter, Skilling 2019. "A clay Tablet from U Thong inscribed in old mon". *In Defining Dvāravatī*, pp.94–97. Edited by Anna Bennett and Hunter Watson. Bangkok: Silkworm books.

Whitehouse, David 1973. "Chinese Stoneware from Siraf: The Earliest Finds." In *South Asian Archaeology: Papers from the First International Conference of South Asian archaeologies held in the University of Cambridge*, pp.227–283. Edited by N. Hammond, London: Duckworth.

Wolters, Oliver 1982. *History, Culture, and Region in Southeast Asian Perspectives*. Singapore: Insitute of Southeast Asian Studies.

Peter Skilling (Bhadra Rujirathat)
DVĀRAVATĪ IN INSCRIPTIONS AND MANUSCRIPTS

Aymonier, Étienne 1900. *Le Cambodge* I: *Le royaume actuel*. Paris: Ernest Leroux.

Baker, Chris and Pasuk Phongpaichit (eds., trans.) 2016. *The Palace Law of Ayutthaya and the Thammasat: Law and Kindship in Siam*. Southeast Asia Program Publications. Ithaca, New York: Cornell University.

Beal, Samuel 1884. *Si-Yu-Ki: Buddhist Records of the Western World*. Translated from the Chinese of *Hiuen Tsiang* (A.D. 629) by Samuel Beal. London. [Reprinted Delhi: Motilal Banarsidass,1981].

Boeles, Jan J. 1964. "The King of Śrī Dvāravatī and his Regalia." *The Journal of the Siam Society 52 (1):* 99–114.

Boeles, Jan J. 1986. 'A note on Tamil relations with southern Thailand and the identification of Ptolemy's Tacola.' In *The Archaeology of Peninsular Siam: Collected articles from The Journal of the Siam Society, 1905–1983*, pp.118–122. Bangkok: The Siam Society. [Originally published in the Journal of the Siam Society 54 (2) (1966): 221–227].

Chalerm Yongboonkerd 1964 [2507 BE]. "Dvāravatī?" *Sam Tahan* 3 (2): 39–43 *Phataraphong Kaongoen* 2002 [2545 BE]. โบราณคดีคอกช้างดิน (*The archaeology of Khok Chang Din*). Bangkok: 2nd Office of the FAD, Suphan Buri.

Coe, Michael D. and Damian Evans 2018. *Angkor and the Khmer Civilization*. London: Thames & Hudson.

Cœdès, George 1929. *Receuil des inscriptions du Siam, deuxième partie : Inscriptions de Dvāravatī, de Çrīvijaya et de Lăvo', deuxième édition revue et mise à jour*. Bangkok.

Cœdès, George 1989. *Les états hindouisés d'Indochine et d'Indonésie*. [de Boccard, Paris, 1948, in the series *Histoire du monde*, no. 13, reprint]. Paris: De Boccard.

Cœdès, George 1954. *Inscriptions du Cambodge*, Vol. VI. Paris: École française d'Extrême-Orient.

Coedès, George 1961. *Recueil des Inscriptions du Siam, Deuxième partie: Inscriptions de Dvāravatī, de Çrīvijaya, et de Lāvo*, 2nd edition. Bangkok: Department of Silpakorn.

Cœdès, George 1963. "Découverte numismatique au Siam intéressant le royaume de Dvāravatī." *Comptes rendus des séances de l'Académie des Inscriptions et Belles-Lettres*, 107–103, pp. 285–291.

Cœdès, George 1964. "A la recherche du royaume de Dvaravati." *Archeologia : fouilles et découvertes* 1: 58–63.

Cœdès, George 1992. 'La stèle du Práḥ Khan d'Aṅkor.' In *Réimpression des articles de George Cœdès parus dans le B.E.F.E.O*, Tome II, *Articles divers*, pp.119–165, 4 plates. [Originally published in *Bulletin de l'École française d'Extrême-Orient* 41: 255–301].

Cœdès, George 1996. *The Indianized State of Southeast Asia*. Edited by W.F. Vella, translated by S.B. Cowing. Honolulu: The University Press of Hawai'i.

Das, Sudhir Ranjan 1968. *Rājbāḍīdāṅgā: 1962 (Chiruṭī: Jadupur). An Interim Report on Excavations at Rājbāḍīdaṅgā and Terracotta Seals and Sealings*. The Asiatic Society Monograph Series Volume XIV. Calcutta: The Asiatic Society.

Damrong Rajanubhab, Prince 1973. *Monuments of the Buddha in Siam*. Translated by Sulak Sivaraksa and A.B. Griswold with footnotes by Prince Subhadradis Diskul and A.B. Griswold. Bangkok: The Siam Society. Second revised edition (first edition published 1962 under title A History of Buddhist Monuments in Siam).

Dhani Nivat, H.H. Prince 1969 [2512 BE]. "Early Trade Relations between Denmark and Siam." In *Collected Articles by H.H. Prince Dhani Nivat Kromamun Bidayalabh Brdihyakorn, Honorary President, The Siam Society, reprinted from the Journal of the Siam Society on the occasion of his eighty-fourth birthday*, pp.35–49. Bangkok: The Siam Society. [Originally published in the Journal of the Siam Society 31 (1) (1939)].

Dhani Nivat, H.H. Prince 1969 [2512 BE]. "The City of Thawarawadi Sri Ayudhya." In *Collected Articles by H.H. Prince Dhani Nivat Kromamun Bidayalabh Brdihyakorn, Honorary President, The Siam Society, reprinted from the Journal of the Siam Society on the occasion of his eighty-fourth birthday*, pp.51–56. Bangkok: The Siam Society. [Originally published in the Journal of the Siam Society 31 (2) (1939)].

Dupont, Pierre 1959. *L'Archéologie mône de Dvāravatī*. Paris: École française d'Extrême-Orient.

Filliozat, Jacqueline 1997. "Une nouvelle lecture du Syāmasandesa de 1756 A.D. conservé au Malvatte Vihāraya de Kandy, Sri Lanka." In *Dharmadūta—Mélanges offerts au Vénérable Thích Huyên- Vi à l'occasion de son soixante-dixième anniversaire*, pp. 95–114. Edited by Bhikkhu Tampalawela Dhammaratana and Bhikkhu Pāsādika. Paris: Editions You-Feng.

Finot, Louis 1915. "Notes d'épigraphie." *Bulletin de l'École française d'Extrême-Orient*:28–36.

Jacques, Claude 1969. "Piédestal circulaire de Chanto'k, K, 1009." In "Études d'épigraphie cambodgienne. II. Inscriptions diverses récemment découvertes en Thailande. III. Quatre fragments d'inscription récemment découverts au Cambodge." *Bulletin de l'École française d'Extrême- Orient* 56: 57–74.

Jacques, Claude (n.d.). *Corpus des inscriptions du pays khmers*. Planches. Tome 1, *Inscriptions préangkoriennes nommant un roi*. New Delhi: International Academy of Indian Culture, New Delhi, (Śata-Piṭaka Series Indo-Asian Literatures Vol. 341, pp. 203–205, with pls. 74[a] and74[b]).

Kannika Wimonkasem and Chirapat Prapandvidya 1999 [2542 BE]. "ชื่อ "ทวารวตี" ในจารึกวัดจันทึก" (Inscription of Wat Chan Thuek Mentioning the name Dvāravatī). In *Thailand: Culture and Society*, pp.389–394. Bangkok: Princess Maha Chakri Sirindhorn Anthropology Centre.

Li Rongxi (trans.) 1995. *A Biography of the Tripiṭaka Master of the Great Ci'en Monastery of the Great Tang Dynasty*. Berkeley: Numata Center for Buddhist Translation and Research (BDK English Tripiṭaka 77).

Li Rongxi (trans.) 1996. *The Great Tang Dynasty Record of the Western Regions*. Berkeley: Numata Center for Buddhist Translation and Research, (BDK English Tripiṭaka 79).

Lunet de Lajonquière, E. 1902. *Inventaire descriptif des monuments du Cambodge*. Paris: Leroux.

Miksic, John N. and Geok Yian Goh 2017. *Ancient Southeast Asia*. London and New York: Routledge.

National Library, FAD 1986a [2529 BE]. *จารึกในประเทศไทย เล่ม 1: อักษรปัลลวะ หลังปัลลวะ พุทธศตวรรษที่12–14* (*Inscriptions in Thailand, Vol.1: Pallava Script, Post-Pallava Script 12–14th BE*). Bangkok. [In Thai]

National Library, FAD 2016a [2559 BE]. *จารึกในประเทศไทย เล่ม 1: อักษรปัลลวะ หลังปัลลวะ พุทธศตวรรษที่ 12–14*, พิมพ์ครั้งที่ 2 แก้ไขเพิ่มเติม(*Inscriptions in Thailand, Vol.1: Pallava Script, Post-Pallava Script 12–14th BE*, Second edition, revised and expanded). Bangkok. [In Thai]

Phonarat, Somdet Phra 2015 [2558 BE] *พระราชพงศาวดาร ฉบับสมเด็จพระพนรัตน์ วัดพระเชตุพน* (*Phra ratchaphongsawadan chabap somdet phra phonarat wat phra chetuphon*). Edited by Santi Pakdeekham. Bangkok.

Piriya Krairiksh 1977. *Art Styles in Thailand: A Selection from National Provincial Museums, and an Essay in Conceptualization*. Bangkok: FAD.

Piriya Krairiksh 2012. *The Roots of Thai Art*. Translated by Narisa Chakrabongse. Bangkok: River Books.

Ronachai Krisadaolarn and Vasilijs Mihailovs 2002. *Siamese Coins from Funan to the Fifth Reign*. Bangkok: River Books.

Sastri, Hiranand 1923–1924. "The Nalanda Copper-plate of Devapāladeva." *Epigraphia Indica* XVII: 310–327.

Skilling, Peter 2003. "Dvāravatī: Recent Revelations and Research." In *Dedications to Her Royal Highness Princess Galyani Vadhana Krom Luang Naradhiwas Rajanagarindra on her 80th birthday*, pp. 87–112. Bangkok: The Siam Society.

Skilling, Peter 2015. "An Untraced Buddhist Verse Inscription from (Pen)insular Southeast Asia." In *Buddhist Dynamics in Premodern and Early Modern Southeast Asia*, pp.18-79. Edited by D.C. Lammerts. Singapore: Institute of Southeast Asian Studies.

Subrahmanyam, B. 1985. "On the Utilization of Epigraphs for Art History: Some Andhra Examples." In *Indian Epigraphy: Its Bearing on the History of Art*, pp. 25–27. Edited by F.M. Asher and G.S. Gai. New Delhi: Oxford & IBH Publishing Co./American Institute of Indian Studies.

Peter Skilling (Bhadra Rujirathat)
DVĀRAVATĪ IN INSCRIPTIONS AND MANUSCRIPTS

Suphaphan Na Bangchang 1988. "A Pāli letter sent by the Aggamahāsenāpati of Siam to the royal court at Kandy in 1756." *Journal of the Pali Text Society* 12: 185–212.

Wheatley, Paul 1980. *The Golden Khersonese, Studies in the Historical Geography of the Malay Peninsula before A.D. 1500.* [Kuala Lumpur: University of Malaya Press, 1961] Kuala Lumpur: Penerbit Universiti Malaya.

Wicks, Robert S. 1992. *Money, Markets, and Trade in Early Southeast Asia: The development of indigenous monetary systems to AD 1400.* Ithaca, New York: Cornell University.

Hunter Watson
OLD MON INSCRIPTIONS AND THE EXTENT OF DVĀRAVATĪ

Aymonier, Étienne 1901. *Le Cambodge II: Les provinces siamoises*. Paris: E. Leroux.

Barram, Andrew and Ian Glover 2008. "Re-thinking Dvāravatī." In *Archaeology in Southeast Asia - from Homo erectus to the Living Traditions, Choice of papers from the 11th International Conference of the European Association of Southeast Asian Archaeologists, Bougan, 25–29th September 2006*, pp.175–182. Edited by J.P. Pautreau, A.S. Coupey, V. Zeitoun & E. Rambault, Chiang Mai: Silkworm.

Bauer, Christian 1987-1988. "Numismatics, dialectology and the periodization of Old Mon." *Mon-Khmer Studies Journal* 16–17: 155–176.

Bauer, Christian 1991a. "Notes on Mon Epigraphy." *Journal of the Siam Society* 79 (1): 31–83.

Bauer, Christian 1991b. "Notes on Mon Epigraphy II." *Journal of the Siam Society* 79 (2): 61–79.

Beal, Samuel 1884. *Buddhist Records of the Western World: Translated from the Chinese of Hiuen Tsiang (A.D. 629), Vol.2*. London: Trübner & Co.

Boeles, Jan Jetso 1964. "The king of Śri Dvāravatī and his regalia." *Journal of the Siam Society* 52 (1): 99–114.

Briggs, Lawrence P. 1945. "Dvāravatī, the Most Ancient Kingdom of Siam." *Journal of the American Oriental Society* 65 (2): 98–107.

Brown, Robert L. 1996. *The Dvāravatī Wheels of the law and the Indianization of South East Asia*. Leiden, New York, Köln: EJ. Brill.

Cha-em Kaeokhlai and Champa Yueangcharoen 1986 [2529 BE]. "จารึกวิหารโพธิ์ลังกา" (Wihan Pho Langka Inscription). In *จารึกในประเทศไทย เล่ม 2: อักษรปัลลวะ อักษรมอญ พุทธศตวรรษที่ 12–21* (*Inscriptions in Thailand, Vol.2: Pallava Script, Mon Script 12–21th BE*), pp.112–118. Edited by K. Veeraprajak. Bangkok: National Library, Department of Fine Arts. [In Thai]

Champa Yueangcharoen 1980 [2523 BE]."ศิลาจารึกวิหารโพธิ์กา เลขที่ น.ศ. 2 ระหว่าง พ.ศ.1775–1825" (The Wihan Pho Langka Inscription, Number N.S. 2, between 1775–1825 B.E.). *Silpakorn Journal* 23 (5): 94–96. [In Thai]

Champa Yueangcharoen 1981 [2524 BE]. "คำอ่านและคำแปลอักษรตัวเขียนด้านหลังพระพิมพ์ดินเผากู่สันถรัตน์ กิ่งอำเภอนาดูน จังหวัดมหาสารคาม" (Reading and translation of writing behind a clay votive tablet from Kusanrat, Na Dun District, Maha Sarakham Province). *Silpakorn Journal* 23 (6): 63–66. [In Thai]

Champa Yueangcharoen, Thoem Mitem and Khongdecha Praphatthong (eds.) 1977 [2520 BE]. *"วิเคราะห์ศิลาจารึกในพิพิธภัณฑสถานแห่งชาติหริภุญไชย"* (*Analysis of inscriptions in the Hariphunchai Museum*). Bangkok: National Library, Department of Fine Arts. [In Thai]

Cœdès, Georges 1925. "Documents sur l'histoire politique et religieuse du Laos occidental." *Bulletin de l'École française d'Extrême-Orient* 25: 1–201.

Cœdès, Georges 1928. *Les collections archéologiques du Musée National de Bangkok*. Paris & Bruxelles: G. Van Oest.

Cœdès, Georges 1929. *Recueil des inscriptions du Siam, Deuxième partie: Inscriptions de Dvāravatī, de Çrīvijaya et du Lăvo*. Bangkok: Bangkok Times Press.

Cœdès, Georges 1952. "A propos de deux fragments d'inscription récemment découverts à P'ra Pathom (Thaïlande)." *Académie des Inscriptions et Belles-Lettres* 96 (1): 146–150.

Cœdès, Georges 1966. "Les Môns de Dvāravatī." In *Artibus Asiae. Supplementum, Vol.23, Essays Offered to G.H. Luce by his Colleagues and Friends in Honour of His Seventy- Fifth Birthday. Volume 1: Papers on Asian History, Religion, Languages, Literature, Music Folklore, and Anthropology*, pp.112–116.

Dhida Saraya 1999. *(Sri) Dvaravati: The Initial Phase of Siam's History*. Bangkok: Muang Boran Publishing House.

Diffloth, Gérald 1984. *The Dvaravati Old Mon Language and Nyah Kur*. Bangkok: Chulalongkorn University Printing House.

Dupont, Pierre 1959. *L'archéologie Mône de Dvāravatī*, 2 Volumes. Publications de l'École Française d'Extrême-Orient 41. Paris: École française d'Extrême-Orient.

Hunter Watson
OLD MON INSCRIPTIONS AND THE EXTENT OF DVĀRAVATĪ

FAD 2000 [2543 BE]. "*ทุ่งเศรษฐี: โบราณสถานทวารวดีชายฝั่งทะเลเพชรบุรี*" (*Tung Setthi: Dvāravatī Archaeological site on the coast of Phetchaburi*). Ratchaburi: 1st Office of Archaeology and National Museums. [In Thai]

FAD 2002 [2545BE]. "*ประวัติศาสตรโบราณคดีสุราษฎร์ธานี*" (*History and Archaeology of Surat Thani*). Nakhon Si Thammarat: 11th Office of Archaeology and National Museums. [In Thai]

FAD. n.d. "*ประวติศาสตรโบราณคดี นครศรีธรรมราช*" (*History, Archaeology, Nakhon Si Thammarat*). Nakhon Si Thammarat: 11th Office of Archaeology and National Museums. [In Thai]

Glover, Ian 2010. "The Dvāravatī Gap - Linking prehistory and history in early Thailand." *Bulletin of the Indo-Pacific Prehistory Association* 30: 79–86.

Guillon, Emmanuel 1974. "Recherches sur quelques inscriptions môn." *Bulletin de l'École française d'Extrême-Orient* 61: 339–348.

Griffiths, Arlo 2014. "Early Indic Inscriptions of Southeast Asia." In *Lost Kingdoms: Hindi-Buddhist sculpture of early Southeast Asia*, pp.53–57. Edited by J. Guy. New York: The Metropolitan Museum of Art.

Griffiths, Arlo and D. Christian Lammerts 2015. "Epigraphy: Southeast Asia." In *Brill's Encyclopedia of Buddhism, Vol.1: Literature and Languages*, pp.988–1009. Edited by Jonathan A. Silk. Leiden: Brill.

Griswold, Alexander B. and Prasert ṇa Nagara 1971. "An Inscription in Old Mòn from Wieng Manó in Chieng Mai Province." Epigraphical and Historical Studies, No. 6. *Journal of the Siam Society* 59 (1): 153–156, fig.1.

Halliday, Robert and Charles Otto Blagden 1930. "Les inscriptions môn du Siam." *Bulletin de l'École française d'Extrême-Orient* 30: 81–105.

Hennequin, Laurent 2010. "The French Contribution to the Rediscovery of Dvāravatī Archaeology." *Journal of the Siam Society* 98: 1–48.

Higham, Charles and Rachanie Thosarat 2012. *Early Thailand: From Prehistory to Sukhothai*. Bangkok: River Books.

Kannika Wimonkasem 1999 [2542 BE]. "พัฒนาการของอักษรโบราณในประเทศไทย" (The development of ancient scripts in Thailand). In *สังคมและวัฒนธรรมในประเทศไทย* (*Thailand: Culture and Society*), pp.309–387. Bangkok: Princess Maha Chakri Sirindhorn Anthropology Centre. [In Thai]

Kannika Wimonkasem and Phongkasem Santhithai 1999 [2542 BE]. "จารึกฐานสถูปดินเผาวัดหนองกระโดน"(Inscriptiononthebaseofa claystupa fromWat Nong Kradon). In *ภาษา-จารึก ฉบับที่6* (*Language-Inscriptions, Vol.6*), pp.143–149. Bangkok: Department of Oriental Languages, Faculty of Archaeology, Silpakorn University. [In Thai]

Khomsi Saenchit 2009 [2552BE]. *เมืองโบราณหริภุญไชย จากหลักฐานโบราณคดี* (*The Haripunchai Ancient City from archaeological evidence*). PhD Diss., Silpakorn University, Bangkok. [In Thai]

Kongkaew Veeraprajak 1986a. "Inscriptions from South Thailand." *SPAFA Digest* 7 (1): 7–21.

Kongkaew Veeraprajak (ed.) 1986b [2529 BE]. *จารึกในประเทศไทย เล่ม 1: อักษรปัลลวะ หลังปัลลวะ พุทธศตวรรษที่ 12–14* (*Inscriptions in Thailand, Vol.1: Pallava Script, Post-Pallava Script 12–14th BE*). Bangkok: National Library, Department of Fine Arts. [In Thai]

Kongkaew Veeraprajak (ed.) 1986c [2529 BE] *จารึกในประเทศไทย เล่ม 2: อักษรปัลลวะ อักษรมอญ พุทธศตวรรษที่ 12–21* (*Inscriptions in Thailand, Vol.2: Pallava Script, Mon Script 12–21th BE*). Bangkok: National Library, Department of Fine Arts. [In Thai]

Kongkaew Veeraprajak and Champa Yeungcharoen 1984 [2527 BE]. "จารึกวัดมหาธาตุ เมืองนครศรีธรรมราช เลขที่ นศ.3" (The Wat Mahathat Inscription of NakhonSi Thammarat, number NS.3). *Silpakorn Journal* 28 (2): 85–88. [In Thai]

Lefèvre-Pontalis, Pierre 1897. "L'invasion Thaïe en Indo-Chine." *T'oung Pao* 8 (1): 53–78.

Le May, Reginald 1938. *A concise history of Buddhist art in Siam*. Cambridge: University Press. Lefèvre-Pontalis, Pierre 1897. "L'invasion Thaïe en Indo-Chine." *T'oung Pao* 8 (1): 53–78.

Lorrillard, Michel 2014. "La plaine de Vientiane au tournant du second millénaire: Données nouvelles sur l'expansion des espaces khmer et môn anciens au Laos (II)." *Bulletin de l'École française d'Extrême-Orient* 100: 38–107.

Lunet de Lajonquière, Étienne 1907. *Inventaire descriptif des monuments du Cambodge, Tome deuxième*. Paris: Imprimerie Nationale.

Mudar, Karen M. 1999. "How many Dvaravati kingdoms? Locational analysis of first millennium A.D. moated settlements in Central Thailand." *Journal of Anthropological Archaeology* 18: 1–28.

Murphy, Stephen A. 2013. "The distribution of *sema* stones throughout the Khorat Plateau during the Dvaravati Period." In *Unearthing Southeast Asia's Past: Vol.1*, pp.215–266. Edited by M.J. Klokke and V. Degroot. Singapore: National University of Singapore Press.

Murphy, Stephen A. 2016. "The case for proto-Dvāravatī: A review of the art historical and archaeological evidence." *Journal of Southeast Asian Studies* 47 (3): 366–392.

Pan Hla, Nai 1988–1989. *An Introduction to Mon Language*. Kyoto: The Center for Southeast Asian Studies, Kyoto University.

Peleggi, Maurizio 2013. "From Buddhist Icons to National Antiquities: Cultural Nationalism and Colonial Knowledge in the Making of Thailand's History of Art." *Modern Asian Studies* 47 (5): 1520–1548.

Pelliot, Paul 1904. "Deux itinéraires de Chine en Inde à la fin du VIIIe siècle." *Bulletin de l'École française d'Extrême-Orient* 4: 131–413.

Phasook Indrawooth 1999 [2542 BE]. *ทวารวดี: การศึกษาเชิงวิเคราะห์จากหลักฐานทางโบราณคดี* (*Dvaravati: A critical study base on archaeological evidence*). Bangkok: Faculty of Archaeology, Silpakorn University. [In Thai]

Phuthorn Bhumadhon and Somchai Na Nakhonphanom (eds.) 1981 [2524 BE]. *จารึกโบราณรุ่นแรกพบที่ลพบุรีและใกล้เคียง* (*The earliest inscriptions discovered at Lop Buri and nearby*). Lop Buri: Department of Fine Arts. [In Thai]

Piriya Krairiksh 2012 [2555 BE]. *รากเหง้าแห่งศิลปะไทย* (*Roots of Thai Art*). Bangkok: River Books. [In Thai]

Prapod Assavavirulhakarn and Peter Skilling 2006–2007. "New Readings of Early Indic- language Inscriptions from Nakhon Si Thammarat, Southern Thailand." *Bulletin d'Études Indiennes* 24–25: 11–24.

Prasan Bunprakhong and Cham Thongkhamwan 1968 [2511BE]. "คำอ่านจารึกที่ฐานพระพุทธรูปอักษรและภาษามอญโบราณได้มาจากเมืองฟ้าแดดสูงยาง ตำบลหนองแปน อำเภอกมลาไสย จังหวัดกาฬสินธุ์" (Reading of inscription on the base of a Buddha image, Old Mon script and language, from Mueang Fa Daet Sung Yang, Nong Paen District, Kalasin Province.). *Silpakorn Journal* 11 (6): 108–111. [In Thai]

Prasan Bunprakhong, Champa Yueangchroen, and Thoem Mitem 1981 [2524 BE]. "จารึกหลัง พระพิมพ์ดินเผานาดูน เลขทะเบียน 712/2522 และ 1106/2522" (Inscriptions behind Na Dun votive tablets registration numbers 712/2522 and 1106/2522). *Silpakorn Journal* 25 (1): 51–55. [In Thai]

Rawi Siri-issaranan (ed.) 2014 [2557 BE]. ตำนานมูลศาสนา (Mulasasana Chronicle). Nonthaburi: Sripanya Publishing. [In Thai]

Revire, Nicolas 2014. "Glimpses of Buddhist Practices and Rituals in Dvāravatī and its Neighbouring Cultures." In *Before Siam: Essays in Art and Archaeology*, pp.240–271. Edited by N. Revire and S. Murphy, Bangkok: River Books and The Siam Society.

Revire, Nicolas 2016. "Dvāravatī and Zhenla in the seventh to eighth centuries: A transregional ritual complex." *Journal of Southeast Asian Studies* 47 (3): 393–417.

Hunter Watson
OLD MON INSCRIPTIONS AND THE EXTENT OF DVĀRAVATĪ

Sarasawadee Ongsakul 2000 [2543 BE]. *ชุมชนโบราณในแอ่งเชียงใหม่-ลำพูน* (*Ancient communities in the Chiang Mai-Lamphun Basin*). Bangkok: Amarin Printing and Publishing. [In Thai]

Sarasawadee Ongsakul 2009 [2552 BE]. ประวัติศาสตร์ล้านนา,พิมพ์ครั้งที่ 6 (History of Lan Na, 6th ed.). Chiang Mai: Chiang Mai University. [In Thai]

Seidenfaden, Erik 1951. "Kanôk Nakhon, an ancient Mon Settlement in Northeast Siam (Thailand) and its treasures of art." *Bulletin de l'École française d'Extrême-Orient* 44 (2): 643–648.

Shorto, Harry Leonard 1971. *A Dictionary of the Mon Inscriptions from the sixth to the sixteenth centuries: Incorporating materials collected by The Late C.O. Blagden*. London: Oxford University Press.

Skilling, Peter 2003. "Dvāravatī: Recent revelations and research." In *Dedications to Her Royal Highness Princess Galyani Vadhana Krom Luang Naradhiwas Rajanarindra on her 80th birthday*, pp.87–112. Edited by C. Baker. Bangkok: The Siam Society.

Stargardt, Janice 2001. "Behind the Shadows: Archaeological data on two-way sea-trade between Quanzhao and Satingpra, South Thailand, 10th–14th century." In *The Emporium of the World: Maritime Quanzhou, 1000–1400*. Edited by A. Schottenhammer. Leiden, Boston, Köln: Brill.

Uraisi Varasarin 1988. "Les Inscriptions mones decouvertes dans le nord-est de la Thailande." In *Le Premier Symposium Franco-Thai: La Thaïlande des débuts de son histoire jusqu'au xve siècle*, pp.196–211. Bangkok: Silpakorn University.

Wales, Quaritch 1969. *Dvāravatī: The earliest kingdom of Siam (6th to 11th century A.D.)*. London: Bernard Quaritch.

Wannasarn Noonsuk 2013. *Tambralinga and Nakhon Si Thammarat: Early Kingdoms on the Isthmus of Southeast Asia*. Nakhon Si Thammarat: Nakhon Si Thammarat Rajabhat University.

Watson, Hunter I. 2013 [2556 BE]. *การศึกษารูปคำภาษามอญโบราณจากจารึกที่พบในประเทศไทยระหว่างพุทธศตวรรษที่ 12–17* (*A Study of OldMon word forms from inscriptions found in Thailand dating between the 6th–11th centuries CE*). MA Thesis, Silpakorn University, Bangkok. [In Thai]

Watson, Hunter I. 2018. "A group of clay artefacts from Tap Chumphon inscribed in Pali and Old Mon." In *Advancing Southeast Asian Archaeology 2016: Selected Papers from the Second SEAMEO SPAFA International Conference on Southeast Asian Archaeology*, pp.118–129, 329–335 Edited by N.H. Tan. Bangkok: SEAMEO SPAFA.

Wyatt, David K. 2001. "Relics, Oaths and Politics in Thirteenth-Century Siam." *Journal of Southeast Asian Studies* 32 (1): 3–65.

Hunter Watson and Peter Skilling
(Bhadra Rujirathat)
A CLAY TABLET FROM U THONG INSCRIBED IN OLD MON

FAD 2018 [2561 BE]. *พุหางนาค และดอกช้างดิน: ร่องรอยพุทธและพราหมณ์บนเขาศักดิ์สิทธิ์ (Phu Hang Nak and Dok Chang Din: Traces of Buddhism and Brahmanism on a sacred mountain)*. Suphan Buri: FAD Office 2

Jenner, Philip 2009. *A Dictionary of Pre-Angkorian Khmer*. Canberra: Pacific Linguistics.

Prachya Rungsaengthong 2017 [2560BE].“โบราณสถานพุหางนาคคือหินตั้งจริงหรือ?” (Is the Phu Hang Nak Archaeological Site really a standing rock?) *Silpakorn Magazine* May-June: 21–31. [In Thai]

Prachya Rungsaengthong 2018 [2561BE].“ผลการขุดแต่งโบราณสถานพุหางนาค หมายเลข 2 กับการตอบคำถามเรื่อง “หินตั้งที่อำเภออู่ทอง จังหวัดสุพรรณบุรี” (Excavation report from the archaeological site Phu Hang Nak Site 2 and an answer to the question of a standing rock at U Thong District, Suphan Buri Province). In พุหางนาคและดอกช้างดินร่องรอยพุทธและพราหมณ์บนเขาศักดิ์สิทธิ์ (Phu Hang Nak and Khok Chang Din: Traces of Buddhism and Brahmanism on a sacred hill), pp.10–22. Suphan Buri: U Thong National Museum. [In Thai]

Shorto, Harry Leonard 1971. *A Dictionary of the Mon Inscriptions from the sixth to the sixteenth centuries: Incorporating materials collected by The Late C.O. Blagden*. London: Oxford University Press.

Watson, Hunter I. 2013 [2556 BE]. การศึกษารูปคำภาษามอญโบราณจากจารึกที่พบในประเทศไทยระหว่างพุทธศตวรรษที่ 12–17 (*A Study of OldMon word forms from inscriptions found in Thailand dating between the 6th–11th centuries CE*). MA Thesis, Silpakorn University, Bangkok. [In Thai]

Anna Bennett
PRECIOUS METALS IN DVĀRAVATĪ CULTURE

Baptiste, Pierre, and Thierry Zéphir 2009. *Dvāravatī: Aux sources du Bouddhisme en Thaïlande*. Exhibition catalogue. Paris: Réunion des Musées Nationaux and Musée Guimet.

Barram, Andrew 2003. "Dating Dvāravatī." *Bulletin of the Indo-Pacific Prehistory Association* 23: 59–62.

Barram, Andrew, and Ian Glover 2008. "Re-thinking Dvavarati." In *Archaeology in Southeast Asia—from Homo erectus to the Living Traditions, Selected papers from the 11th International Conference of the European Association of Southeast Asian Archaeologists, Bougan, 25–29th September 2006*, pp.175–182. Edited by J.P. Pautreau et al. Chiang Mai: Silkworm.

Bellina, Bérenice (ed.) 2017. *Khao Sam Kaeo. An Early Port-City between the Indian Ocean and the South China Sea.* Paris: École française d'Extrême-Orient.

Bellina, Bérenice and Ian Glover 2004. "The Archaeology of Early Contact with India and the Mediterranean World, from the Fourth Century BC to the Fourth Century AD." In *Southeast Asia: From Prehistory to History*, pp.68–88. Edited by I. Glover and P. Bellwood. London: Routledge-Curzon.

Bellina, Bérénice et al. 2014. "The Early Development of Coastal Polities in the Upper Thai-Malay." In *Before Siam: Essays in Art and Archaeology*, pp.69–89. Edited by N. Revire and S.A. Murphy. Bangkok: River Books & The Siam Society.

Bennett, Anna 1988. *Copper Metallurgy in Central Thailand*. PhD dissertation, Institute of Archaeology, University College London.

Bennett, Anna. 2010. Gold in early Southeast Asia. Proceedings of workshop AURUM, the authentication and analysis of gold work. *ArcheoSciences* 33.

Bennett, Anna 2015. "Ancient Gold and Modern Fakes in Southeast Asia." In *Gold in Early Southeast Asia: Selected papers from the symposium Gold in Southeast Asia, Yale University Art Gallery 13–14 May 2011*, pp.183–236. Monograph 64. Edited by R. Barnes, E.N. Stein. and B. Diebold. New Haven: Yale Southeast Asia Studies.

Bennett, Anna 2016 [2559 BE]. "Gold finds from the Lopburi area." In สรรพศาสตร์ สรรพศิลป์ ถิ่นลพบุรี (Multidisciplinary Studies on Lopburi), pp.620-637. Edited by Wanna Nawikamon. Lop Buri: Faculty of Management Science, Thepsatri Rajabhat University, and affiliates. [In Thai]

Bennett, Anna 2017. *The Ancient History of U Thong City of Gold: A scientific study of the Gold from U Thong.* Bangkok: River Books.

Bennett, Anna forthcoming. "Mauryan–Śuṅga Period objects found on the Myanmar-Thai-Malay Peninsula". In *Archaeology in South Asia—, Selected papers from the 24th International Conference of the European Association of South Asian Archaeologists, Naples, 2018*

Bennett, Anna 2019. "Suvarṇabhūmi Land of Gold." In *Suvarnabhumi: The Golden Land*, pp.81–116. Edited by B. Pongpanich & S. Thinapong. Bangkok: GISTDA.

Boeles, Jan J. 1964. "The king of Sri Dvāravatī and His Regalia." *Journal of the Siam Society* 52 (1): 99–114.

Borell, Brigitte, et al. 2014. "Contacts between the Upper Thai-Malay Peninsula and the Mediterranean World." In *Before Siam: Essays in Art and Archaeology*, pp.98–117. Edited by N. Revire and S.A. Murphy. Bangkok: River Books & The Siam Society.

Borell, Brigitte. 2017a. "Gold Coins from Khlong Thom." *Journal of the Siam Society* 105: 151–177.

Borell, Brigitte. 2017b. "Gemstones in Southeast Asia and Beyond: Trade along the Maritime Networks." In *Gemstones in the first Millenium AD: Mines, Trade, Workshops and Symbolism*, pp.21–44. RGZM Tagungen. Mainz: Römisch-Germanisches Zentralmuseum.

Borell, Brigitte. 2017c. *Traces of the Roman World in U Thong and Southern Thailand*. Bangkok: DASTA and BIA. [in Thai]

Borell, Brigitte. 2018. "A Roman gold coin found in Peninsular Thailand." In *Suvarnabhumi: The GoldenLand*, pp.59–68. Edited by Pongpanich & Thinapong. Bangkok: GISTDA.

Bostock John and Henry Riley 1847–1848. *Full text of Pliny's Natural History. In thirty-seven books.* London.

Bronson, Bennet 1986. "Glass and Beads at Khuan Lukpad." In *Southeast Asian Archaeology, 1986: Proceedings of the First Conference of the Association of Southeast Asian Archaeologists in Western Europe*, pp.139–183. Institute of Archaeology, University College London, 8–10th September 1986. Edited by Ian Glover and Emily Glover. Oxford: British Archaeological Series [BAR] 561.

Brown, Robert L. 1996. *The Dvāravatī Wheels of the law and the Indianization of South East Asia.* Leiden, New York, Köln: EJ. Brill.

Brown, Robert 2014. "Dvāravatī Sculpture." In *Lost Kingdoms: Hindu Buddhist Sculpture of Early Southeast Asia*, pp.189–191. The Metropolitan Museum of Art. Yale: University Press.

Brown, Robert 2017. "The Trouble with Convergence." In *India and Southeast Asia Cultural Discourses*, pp.37–50. Edited by A.L. Dallapiccola. Mumbai: K.R. Cama Oriental Institute.

Bunchar Pongpanich 2009 [2552 BE]. รอยลูกปัด *(Beyond Beads)*. Bangkok: Matichon Publishing House. [In Thai]

Bunchar Pongpanich and Phuthorn Bhumadhon 2015 [2558 BE]. อู่ทอง... ที่รอการฟื้นคืน ผ่านรอยลูกปัด และพระพุทธศาสนาแรกเริ่มในลุ่มน้ำแม่กลอง–ท่าจีน (*The Beads of and Archaeology of U Thong)*. Bangkok: DASTA and BIA. [In Thai]

Bunchar Pongpanich and Somchet.Thinapong (ed.) 2019 (forthcoming). *Suvarnabhumi The Golden Land.* Bangkok: GISTDA Geo-Informatics and Space Technology Development Agency.

Coedès, George 1963. "Decouverte numismatique au Siam interessant le royaume de Dvāravatī." *Comtes rendues de l'Academie des Inscriptions et Belle-Lettres* 107 (3): 285–291.

Dube, R.K. 2003. "Suvarnabhumi, and Suvarnadvipa: Origin, identity, and its richness in gold in ancient and medieval Times." *Bulletin of the Metals Museum* 36: 3–23.

Gallon, Mathew 2014. "Monuments and Identity at the Dvāravatī Town of Kamphaeng Saen." In *Before Siam: Essays in Art and Archaeology*, pp.331–351. Edited by N. Revire and S.A. Murphy. Bangkok: River Books & The Siam Society.

Glover, Ian 1990. *Early Trade between India and Southeast Asia: A Link in the Development of a World Trading system.* Occasional Paper No 16, University of Hull: Centre for South-East Asian Studies. 2nd revised edition.

Glover, Ian 1996a. "The Southern Silk Road: Archaeological Evidence for Early Trade between India and Southeast Asia." In *Ancient Trades and Cultural Contacts in Southeast Asia*, pp.57–95. Bangkok: The Office of the National Culture Commission.

Glover, Ian 1996b. "The Archaeological Evidence for Early Trade between India and Southeast Asia." In *The Indian Ocean in Antiquity,* pp.365–400. London: Kegan Paul International.

Glover, Ian 2010a. "The Dvāravatī Gap—Linking Prehistory and History in Early Thailand." *Bulletin of the Indo-Pacific Prehistory Association* 30: 79–86.

Glover, Ian 2010b. "Thinking about Dvāravatī." In *Abhinandanamālā: Nandana Chutiwongs Felicitation Volume*, pp.47–65. Edited by L. Prematilleke et al. Bangkok: SEAMEO SPAFA, in collaboration with the Abhinandanamālā Committee, Colombo.

Glover, Ian and Bérénice Bellina, 2011. "Ban Don Ta Phet and Khao Sam Kaeo: The Earliest Indian Contacts Re-assessed." In *Early Interactions between South and Southeast Asia: Reflections on Cross- Cultural Exchange*, pp.17–45. Edited by P-Y. Manguin, A. Mani, and G. Wade, Nalanda-Sriwijaya Series 2. Singapore: Institute of Southeast Asian Studies; New Delhi: Manohar India.

Gutman, Pamela 1978. "The Ancient Coinage of Southeast Asia." In *Journal of the Siam Society* 66, (1): 8–21.

Guy, John (ed.) 2014. *Lost Kingdoms: Hindu Buddhist Sculpture of Early Southeast Asia.* New York: The Metropolitan Museum of Art.

Anna Bennett
THE ROLE OF THE TRADE IN PRECIOUS METALS

Guy, John 2017. "The Phanom Surin Shipwreck, a Pahlavi Inscription, and their Significance for the History of Early Lowe Central Thailand." *Journal of the Siam Society* 105.

Higham, Charles 2014. *Early Mainland Southeast Asia From First Humans to Angkor*. River Books, Bangkok.

Jacq-Hergoualc'h 2002. *The Malay Peninsula: Crossroads of the Maritime Silk-Road (100 BC–1300 AD)*. Leiden: Brill.

Krahl, Regina and John Guy 2011. *Shipwrecked: Tang Treasures and Monsoon Winds*. Exhibit catalogue. Edited by Arthur M. Sackler Gallery et al. Singapore: Smithsonian Books.

Kulke, Hermann and Dietmar Rothermund. *A History of India*, 4th ed. London and New York: Routledge, 2004.

Majumdar, Ramesh Chandra 1953. *Inscriptions of Kambuja*. Calcutta: The Asiatic Society.

Majumdar, Ramesh Chandra [1936] 1986 *Suvarṇadvīpa: Ancient Indian Colonization in the Far East*, New Delhi: Gian.

McCrindle (1927) *Ancient India as described by Ptolomy*. Calcutta

Meltzer, Gudrun and Lore Sander 2006. "A Copper Scroll Inscription from the Time of the Alchon Huns In Buddhist Manuscripts." In *Schøyen Collection*, Vol. 3, pp.251–78. Edited by J. Braarvig et al. Oslo: Hermes Publishing.

Miksic, John 2003. "The Beginning of Trade in Ancient Southeast Asia: The Role of Oc Eo and Lower Mekong River." In *Art and Archaeology of Fu Nan: pre-Khmer Kingdom of the lower Mekong Valley, pp.*1–34. Edited by J.C.M. Khoo. Bangkok: Orchid Press.

Miksic, John 2011. *Old Javanese Gold: The Hunter Thompson Collection at Yale University Art Gallery*. New Haven: Yale University Press.

Mitchiner, Michael and Mark Pollard 1990. Early South-East Asian Currency Systems. *Annali - Istituto Universitario Orientale, Supplemento* no. 65. Napoli: Instituto Istituto Universitario Orientale.

Moore, Elisabeth 2007. *Early Landscape of Myanmar*. Bangkok: River Books.

Mudar, Karen 1999. "How Many Dvāravatī Kingdoms? Locational Analysis of First Millennium AD. Moated Settlements in Central Thailand." *Journal of Anthropological Archaeology* 18: 1–28.

Murphy, Stephen. 2016. "The case for proto-Dvāravatī: A review of the art historical and archaeological evidence." *Journal of Southeast Asian Studies* 47 (3): 366–392.

Nareerat Preecharpeechagupt 2014 [2557 BE]. "เรือ โบราณพนมสุรินทร์" (The Phanom Surin Shipwreck). *Silpakorn Journal* 57 (3): 22–35. [In Thai]

Phasook Indrawooth 2004. "The Archaeology of the Early Buddhist Kingdoms of Thailand". In *Southeast Asia from Prehistory to History*, pp.120–148. Edited by I. Glover and P. Bellwood. London: Routledge/Curzon.

Phasook Indrawooth 2008. "Recent research on Dvaravati cultural workshop sites in Petchaburi province, Central Thailand." In *Interpreting Southeast Asia's Past: Monument, Image, and Text*, pp.306–322. Edited by E. Bacus, I. Glover, and P. Sharrock. European Association of Southeast Asian Archaeologists 10. Singapore: National University of Singapore Press.

Phasook Indrawooth 2009. "Un antique royaume urbanisé de Thaïlande." In *Aux sources du bouddhisme en Thaïlande*, pp.31–45. Edited by P. Baptiste and T. Zéphir. Dvāravatī, Paris: Réunion des musées nationaux.

Phattharaphong Kaongoen 2002 [2545 BE]. *โบราณคดีคอกช้างดิน* (*The Archaeologyof Khok Chang Din*). Suphan Buri: FAD, Office 2. [In Thai]

Phuthorn Bhumadhon 1984 [2527]. "Dvāravatī Silver Coins at Lop Buri Province. "*Silpakorn Journal* 28 (4): 55-63. [In Thai]

Phuthorn Bhumadhon 1987 [2530 BE]. "โบราณคดีเมือง ดงคอน อำเภอสรรคบุรี จังหวัดชัยนาท" (*The Archaeology of Dong Khon*). Bangkok: Amulet Council and Subcommittee of Culture, Chai Nat Province. [In Thai]

Phuthorn Bhumadhon 2015 "Interaction Place since the Buddist Era" In *The Beads of and Archaeology of U Thong*. Bangkok: DASTA and BIA. [In Thai]

Preeyanuch Jumprom 2019 [2562 BE]. "Recovery of a Lost Arab-styled Ship at Phanom-Surin, the Wetland Excavation Site in Central Thailand". In *Ancient Maritime Cross-cultural Exchanges, Archaeological Research in Thailand*. FAD [In Thai]

Pryce, Oliver, Bellina Bérénice and Anna Bennett 2008. "*The Development of Metal Technologies in the Upper Thai-Malay Penininsula: Initial Interpretation of the Archae-ometallurgical Evidence from Khao Sam Kaeo.*" Paris: *Bulletin de l'École française d'Extrême-Orient* 93: 295–315.

Ramesh K.V. 2012. "Recent Studies in Indian Epigraphy History, Archaeology and Art." In *Essays in honour of Prof. Shrinivas Ritti.* Edited by P. Shrinivas and V. Shivananda. Delhi: Agam Kala Prakashan.

Ray, Himanshu Prabha 1994. *Winds of Change: Buddhism and the Maritime Links of Early South Asia.* New Delhi: Oxford University Press.

Ray, Himanshu Prabha 2014. "Multi-religious Linkage across the Bay of Bengal during the First Millenuium CE." In *Before Siam: Essays in Art and Archaeology*, pp.134–151. Edited by N. Revire and S.A. Murphy. Bangkok: River Books & The Siam Society.

Reinecke, Andreas 2015. "Ancient Gold and Silver Jewellery and the Beginnings of Gold Working in Mainland Southeast Asia." In *Gold in Early Southeast Asia.* Edited by Barnes R, Stein E.N. and Diebold B, selected papers from the symposium *Gold in Southeast Asia*, pp.125–166. Yale University Art Gallery 13–14 May 2011. Monograph 64. New Haven: Yale Southeast Asia Studies.

Richter, Anne 2000. *The Jewelry of Southeast Asia. London*: Thames and Hudson.

Ronachai Krisadolarn 2016. *The evolution of Thai money from its origins in ancient kingdoms.* Bangkok: River Books.

San Thaiyanonda 2011. การศึกษาลำดับพัฒนาการวัฒนธรรมทาง โบราณคดีเมืองอู่ทอง (*Cultural development of ancient communities at Mueang U Thong*). PhD Diss., Silpakorn University, Bangkok. [In Thai]

Saritphong Khunsong 2015. *The Ancient City of U Thong: Report from the Archaeological Excavation at Nern Plub Pla.* Bangkok: Department of Archaeology, Faculty of Archaeology, Silpakorn University. [In Thai]

Sawang Lertrit 2001. *Ceramic Chronology for Central Thailand: A View from the Pa Sak River Valley*. PhD Diss., Department of Anthropology, Washington State University.

Skilling, Peter 2003. "Dvāravatī: Recent Revelations and Research." In *Dedications to Her Royal Highness Princess Galyani Vadhana Krom Luang Naradhiwas Rajanagarindra on her 80th birthday*, pp.87–112. Edited by C. Baker. Bangkok: Siam Society.

Skilling, Peter 2011. "Buddhism and the Circulation of Ritual in Early Peninsula Southeast Asia." In *Early Interactions between South and Southeast Asia: Reflections on Cross-Cultural Exchange*, pp.371–384. Edited by P-Y. Manguin et al. Series 2. Singapore: Institute of Southeast Asian Studies. New Delhi: Manohar India.

Skilling, Peter 2015. "The Circulation of Artefacts Engraved with 'Apram da' and Other Mottos in Southeast Asia and India: A Preliminary Report." In *Annual Report of The International Research Institute for Advanced Buddhology at Soka University for the Academic Year 2014, 5 (18)*, pp. 63–77. Tokyo: Soka University.

Stückelberger Alfred and Gerd Grasshoff 2017 *Klaudios Ptolemy. Handbook of Geography.* Schwabe publishing group AG

Srisakra Vallibhotoma 2018 [2561 BE]. "ความก้าวหน้าเรื่อง "สุวรรณภูมิ"" (Progress in the matterof "Suvannabhumi"). *Mueang Boran* 44 (2): 30–41. [In Thai]

Anna Bennett
THE ROLE OF THE TRADE
IN PRECIOUS METALS

Supamas Doungsakun 2005. *Paleo-environmental study at Khok Chang Din Ruins, U Thong district, Suphanburi Province.* M.Sc. Thesis, Mahidol University, Bangkok. Dynasty

van Cutsem, Anne 2001. *A world of Earrings–Africa, Asia, America*. Milano: Skira editore.

Vickery, Michael 1998. *Society, Economics, and Politics in Pre-Angkor Cambodia: The 7th–8th Centuries*. Tokyo: The Centre for East Asian Cultural Studies for UNESCO, The Tokyo Bunko.

Wang, Gungwu 1958. "The Nanhai Trade: A Study of the Early History of Chinese Trade in the South China Sea." *Journal of the Malayan Branch of the Royal Asiatic Society* 31 (2): 1–135. (Reprinted Singapore: Times Academic Press, 1998).

Wicks, Robert S. 1992. *Money, Markets, and Trade in Early Southeast Asia: The development of indigenous monetary systems to AD 1400*. Ithaca, New York: Cornell University.

Woodward, Jr. Hiram Woods 1997. *The Sacred Sculpture of Thailand, The Alexander B. Griswold Collection*. Maryland: The Walters Art Gallery.

Xiong Zhaoming 2014. "The Hepu Han tombs and the maritime Silk Road of the Han Dynasty." *Antiquity* 88 (342): 1229–1243

Xiong Zhaoming 2017. *Archaeological Discovery: The Hepu Port on the Maritime Silk Road.* Beijing: Cultural Relics Press.

Lin Ying and Huang Jiaxin
THE REQUEST FROM DVĀRAVATĪ
FOR FINE HORSES

Revire, Nicolas and Stephen A. Murphy (eds.) 2014. *Before Siam. Essays in Art and Archaeology*. Bangkok: The Siam Society and River Books.

Wade, Geoff 2014. "Beyond the Southern Borders: Southeast Asia in Chinese Texts to the Ninth Century." In *Lost Kingdoms. Hindu-Buddhist Sculpture of Early Southeast Asia*, pp.25–32. Edited by J. Guy. New York, Bangkok: The Metropolitan Museum of Art, Yale University Press and River Books.

Wheatey, Paul 1961. *The Golden Khersonese*. Kuala Lumpur: University of Malaya Press.

U-tain Wongsathit, Kangvol Katshima, and Chatupohn Khotkanok

THE FALL OF DVĀRAVATĪ

Bhattacharya,Kamaleswar1961. *Les Religions brahmaniques dans l'ancien Cambodged'apresl'ep igraphie et l'iconographie.* Publications de l'École Française d'Extrême-Orient 49. Paris: École Française d'Extrême-Orient.

Briggs, Lawrence P. 1951. *The Ancient Khmer Empire*. Philadelphia: Transactions of the American Philosophical Society.

Chakravarti, Adhir 1978. *The Sdok Kak Thom Inscription Part I: A Study in Indo-Khmer Civilization*. Calcutta: Sanskrit College.

Chakravarti, Adhir 1980. *The Sdok Kak Thom Inscription Part II: Text, Translation and Commentary*. Calcutta: Sanskrit College.

Cœdès, George 1937–1966. *Inscriptions du Cambodge*, 8 Volumes. Hanoi: Imprimerie d'Extrême- orient.

Cœdès, George 1968. *The Indianized State of Southeast Asia.* Edited by W.F. Vella, translated by S.B. Cowing. Honolulu: The University Press of Hawai'i.

Huffman, Franklin E. 1978. *Khmer-English Dictionary.* New Haven: Yale University Press. Majumdar.

Ramesh Chandra 1953. *Inscriptions of Kambuja*. Calcutta: The Asiatic Society. Mani, Vettam 1975. *Puranic Encyclopaedia*. Delhi: Motilal Banarsidass.

Monier-Williams, Monier 1899. *A Sanskrit-English Dictionary: Etymologically and Philologically Arranged with Special Reference to Cognate Indo-European languages.* Delhi: Motital Banarsidass.

Pou, Saveros 1989. *Nouvelles Inscriptions du Cambodge I.* Paris: École française d'Extrême-Orient.

Pou, Saveros 1992. *Dictionnaire Vieux Khmer-Français-Anglais*. Paris: Cedoreck.

Pou, Saveros 2001. *Nouvelles Inscriptions du Cambodge 2 & 3*. Paris: École française d'Extrême- Orient.

Sak-Humphry, Chhany 2005. *The Sdok Kak Thom Inscription*. Phnom Penh: Buddhist Institute Printing House.

Seam, Long 1997. *Toponymie Khmer*. Phnom Penh: Buddhist Institute.

Seam, Long 2000. *Dictionnaire du Khmer Ancien*. Phnom Penh: Phnom Penh Printing House.

U-tain Wongsathit 2012. *Sanskrit Names in Cambodian Inscriptions.* PhD Diss., Department of Sanskrit and Prakrit Languages, University of Pune.

U-tain Wongsathit 2015. "Wat Chongko Inscription: The Newly found Inscription of Jayaviravarman." In *The Proceedings of the 11th International Conference on Southeast Asian Culture Values "Culture-Green Growth and Tourism,"* pp.102–113. December 2015. Siem Reap, Cambodia.

Vickery, Michael 1998. *Society, Economics, and Politics in Pre-Angkor Cambodia: The 7th–8th Centuries*. Tokyo: The Centre for East Asian Cultural Studies for UNESCO, The Tokyo Bunko.

Vickery, Michael 2000. "Cœdès' Histories of Cambodia." *Silpakorn University International Journal* 1 (1): 61-108.

Vickery, Michael 2002. *History of Cambodia.* Phnom Penh: Pre-Angkor Studies Society.

Vong Sotheara, Chuon Sounthy et al. 2002. *Ancient Inscriptions of Cambodia*, 4 Volumes. Phnom Penh: UNV/UNESCO.

Appendix 1: English–Thai List of Place names

Thailand

Geographic features in Thailand mentioned in the texts

Andaman Sea	ทะเลอันดามัน
Central Plain	ที่ราบภาคกลาง
Gulf of Thailand	อ่าวไทย
Khorat Plateau	ที่ราบสูงโคราช
Kra Isthmus	คอคอดกระ
Phetchabun Range	ทิวเขาเพชรบูรณ์
Dangrek Range	เทือกเขาพนมดงรัก

Rivers in Thailand mentioned in the texts

Bang Pakong River	แม่น้ำบางปะกง
Chao Phraya River	แม่น้ำเจ้าพระยา
Chi River	แแม่น้ำชี
Chorakhe Sam Phan River	คลองจระเข้สามพัน
Khwae Noi River	แม่น้ำแควน้อย
Khwae Yai River	แม่น้ำแควใหญ่
Mae Klong River	แม่น้ำแม่กลอง
Mekhong River	แม่น้ำโขง
Mun River	แม่น้ำมูล
Nan River	แม่น้ำน่าน
Pa Sak River	แม่น้ำป่าสัก
Pattani River	แม่น้ำปัตตานี
Ping River	แม่น้ำปิง
Tha Chin River	แม่น้ำท่าจีน
Wang River	แม่น้ำวัง
Yom River	แม่น้ำยม

Cities and provinces in Thailand mentioned in the texts

Ayuthaya	อยุธยา
Bangkok	กรุงเทพมหานคร
Buri Ram	บุรีรัมย์
Chai Nat	ชัยนาท
Chaiyaphum	ชัยภูมิ
Chiang Mai	เชียงใหม่
Chon Buri	ชลบุรี
Chumphon	ชุมพร
Kalasin	กาฬสินธุ์
Kanchanaburi	กาญจนบุรี
Khon Kaen	ขอนแก่น
Krabi	กระบี่
Lamphun	ลำพูน
Lop Buri	ลพบุรี
Maha Sarakham	มหาสารคาม
Nakhon Pathom	นครปฐม
Nakhon Ratchasima	นครราชสีมา
Nakhon Sawan	นครสวรรค์
Nakhon Si Thammarat	นครศรีธรรมราช
Phang Nga	พังงา
Phetchabun	เพชรบูรณ์
Phetchaburi	เพชรบุรี
Prachin Buri	ปราจีนบุรี
Ranong	ระนอง
Ratchaburi	ราชบุรี
Sakon Nakhon	สกลนคร
Samut Sakhon	สมุทรสาคร
Saraburi	สระบุรี
Sing Buri	สิงห์บุรี
Songkhla	สงขลา
Suphan Buri	สุพรรณบุรี
Surat Thani	สุราษฎร์ธานี
Udon Thani	อุดรธานี
Uthai Thani	อุทัยธานี

Appendix 2: Archaeological sites and areas in Thailand mentioned in the texts

Ban Don Ta Phet, Kanchanaburi P.	บ้านดอนตาเพชร จ.กาญจนบุรี
Ban Kao, Kanchanaburi P.	บ้านเก่า จ.กาญจนบุรี
Ban Pong Manao, Lop Buri P.	บ้านโป่งมะนาว จ.ลพบุรี
Bang Kluai Nok, Ranong P.	บางกล้วยนอก จ.ระนอง
Bueng Khok Chang, Uthai Thani P.	บึงคอกชาง จ.อุทัยธานี
Chan Sen, Nakhon Sawan P.	จันเสน จ.นครสวรรค์
Chai Badan, Lop Buri P.	ชัยบาดาล จ.ลพบุรี
Chaiya, Surat Thani P.	ไชยา จ.สุราษฎร์ธานี
Chum Phae, Khon Kaen P.	ชุมแพ จ.ขอนแก่น
Fa Daet Song Yang, Kalasin P.	ฟ้าแดดสงยาง จ.กาฬสินธุ์
Hariphunchai, Lamphun P.	หริภุญชัย จ.ลำพูน
Huai Chorakhe, Nakhon Pathom P.	ห้วยจระเข้ จ.นครปฐม
In Buri, Sing Buri P.	อินทร์บุรี จ.สิงห์บุรี
Kamalasai, Kalasin P.	กมลาไสย จ.กาฬสินธุ์
Kamphaeng Saen, Nakhon Pathom P.	กาแพงแสน จ.นครปฐม
Kaset Sombun, Chaiyaphum P.	เกษตรสมบูรณ์ จ.ชัยภูมิ
Khao Chamuk, Ratchaburi P.	เขาจมูก จ.ราชบุรี
Khao Khok, Suphan Buri P.	เขาคอก จ.สุพรรณบุรี
Khao Phra, Suphan Buri P.	เขาพระ จ.สุพรรณบุรี
Khao Ngu Hermit Cave, Ratchaburi P.	ถ้ำฤษีเขางู จ.ราชบุรี
Khao Rang Kapit, Suphan Buri P.	เขารางกะปิด จ.สุพรรณบุรี
Khao Sam Kaeo, Chumphon P.	เขาสามแก้ว จ.ชุมพร
Khao Sam Pot, Lop Buri P.	เขาสมโภชน์ จ.ลพบุรี
Khao Tham Thiam, Suphan Buri P.	เขาทำเทียม จ.สุพรรณบุรี
Khon Sawan, Chaiyaphum P.	คอนสวรรค์ จ.ชัยภูมิ
Khlong Thom, Krabi P.	คลองถม จ.กระบี่
Khuan Luk Pat, Krabi P.	ควนลูกปัด จ.กระบี่
Khok Chang Din, Suphan Buri P.	คอกช้างดิน จ.สุพรรณบุรี
Khok Mai Den, Nakhon Sawan P.	โคกไม้เดน จ.นครสวรรค์
Khu Bua, Ratchaburi P.	คูบัว จ.ราชบุรี
Kumphawapi, Udon Thani P.	กุมภวาปี จ.อุดรธานี
Lan Sak, Uthai Thani P.	ลานสัก จ.อุทัยธานี
Mueang Phet, Nakhon Ratchasima P.	เมืองเพ็ด จ.นครราชสีมา
Na Dun, Maha Sarakham P.	นาดูน จ.มหาสารคาม
Nam Nao, Phetchabun P.	น้ำหนาว จ.เพชรบูรณ์
Narai Cave, Wat Khao Wong, Saraburi P.	ถ้ำนารายณ์ วัดเขาวง จ.สระบุรี
Noen Phra, Nakhon Pathom P.	เนินพระ จ.นครปฐม
Phanom Wan Temple, Nakhon Ratchasima P.	พนมวัน จ.นครราชสีมา
Phanat Nikhom, Chon Buri P.	พนัสนิคม จ.ชลบุรี
Phanom Surin shipwreck, Samut Sakhon P.	พนมสุรินทร์ จ.สมุทรสาคร
Phanom Rung, Buri Ram P.	พนมรุ้ง จ.บุรีรัมย์
Phimai, Nakhon Ratchasima P.	พิมาย จ.นครราชสีมา
Phong Tuek, Kanchanaburi P.	พงตึก จ.กาญจนบุรี
Phu Hang Nak, Suphan Buri P.	พุหางนาค จ.สุพรรณบุรี
Phukhao Thong, Ranong P.	ภูเขาทอง จ.ระนอง
Prasat Mueang Sing, Kanchanaburi P.	ปราสาทเมืองสิงห์ จ.กาญจนบุรี
Promthin Tai, Lop Buri P.	บ้านพรหมทินใต้ จ.ลพบุรี
Sam Phran, Nakhon Pathom P.	สามพราน จ.นครปฐม
Sankhaburi, Chainat P.	สรรคบุรี จ.ชัยนาท
Sawang Daen Din, Sakon Nakhon P.	สว่างแดนดิน จ.สกลนคร
Sawang Arom, Uthai Thani P.	สว่างอารมณ์ จ.อุทัยธานี
Si Mahaphot, Prachin Buri P.	ศรีมหาโพธิ จ.ปราจีนบุรี
Si Mahosot, Prachin Buri P.	ศรีมโหสถ จ.ปราจีนบุรี
Si Thep, Phetchabun P.	เมืองศรีเทพ จ.เพชรบูรณ์
Takua Pa, Phang Nga P.	ตะกั่วป่า จ.พังงา
Thap Chumphon, Nakhon Sawan P.	ทัพชุมพล จ.นครสวรรค์
Tha Muang, Kanchanaburi P.	ท่าม่วง จ.กาญจนบุรี
U Thong, Suphan Buri P.	อู่ทอง จ.สุพรรณบุรี
Wat Cong Ko, Nakhon Ratchasima P.	วัดจงกอ จ.นครราชสีมา
Wat Khao Noi, Songkhla P.	วัดเขาน้อย จ.สงขลา
Wat Khoi, Singburi P.	วัดข่อย จ.สิงบุรี
Wat Si Wanaram, Suphan Buri P.	วัดศรีวรรณาราม จ.สุพรรณบุรี
Wiang Kum Kam, Chiang Mai P.	เวียงกุมกาม จ.เชียงใหม่
Wiang Mano, Chiang Mai P.	เวียงมะโน จ.เชียงใหม่
Wiang Tho, Chiang Mai P.	เวียงเถาะ จ.เชียงใหม่